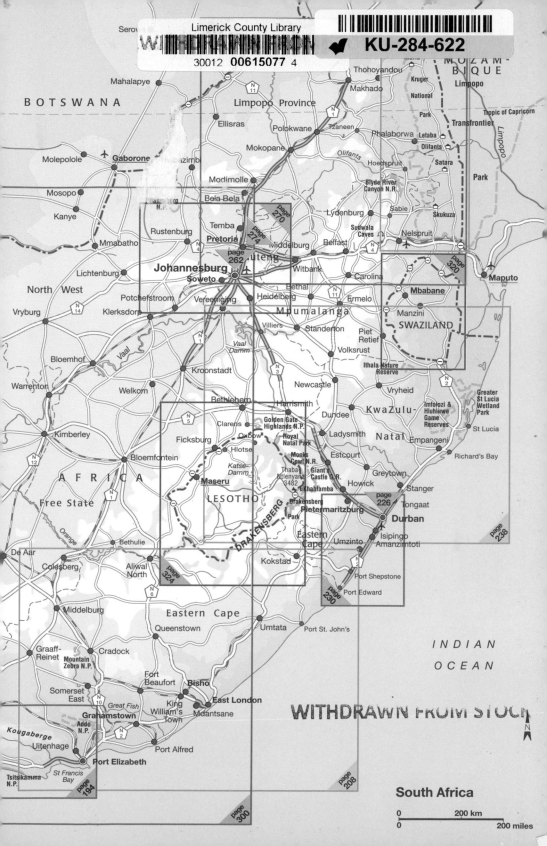

South Africa

INSIGHT GUIDES

SOUTH AFRICA

Discovery
CHANNEL

APA PUBLICATIONS L
Part of the Langenscheidt Publishing Group

INSIGHT GUIDE
SOUTH AFRICA

Editorial
Project Editor
Jason Mitchell
Editorial Director
Brian Bell

Distribution

UK & Ireland
GeoCenter International Ltd
Meridian House, Churchill Way West
Basingstoke, Hampshire RG21 6YR
Fax: (44) 1256 817988

United States
Langenscheidt Publishers, Inc.
36–36 33rd Street, 4th Floor
Long Island City, New York 11106
Fax: 1 (718) 784 0640

Australia
Universal Publishers
1 Waterloo Road
Macquarie Park, NSW 2113
Fax: (61) 2 9888 9074

New Zealand
Hema Maps New Zealand Ltd (HNZ)
Unit D, 24 Ra ORA Drive
East Tamaki, Auckland
Fax: (64) 9 273 6479

Worldwide
Apa Publications GmbH & Co.
Verlag KG (Singapore branch)
38 Joo Koon Road, Singapore 628990
Tel: (65) 6865 1600. Fax: (65) 6861 6438

Printing

Insight Print Services (Pte) Ltd
38 Joo Koon Road, Singapore 628990
Tel: (65) 6865 1600. Fax: (65) 6861 6438

CONTACTING THE EDITORS
We would appreciate it if readers
would alert us to errors or out-
dated information by writing to:
**Insight Guides, P.O. Box 7910,
London SE1 1WE, England.
Fax: (44) 20 7403 0290.
insight@apaguide.co.uk**

www.insightguides.com

ABOUT THIS BOOK

The first Insight Guide pioneered
the use of creative full-colour photography in travel guides in 1970.
Since then, we have expanded our
range to cater for our readers' need
not only for reliable information about
their chosen destination but also for
a real understanding of the culture
and workings of that destination.
Now, when the internet can supply
inexhaustible (but not always reliable)
facts, our books marry text and pictures to provide those much more
elusive qualities: knowledge and dis-
cernment. To achieve this, they rely
on the authority of locally
based writers and photo-
graphers.

How to use this book

The book is carefully
structured both to

convey an understanding of South
Africa and to guide readers through
its sights and activities:

◆ To understand South Africa today,
you need to know about its past.
The first section covers the country's History and People, with Features on South African culture and
nature. These lively, authoritative
essays are written by specialists.

◆ In addition to this unique history,
South Africa is a destination for
nature lovers. Our gazetteer provides you with an on-the-spot reference source to help you identify
animals on safari.

◆ The main Places section provides a full run-down of all the
attractions worth seeing. The
principal places of interest
are coordinated by number
with full-colour maps.

ABOVE: a sandcastle dinosaur in Camp's Bay, near Cape Town.

◆ The Travel Tips listings section provides a convenient point of reference for information on travel, hotels, restaurants, sports and festivals. Information may be located quickly by using the index printed on the back cover flap – and the flaps also serve as bookmarks.

◆ Photographs are chosen not only to illustrate geography and attractions but also to convey the moods of the country and the activities of the people.

The contributors

This edition, produced by **Jason Mitchell**, an editor in Insight Guides' London editorial headquarters, builds on previous best-selling editions

edited by **Johannes Haape** and **Melissa de Villiers**.

Philip Briggs, an acknowledged expert on African travel, was the main writer for this new edition. He restructured, updated and provided new materials to reflect the new developments in this rapidly changing country. In addition to work on other Insight Guides, including *Tanzania* and *East African Wildlife*; Briggs wrote the first travel guide to South Africa following the release of Nelson Mandela and is a regular contributor to travel magazines. Briggs and **Sally Munro**, who updated the Cape Town, Western Cape and Garden Route information, keeps this book up-to-date.

Original writers include: **David Bristow**, who covered Cape Town, Durban, Swaziland and Lesotho. **Wendy Toerien**, staffer on South Africa's acclaimed *Wine* magazine, wrote on the Cape's grape. Writer and television producer/director **Gary Rathbone's** original essay provided the basis for "Living Together", plus chapters on sports and Johannesburg. **Bridget Hilton-Barber** covered Zulu culture, township life, and dorps. Other writers included **Christopher Till**, former director of the Johannesburg Art Gallery; **Ian MacDonald**, chief executive of WWF South Africa; and ecotourism management consultant **Vincent Carruthers**. **Sabine Marschall** wrote on architecture. Author **Stephen Gray** contributed the chapter on South African literature.

The History section was written by **Jeff Peires**, former ANC MP and the author of two books on the history of the Xhosa people, and **Rodney Davenport**, emeritus professor and editor of the standard work, *A Modern History of South Africa*.

Map Legend

—— ··	International Boundary
————	Province Boundary
⊖	Border Crossing
—·—·—	National Park/Reserve
————	Ferry Route
✈ ✈	Airport: International/ Regional
🚌	Bus Station
❶	Tourist Information
✉	Post Office
🛉 † ⛪	Church/Ruins
†	Monastery
☾	Mosque
✡	Synagogue
⛫ 🏚	Castle/Ruins
🏠	Mansion/Stately home
∴	Archaeological Site
∩	Cave
⚲	Statue/Monument
★	Place of Interest

The main places of interest in the Places section are coordinated by number with a full-colour map (e.g. ❶), and a symbol at the top of every right-hand page tells you where to find the map.

INSIGHT GUIDE
SOUTH AFRICA

Maps

A map of Cape Town is on
the inside back cover.

CONTENTS

Face to face
with the wild.

Information panels

Places

Insight on....

THE BEST OF SOUTH AFRICA

From watching the most savage of beasts to sampling the subtle bouquet of a shiraz wine, the experiences available in South Africa are as vast as the country's never-ending landscape

SPECTACULAR GAME VIEWING

- **Kruger Park**
  One of Africa's truly great wildlife sanctuaries, and well suited to a DIY safari, the Kruger hosts some of the world's highest concentrations of lions, elephants, zebra, giraffe, antelope and rhinos. Adjacent Sable Sands Reserves, provide the best chance of leopard sightings anywhere in Africa. *See page 288.*
- **Hluhluwe-Imfolozi**
  The largest of the Zululand reserves, and the best place to spot rhinos. *See page 242.*
- **Kgalagadi Park**
  Protecting the red dunes and dry water-courses of the Kalahari, this fabulously remote park offers some of the country's best predator viewing. *See page 308.*
- **Addo Elephant Park**
  Known primarily for its excellent elephant viewing, Addo has recently introduced lions and expanded to the Indian Ocean. It now protects the most varied habitats of any South African reserve. *See page 208.*
- **De Hoop Reserve**
  De Hoop is the largest protected area of *fynbos* in the Cape, and harbours bontebok and Cape mountain zebra. *See page 190.*

WINING AND DINING

- **Cape Winelands**
  Chill out at estates such as Boschendal or Groot Constantia, which offer the intoxicating combination of fine food, first-class wine and superb mountain scenery. *See page 182.*
- **Oyster Company, Knysna**
  More succulent seafood in the form of oysters – and if the wine is starting to pall, try the excellent ale served at nearby Mitchell's Brewery. *See pages 200 & 351.*
- **V&A Waterfront, Cape Town**
  Fair enough, it's a bit too commercialised for some tastes, but "the waterfront" is a great place to enjoy the local crayfish and a bottle of chilled white wine, while seals and gulls frolic and soar in the harbour. *See page 161.*
- **Kapitan's, Johannesburg**
  A legendary Indian restaurant that was regularly frequented by Nelson Mandela and Oliver Tambo back in the 1950s. *See page 264.*
- **Le Must, Upington**
  Tucked away in remote Upington, Le Must is one of the finest exponents of Cape cuisine in the country – the Karoo lamb is superb. *See page 347.*

LEFT: a close-up rendezvous with a hungry lion.

TOP SCENERY

● **uKhahlamba-Drakensberg**
The Royal Natal Park and more remote Giant's Castle rank high among the scenic reserves that protect the region's largest and tallest mountain range. *See page 253.*

● **Table Mountain**
The panorama from the peak of the 1,000-metre high mountain standing sentinel over

Cape Town is breathtaking. *See page 163.*

● **Namaqualand**
The arid plains along the West Coast support an extraordinary diversity of succulents that burst into magnificent flower in the spring. *See page 313.*

● **Storm's River Mouth**
Crossed by suspension bridge, this is the scenic highlight of the Garden Route. *See page 202.*

LEFT: under the shadow of the Drakensberg Mountains lies the magical beauty of the Royal Natal Park
ABOVE: a highlight of any trip to South Africa is hunting for authentic souvenirs to bring home.

HISTORY AND CULTURE

● **Drakensberg rock art**
Arguably the world's best open-air gallery, the caves and shelters contain thousands of rock paintings, some thousands of years old. *See page 255.*

● **Robben Island**
Now a nature reserve and museum, this small island in Table Bay is where Nelson Mandela and other ANC members were imprisoned – guided tours are conducted by former prisoners. *See page 162.*

● **Museum Africa**
Set in Johannesburg, this museum offers a panoramic overview of South Africa's past. *See page 266.*

● **Cradle of Humankind**
Best known for Sterkfontein Caves, where a near-complete 3½ million year old skeleton is the oldest hominid fossil in the region. *See page 272.*

ADVENTURE ACTIVITIES

● **Imfolozi Trail**
A great overnight hike through the Hluhluwe-Imfolozi Game Reserve. *See page 242.*

● **Caged Shark Dive, Mossel Bay**
Just a few steel bars protect viewers from the rapacious "great white". *See page 194.*

● **White-water Rafting, Swaziland**
The best white-water rafting south of the Zambezi is on the Great Usutu

River, southern Swaziland. *See page 322.*

● **Bloukrans Bridge Bungy Jump**
Reputedly the highest bungy jump in the world plummets from the 215-metre high Bloukrans Bridge. *See page 202.*

● **Otter Trail**
The most popular of hundreds of hiking trails through South Africa, the Otter Trail follows the stunning Tsitsikama coastline over five days. *See page 203.*

RIGHT: Robben Island.

OFF THE BEATEN TRACK

● **Northern Cape**
The province that tourism forgot is actually one of the most rewarding parts of South Africa to explore, highlights being Kgalagadi, Augrabies Falls and the Namaqualand flowers. *See page 307.*

● **Hogsback**
This remote mountain village in the Eastern Cape offers fine hiking opportunities, as well as excellent forest birding and – in midsummer – refuge from the muggy coastal climate. *See page 213.*

● **Graaff-Reinet**
The fourth-oldest town in South Africa, Graaff-Reinet boasts some superb Cape Dutch architecture, as well as walks and drives through the scenic Karoo Nature Reserve that surrounds it. *See page 210.*

● **KwaZulu-Natal South Coast**
A nightmare in season, when domestic tourists descend on it en masse, the south coast of KwaZulu-Natal tends to be quiet for the rest of the year, when it has much to commend it, including beaches, good accommodation deals, a year-round subtropical climate and a clutch of small nature reserves. *See page 231.*

● **Northern Kruger Park**
Far north of the traditional tourist trail, camps such as Letaba, Shingwedzi and Punda Maria are among the most remote accessible by surfaced road, and offer some excellent game viewing. *See page 292.*

BELOW: keeping the coast safe for visitors.

ABOVE: Cape Town's Minstrel Carnival is one of South Africa's biggest festivals, but in a country with so many cultures, you've never long to wait for the next one.

CONTEMPORARY CULTURE

● **Grahamstown Arts Festival**
Worthwhile at any time of year, with its numerous museums and old churches, the university town of Grahamstown comes into its own in June, when it hosts a nine-day arts and fringe festival that attracts hundreds of theatrical, musical and other acts. *See page 213.*

● **Johannesburg/ Soweto**
High crime rates notwithstanding, the cultural hotchpotch that is Johannesburg stands at the cultural vanguard of the new South Africa whether you hang out in the bustling street cafés of Melville, catch a play at the central Market Theatre complex, or take a guided tour into Soweto. *See page 261.*

● **Cape Minstrel's Carnival, Cape Town**
One of the most vibrant events in the Cape calendar is this street festival, which takes place every January. *See page 168.*

● **Pink Loerie Mardi Gras, Knysna**
South Africa's premier gay, lesbian, transsexual and transgender carnival takes place every May in the lovely resort town of Knysna on the Garden Route. *See page 199.*

● **Lesotho**
The remote mountains of the "Kingdom in the Sky", best explored on horseback, offer a great opportunity to experience contemporary rural Africa culture in the company of the welcoming Basotho people. *See page 324.*

TOP FAMILY ATTRACTIONS

- **Lion Park** Dense with lions and other game, Johannesburg's safari-style drive-through zoo is the ideal alternative to visiting a game reserve (where wildlife must actively be sought) for youngsters with low boredom thresholds. *See page 271.*
- **Two Ocean's Aquarium, Cape Town** With everything from seahorses and squids to dolphins and penguins represented, this excellent aquarium will appeal to children of all ages, as will its equally worthwhile counterparts in Durban, East London and Port Elizabeth. *See page 162.*
- **Monkeyland, Plettenberg Bay** Guided walks through the large forested enclosure, which contain monkeys and lemurs from around the world. *See page 201.*
- **Waterworld, Durban** Offering exciting splashy water rides, this is the centrepiece of Durban's child-friendly waterfront, which also boasts a snake park and aquarium. *See page 226.*
- **Ostrich Farms** Several farms around Oudtshoorn let you ride, eat and buy the hollowed eggs of the world's largest – and most bird-brained – feathered creature. *See page 195.*

ABOVE: South Africa is a temporary home to many exotic birds – Bird Island is favoured by the Cape Gannet.

BEST FOR BIRDWATCHING

- **Kruger Park** With over 500 bird species recorded, the Kruger offers the best all-round introduction to South Africa's avifauna. *See page 288.*
- **Ndumo Reserve** Any of Zululand's reserves offers good birdwatching, but Ndumo is the pick, both for tropical water birds and for species otherwise restricted to Mozambique. *See page 245.*
- **Wilderness Park** One of the best birdwatching spots in the Cape, this park supports a good variety of birds, as well as the brilliant Knysna loerie. *See page 197.*
- **Barberspan Sanctuary** Regarded to be South Africa's most important avian wetland habitat, it is home to flamingos, ibises and waders. *See page 307.*
- **Bird Island** Over 100,000 Cape gannets breed on this small island in Lambert's Bay, reached on foot via a causeway. *See page 180.*

MONEY-SAVING TIPS

Whale-watching, Walker Bay Between July and November, over 500 southern right whales congregate in this pretty bay, offering the world's most reliable, and cheapest, land-based whale-viewing from picturesque towns such as Hermanus and Gansbaai. *See page 174.*

St Lucia Township Possibly the last urban settlement in South Africa to harbour wild hippos, crocodiles and antelope, with no fee to see them. There are also great day trip possibilities from its location at the mouth of the jungle-fringed St Lucia Estuary. *See page 241.*

Bloubergstrand A short drive north of Cape Town, this long, sandy beach is where those stunning photos showing Table Mountain towering above the city bowl were taken. *See page 177.*

Orange River Winery Free wine-tasting at the world's largest wine co-operative (what could be better), set rather improbably in the middle of the arid Kalahari, but watered by an irrigation scheme emanating from the Orange River. *See page 310.*

Panorama Route Assuming you have wheels, you don't pay a cent to park at the likes of the Three Rondavels and God's Window viewpoints and soak up the spectacular scenery. *See page 284.*

THE SHAPE OF GOOD HOPE

South Africa's natural beauties are legendary. Now it also

offers visitors the chance to witness a nation reborn

The news from South Africa, wrote one observer after a visit, "is absorbingly interesting at the moment". The writer was Matthew Arnold, and the year 1879, but the remark is particularly relevant today. Perhaps no other country in the world is undergoing quite such dramatic change as South Africa, where, after 40 years of white minority rule, a clutch of cultures – interlinked, but powerfully divergent – try to heal the wounds of apartheid and find a communal voice.

Today's visitors have the chance to be present as a new nation evolves in all its richness and diversity, rooted in the indigenous cultures that suffered such dismal neglect during the apartheid years. Now, instead of relying on the United States and Europe for inspiration, there is much-welcome official support for African art, music, dance, drama, crafts – and political debate.

For many first-time visitors fed by media coverage of the country's political dramas, South Africa's pristine natural beauty and remarkable ecological variety comes as a welcome surprise. For several years, the South African Tourist Board's pet marketing catchphrase was "A World In One Country" – a slogan that might justifiably raise the hackles of any self-respecting sceptic, but does nevertheless possess a significant grain of truth.

Game parks and beaches

You want vast stretches of savannah studded with flat-topped acacia and teeming with herds of big game? Well, South Africa's Kruger National Park, extending over an area larger than Wales or Massachusetts, more than fits the bill, as does the relatively compact Hluhluwe-Imfolozi and other game reserves of KwaZulu-Natal. You want sun-drenched palm-lined beaches, or windswept islands adorned with breeding colonies of seals and marine birds, or craggy peninsulas overlooking wide bays frequented by dolphins and whales – check, check, and check again.

Then there's the wild red dunefields of the vast Kgalagadi Transfrontier Park in the northwest, the misty forests of the southeastern coastal belt, the sedate old-world architecture and winelands of the Western Cape, the breathtaking magnificence of Table Mountain, the peerless spring wildflower displays of Namaqualand, and the towering rock amphitheatres and grassy slopes of the uKhahlamba-Drakensberg Mountains, which even, incredibly, support a low-key seasonal ski resort at Rhodes.   ▷

PRECEDING PAGES: surfing into Cape Town; Long Street, Cape Town; the vibrant fabrics of Greenmarket Square, Cape Town.
LEFT: a modern face of South Africa.

Evidence of prehistoric human occupation of South Africa includes the abandoned mediaeval gold-trading emporium at Mapungubwe Hill, as well as the world's finest and most prolific rock art, some of it thought to be around 20,000 years old; while the hominid fossil record at the Cradle of Humankind west of Johannesburg stretches back 3½ million years. And modern South African culture, with significant roots in three continents, is increasingly developing into something far more exciting than the sum of its once fractious parts – most clearly in urban melting pots such as the brash, business-orientated Johannesburg and funkier chilled-out Cape Town.

South Africa was starved of tourists under the apartheid regime, whose discriminatory policies and oppressive methods of enforcing them repelled most potential visitors, and it has largely escaped the sort of environmental degradation common to places with developed holiday industries. Consequently, a good deal of debate goes on in the press on how best to preserve the natural heritage while ensuring that the economic benefits of tourism are passed on to underdeveloped communities and conservation agencies. "Ecotourism" is a buzzword visitors will hear often; it's the strategy promoted by the government on the basis that the gross returns per hectare from wildlife tourism are much higher than from any other form of land use. The concept also embraces a move towards community-based tourist developments, which provide all South Africans with a real incentive to conserve the country's wildlife and wild places.

What of the future?

In the mid-1990s, apartheid's legacy loomed large as Nelson Mandela's government struggled to create jobs, improve health and education, and remove the last vestiges of racial discrimination. Since Mandela's retirement in 1999, the biggest test faced by his successor, Thabo Mbeki, has been to make good on the ANC's promises without being able to rely on the so-called "Madiba Magic" – the singular natural charisma and authority possessed by Mandela – to win himself more time and goodwill.

It's probably fair to say that expectations have not been met fully at grassroots level, while on the broader political arena Mbeki has incurred widespread criticism for his handling of the crisis of government in neighbouring Zimbabwe and the HIV pandemic at home. Then again, few prominent politicians will finish their career without having pursued the odd unpopular, divisive or plain misguided policy – the most important thing, in direct contrast to the oppressive atmosphere under apartheid, is that such policies are pursued in an atmosphere of free political debate and a national mood that remains broadly optimistic.

What is clear from a visitor's point of view is that South Africa has much to offer, and that few will leave disappointed. The news is indeed absorbingly interesting.   ❏

RIGHT: even the fastest of predators must keep an eye on what lies behind them.

Decisive Dates

Circa **8000 BC:** San hunter-gatherers inhabit the south-western regions of southern Africa.

From AD 200: The semi-nomadic Khoikhoi begin farming the land.

From 1100: Other African peoples migrate into the southern African region from the north.

1486: Portuguese navigator, Bartholomeu Diaz, circumnavigates the Cape and lands at Mossel Bay.

1497: Another Portuguese explorer, Vasco da Gama, discovers a sea route to India via the Cape.

1652: Jan van Riebeeck sets up a supply station at

the Cape for the Dutch East India Company, thus founding Cape Town.

1659: The first wine from Cape grapes is pressed.

1667: The first Malays arrive at the Cape as slaves.

1688–1700: Huguenot refugees settle in the Cape.

1779: First skirmishes between the settlers and the Xhosas, followed by eight further frontier wars.

1795: The British annex the Cape.

1803: The Cape Colony reverts to Dutch rule.

1806: Britain reoccupies the Cape, the start of 155 years of British rule.

1814: The Cape is formally ceded to Britain by the Dutch government.

1818: Shaka becomes king of the Zulus.

1820: British settlers arrive in the Eastern Cape.

1820–28: Shaka extends his territory, vanquishing other tribes and leaving large areas devastated and depopulated in his wake.

1824–25: Port Natal (later renamed Durban) is established in Shaka's kingdom by British traders.

1828: Shaka is murdered by his brothers, one of whom – Dingane – becomes king.

1834: Slavery is abolished in South Africa.

1836–54: The Great Trek. Over 16,000 Voortrekkers travel northwards in wagons from the Cape in order to escape British domination, settling mainly in the north and what is now KwaZulu-Natal.

1838: On 16 December, a party of Voortrekkers under Andries Pretorius defeat the Zulus under Dingane at Blood River in Natal.

1845: Natal becomes a British colony.

1848: British sovereignty is proclaimed between the Vaal and the Orange rivers.

1852: Several parties of Boers move further east and found the Zuid-Afrikaansche Republiek.

1854: The Boer Independent Republic of the Orange Free State founded.

1860: The first Indian indentured workers arrive in Natal to work in the sugar-cane industry.

1867: Diamonds are found near Kimberley.

1877: Britain annexes the South African Republic.

1879: Zulu *impis* wipe out a British force at Isandlwana. The British retaliate by defeating the Zulus at Ulundi, in what is now KwaZulu-Natal.

1880–81: The Transvaal declares itself a republic. The first Anglo-Boer War.

1883: Boer leader Paul Kruger becomes the first president of the Transvaal.

1886: Gold mining begins in the Transvaal and the mining town of Johannesburg is founded.

1899–1902: The second Anglo-Boer War, in which the Boers are beaten and their settlements destroyed.

1910: The Union of South Africa is proclaimed.

PARTIES AND ORGANISATIONS	
AWB:	Afrikaner Resistance Movement, a neo-Nazi white group.
COSATU:	Congress of South African Trade Unions.
IFP:	Inkatha Freedom Party, the Zulu political party which clashed violently with the ANC in the 1980s and 1990s.
NP:	National Party, the white, mainly Afrikaner political party which ruled South Africa from 1948–94.
NUM:	National Union of Mineworkers.
SACP:	South African Communist Party, formed 1921, banned 1950–90.

1912: A Black civil rights movement, the South African Native National Congress is formed, known after 1923 as the African National Congress (ANC).

1913: The Native Land Act is passed, limiting land ownership for Blacks.

1920: South African Indian Congress founded.

1925: Afrikaans replaces Dutch as the official "second language" after English.

1948: National Party under D.F. Malan wins general election. Acts enforcing apartheid follow.

1950–53: Apartheid is entrenched still further via such legislation as the Group Areas Act, and the forced removal of numerous communities.

1952: The ANC launches the Defiance Campaign.

1960: On 21 March the police shoot and kill 67 participants in a demonstration staged against the pass laws in Sharpeville, Transvaal. The government bans the ANC.

1961: South Africa becomes a republic and leaves the Commonwealth. The ANC launches its armed struggle; leader Albert Luthuli is awarded the Nobel Peace Prize.

1964: Following the 1962 arrest of lawyer and ANC president Nelson Mandela, his original prison sentence of five years is commuted to life for "high treason and sabotage" in the Rivonia Treason Trial.

1966: Apartheid's chief architect, Hendrik Verwoerd, is assassinated in Parliament. B.J. Vorster succeeds him as Prime Minister.

1967: The world's first human heart transplant is performed at Cape Town's Groote Schuur Hospital.

1975: The Zulu cultural movement *Inkatha* is revived by Chief Mangosuthu Buthelezi in Natal.

1976: On 16 July, Soweto school children protest against Afrikaans as the medium of instruction in Black schools. Police violence ignites resistance across the country. At least 600 people lose their lives.

1976–81: The homelands of Transkei, Bophuthat-swana, Venda and Ciskei are given nominal independence from South Africa and become so-called "separate countries".

1983: A new Constitution provides for a tricameral Parliament for "whites, Coloureds and Indians". The anti-apartheid United Democratic Front is founded.

1984: Anglican Archbishop Desmond Tutu is awarded the Nobel Peace Prize. Various "petty apartheid" acts are abolished, including the ban on mixed marriages.

1986: State repression is stepped up nationwide and a state of emergency is declared.

1989: F.W. de Klerk succeeds P.W. Botha as President.

1990: De Klerk announces plans to scrap apartheid and releases Nelson Mandela. The state of emergency is

ended, and organisations including the ANC unbanned. The ANC suspends its armed struggle. *Inkatha* becomes a political party, the Inkatha Freedom Party.

1991: All apartheid laws are repealed. Declaration of Intent signed at the Convention for a Democratic South Africa (CODESA).

1993: President de Klerk and Nelson Mandela receive the Nobel Peace Prize;·international sanctions are lifted.

1994: The first democratic election is held. On 10 May, Nelson Mandela is sworn in as the first Black President of South Africa. De Klerk and Thabo Mbeki become joint Deputy Presidents.

1995: A Truth and Reconciliation Commission appointed under Archbishop Desmond Tutu.

1996: De Klerk pulls the NP out of government and joins the Opposition benches.

1997: South Africa's new Constitution comes into effect on 3 February. De Klerk steps down as NP leader. Nelson Mandela steps down as ANC leader.

1998: The Truth and Reconciliation Commission ends.

1999: The second democratic general election is held and the ANC are returned to power. Mandela retires as President to be succeeded by his deputy, Thabo Mbeki.

2002: A National AIDS Council is created (SANAC).

2004: In South Africa's third democratic election, Mbeki and the ANC win a 70 percent majority.

2005: Over 100,000 gold miners go on strike.

2006: Former Deputy President Jacob Zuma is aquitted of rape and corruption charges. South Africa becomes the first African country to allow same-sex unions. ❑

PRECEDING PAGES: San rock art. **LEFT:** Stone Age tools found at Thulamela. **RIGHT:** the unlikely architects of a revolution: F.W. de Klerk and Nelson Mandela.

BEGINNINGS

The first African cultures were established much earlier – and were more sophisticated – than the apartheid theorists cared to admit

Apartheid theorists liked to describe South Africa as an empty land, peopled by immigrants. Apartheid maps showed fat black arrows depicting waves of Africans migrating into South Africa from the far north, while much thinner white arrows discreetly indicated the European incursions from the sea. The intention, of course, was to give the impression that all South Africans, equally, were intruders of alien origin, and that the white minority had the same moral right to the land as the black majority.

For similar reasons, apartheid theorists were at pains to stress the cultural differences between different kinds of Africans. Black Africans were alleged to belong to "tribes", culturally monolithic and mutually incompatible. These could not be trusted to live in peace, and had to be sharply segregated from each other. One of the ways this was achieved was by dividing South Africa up into ethnically distinct tribal "homelands".

Apartheid theory also sought to divide this African majority into much smaller components so that the white minority no longer seemed like a white minority, but more like one tribe among many other tribes. The fact that the white tribe, a mere 13 percent of the total population, occupied more than 80 percent of the total land surface of the country was shrugged off as a mere historical coincidence.

Such crude apartheid theories are rarely met with in South Africa these days, but the underlying stereotypes still persist to a surprising extent. Many of them are the by-products of attempts to romanticise African culture and the African past for the sake of making a fast tourist buck. The stereotype of the "proud Zulu" is a good example.

South Africa's people are naturally conscious of their diverse origins, and actively seek to pre-serve all that is positive in their heritage. The importance attached to the country's 11 official languages in the very first chapter of the 1996 Constitution is a case in point.

However, the industrial revolution which followed the discovery of gold in 1886 and created Johannesburg, South Africa's first non-racial

city, fused all these diverse, pre-existing elements into a single social formation with a common destiny. The white ruling class joined together in the Union of South Africa in 1912. The black majority joined together in the African National Congress of 1912. Ever since then, South Africans have been South Africans first and foremost, although it is true that every now and then, glimpses of more retrograde tribalisms do appear.

Moreover, having suffered for so long at the hands of a government which tried to slot everybody into ethnic boxes, most South Africans today rightly resent the question "Which tribe do you belong to?"

LEFT: a ceramic head, dated to AD 500, found on an Early Iron Age site near Lydenburg, Mpumalanga.
RIGHT: San hunters armed for an expedition from a painting by Samuel Daniell, about 1830.

The first inhabitants

The earliest known varieties of humankind emerged in Africa. Physical anthropologists call them hominids, meaning that they were more than apes but less than humans. More than 300 hominid remains, some dating back about 3.5 million years, have been found at the Sterkfontein Caves and other sites in the Cradle of Humankind, a UNESCO World Heritage Site in Gauteng.

But not all hominids were the same. The *Australopithecus* (an "upright-walking small-brained creature") co-existed in South Africa with the more sophisticated *Homo Habilis* for more than a million years before finally biting

in relative isolation in the southwestern corner of the continent for about 40,000 years. These are the so-called Khoisan peoples, who once inhabited substantial parts of what is now South Africa, Namibia and Botswana.

The Khoisan were shorter and lighter skinned than most other Africans, their languages contained clicks and other unusual consonants, and they knew nothing of agriculture or iron-working. They were mostly hunter-gatherers, and they lived in very small nomadic bands following the migration patterns of wild game.

The Khoisan peoples concentrated mainly in what are today the Western Cape and Northern

the dust – surely a worthy theme for a high-tech, big budget movie.

Remains of our own direct ancestor, *Homo Sapiens Sapiens*, have also been found widely distributed throughout South Africa. African variants of *Homo Sapiens Sapiens* display genetic markers which are called Negroid by comparison with the Mongoloid and Caucasoid variants found elsewhere. Crudely put, this implies that black people have been living in South Africa for at least 100,000 years.

Within the Negroid genetic constellation, however, different groups developed in relative isolation from each other. One sub-group which we particularly need to notice must have lived

ENTER THE "MEN OF MEN"

About 3,000 years ago, a group of Khoisan living in northern Botswana were initiated into cattle-keeping by other Africans. Being herders, not hunters, they began to call themselves *Khoikhoi* ("men of men"), to distinguish themselves from the remaining hunter-gatherers, now called the San. The Dutch nicknamed them Hottentots and Bushmen, terms now regarded as insulting. Similarly, the word *Bantu*, a linguistic term embracing South Africa's extant indigenous languages, has been rendered dubious at home as a result of its misappropriation by the apartheid government.

Cape provinces. Most of South Africa was occupied by other African peoples who were darker skinned and more technologically sophisticated. They spoke languages which clearly indicate their cultural links with the rest of Sub-Saharan Africa.

Internationally, these languages are known as Bantu languages, a perfectly respectable term outside South Africa. But in South Africa the word "Bantu" was so abused by the apartheid governments that it is not socially acceptable in any context.

Today, most black South Africans speak either the Sotho-Tswana languages, which are

which they lived. Water is relatively scarce in the interior. Hence the Sotho-Tswana tended to live in bigger settlements and to build in stone. The coastal lands, however, are punctuated by many rivers running from the mountains to the sea. This permitted the Nguni to live in more dispersed settlements, and to change their dwellings more frequently.

Marriage practices are another example of the way in which environment influenced traditional customs. Among the Sotho-Tswana, cattle were relatively scarce and society was more hierarchical. It therefore made good sense to marry one's cousins and keep the cattle in the

found mainly on the interior plateau, or else they speak the Nguni languages (Zulu, Xhosa, Swazi), which are found mainly along the coast. In Limpopo Province one also finds Venda, which is a relative of Shona in Zimbabwe, and Tsonga, which is related to the languages of southern Mozambique.

Social scientists attribute the many cultural differences between the Sotho-Tswana and the Nguni to the different natural environments in

LEFT: Zulu Kraal near Umlazi, Natal, by G.F. Angas.
ABOVE: Ndebele warriors attacking, by C.D. Bell. The Ndebele troops carried large, oval, Nguni-type shields and short stabbing spears.

family. Among the Nguni, however, homesteads were more dispersed, and it made more sense to forge alliances by marrying into other families and exchanging cattle with them.

These examples show that South Africa's indigenous black cultures were well adapted to their local circumstances. The strong emphasis placed on custom and tradition was a natural recourse of people who lacked the means to record their political and legal codes on paper, but it did not prevent innovation or change. Far from being culturally monolithic and mutually incompatible, these cultures were a great deal more flexible than the apartheid theorists cared to admit. ❏

THE COLONISATION OF THE CAPE

Two centuries of European settlement failed to unite South Africa – yet the seeds of apartheid were sown

Europonolonisation of South Africa began in 1652 when the Dutch East India Company opened a refreshment station at Cape Town. The first Commandant, Jan van Riebeeck, was unable to maintain good relations with the neighbouring Khoikhoi, and he took two decisions of great importance to the future of South Africa: he established a class of permanent white settlers, and he imported slave labour. He also went to war with the Khoikhoi, and he imprisoned their leaders on Robben Island. This was the beginning of South Africa's most notorious penal settlement.

The slaves at the Cape soon came to outnumber the white population. They came mostly from the Dutch East Indies (modern Indonesia), and they intermarried with Khoisan, other African tribes and renegade whites to form a new community, known today as the Coloured people. There were no slave plantations at the Cape, and very few big farms. Most of the slaves lost their indigenous cultures and adopted the language and religion of their masters.

However, a minority of slaves, mostly political exiles and skilled artisans who had bought their freedom, adhered to their Islamic heritages. This "Cape Malay" community still predominates in parts of Cape Town such as the Bo-Kaap, which has a distinctive style of architecture.

The first white settlers farmed wheat and wine on relatively small holdings near Cape Town. But as soon as settlement expanded beyond the mountains into the drier grazing-lands of the interior, it accelerated at a frightening speed. The settlers referred to themselves as "Boers" (farmers) or "Afrikaners" (Africans) to distinguish themselves from the Netherlands officials. They took whatever land they pleased and treated the Khoisan as vermin, killing the adults and raising the children as servants. There was very little control by the feeble

Dutch East India Company, and Boer interests were well served by their local *Heemraaden* (magistrates' council).

The Huguenots

Meanwhile, the colony continued to expand. In 1688, the first of 220 French Protestants, known

as Huguenots, arrived at the Cape. They were fleeing religious persecution because Louis XIV of France had revoked the Edict of Nantes, the last guarantee of immunity for Calvinists living in France.

The impact of this small group was more significant than might be imagined: for one thing, it increased the colony's European population by about 15 percent. The Huguenots also brought with them valuable know-how, including the ability to cultivate wine. The names of some of the wine farms (La Motte, Cabrière, Mont Rochelle) in the vicinity of Franschhoek ("French Corner") still recall the places of origin of these settlers.

LEFT: the arrival of the Dutch East Indiaman *Noordt Nieuwlandt* in Table Bay on 21 August 1762.
RIGHT: a typical Boer frontier family with Khoisan servants in attendance.

Britain takes control of the Cape

The British presence at the Cape was initially strategic. During the War of American Independence, an increasing number of French vessels visited the Cape on their way to India. This development greatly disturbed the British government, then on the brink of hostilities with Napoleon. When the Dutch East India Company was finally liquidated in 1795, British forces took control of the Cape as allies of the Prince of Orange, and, although briefly returning it to the Netherlands in 1803–1806, they eventually decided to keep it.

The British were infinitely more powerful than their feeble Dutch predecessors. One of the

first loose ends they decided to tie up was the Eastern Frontier. Several Xhosa chieftains, headed by a rebellious ex-Regent named Ndlambe, had penetrated deep into colonial territory, defying all the attempts of the Dutch authorities to dislodge them. Colonel John Graham was instructed to inspire "a proper degree of terror" in "these savages", and to chase them over the colonial boundary. He did just that, also founding, in 1812, the town which still bears his name today.

To accelerate the region's integration into the British colonial system, the government in London decided to sponsor emigration programmes to the Cape. Accordingly, in 1819, some 4,000 people – mostly artisans and ex-soldiers – were granted land in the area known as the Zuurveld, bordering on the Great Fish River. Between 1820 and 1824, the settlers were shipped out from the mother country, issued with basic rations, tents and farming tools and quickly dispatched to their new frontier "farms".

The settlers were, on the whole, a literate and articulate group who were to make a lasting impression on the development of education, the press and the legal system in South Africa. However, frontier life was harsh and uncompromising. Few of the settlers were experienced farmers, and many drifted towards towns such as Bathurst and Grahamstown. Those who remained on the land had to contend with a fickle climate, regular crop failures and constant raids on their stock by marauding Xhosas.

Despite petitioning the government in the Cape to provide them with adequate protection, the settlers' pleas were to no avail. Instead, the government decreed they should use their own horses and equipment while engaged in punitive expeditions. What's more, farmers were still expected to pay their normal taxes, which only added to their grievances.

The Boers shared with the new immigrants a common resentment against the administration in Cape Town. Beforehand, as already noted, they had done more or less whatever they wanted and taken more or less whatever they could, particularly land and labour. But from 1822 onwards, a British Commission of Inquiry initiated a series of reforms designed to destroy the Boer's preferred way of life. These included more effective taxation, land allocation and more determined magisterial authority. Ordinance 50 of 1828 abolished forced labour and proclaimed authority before the law regardless of colour, paving the way for the abolition of slavery in 1834.

The Boers could read the writing on the wall, and they turned their eyes to the lands beyond the Orange River which were still outside the British sphere of control. Already, small bands of Coloured people known as Griquas, who had left the colony to escape racial discrimination, had set up de facto states beyond the River Orange. They dominated the surrounding Black nations by virtue of their access to horses and guns. From about 1834, Boer leaders such as Piet Uys and Louis Trichardt started to send out exploratory parties to reconnoitre new territories. By 1836 the mass migration of Boers, known to history as the Great Trek, was under way.

A time of troubles

Meanwhile, a very different kind of revolution was taking place north of the Thukela River in the present province of KwaZulu-Natal. It culminated in the reign of Shaka Zulu (1818–28), but it did not begin with him. The critical element in the rise of the Zulu kingdom was the militarisation of youth associations called in Zulu *amabutho*, and usually translated as "regiments". Some recent historians have maintained that this militarisation was due to the presence of Portuguese slave traders at nearby Delagoa Bay (now Maputo). But this argument falls down on chronological grounds, because the slave trade only began in the 1820s, at least 25 years after the events which led up to the formation of the Zulu state.

The decade of the 1790s saw a series of increasingly ferocious wars fought between increasingly ferocious chiefs, concluding with the establishment of the Shakan despotism in 1818. Shaka did not originate the regimental system, but he elaborated it to its highest point of perfection. He erected military headquarters throughout his kingdom, in which the various regiments were housed.

The nature of these establishments has been greatly misunderstood by romantic and reactionary writers alike, more especially the fact that Zulu warriors were not allowed to marry

LEFT: a private from the Dutch East India Company.
RIGHT: Table Bay in 1683, by Aernaut Smit, with the ship *Africa* in the foreground. The castle is depicted with the original entrance facing the beach.

until their regiment was dissolved by the king. Male regiments were, in fact, twinned with female regiments and their deprivation was social rather than sexual in nature. Although the Zulu warriors were physically mature men, they were not regarded as independent adults but as the children of the king and had to be available at all times to do his bidding.

Shaka thus obtained a degree of despotic control over his people which was unprecedented in southern African history. Legends of his cruelty abound, and although these must be treated with caution, it does seem that he became increasingly erratic as time went on. It is quite

certain that his nearest and dearest conspired against him, which tells us something. Shaka was assassinated in 1828 by his brother Dingane, with the active assistance of his other brother, his father's sister and his personal manservant.

By this time, the Shakan method had become well understood, and it was copied by a number of mini-Shakas who carved out their own despotism in diverse parts of southern Africa, including Mozambique, Swaziland, Zimbabwe, Zambia, Malawi and Tanzania. On the other hand, wiser and more tolerant chiefs built up their power by offering succour and defence to homeless refugees. Moshoeshoe, the founder of Lesotho, is the most famous example of this kind of chief. This period of South African history is sometimes called the *Mfecane*, after a word meaning "crushing", but this term has lately fallen out of favour.

Piet Retief, leader of the Boer trekkers, or "Voortrekkers", attempted to negotiate with Dingane to obtain land in Natal south of the Thukela River. But Dingane distrusted the Boers and ordered the murder of Retief and his negotiating party. The Boers rallied their forces under Andries Pretorius, who gave his name to South Africa's administrative capital. They defeated the Zulus in 1838 at the Battle of Blood River.

Later, in the 1930s, Afrikaner historians and politicians turned the events of 1838 into a nationalist and racist myth. Retief's murder became an act of primitive savagery, and Pretorius's "miraculous" victory over the Zulus a sign that the Voortrekkers and their descendants were God's people who alone had the right to rule South Africa.

The birth of the Boer republics

After their victory, the Boers in Natal set up a new republic which proved short-lived. The British were not yet ready to surrender their imperial hegemony over southern Africa, and so they annexed Natal in 1845. The Boers, however, refused to accept this. They headed across the Drakensberg into the far interior, where they founded two republics, the Orange Free State and the South African Republic (later known as the Transvaal).

The independence of these republics was soon challenged by the British. Claiming that their jurisdiction extended to the 26th south parallel, in 1848 a British invasion force annexed the entire territory between the Orange and the Vaal rivers. Eventually, however, a change of government in London contributed to the British recognising Boer independence north of the Vaal in 1852, and south of the river in 1854. The move effectively awarded sovereignty to the Boer republics.

The character of these republics may be inferred from Article 9 of the Constitution of the South African Republic (1858). This stated unequivocally that "the people are not prepared to allow any equality of the non-white with the white inhabitants, either in Church or State".

Other laws of the South African Republic also show very clearly the goals which the Boers set themselves when they embarked on the Great Trek. Every Boer who had participated in the Trek was entitled by right to two farms, which he demarcated himself. Black chiefdoms defeated by the Boers were obliged to supply them with tribute labour. The old tradition of child labour in the form of indentures (called the *inboekstelsel* because the names of the children were recorded in a book) was continued.

And if that was not enough, in 1870 the SAR legislature passed a law called the *kaffer wet,* whereby each farmer was entitled to labour service from five Black families living on his farm. This was the origin of the system of labour tenancy which still faces the post-apartheid government in the present day.

The frontier wars

Back in the Cape, Britain was still continuing what is now known as the Hundred Years War against the Xhosa people on its eastern frontier. Both the Xhosa and the settlers were stock farmers, dependent on sufficient grazing. After a series of devastating droughts, the white farmers started trekking eastwards, encroaching on tribal land. Subsequently, they were subjected to stock raids of increasing intensity.

The settlers, blaming the British administration for the lack of adequate protection, took matters into their own hands. Between 1819 and 1853 four frontier wars erupted in the border area, claiming thousands of lives and debilitating traditional Xhosa society for generations to come. Attempts by the British administration to reassert its authority were met by equally strong resistance from the farmers. Their feeling of alienation from the Cape was aggravated by their anger over lack of compensation for their losses.

From 1856 to 1857, the extraordinary incident known as the Xhosa Cattle-Killing occurred. A young girl, Nongqawuse, prophesied that if the people killed all their cattle and destroyed all their crops, the dead would rise, new cattle

The manifest failure of Xhosa traditionalism following the cattle-killing set the scene for increased co-operation between settler traders and progressive Xhosa farmers. British missionaries were very active in the Eastern Cape and they encouraged the growth of an African peasant class. Here, British commercial interests led to the liberalisation of the laws of the Cape Colony – there was even a non-racial franchise, although it included only the very well-educated.

In the British colony of Natal, however, the situation was very different, and policy was not at all liberal. Here, the British established sugar plantations which were voracious of land and

would rise, and nobody would ever again lead a troubled life. Hard-pressed by the rapid disintegration of their traditional culture under severe pressure from the settlers (claimants of their ancestral lands) and the missionaries (breakers of their traditional customs), the Xhosa resorted to desperate measures. The failure of the prophecies was manipulated by a particularly ruthless governor named Sir George Grey to ensure that Xhosa power was finally destroyed.

LEFT: the Boer leader, Andries Pretorius.
ABOVE: C.D. Bell's depiction of a surprise attack by Zulu warriors on a small party of Voortrekkers encamped near the Bloukrans River.

labour. Segregation and "native reserves" were consequently established in the colony before they were even thought of in the Boer republics. And because labour was so scarce, the British added another twist to South Africa's social fabric by introducing indentured Indian labour.

As recently as 1867 – indeed, for several decades after that – South Africa was not the unified political entity we know today. There were four white-ruled colonies and innumerable Black kingdoms and chiefdoms. Britain was the dominant imperial power, but even she had more pressing concerns elsewhere.

Then diamonds were discovered and everything changed. ❑

WEALTH AND WELFARE

The discovery of diamonds and gold created wealth,
cities and jobs. It also sparked war

South Africa prior to the mid-19th century was a rather thinly populated land with limited economic resources and a small export trade in such items as wool, ivory and hides. Before 1848 there were few roads, before 1860 no substantial banks, and until 1880 almost no railway lines. Such towns as existed,

apart from the ports, were either seats of magistracy like Graaff-Reinet, or meeting places for the quarterly *nachtmaal* of the Dutch Reformed Church.

Diamond rush

All this changed after 1867, when the first diamond was found north of the Orange River. Speculators from the Cape and Natal, a few Afrikaner farmers, and local Griqua and Tlhaping tribesmen sought to benefit from the river diggings on the Vaal and the dry diggings that soon turned into the vast prospectors' camp of Kimberley. The region became a bone of contention among the British, Free State and Trans-

vaal governments because of its strategic position. That problem was resolved, amid much controversy, by an arbitration court which ordered the proclamation of the diamond fields as the crown colony of Griqualand West.

Successful diamond mining depended on the ability of the claim-holders to control marketing, and this necessity led between 1870 and 1888 to a step-by-step amalgamation of individual claims, which was made more urgent as the mines went deeper and the work became more expensive. Cecil John Rhodes' De Beers Company eventually emerged as the pre-eminent mining house, a position it still holds.

The Kimberley mines drew in the skills of well-paid immigrants and the manual labour of low-paid Africans. The latter were recruited on contract by labour touts in collusion with chiefs, who in turn required payment of their subjects in firearms as well as other goods. The black miners were in due course housed in compounds under strict control, and subjected to close body searches to prevent diamond smuggling. The white diggers won exemption from these searches. Thus there developed a pattern of labour differentiation and control which would set a precedent for much of the industrial life of South Africa in later years.

With the birth of Kimberley, industrial South Africa came into being. It provided an urban market for foodstuffs, at first supplied largely by African farmers. Kimberley's needs also set in motion the railway age.

Gold fever

Gold, like diamonds, had been discovered in 1867, at Tati on the Transvaal border of Bechuanaland, and subsequently in various parts of the eastern Transvaal from 1874. But it was only with the location of the main reef on the Witwatersrand in 1886 that South African gold mining began in earnest. Kimberley supplied the entrepreneurs, the initial capital and some of the expertise to set Rand mining going. But the monopoly conditions necessary for diamond mining did not develop on the Rand.

The Chamber of Mines, established in 1887, went some way to regulate the competition, above all by ensuring that labour was made extremely cheap, and housed in compounds as a control device. But by 1890 the Chamber found itself in opposition to Paul Kruger's government for both political and economic reasons.

The republicans resented the intrusion of foreigners *(uit-landers)*, especially when they demanded political rights, which they were reluctant to grant. It sought to profit from gold

A WHITE LAND

By the end of the 19th century nearly all the land in southern Africa was owned by whites, either through surveyed titles, or through government control.

carved out farms and worked the mineral deposits they had acquired through victory in frontier wars. On the other, there was a contest between Great Britain as the paramount power in the region and the Boer republics for the political control of territory.

The first phase of the Anglo-Boer conflict over territory, which developed after the recognition of republican sovereignty by Britain, was a dispute between Britain and the Free State over the control of Basutoland (current-day Lesotho) and

mining but drove up production costs by, among other means, the inefficient taxing of explosives. By 1895 it was becoming clear to governments in Europe that the Transvaal had become a focal point of power, just at a moment when the international partition of Africa was gradually moving towards a climax.

The imperial factor

The European occupation of southern Africa was a double process. On the one hand, there was the physical appropriation of the greater part of the land by white colonists as they

LEFT: a miner's life. ABOVE: diamonds are forever.

the diamond fields. Both territories passed under British control and both were later transferred to the Cape Colony, but Basutoland was made a British protectorate in 1884, as were Bechuanaland (Botswana) in 1885 and Swaziland in 1902.

From 1868 it became a stated objective of British policy to amalgamate the South African territories politically for reasons of defence and economy. In 1875 Disraeli's Colonial Secretary, Lord Carnarvon, sought to do this, but he forced the pace, and failed to win the backing of the Cape government. In 1877 he did, however, succeed in annexing the Transvaal in an adroit move designed to put pressure on the Free State.

The annexation proved a fiasco, partly because of poor administration, partly because the Afrikaner leadership under Paul Kruger organised a successful rebellion in 1880–81 and persuaded Gladstone that it would be wise to withdraw. Conventions signed in 1881 and 1884 restored the Transvaal's independence on terms which gave Britain, at best, an ambiguous right to intervene in its affairs.

When gold mining developed on the Witwatersrand, it became apparent that the economic balance had shifted to the north, and that whoever ruled the Transvaal would dominate South Africa. Deep-level mining on the Rand pro-

duced only narrow profit margins, partly due to Kruger's fiscal policy, and this created at least a temptation to overthrow his government.

Cecil Rhodes, prime minister of the Cape from 1890 to 1896, had already unsuccessfully attempted to incorporate the Transvaal in a South African railway and customs union, and then to encircle the republic by purchasing Lourenço Marques (Maputo) from the Portuguese. In 1895 he plotted a rebellion on the Rand to be assisted by an invasion by his British South Africa Company forces from across the border. But the Jameson Raid, planned with the knowledge of the British Government, also failed, and seriously undermined Kruger's

willingness to trust the British. Rhodes was therefore discredited and resigned.

The Anglo–Boer War

In a sustained diplomatic face-off in 1899, the British drove Kruger to the brink of war by insisting on the full recognition of *uitlander* rights. Kruger yielded ground to the point at which his pride could yield no more, and anticipated a British ultimatum by invading the coastal colonies in October.

The Anglo–Boer War of 1899–1902 at first went well for the Boers, who scored major victories against a heavily equipped, well-trained enemy. Only when the main British forces arrived were they able to invade the allied republics, occupying Bloemfontein and Pretoria by June 1900. However, the war dragged on for two more years. Boer guerrilla forces raided across the plateau. The British commander, Kitchener, responded by moving Boer women and children into concentration camps. These were a disaster, their poor sanitation causing the deaths from disease of close on 28,000 Boers and many thousands of black refugees. Finally, and bitterly, the Boers surrendered in 1902. Their two republics, and the gold fields, became part of the British Empire.

The conflict had a profound effect on the moulding of South African political attitudes. Most Boers believed that they were the victims of a monstrous British injustice; that the British had set out to destroy them as a people. Latter-day Afrikaner nationalism was born out of a determination to put right these wrongs by making sure that South Africa became an Afrikaner country, not a British one.

However, the myth that it was a "white man's war" which didn't affect blacks has little historical evidence to support it: blacks were recruited as labourers and scouts by both sides in the conflict, though the Boers were more reluctant than the British to issue them with arms. Blacks also suffered directly and in large numbers during the sieges and from the destruction of farms, as well as from the concentration camps, where more than 14,000 died. But their hardships went relatively unnoticed in the published accounts, and, when the war was over and the peace treaty signed, they had little to expect for their sufferings. ❑

LEFT: for three years, the Boers kept the British at bay.

Kruger and Rhodes

With his baggy black suit, straggly beard and enormous pipe, Paul Kruger was caricatured by the world press as a typical "backveld" Boer, but critics who underrated his undoubted political skills did so at their peril.

Born in 1825 in the Cape Colony to a Boer family of German origin, Kruger was a veteran of the Great Trek. As he liked to remind his audiences, he had seen the circle of wagons, the children melting lead to make bullets, and the women hacking off the arms of those Zulus who tried to break through the thorn bushes between the wagons at the Battle of Blood River.

With no formal education, his first "profession" was that of lion hunter, but he quickly rose within Voortrekker ranks by showing his mettle on command, as the Boers battled to wrest land from Black chiefdoms north of the Cape. By the age of 36 he had been appointed to the rank of commandant-general. In 1877, when Britain annexed the Transvaal Republic, Kruger emerged as the Boer's national champion, and was twice sent to London to try to persuade the British to abandon their policy. Finally, in 1883 he was elected president of the Transvaal, now known as the South African Republic – an office he was to hold for four terms.

A Calvinist to the core, with an unshakeable belief that his "volk" were God's chosen people who alone had the right to rule South Africa, Kruger was a forceful personality, but Afrikaner as well as British opponents found him headstrong and autocratic.

Provoked into declaring war on Britain in 1899, it was Kruger's misfortune to lead his beloved republic to defeat. When the war started to go badly he went into voluntary exile, following events closely to the final defeat of the Boer forces in 1902. Refusing to submit to British rule, he remained in exile, dying in Clarens, Switzerland in 1904. His remains were brought home for burial at Heroes Acre in Pretoria.

If ever there was a *bête noire* almost custom-made for Kruger, it was Cecil John Rhodes. Born in Hertfordshire, England in 1853, the son of a vicar, Rhodes was first sent out to Natal to recuperate from tuberculosis. The sickly youngster soon found his way to the new diamond fields at Kimberley, where he conceived an ambitious plan to gain total control of the entire diamond industry. By 1889, Rhodes and his mining company, De Beers Consolidated, had achieved his goal.

Obsessed with furthering the cause of British imperial expansion, Rhodes combined his commercial genius with an equally ruthless career in politics. Made prime minister of the British Cape Colony in 1890, he used intrigue and war to grab the lands of the Matabele and Shona north of the Limpopo, and establish under royal charter his personal states of Northern and Southern Rhodesia (now Zambia and Zimbabwe). This effectively blocked Kruger's South African Republic from expanding north of the Limpopo.

But a scheme to topple Kruger and seize the republic's goldfields for the British led to Rhodes' downfall. The Jameson Raid of 1895, in which Rhodes tried to organise a committee of leading *uitlanders* (dissatisfied immigrants) to overthrow the Transvaal government with the help of a column of British police, failed dismally – Kruger's government got wind of the plot before it even took place. This fiasco not only marked the end of Rhodes's political career, it also helped to alienate British and Afrikaners across the whole of South Africa.

Rhodes died in his Muizenberg cottage (now a museum) in 1902, his dreams of a British "Road to the North" unrealised. Paradoxically, the glittering financial empire he built continues to be a mainstay of South Africa's economy. ❏

RIGHT: Paul Kruger, the "Wounded Lion".

UNION AND RESISTANCE

By the early 20th century, whites dominated South Africa –
despite the fact that blacks far outnumbered them

The Peace of Vereeniging registered the victory of the Empire over the Boers shortly after white domination of South Africa was finally achieved. The 20th century would witness a speedy Afrikaner return to power, and then – after 90 years of assertive white dominance – the start of an impressive Black resurgence.

Britain annexed the former Boer republics in 1902, but made it possible for them to regain autonomy. This was largely the achievement of generals Louis Botha and Jan Smuts, who saw the need for conciliation among whites – between Empire and Boer, Boer and English speaker, and rival groups within Afrikanerdom – but left the problem of dealing with Blacks to the "stronger shoulders" of the future. The British government thought that extending the vote to Blacks would jeopardise their aim of conciliating the whites.

Meanwhile, Black political organisations watched resentfully as Britain first allowed the Transvaal and Orange River Colony to acquire white-controlled constitutions in 1907–8, and then agreed after the national convention of 1908–9 to a Constitution for a united South Africa, which did substantially the same thing.

Britain aimed to restore the South African economy by bringing the mines back into production and resettling the uprooted on the land, thereby coaxing the Afrikaner back into the imperial fold. Black labour might be essential for this task, but not Black voters. Reconstruction therefore took place, conciliation among whites began to work, and the Union of South Africa took its seat with the other white dominions in the British Commonwealth of Nations.

As a member of that imperial system, South Africa took part in two world wars and played a leading role in the evolution of dominion autonomy between 1917 and 1934. The involvement of prime ministers Louis Botha, Jan Smuts and Barry Hertzog in the consultations of the Empire were themselves a clear indication of how well conciliation had worked. However, it operated only on the surface, and was not able to contain the groundswell of opposition underneath.

The Union of South Africa in 1910 was an embryonic industrial state, with mineral exports (especially gold) far exceeding agricultural, and with a developing manufacturing industry producing mainly for the local market. These years also witnessed a parallel townward movement by both Afrikaners and Black South Africans.

Resurgence of Afrikaner power

Afrikaner republicanism was reborn soon after union, on a platform of opposition to the imperial connection and a demand for the effective recognition of Afrikaans language rights. The former found expression in the rebellion of

LEFT: the proudly named "Union Express", symbol of a newly united country, carried passengers from Cape Town to Johannesburg.
RIGHT: mineral wealth fuelled the colonial economy.

1914, triggered by the government's decision to invade German South West Africa, while the founding of the secretive Broederbond in 1918 led to a spread of Afrikaner cultural and economic organisations, the latter with a focus on the rescue of poor whites.

Both found a political mouthpiece in the National Party governments of General Barry Hertzog between 1924 and 1939: first in alliance with the white Labour Party and after 1932 in alliance with General Smuts (until their fused United Party was split asunder when Hertzog tried to keep South Africa neutral in World War II).

Hertzog's strident nationalism was toned down once he had seen that South Africa could remain within the British Commonwealth without the rights of the Afrikaner necessarily being threatened. But this wasn't the view of a new "purified" National Party, which grew after 1934 under the leadership of Dr D.F. Malan.

Malan's party, the voice no longer just of the poor whites but also of a new brand of Afrikaner entrepreneur seeking economic power, won the 1948 election and remained in power without a break until the first democratic elections for all South Africans in April 1994. Afrikaner voters, some of whom had been

attracted to Leninism in their poverty of the 1920s, had entrenched themselves not only on the land but also in the civil service and the professions, and more recently in business too. English speakers, by contrast, remained politically marginal, though their business dominance remained strong.

Roots of Black opposition

But the main catalyst for change, which gradually came to monopolise the attention of the white political establishment, was the numerical growth and urban drift of Black South Africans. A small minority in all urban areas at the time of union, Blacks were in the majority in nearly all of them by the mid-century, though they were required nearly everywhere to reside in "locations" away from the towns proper.

Blacks were also effectively debarred by law from political and trade-union activities, and controlled in their movements by pass laws. This ensured that many could not move from white-owned farms to towns. The majority, who remained in the tribal reserves, were also prohibited from acquiring land outside the reserves by the Land Acts of 1913 and 1936. Thus tied down, Blacks found it hard to organise themselves effectively to promote political or economic change.

During World War II, it seemed that segregationist policies might be reduced under pressures generated by the Atlantic Charter. The wartime government of General Smuts tried to ameliorate the conditions of urban Blacks, ceased briefly to enforce the pass laws, began to build Black secondary schools, made a start with Black pensions and disability benefits, and professed its rejection of the principle of segregation.

But in the run-up to the general elections of 1943 and 1948, the Smuts government could not contain the rising propaganda of the National Party. Smuts's failure to initiate a change of direction led to a major confrontation with the African Mineworkers' Union in 1946, in which lives were lost. This broke Black trust in Smuts. His government's attempts at policy changes, on the eve of the 1948 election, were neither sweeping enough to attract Black backing nor cautious enough to prevent the white electorate from casting their votes decisively for Malan. ❑

LEFT: Afrikaner general Smuts.

Gandhi

The development of the sugar cane industry in the 1860s in what is now KwaZulu-Natal meant that large numbers of indentured Indian labourers were imported by the British colonial authorities to work in the plantations. Many settled in South Africa after finishing their contracts, establishing small businesses. Thus trade connections with India grew, and Durban, in turn, developed into South Africa's most distinctively multi-cultural city.

In 1893 a 24-year-old advocate named Mohandas Karamchand Gandhi came to South Africa to act in a lawsuit between two Indian trading firms. Having landed at Durban, he caught a train to Pretoria in connection with the suit. He had a first-class ticket, but during the journey a white passenger objected to his presence in the compartment, and he was ordered to move to a third-class coach.

Ignorant of South African racial prejudice, he refused – and was promptly ejected from the train for his pains. He spent the night at Pietermaritzburg station. The incident made such an impression on Gandhi that in later life he declared it had been the single most important factor in rousing his spirit of protest and determining his political career.

Gandhi's subsequent involvement in the Indian community's struggle for civil rights kept him in South Africa for 21 years. It was here that he first developed the philosophy of *satyagraha* which made him world-famous, and which later played such a key role in India's struggle against British colonial rule.

Satyagraha means "keep to the truth". Gandhi considered truth a central life-principle – one which meant, in practice, resisting injustice not with force, but with the superior powers of love and spiritual conviction. Hence his conception of passive resistance as a form of political protest.

The community of Indian entrepreneurs in Natal was a flourishing one, but deeply resented by white traders who disliked undercutting. Attempts to establish Indian businesses in the Transvaal were met with restrictions on residential and trading rights; Natal also imposed a hugely unpopular £3 tax on Indians who wished to stay in the colony after the expiry of their indentures.

The young Gandhi quickly became one of the Indian community's most articulate and influential

leaders, founding the Natal Indian Congress in 1894. He also pursued his professional career with great success, first in Durban, then in Johannesburg.

But it was in protests against the Immigration Act of 1913, restricting Indian settlement in the Transvaal, that his passive resistance campaign reached its climax. Strikes were organised in the coal mines of northern Natal, which soon spread to sugar and other plantations. Finally, on 1 November, more than 2,000 *satyagrahis* started a march to the Transvaal with the intention of breaking the law and being arrested and imprisoned. The authorities could do little beyond make mass arrests,

God is Truth

MKGandhi

thereby seriously threatening work on the sugar estates. Gandhi himself was sentenced to 9 months' imprisonment.

The net result of all the upheaval, the Indians' Relief Act of 1914, addressed some of the community's chief grievances, such as the hated £3 tax and the fact that Indian marriages were not recognised. However, Indians were still denied any sort of official political representation.

Nonetheless, Gandhi considered his work in South Africa completed and returned to India, where he immediately threw himself into the struggle against British rule. His ideal was finally realised in August 1947, when India became independent. Tragically, only a few months later in January 1948, he was assassinated by a Hindu fanatic. ❑

RIGHT: the philosopher-politician Mahatma Gandhi.

THE RISE AND FALL OF APARTHEID

The 1950s saw segregationist policies entrenched into a system
that would stain the subcontinent for nearly half a century

The National Party headed by Dr Daniel François Malan, a preacher and journalist before becoming a politician, won the 1948 general election by a narrow margin and against expectations. The bulk of support came from recently urbanised whites who feared the challenge of blacks in the marketplace, espe-

cially as the African National Congress (ANC), in association with the African Mineworkers' Union, showed signs of growth during the 1940s.

The new government's response was to bring out a legislative programme designed to entrench white (and by implication Afrikaner) dominance. The principles of apartheid (separateness) dominated the government's legislative programme from the start. It enacted a Population Registration Act to slot everybody into an appropriate race group, as well as to outlaw interracial matrimony or sexual relations, and a Group Areas Act to divide every town in South Africa into defined sectors where only members of particular groups could own or occupy property. This required the physical removal of many coloured and Asian households, but few whites. Most resented of all were the "pass laws" which restricted the movements of blacks. The legislation was buttressed by laws designed to undercut political resistance, beginning with the Suppression of Communism Act. It was followed by measures which would restrict individuals and organisations, while denying them right of appeal to the courts.

Growing black resistance

After Dr Hendrik Frensch Verwoerd – a chief promoter of apartheid legislation – became prime minister in 1958, the policy was developed to promote territorial partition so that the African reserves could be turned into "independent homelands" whose citizens could on that pretext be deprived of access to political rights in the South African heartland. Verwoerd tried to establish border industries to enable blacks living in the homelands to find employment in "white" South Africa with minimal daily travel; but he would not allow white capital to finance such development. His successor, Balthazar Johannes Vorster, a lawyer and staunch supporter of traditional Boer principles, removed this restriction; but by 1970 it was clear that job creation in the homelands fell far short of providing a living for the number of Africans required by government policy to live there.

PASSIVE RESISTANCE

A campaign against the pass laws (which restricted the movements of blacks throughout white areas) during the war eventually led to the launching of a Defiance Campaign in 1952, a well-orchestrated passive resistance tactic by African, Asian and Coloured movements to offset the white tercentenary celebrations. Its forceful suppression led to the public adoption of a freedom charter at Klipfontein, near Johannesburg, in 1955 – a broad social democratic affirmation designed to achieve widespread public support.

Such policies strengthened support for the ANC. The oldest existing political party in the country, it had formed for six decades the vanguard of black political aspirations. It was in January 1912 that representatives of the country's major African organisations met in Bloemfontein to form the South African Native National Congress. The movement, which was soon renamed the African National Congress, had its agenda cut out. Two years earlier the Union of South Africa had been forged out of the ashes of the Boer–British struggle, but had ignored the position of the vast majority of the country's citizens.

Mandela. They were soon strong enough to stage an internal coup and to get their candidate, Dr James Moroka, elected president. This marked the beginning of a new strategy of direct, non-violent confrontation.

Documents confiscated by the police when they broke up the Klipfontein gathering *(see box opposite)* formed the basis for the first of a number of "treason trials" which marked the next 35 years. The defendants were all found innocent in 1961, but in the meantime divisions opened up within the ANC. A group of "Africanists" led by Robert Sobukwe was disturbed by communist influences on ANC policy, arguing

The ANC spent its first years protesting the historical errors committed at the Union. But its critics accused it of being an organisation of elderly men fighting to preserve their hard-won, middle-class privileges. Impatient activists joined the fledgling labour movements that advocated more radical action. In 1943 the ANC Youth League was formed by a group of young men whose political legacy is still felt: the brilliant Anton Lembede, Oliver Tambo, Walter Sisulu and an enigmatic young lawyer, Nelson

LEFT: Grand Vizier of apartheid, Dr Hendrik Verwoerd.
ABOVE: Sharpeville, 1961. Police bullets killed 69 protestors, hitting many in the back.

that if a racist government was in power the assertion of African nationalism was the real note to strike. Driven out of the ANC in 1958, they broke away to form the Pan-Africanist Congress (PAC).

When the government launched its campaign for a republic in 1960, the ANC and PAC were at daggers drawn, yet both were angling for mass support by promoting anti-pass demonstrations linked to wage demands. Some 30,000 Africans marched on the Houses of Parliament in Cape Town. Police bullets killed 69 protesters at Sharpeville, near Vereeniging on the South Rand, on 21 March, and the government, clearly frightened, banned both the

PAC and the ANC, driving them underground. The world condemned the Sharpeville shootings, and South Africa's ostracism in world affairs began.

White responses

In a whites-only referendum, Dr Verwoerd obtained a narrow victory to proclaim a republic and his government subsequently decided to leave the British Commonwealth. Sharpeville had shown the inadequacy of passive resistance and drove the African resistance movements into violent opposition. In 1962, however, the police captured the underground leaders of the

ANC, headed by Nelson Mandela, in Rivonia, outside Johannesburg, as they were planning to disrupt public life. After an eight-month trial, they received life sentences in the notorious Robben Island prison.

The ANC and the PAC set up bases in exile in Lusaka, Dar-es-Salaam and London, but found it hard to make much impact locally or internationally. For almost 10 years the South African government managed to keep a lid on black political activity. Activists were rounded up and held under detention without trial.

In September 1966, Hendrik Verwoerd was stabbed to death in the House of Assembly by a parliamentary messenger. His successor, B.J.

Vorster, was better at silencing opposition than developing strategies for change. But, when capital started to flow back into South Africa, he tried to revive the socio-economic aspects of apartheid. Investment corporations were set up to develop the homelands. The expansion of black businesses, black housing, black schools and black immigration into the white area was made harder.

By 1970 the number of jobs created in the homelands was seen to be nowhere near that required if Africans were to be able to "flow back" from the white areas. The government decided to press ahead with homeland "independence", starting with the Transkei in 1976. The aim was to create alternative allegiances, thus depriving all citizens of "independent" homelands of their South African citizenship even if they still lived in the republic.

The tide turns

On a cold winter's day, 16 June 1976, Soweto, the large African residential location outside Johannesburg, erupted after a government decision to enforce the use of Afrikaans as a language medium in schools, though the grievances were far wider and included objections to homeland independence. Much of the drive came from a new Black Consciousness Movement led by Steve Biko, an activist from the Eastern Cape.

Over a period of 18 months the burning of public buildings, schools, liquor outlets and cars had most of the African townships in flames and the conflagration soon also spread into coloured and Indian residential areas. The government again clamped down heavily. On 18 August 1977, Biko was arrested by the security police. Twenty-six days later he died from head injuries sustained during interrogation.

Black consciousness was too well-rooted to be effectively extinguished; it re-emerged in other forms, linking Africanist aspirations to a socialist ideal. Many young activists fled the country, joining the waiting structures of the ANC in exile. This influx of new blood rejuvenated and strengthened the movement considerably. Led by Oliver Tambo, the ANC redoubled its onslaught against the government on two fronts: the military, where they achieved moderate successes with sabotage attacks on strategic installations; and international isolation, where they continuously pushed for strong punitive measures – economic sanctions, arms embargoes and cultural and sporting boycotts.

Internally, black opposition re-emerged in 1985 with the formation of the United Democratic Front (UDF), a loose federation of anti-apartheid movements, linked ideologically to the ANC. A new generation of black leadership – "the '76 generation" – came to the fore. When they were restricted, trade unions became a focal point of political activity, leading to the creation of the giant Congress of South African Trade Unions (COSATU). Church leaders emerged as vocal spokesmen for black aspirations, with men like Archbishop Desmond Tutu and Dr Allan Boesak becoming household names across the world. Tutu became the second South African to

Namibia), in a dispute with the United Nations which had started soon after World War II. Talk of international sanctions, beginning with an arms embargo in 1963, was spreading to include economic and cultural boycotts. Almost the whole world condemned the republic's policies.

Vorster's government fell after disclosures of serious financial mismanagement in the running of its propaganda activities. The scandal divided the ruling National Party and propelled the defence minister, Pieter Willem Botha, to the premiership. Botha restored effective control over government. He also tried to rebuild the economy, which went into deep recession from

win the Nobel prize for peace (the first, in 1961, was Albert Luthuli, a Natal teacher who had become leader of the ANC in the 1950s).

World opinion

In the 1960s and 1970s, Vorster's government had offended world opinion by refusing to support sanctions against the white rulers of Rhodesia, and by holding out against the transfer of power in South West Africa (present-day

LEFT: Hector Pietersen, the first victim of the riot police at Soweto, 16 June 1976.
ABOVE: a groundswell of public violence was a hallmark of the apartheid years.

1982 as a result of a sustained drought and a dramatic fall in the gold price, aggravated by a move among the world's banks to impose a stranglehold on South Africa's borrowing.

Far from trying to abolish apartheid, Botha attempted in 1983 to make it irremovable. He secured white electoral support for a new Constitution, which not only made him an executive president (as distinct from the largely formal office created in 1961) but also created ethnically distinct Houses of Parliament for whites, coloured people and Indians, with no representation for Africans.

This led to renewed violence in the new coloured and Indian constituencies when a general election was held in 1983. By then, the ability of black organisations to conduct effective resistance had markedly increased as industrial workers and resistance leaders in the townships began to act together.

The ANC, for its part, was now concentrating on building up its links with the international community, setting up missions in many parts of the world where the South African government was not represented, even acquiring diplomatic recognition in some.

Furthermore, the homeland structures, Verwoerd's brainchild, were beginning to collapse as "independent" states – in some instances

thrown into confusion on the eve of a general election which had been forced upon it by a deadlock with the Coloured House of Representatives arising out of the terms of the 1983 Constitution.

Apartheid in reverse

Botha's mantle fell on the shoulders of the Transvaal leader of the National Party, Frederik Willem de Klerk, who won the 1989 white general election by an outright majority over opponents of both left and right after seeking a mandate for unspecified reform. Educated and confident, de Klerk was an example of a new

through the exposure of corruption, in others through the overthrow of ruling dynasties – ground to a standstill. In Natal, even though KwaZulu's Inkatha movement had opposed independence, something like open warfare developed between Inkatha and ANC supporters as each side attempted to build up its constituency in anticipation of an eventual redistribution of political power.

Paralysed by a manifest inability to keep his policies on course and in the face of a growing threat from a new Afrikaner right wing, P.W. Botha was forced out of office by a ministerial rebellion in September 1989. The future direction of the National Party was thus

"BLACK-ON-BLACK" VIOLENCE

During the 1980s and early '90s, parts of KwaZulu-Natal and Gauteng turned into battlegrounds as something like open warfare raged between members of the Zulu Inkatha movement (later, the Inkatha Freedom Party) and the Xhosa-dominated UDF (sympathisers of the then-banned ANC). Mostly, UDF-backed "civic" movements were fighting to discredit Inkatha councillors elected under the unpopular local government legislation of 1983. Thankfully, this form of civil unrest has now declined almost to the point of non-existence.

generation of Afrikaners who came of age after the introduction of apartheid and began to question the very basis of the system they inherited.

Because he was known to be a supporter of narrow, white "group interests", many doubted his will to go for real change. But South Africa could no longer afford to maintain apartheid in an increasingly hostile world, with a weakened economy, and with a ruinously expensive war which had broken out on the South West African border against members of the South West African People's Organisation (SWAPO).

Opening the parliamentary session of 1990, de Klerk undertook to remove apartheid,

another source of international protest: he attended the independence celebrations as South West Africa became Namibia, ending a deadlock that had lasted more than 40 years.

De Klerk found a willing negotiating partner in the pragmatic Mandela. Opening the South African Parliament in February 1990, he said the government wished to negotiate a new Constitution with equal political rights for all. The ban on political opponents was lifted and the leaders of the liberation movements released from jail or allowed to return from exile. Even so, a groundswell of public violence was a constant reminder that the transition would not be easy.

promising sweeping reforms. He planned to move cautiously, consulting the ANC leadership step by step. On 11 February 1990 he unconditionally released Nelson Mandela, the last of the imprisoned ANC leaders, after he had served 27 years in jail. It was a momentous decision because it signalled to a world which had long regarded Mandela's imprisonment as a symbol of apartheid's evil that a milestone had been passed. Six weeks later de Klerk removed

LEFT: ANC supporters campaign for non-racial, democratic elections.
ABOVE: a first-time voter proudly displays proof of her newly won democratic rights.

The odd couple

Hopes for the country's future centred to a remarkable degree around de Klerk and Mandela – a fact the outside world recognised by awarding them jointly the 1993 Nobel Peace Prize. But could de Klerk neutralise groups such as the Afrikaner Resistance Movement, who still referred to the ANC as "the Antichrist"? And could Mandela reconcile the ethnic rivalries cemented by centuries of violence?

Mandela called his election manifesto "A Better Life for All". It promised 10 years of free education for all children, a million new homes, and a public works programme to provide jobs for 2½ million people. These were unrealistic promises, according to de Klerk, who knew better than most that there had been little significant investment in infrastructure for years, and that the annual 6 percent growth of the 1960s had turned into negative growth by the 1990s.

After prolonged multi-party negotiations, South Africa's first democratic elections took place in April 1994. They were described by one official as "unmitigated chaos": many ballot papers went missing, while allegations of fraud and malpractice were rife. Yet millions of people who had never seen a ballot paper before queued for hours under a hot sun to cast their vote. Old women, some aged more than

National Party out of government and into opposition. Mandela remained an international hero, being accorded a state visit to Britain in 1996. At home, however, there were accusations of ANC corruption and authoritarianism, while the big question was how long the black majority would wait for the president to make good his promises to improve their economic wellbeing.

"The wheels of government grind slowly," was all Mandela would say. But at least they *were* grinding, and the transition to black majority rule – an event which only a few years before had seemed utterly improbable – had been

100, were pushed in their wheelchairs to the booths. White women lined up alongside their maids. Archbishop Desmond Tutu danced a jig for the cameras after voting in Cape Town. A Johannesburg radio station played Louis Armstrong's *What a Wonderful World*. After 342 years and 23 days, white rule had come to an end.

Despite the allegations of chicanery, the election was declared free and fair, and the ANC emerged with 62 percent of the vote. On 10 May 1994, Nelson Mandela, former prisoner 466/64, became president. F.W. de Klerk, meanwhile, became one of two vice-presidents.

The "marriage" between Mandela and de Klerk lasted until 1996, when de Klerk took the

achieved without the predicted bloodbath. What's more, South Africans, white and black, had accomplished the miracle themselves, without the intervention of international tribunals or peace-keeping forces. Hope, although still fragile, had begun to bloom again.

In 1999, the ANC was re-elected but Mandela retired to make way for his deputy, Thabo Mbeki. In April 2004, South Africa celebrated a decade of democratic rule as the ANC remained in power with a 70 percent majority. Weeks later South Africa was chosen to host the 2010 FIFA World Cup. ❑

ABOVE: people queue to reach the voting booths, 1994.

Mandela

Born the son of a chief in 1918 in rural Qunu, Transkei (now the Eastern Cape), a member of the Thembu royal household, Nelson Rolihlahla Mandela first became involved in politics as a student at the University of Fort Hare. It was here that he met Oliver Tambo, later to become the African National Congress's first president-in-exile.

After being expelled from Fort Hare for their role in student strikes, both young men moved to Johannesburg. Here, Mandela met Walter Sisulu, and the three – Tambo, Sisulu and Mandela – became key movers in ANC politics, helping to found the ANC Youth League in 1944. The League was extremely influential in pushing the ANC towards adopting a more radical stance on protest action, and, in particular, founding the 1952 Defiance Campaign. Based largely on Gandhian principles of non-violence, the Defiance Campaign involved the deliberate breaking of apartheid legislation, such as the hated "pass laws".

Mandela completed a BA degree by correspondence and then studied for an LLB at the University of the Witwatersrand, before establishing (with Tambo) Johannesburg's first black law firm in 1952. In 1958 he married Winnie Madikizela, a social worker, and the couple had two daughters.

When the ANC was banned in 1960, the organisation decided that the time for peaceful protest was over. Mandela went underground to form *Umkhonto we Sizwe* (the Spear of the People, commonly known as MK), and to organise a campaign of sabotage. Tambo left the country to re-establish the ANC in exile.

Mandela survived "underground" for 17 months, training as a guerrilla fighter in Algeria and visiting Britain and many African states in search of support for MK. He became famous for staying a step ahead of the police, earning himself the nickname "the Black Pimpernel". But his luck ran out in 1962 when he was caught in a police trap. His links with MK as yet unknown, he was charged with "leaving the country without permission" and given a five-year jail sentence. Then, in 1963, the police raided MK's Rivonia headquarters and discovered evidence of Mandela's role in the organisation. On 12 June 1964 he and eight others, including his old friend Sisulu, were found guilty of plotting to overthrow the state and sentenced to life imprisonment. Mandela was sent to Robben Island.

RIGHT: South Africa's first black president.

For the next 26 years, the ANC's leaders in exile struggled to keep the organisation active and united. They were helped in no small measure by Mandela's fame as an internationally respected leader and symbol for human rights, which grew the longer he remained in prison.

After his release in 1990, Mandela went on to play a central role during the four long, troubled years of multi-party negotiations, which finally culminated in South Africa's first democratic elections in April 1994. On 10 May of that year he was inaugurated as South Africa's first black president, a position he held until his retirement at the next election in 1999.

In 1996, Mandela divorced his wife, Winnie, a loyal ANC member whose reputation had become increasingly tarnished by scandal, including a conviction for kidnapping. Two years later he married Graca Machel, widow of the former Mozambican president, and set about building himself a retirement home back in Qunu.

Despite the problems his government had trying to implement an ambitious programme of reform, Mandela remained enormously popular throughout his term of office, not least with many white South Africans who had once regarded him as a terrorist. He had come to be seen as the living embodiment of new, longed-for standards and values in post-apartheid South Africa, and his departure marked the passing of an era. ❑

LIVING TOGETHER

The transition to majority rule wasn't easy. But it has produced a fascinating and complex Rainbow Nation characterised by diverse origins and a united purpose

It has become one of the most difficult questions to answer. Indeed, sensible people have simply stopped asking it: who or what is the typical South African? Other countries might have a stock of comfortable national stereotypes to fall back on, but in South Africa cultural clichés change from suburb to suburb, never mind city to city.

For many, the stock image of Africa starts with the stereotypical "noble savage": people and cultures both primitive and vibrant, still magically in touch with the ways of the natural world. And let's not forget that crucial sense of rhythm, honed after generations of dancing around ceremonial fires.

South Africa has an extra element. The white settlers, the people responsible for inventing apartheid, live here too: burly, bearded, khaki-clad folk who clutch rifles to keep marauding lions, rhinos and the occasional restless native at bay. It's the image most people have of the Afrikaner, and it's the way many people imagine all white South Africans to be.

But these stereotypes have little basis in reality. South Africa is an extraordinary tapestry of race and culture. And despite the problems of the past, it's a society that's beginning to find great strength in diversity.

A complex culture

Diversity is what South Africa's young democracy is all about. No fewer than 19 different parties participated in the first democratic election in 1994, collectively representing practically every aspect of the country's political, religious and social spectrum. Following that election, linguistic diversity was recognised when the ANC accorded official status to 11 languages: English, Afrikaans, Zulu, Xhosa, Sotho, Venda, Tswana, Tsonga, Pedi, Shangaan and Ndebele.

PRECEDING PAGES: traditional Ndebele dancers; sport attracts South Africans from all walks of life.
LEFT: a new generation hopes for further reconciliation.
RIGHT: an everyday transaction in Franschhoek.

Switch on the television in South Africa today and you'll find news broadcasts coming at you in each of the four main language groups – English, Nguni (Zulu and Xhosa), Afrikaans and Sotho – while radio tells it like it is in all 11 languages. Switch over to a local football match and you'll get your commentary broken up into

15-minute slots, alternating between Zulu and Xhosa, English and Sotho. Diversity? South Africa surely invented the term. So the one thing first-time visitors shouldn't pack is the preconception of a nation divided into two basic groups of blacks and whites. Nothing is simple in South Africa; it's a far more fascinating place than that.

Melting-pot – or divided society?

South Africa's 48 million inhabitants are comprised of four main elements. Indigenous Africans form the overwhelming majority, but 9 percent of South Africans are of European descent, while another 9 percent consists of people of mixed origin (known as coloureds), and one in 40 South Africans claims Asian descent.

The key division within black South African society is between the Sotho (South Sotho, Bapedi, Tswana), and the Nguni (Zulu, Xhosa and Swazi). Originally, academics split nations between these two groups on the basis of language, location and population patterns – early Nguni settlements tended to be dispersed, whereas the Sotho lived in concentrated towns. Additionally, societies such as the Shangaan-Tsonga belong to neither group. Nor do the people of Venda, whose 30 independent chiefdoms include the Lemba, who claim to be a lost tribe of Israel.

in the establishment of the mining industries. A sizeable group of Jewish refugees from the Baltic settled in the country after World War I and became involved in trading and manufacturing, laying the foundations for one of the most prosperous sectors of the local economy.

More recently, the 1960s saw an influx of Lebanese, Italian and Greek Cypriot settlers, as well as Portuguese from Madeira, Mozambique and Angola. The Soviet invasions of Hungary (1956) and Czechoslovakia (1968) also brought new immigrants. All these people played an important role in the economy by supplying new skills and helping to create job opportunities.

The main cultural divide among white South Africans is along linguistic lines. There are the English-speakers, many of whom descend from the 4,000 British who settled in the Eastern Cape in 1820, And there are the Afrikaners, whose mother tongue Afrikaans is regarded to be the world's most modern language, having evolved from the archaic Dutch spoken by early Cape settlers and spiced with various European, African and Oriental influences.

Other, smaller groups abound. South Africa's Jewish community (about 130,000 strong) has made an indelible impression on cultural and economic life, with the likes of Barney Barnato and Alfred Beit having played an important role

The term "Coloureds" refers to those of mixed descent, most of whom speak Afrikaans as a first language, but it also includes a number of other sub-groups such as the 200,000-strong Malay community centred on Cape Town's Bo-Kaap district. More recent arrivals from Asia were the indentured labourers – Indians to the sugar farms of KwaZulu-Natal in the 1860s, and the Chinese as mineworkers on the Witwatersrand in 1904 – whose descendants now number about 1 million.

Shaped by conflict

A series of wars – including the frontier wars of the Eastern Cape, the Zulu Wars and the Boer Wars – originally established the basis of the relationship between South Africa's different communities, both black and white. This bleak history, along with the 1913 Land Act and the brutal legacy of apartheid, pretty much defined South African society as it is today. Most of South Africa's socio-linguistic groupings are traditionally associated with a specific location, a situation that was exploited by the engineers of apartheid, who attempted to confine 42 percent of the population to the 13 percent of the land designated as nominally self-governing homelands.

Today, most Zulus still inhabit the province of KwaZulu-Natal, while the Eastern Cape and parts of the Western Cape remain Xhosa terri-

a distinctly English flavour, and is home to the majority of the country's Indian population, while the Eastern Cape is split quite evenly between English- and Afrikaans-speaking whites.

Of course, these are just simplistic outlines. Numerous farming communities in northern KwaZulu-Natal, for instance, possess a strong Afrikaans element, while the Western Cape – the domain of Afrikaans speakers, both coloured and white – has a significant English-speaking population centred on Cape Town. Finally, there's Gauteng – multicultural South Africa at its most vibrant and diverse, and home to everyone and anyone.

tory, and the Northern Cape, North Western Province and Free State are inhabited by the Sotho and Tswana. Different parts of Mpumalanga and Limpopo provinces are variously home to the Venda, Pedi, Shangaan and Ndebele peoples.

Regional bias can be noted among the non-indigenous communities. The Western Cape, Northern Cape, North West, Free State, Limpopo and Mpumalanga are all strongly Afrikaans, with the first two also forming important strongholds for the coloured community. KwaZulu-Natal has

LEFT: the annual Queer Party in Cape Town.
ABOVE: township kids taking a break.

SURVIVING AGAINST THE ODDS

The last surviving San and Khoikhoi communities fall into the coloured category, although their numbers are now so small that they can no longer be said to represent distinct social groupings. A few small bands of San still roam the arid Kalahari desert, pursuing their traditional nomadic hunter-gatherer lifestyle. Of the Khoikhoi, several communities of Griqua (one of the main clans) have settled around Kimberley in the Northern Cape Province; while the last surviving Nama, another key group in this category, live in an area situated near Steinkopf on the northwest coast.

So how does this social jigsaw fit together? Well, it's a relatively new experience for most. Apartheid tried to confine everyone to discrete ethnic boxes, so that the only black faces one would have encountered in a middle-class white suburb belonged to the people who hung out the laundry or mowed the lawn. Back then, most whites would have regarded a trip to a black township as akin to visiting hell – a hostile land filled with angry people ready to rob, mug or roast alive the white oppressor. But the Afrikaner Nationalists who devised apartheid failed to grasp that this diverse conglomeration of people at the southern end of the continent actually belong together. Paradoxically, years of conflict has only created a stronger sense of shared history. And the advent of democracy has heralded a new openness to cultural mixing – indeed, post-millennial South Africa is not merely accepting its multicultural identity, but actually starting to embrace and thrive on it.

Land of many tongues

South Africans are faced with a linguistic scenario that makes the lot of those ancient Babylonian tower builders seem relatively simple. Indeed, language is the first clue you get that the differences between people here are not simply a matter of skin colour – the Xhosa language is as different to Venda as German is to Spanish, while English has as much in common with Afrikaans as Italian does with French. In practice, however, English is increasingly the main lingua franca, both officially and unofficially, though Afrikaans still retains this role in many rural areas. Of the other official languages, Zulu is probably the most widely used nationally, and Sotho and Xhosa are also used on a wider scale, but the others are more or less confined to their regional bases.

The major cities have attracted people from all over the country since the turn of the 21st century,

thanks to mines and industries, and have their own distinctive styles of communication. The townships of Gauteng gave rise to the colourful street-slang known as Tsotsi-taal (gangster, or bad-boy language), which combines elements of Afrikaans and African languages with expressive North American gangster slang, and typifies the style of the ultra-cool modern youth.

Today it's a pervasive part of everyday township lingo, full of coded names and expressions: the ever-present minibus taxis are called "Zola Budds" (because they're always crashing into each other, as athlete Zola Budd did, colliding with Mary Decker at the Los Angeles Olympics). The small, 200-ml bottles of spirits commonly sold at shows and sporting events and in shebeens are called "cellulars", because they fit into your pocket like a cellphone.

When things are named like this, it signifies a lasting cultural acceptance. The same applies to people – a football player without a nickname obviously hasn't touched the hearts of the fans. Popular nicknames include "Chippa", which implies the skill to "chip" a shot beyond an opponent's defence. "Dancing Shoes", or "Shoes", is another, given to players who can "dance" past opponents with the ball.

MIXED METHODS

Today, traditional medicine in South Africa works hand in hand with modern science to tackle problems such as tuberculosis.

ably be late. When this happens, the person stood up is supposed to roll eyes heavenwards and say, "Well, that's African time". It's a generalisation based on two myths. The first is the old racist stereotype of blacks as lazy and uncooperative. The other, often propagated by black South Africans themselves, is that "This is Africa, man. Relax... don't be white and uptight. Everything will get done in good time."

These different understandings of the nature of "African time" are at the heart of a bigger

Former national captain Neil Tovey (a white in a predominantly black team) earned the unique nickname CODESA II after the 1991 negotiations in which the principles of non-racial democracy were hammered out.

Culture clashes

All this "living together" business does create room for misunderstanding. One popular generalisation, referred to as "African time", is that it's pointless making appointments with black South Africans, since they will invari-

LEFT: *kappies* like these are worn to church.
ABOVE: models in the annual Anglo Gold competition.

debate concerning how South African society should be advancing. There are those who argue that a more Afrocentric approach is called for, while others – often called Eurocentric – believe that modern realities require Africa to shift away from the traditional mindset and get into step with the rest of the planet.

While they debate themselves into a meaningless lather, the reality is that South African society already is a fascinating blend of African tradition and modern principles. In the suburbs, a white householder calls in a traditional healer to prepare charms to protect his home after the sophisticated alarm system has failed to do the job. Across town, a black mother-to-be puts her

Zulus

Accrding to South African journalist Khaba Mkhize, "there are two types of Zulus – postcard Zulus, and the type of Zulu who is running away from the postcard". South Africa's largest black nation has been subjected to some particularly crude stereotyping in the past, from the caricature of the cattle-herding peasant to that of the bloodthirsty tribalist, sporting leopardskin and waving a spear.

Based on fragments of apartheid propaganda, bolstered by the "tribal" souvenirs mass-produced for the tourist market, such images have little bear-

ing on reality. Most Zulus today view themselves as citizens of South Africa, rather than identifying themselves first and foremost as members of a tribe. In any case, as more and more people opt for an urban lifestyle, the old customs and traditions are fast being displaced by "Western" ways.

What is certainly true is that the Zulus were once a mighty military power. The late 18th and early 19th centuries were characterised by almost constant Zulu warfare – against neighbouring clans, against the Afrikaner Voortrekkers, and against various British regiments (KwaZulu-Natal's historic "Battlefields Route" bears fascinating and sometimes chilling testament to these torrid times). Legendary leaders such as Shaka

Zulu are still a source of fireside tales and a symbol of both resistance and national pride.

This legacy has been shrewdly exploited by the right-wing Inkatha Freedom Party under the charismatic Mangosuthu Buthelezi, former Minister of Home Affairs. Although he began his political career as an ANC member, he has fallen in and out of bed with the organisation over the years; during the 1980s, the IFP also accepted secret military and financial aid from the apartheid security forces.

With a membership drawn from the most deprived rural areas of KwaZulu-Natal, where the cult of the warrior is still prevalent, the rabidly nationalist IFP was caught up in a series of bloody clashes with the Xhosa-dominated UDF which persisted throughout the 1980s and 90s. Although some analysts sought to crudely characterise this "Black-on-Black" violence as the latest stage in an ancient tribal feud, in fact hostilities first arose out of disputes relating to local government issues. Both black political movements were struggling for control of the townships, each attempting to build up its constituency in anticipation of an eventual redistribution of political power. In the process, thousands lost their lives.

As for urban Zulus, not all have traded in their cultural roots for a briefcase or a factory job. Millions remain faithful to at least some semblance of custom and culture, consulting *nyangas* (traditional healers) and paying *lobola* (the traditional "bride-price" paid by a bridegroom to his father-in-law). Notwithstanding urbanisation and Christianity, a belief in ancestral spirits is still strong.

Today, as the whole issue of ethnicity becomes less of a hot potato in post-apartheid South Africa, something of an indigenous cultural renaissance is getting underway. Post-apartheid, there is official support for all aspects of traditional black culture, from music and theatre to traditional healing. "Cultural villages" have been set up to promote indigenous crafts and customs – at Simunye Pioneer Settlement in KwaZulu-Natal, for example, visitors can spend time listening to tales of battles with the British from a Zulu perspective, filled with "unofficial" oral history. Most importantly, thanks to a post-apartheid update of the history books, black schoolchildren are now able to take pride in their tribal heritage without being patronised or politically branded for it.

At long last, it seems the Zulus can turn their backs on those postcards. ❑

LEFT: Zulu dancer in imaginative headgear.

faith in a Jewish, London-trained, gynaecologist rather than the rural midwife her mother went to.

And at the local stadium, black and white fans urge on a player kitted out by Adidas and anointed with a secret *muti* (traditional medicine) by the team *sangomas* (healers) – the opposing viewpoints in the Afro/Eurocentric debate become partners in the cause of victory.

Not all traditional beliefs make the modern South Africa feel comfortable. Rural black attitudes to homosexuality, for example, are almost

A LONG WAIT

Islam arrived in South Africa in 1658, but repressive conditions meant the first mosque (in the Bo-Kaap) was only erected in 1798.

tianity predominates among both black and white, yet even this common belief was a tool of divisiveness during the apartheid era.

The Dutch Reformed Church (DRC) lay at the heart of the apartheid mindset, citing biblical writ to justify government policy – though it also produced some powerful critics from within its own ranks, most notably Beyers Naude, a former DRC minister who broke away to found the Christian Institute. In 1986, the DRC publicly rescinded apartheid and apologised to black South Africans.

medieval – some conservative elements simply refuse to acknowledge such a thing exists. Still, at least things have come a long way since the days when homosexuals were thrown into the communal cattle-kraal to be trampled to death. In the major urban centres, the majority of black communities now accept gay culture as a part of life.

Religion

Although traditional faiths still have a place, especially in rural areas, most South Africans subscribe to one or other exotic religion. Chris-

By contrast, Anglican church leaders played a leading role in the anti-apartheid movement, most famously Nobel Peace Prize-winner Desmond Tutu, the first black archbishop of Cape Town and head of the Anglican Church in southern Africa. Also critical of apartheid, the Catholic Church's cross was first raised in South Africa by Bartolomeu Diaz at Santa Cruz in 1486 and again by Vasco da Gama in Mossel Bay in 1498, and today it has 2.5 million adherents in South Africa. Also well established are the Methodists, Baptists, the Salvation Army and the Greek Orthodox Church.

Then there are the various African Indigenous Churches (AIC), which broke away from

ABOVE: rugby fans, their faces patriotically painted in the colours of the new South African flag.

the mainstream denominations in the 1880s and still operate independently from them today. Key features of their faith include a belief in prayer healing and baptism by total immersion, along with a general prohibition on tobacco, alcohol, medication and pork. Hundreds of small congregations, each with a different name and colourful uniform, gather for weekend services throughout South Africa. The largest AIC grouping is the Zion Christian Church, which was founded in 1914 and has its own settlement

ANCIENT RELIGION

A 100,000-year-old cave grave in northern KwaZulu-Natal is thought to be the oldest recorded evidence of religious activity.

Healing and religion are closely interrelated. As Christians, however, AIC members make it clear that they do not pray to ancestors for intervention; on the other hand, like followers of indigenous religions, they don't put much store in conventional medicine. Rather, they believe in the power of faith-healers *(umthandazi)* and prayers for the sick. The biggest churches not only have a number of faith-healers with immense reputations and constantly overcrowded consulting rooms, but also have their own range of herbal treatments,

at Zion City Moria, near Polokwane in Limpopo Province.

Many elements of traditional African religion inform the AIC belief system. For instance, the circle is a powerful symbol in both beliefs. Another very significant element taken over from tribal religion is the emphasis on harmony with God and one's fellow man. The AIC isn't rich and its "temples" usually consist of a simple circle of whitewashed stones set around a high tree that mimics a church steeple. AIC members congregate within the circle, sitting and kneeling on simple grass mats. In bad weather, a round hut accommodates the proceedings, its central pole replacing the tree.

coffee, tea and strict rules for healthy living. Although professed Christians, faith-healers do not always undergo training.

Today, the Constitution guarantees complete freedom of worship not only to these varied Christian denominations, but to countless other religious communities – which include Jews, Muslims of mostly Malay or Indian descent, Hindus, and smaller numbers of Buddhists.

Closing the poverty gap

South Africa is in a state of economic transition. Apartheid separated communities, social services, business activity and political life along ethnic lines. Bringing together these disparate threads has been, and remains, a social and economic project comparable to the challenge that faces much of eastern Europe. South Africa has the advantage of comparatively established market networks and economic infrastructure. It has the disadvantage of extreme inequality in wealth, considerable backlogs in education and housing, rapid urbanisation, the lingering effects of the social disruption caused by the migrant labour system, a high rate of HIV infection, and a lack of jobs that enforces more than half of the population to live below the poverty line.

up income-generating opportunities rather than re-engineering a failed interventionist blueprint.

On the social front, the most striking successes of the ANC have been improved electrification and water supplies to low-income communities, and extensions to the network of primary health clinics. In 2007, the country's fifth general household survey estimated that residents in 80 percent of homes could switch on lights and run electrical appliances, a great improvement on the 1999 figure of 60 percent. Similar progress was noted with respect to access to running water, sanitation, education and sufficient food.

The ANC has thus far juggled the dual – and sometimes conflicting – goals of free market economic growth and interventionist wealth redistribution with some adroitness. The flagship Reconstruction and Development Programme has set out ambitious targets for creating jobs, building houses, extending electricity and telecommunications lines, redistributing land and improving basic education, health and welfare services. But the ANC recognises that this policy depends on opening

Land reform has been a slower process. Government has assured local and international communities that it will not tolerate a "land grab" process like the one that has crippled Zimbabwe. But the process is long and slow and, so far, only a small fraction of the farmland earmarked for redistribution by 2014 has been achieved. But if the system works, the outcome of the land reform policy will redress one of the injustices of apartheid, and will foster national reconciliation, underpin economic growth and alleviate hardship and poverty.

The expansion of educational opportunities under the ANC tells a mixed story. South

LEFT: some 20 percent of Indians and Cape Malays follow the Islamic faith.
ABOVE: village life in Arniston.

Traditional Religion

A minority of black South Africans still follow traditional religions, most strongly in rural areas, but there are also many believers who are urbanised and "Westernised".

Traditional African religion is based on a holistic conception of the universe. Religious practices are supposed to preserve and reinforce harmony within the web of an individual's relationship to himself and his family, to his society and environment, to the realm of spirits, both good and evil – and ultimately to God. Keeping damaging influences at

bay and healing damaged relationships is therefore extremely important.

Traditional beliefs and ceremonies are informed by the animistic conviction that natural elements and objects such as rivers, trees and wind possess a soul. But the central tenet is a belief in a Supreme Being, who can only be reached by people on earth through the medium of their ancestors. Because the ancestors are already with the Godhead, they are venerated as the "living dead", and may pass on their descendants' requests regarding such important matters as rain, health and fertility.

But first the ancestors have to receive a sign. Traditionally, this would be given by slaughtering

an animal, which was then divided communally and consumed – with the dead ancestors duly receiving their portion. The head of each household functioned as family priest; in matters concerning the whole community, the chief took the role. He killed the cow or goat with a spear reserved for the purpose, and conveyed the requests of the living to the ancestors.

Diviners and mediums have always played – and still play – an important role in traditional religion. According to popular belief, people are most vulnerable to illness, often caused by sorcery, when their ancestors are "facing away". Traditional healers – *inyangas* or *sangomas* – give instruction in the rituals which will placate the ancestors and ensure good health, as well as prescribing *muti* (medicine).

An estimated 300,000 traditional healers minister to the physical and spiritual needs of South Africa's black community. These include herbalists or *inyangas* (usually male), and diviners or *sangomas* (usually female), who specialise in divining the illness and its causes by spiritual communication with the patient's ancestors. Both kinds of healer have a comprehensive knowledge of herbal remedies and of the medicinal properties of many plant species used to make up pharmaceuticals today.

The most common treatments administered by traditional healers are poultices, lotions, ointments, hot and cold infusions, and powders rubbed into parts of the body where incisions have been made. Healers also prescribe blood-letting, enemas and emetics to flush impurities out of the system. Plants are the basis of most traditional remedies, but some also use animal and bird parts.

Today, traditional healing is enjoying a growing respectability in health-care circles. Many conventional medical practitioners recognise the wisdom of the traditional healer's holistic approach, which incorporates psychological, social, cultural and spiritual facets in the healing process. It is also recognised that, thanks to a critical shortage of qualified doctors, a high proportion of the rural population currently depends on herbal remedies. Some South African universities have therefore introduced traditional healing as a medical-school subject, to train students in the importance of using natural resources in primary health care. ❑

LEFT: a *sangoma*, traditional healer, undergoes an initiation ceremony.

Africa has near-universal enrolment for 10 years or more of schooling, and participation in higher education now exceeds one million. But this rapid growth has resulted in an increase of governmental education spending to around 20 percent of the annual budget – high by any international comparison – and has contributed to strains in management capacity and some glaring qualitative deficiencies. Science and mathematics teaching in particular is woefully inadequate.

Historically, South Africa's fortunes have risen and fallen with those of gold, diamonds and other minerals – the mining of which accounted for 70 percent of export earnings as recently as 1990. The government's economic strategy today centres on supplementing an unhealthy dependence on extracting raw materials from the earth with the greater expansion of manufacturing sectors. Since 1994, manufacturing growth has been steady, and annual investment in plants has grown by 30 percent. Strong export growth in recent years has been spread across a wide range of products, thanks to a more competitive exchange rate, favourable regional and global market trends, and export incentives.

Another welcome economic stimulant has been South Africa's rapid transition from tourist pariah to one of the world's travel hotspots. Tourism is now the world's fastest-growing industry, and it is estimated that one new job is created for every eight tourists who visit South Africa annually. The rapid growth in this sector, sustained even through the post-9/11 international tourist recession, is a potential economic goldmine in which South Africans from all backgrounds are claiming a stake.

As in many developing countries, the official statistics have gaping holes. Household survey data show that total employment is about 10 million, nearly double the total measured by the regular data series. This is because informal trade – heavily repressed a decade ago – now flourishes. Formal industry may not be creating employment, but there is a complex balance to be struck between promoting technological progress and global industrial penetration, and ensuring that casual

RIGHT: years of apartheid laid a foundation of poverty that will take decades of reform to eliminate.

earning opportunities extend into townships and rural areas.

The ANC government has had to balance the need for reform with that of stabilising an economy that was already ailing badly in 1994 and might easily have collapsed after the election due to lack of faith.

It has thus committed itself to a fairly conservative regime of tight public expenditure control and falling budget deficits. Inevitably, this strategy came in for heavy criticism from the ANC's allies in the South African Communist Party, but it has also reaped benefits in terms of increased international investment, a

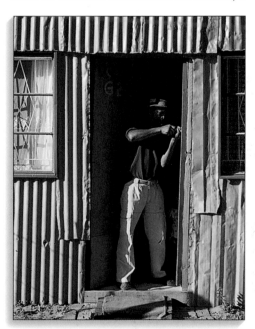

SHIFTS IN POLICY

ANC policy since 1996 has moved away from its former commitment to nationalisation. The government now tends to play down its socialist past and play up the fact that it is committed to a moderate, growth-driven economic programme which will provide for the privatisation of many state assets, as well as a reduction in the size of the civil service. The so-called "route of Africa" – the typical snap replacement of a right-wing settler regime by a left-wing liberation movement which soon displays feet of clay – seems to have been short-circuited in the case of South Africa.

remarkable recent turnaround in the performance of the formerly beleaguered rand, and the slow but sure reversal of the negative balance of debt inherited from the apartheid government.

Undeniably, South Africa has come a long way since 1994. Transformation ideals have given way to the more tedious projects of building institutions and reconciling public spending goals to the available means. Black business interests are rapidly making more money than their unreconstructed competitors. Career prospects are now more prominent than political struggles in the minds of ambitious students.

Furthermore, whatever contradictions might blight its economy, South Africa's GDP exceeds that of the rest of sub-Saharan Africa combined, and the country is also rapidly realising its potential as a continental economic powerhouse. South Africa's past still casts shadows over the country's prospects, but its policy debates are firmly focused on the challenges of the future.

Coming together

On 3 February 1997, exactly seven years after President De Klerk announced his plan to scrap apartheid, South Africa adopted a Constitution that is widely regarded to be among the most liberal in the world. A major democratic milestone, this new Constitution recognised that all South Africans are entitled to a common citizenship in a sovereign and democratic state in which there is equality between men and women of all races, where all can exercise their fundamental rights and freedoms. The Constitution also contained a Bill of Rights which guaranteed freedom of movement; freedom of opinion, religion and belief; and equality and equal protection before the law.

How did things change so quickly? Well, there is the Mandela factor, the fact that this most remarkable political transformation was overseen by a statesman whose gift for reconciliation gained him tremendous respect across all race barriers. Furthermore, it is clear, in hindsight, that most white supporters of apartheid were motivated not by malice towards its victims, but by the fear of an uncertain future as a minority group under black rule. Once that future arrived in all its non-racial benignity, there was little to fear any more, nowhere to go but forward, and the vast majority of South Africans – black or white, male or female, straight or gay – embraced their new democratic identity with remarkable enthusiasm.

This newfound sense of national identity is most evident perhaps in the sporting arena. Supporting your country in sport is something most people take for granted, but under apartheid it was common for black South Africans to support foreign teams over "white" local teams, while their sports-crazed white compatriots became increasingly embittered at the sanctions that prevented South Africa from taking on the world's best. With the end of apartheid came re-admission into international sport, and suddenly South Africans of all colours and political persuasions were united in a frenzy of adulation for their sporting heroes. Furthermore, over the course of almost 15 years of democracy, formerly divided sports have become increasingly racially integrated, so that the hopes of every white cricket supporter might rest on the speed and accuracy of a Xhosa bowler, or those of black football fans on the anticipation and athleticism of an Afrikaner goalie. ❑

LEFT: South Africa's natural beauty attracts tourists who provide much-needed economic stimulus.

Truth and Reconciliation

Yasir Henry is a traitor. He betrayed the whereabouts of his friend, Anton France, to the authorities, and on 4 September 1984, his friend died in a hail of police bullets. Now Henry is seated before a microphone in a gloomy public building somewhere in Gauteng. Tears trickle down his face; the members of the public listening to his testimony are hushed. Yasir Henry betrayed his friend after being tortured by the police. Ever since, he's been tortured by the image of Anton dying with a single unanswered question on his lips: "Who betrayed me?"

The line between victims and criminals is a thin one in South Africa. It seems scarcely possible that the scars left by 40 violent years of apartheid could ever be healed, yet the South African Government attempted to do just that. The Truth and Reconciliation Commission, established in 1995 under the chairmanship of Nobel Peace Prize-winner Archbishop Desmond Tutu, aimed to investigate gross human-rights violations committed by all parties between 1 March 1960 and 10 May 1994. It also aimed to recommend reparation for victims.

The regular televised sittings of the Commission included shocking disclosures of atrocities committed by senior officials in the National Party, the police and the Defence Force, as well as members of the Inkatha Freedom Party, the ANC and PAC and other organisations involved in the anti-apartheid struggle.

Yet, extraordinarily, the Truth Commission was not geared towards punishing offenders. Instead, they were to be granted amnesty and indemnity if their crimes could be proved to have been "politically motivated" – while victims were given the chance to speak out about the injustices done to them and so perhaps liberate themselves to some extent from the burden of their memories.

Tutu's insistence that the Truth Commission's emphasis was less on "settling things legally" and more on allowing all South Africans to come to terms with the past in a cathartic spirit of reconciliation angered some of the families of apartheid victims, who indicated that they would instead prefer to see justice done. Yet Tutu was adamant in his espousal of a Christian philosophy of forgiveness. And while critics said that hearings were also disappointing in

RIGHT: Nobel Peace Prize-winner Archbishop Desmond Tutu.

terms of extracting candid confessions from apartheid's worst sinners, most would nonetheless agree the Commission was a vital first step in the essential process of creating a new national morality. "South Africa cannot step confidently into the future unless and until it has made an honest effort to come to terms with its past. And the TRC is that effort," noted the *Star* newspaper.

Human rights activist Alex Boraine, who structured the Truth Commission, spent several years researching the task. He studied 15 similar bodies worldwide, in countries such as Guatemala, El Salvador, Chile and Argentina, and reached a somewhat depressing conclusion. In most cases, the key perpetrators of

human-rights abuses – high-ranking military officials – had simply ignored the whole process. "Each commission was supposed to help the victims of an unjust regime start a healing process, but in the end, they all gave up trying. Each has left behind an underclass of victims who have never had any reparation for what they went through," he noted.

So far, South Africa's Truth Commission may be unique in having found a solution. Thousands of people voluntarily gave testimony; people like Yasir Henry – forgiven, at last, by his friend's family, after confessing to his crime. The process was a "risky and delicate business", admitted Archbishop Desmond Tutu, but it was "the only alternative to Nuremberg on the one hand, and amnesia on the other". ❑

THE PERFORMING ARTS

Despite drastic cuts in subsidies to performing arts bodies,
a cultural renaissance is slowly getting underway

The growth of indigenous theatre in South Africa has been inextricably linked to the country's harsh political realities. The 1980s, in particular, produced a wealth of "protest plays" focusing on the damaging social and psychological effects of apartheid. Unfortunately protest art loses it's momentum once its cause is won.

Theatre complexes such as the Market Theatre in Johannesburg built their reputations as avant-garde centres staging original works which reflected the lives and aspirations of all South Africans. It was a laborious process, often hampered by state censorship and not always artistically successful. But it produced some memorable theatre that was exported to international stages.

Actors and playwrights to succeed abroad include Athol Fugard *(A Lesson from Aloes)* and the hugely successful partnership of John Kani and Winston Ntshona *(Sizwe Banzi Is Dead* and *The Island)* who were both honoured with the USA theatre's highest accolade, the Tony Award. An expatriate actor, Zakes Mokae, later won the award for his performance in Fugard's *Master Harold and the Boys*.

Often dubbed "the father of Black theatre", Gibson Kente provided through his "theatre of the townships" numerous opportunities for aspiring writers and actors to become major stars. This provided the impetus for talented writers such as Mbongeni Ngema, Barney Simon and Percy Mtwa to take their trailblazing production, *Woza Albert*, onto the international stage.

Works of the playwright Mbongeni Ngema have also been performed across the world. Ngema's *Asinamali* wound up on Broadway in 1987 and won a Tony nomination for best director. In 1988, he took his hit musical, *Sarafina,* to New York's Lincoln Theatre and then to Broadway, where it played to capacity audi-

ences for 11 months. *Sarafina* has also been made into a film starring Whoopie Goldberg.

The arts and the ANC

The end of apartheid has brought enormous changes to the performing arts. The ANC's developmental programme is focussed on housing, edu-

cation, land redistribution, health and the general upliftment of the formerly disadvantaged, but it is also official policy to support indigenous art in every sphere, without detracting from the vitality of the well-established Western tradition. Post apartheid, there has also been a heartening resurgence of interest in South Africa from outside the country, leading to a renewed surge of artistic and cultural exchange.

Opera, theatre and ballet are officially supported in the sense that venues such as Cape Town's Nico Malan Theatre Centre and Pretoria's State Theatre receive state subsidies. In the meantime, South Africa's ballet scene is adapt-

---

LEFT: government subsidies for the classical performing arts – including ballet – have all been slashed.
RIGHT: modern drama.

ing to the challenges of the post-apartheid era. The country's only school of ballet, established at the University of Cape Town in 1934, has now been privatised, as has the high-profile PACT, a former provincial arts council. Both companies continue to mount impressive repertoires of classical works and indigenous ballets, and are committed to maintaining standards of excellence.

Music: a new crossover

Although orchestras have faced particular difficulties as a result of subsidy cuts, they have, in the main, managed to survive. The

Soweto String Quartet which best typifies the exciting new trend towards the merging of Western and African musical forms. Under the leadership of Sandile Khemese, the quartet gained international recognition with their 1996 hit, *Zebra Crossing*; they are still one of South Africa's best-loved classical groups.

Also notable has been the revival of traditional Afrikaans *boeremusiek*. Legendary Afrikaner musicians such as accordion player Nico Carstens are even recording and performing songs which mix the style with the heavy bass rhythms of township *mbaqanga* – an extraordinary fusion which would have been unthinkable before 1994.

independently run Cape Town Philharmonic Orchestra (formed after a merge between the former Cape Town Symphony Orchestra and the CAPAB orchestra) performs regularly and also serves as a pit orchestra for opera, ballet and musicals.

The Natal Philharmonic Orchestra in Durban and the National Symphony Orchestra in Johannesburg (the latter formerly sponsored by the South African Broadcasting Corporation) are now both privately funded and performing at every opportunity, although there is no certainty at this point that their financial futures are secure.

Choral music has found a ready "crossover" market, but perhaps it is the success of the

A stage beyond

As for drama, the disappearance of apartheid and the lifting of the cultural boycott has proved something of a mixed blessing for home-grown theatre – so long reliant on the protest genre – and seems hard-pressed to find fresh themes.

There have been a few interesting departures, among them Athol Fugard's *Valley Song*, which explores issues of individual, rather than simply political, discontent. Paul Slabolepszy's inspired discourse on rugby fever, *Heel Against the Head*, is another noteworthy exception. Yet debacles such as the *Sarafina II* scandal – the Ministry of Health's AIDS education play, commissioned from celebrated playwright Mbongeni Ngema, which eventually cost some R14 million to stage – have done little to provide the local theatre scene with that much-needed spur. Nonetheless, the overall standard of production of works by both local and foreign playwrights remains encouragingly high.

Celebrating a new tradition

Another more positive sign is the flourishing festival scene. Mother of all arts gatherings is the Standard Bank National Arts Festival – South Africa's equivalent of the Edinburgh Festival – which completely swamps the small

Karoo Nasionale Kunstefees, begun in 1994 as an Afrikaans alternative to the mainly English-dominated National Arts affair, this vibrant Oudtshoorn-based event hosts open-air events from music and dance to drama and poetry.

Then there's the North West Cultural Calabash, a four-day celebration of traditional African culture based in the peaceful village of Taung and established 10 years ago. Every September, visitors come to see the amazing displays of traditional dancing (Tswana, Tsonga and Zulu-style) and to soak up the rural atmosphere, as well as for the more conventional offerings of jazz, drama, fine art and ballet. ❏

Eastern Cape town of Grahamstown every July (www.nafest.co.za). Apart from a packed programme from dance, theatre, music and opera to fine art, film, cabaret and jazz, it has craft fairs, flea markets, buskers galore and, of course, a Fringe.

Grahamstown may dominate, but an increasing number of smaller celebrations are now appearing on the festival calendar throughout the year. One of the best-known is the Klein

LEFT: ballroom dancers, Cape Town.
ABOVE: if both Western and African cultural traditions are nourished, so the thinking goes, one rich, multi-faceted culture may one day emerge.

NEW BOUNDARIES, FRESH TALENT

Local opera has seen a remarkable infusion of fresh talent since the early 1990s. Composer Bongani Ndodana's work is especially notable for the way it fuses divergent Western and African traditions – his 1998 opera-oratorio *Uhambo* deploys an *imbongi* or praise singer alongside a chamber orchestra and soloists. Also notable is Cape Town's Michael Williams, whose opera productions draw on a mix of Xhosa, Kenyan and North American Indian folklore. Roelof Temmingh's chamber operas also continue to win prizes both at home and abroad.

THE MUSICAL TRADITION

*With its rich, multicultural musical history, South Africa offers a
potent mix of indigenous and world musical trends*

South Africa is distinguished by one of the richest musical histories and most complex profusion of styles on the continent, and probably has the best-developed recording industry. Its music – although deeply influenced by Europe and the USA – is unique.

Traditional music

Southern Africa's earliest known musicians were San hunter-gatherers who sang in a click-filled language, produced a variety of instruments – rattles, drums and flutes – and adapted forms of their hunting bow for making music.

The Khoikhoi ("men of men"), who arrived in southern Africa some 3,000 years ago, seem to have been more sophisticated in their musical tradition. When the Portuguese explorer Vasco da Gama landed at Mossel Bay in 1497, a Khoikhoi band treated the expedition to a performance on reed flutes. These were rather like a set of dismantled pan pipes, with each player blowing on one reed to produce a single tone at a set point. Probably da Gama heard a set of four different reeds playing a four-note melody.

Five centuries later, the Venda in Limpopo Province follow a similar principle. The only difference is that a large number of players produce each pitch and, since the reeds cannot all have the exact same bore, they create the impression of a conglomerate of microtonal pitches grouped around four notes.

The Bantu-speaking cultures of South Africa were even more musically sophisticated. Their strongly developed vocal tradition included songs to accompany every occasion, from the initiation of adolescents to spirit exorcism, from festival days to education. Yet, whatever the song, the underlying musical structure consisted of two or more linked melodic phrases which were repeated ad infinitum, but staggered in relation to each other, producing a simultaneous polyphony. This is the basis of the "call and response" arrangement

of later African-American styles such as gospel, doo-wop and soul.

Christian missionaries provided the first contact with Western music in the 19th century, and trained pioneers such as Enoch Mankayi Sontonga, who in 1897 composed *Nkosi Sikelel' i Africa* ("God Bless Africa"), a national anthem.

The Cape Malay tradition

The early Dutch settlers at the Cape relied on slave labour; indeed, slaves soon came to outnumber the white population. They came mostly from the Dutch East Indies (Indonesia) and intermarried with Khoisan, Africans and renegade whites to form a new community, known today as Coloureds.

A minority of the slaves, mostly political exiles and skilled artisans who had bought their freedom, adhered to their Islamic heritage. This "Cape Malay" community still predominates in parts of Cape Town such as the Bo-Kaap, and their traditional music still has marked Eastern characteristics: for instance, a couple of rhythmic

---

LEFT: African music: as colourful as it is creative.
RIGHT: the San adapted the traditional bow
and arrow for making music.

instruments (the portable drum, or *gomma*, and the large tambourine, *rebana*), an Eastern singing style marked by *karienkels* ("sound wrinkles" of microtonal decorations surrounding certain melody tones), and also by traditional vocal styles which have survived 300 years of estrangement from their original country.

Some of these are of a religious nature (for example, the *pudjies*, antiphonal singing divided between an imam and members of the congregation), while others are connected with wedding ceremonies (for

> ## THE PEOPLE'S BEAT
>
> As in the United States, township jazz developed as a grassroots genre, rather than the preserve of an elite clique of fans.

a three-chord progression, repeated endlessly in traditional style. A solo voice sang over an organ or guitar, drums were improvised, and pebble-filled condensed-milk tins provided percussive accompaniment.

Marabi was flexible enough melodically to absorb anything from hymns to Tin Pan Alley hits, and skilled musicians added depth by varying the theme and by improvisation. But what really gave the new music its raw potency and edge was its anti-establishment stance, for *marabi* was the authentic sound of the

instance, the antiphonal *minnat* songs which are sung at an extremely slow pace by a leader and a group of male guests). But they also preserved songs reflecting their two centuries of serfdom, which have, ironically, been absorbed into the Dutch repertoire of folk songs.

Township jazz

By the 1930s, a vibrant black urban culture was firmly established in South Africa's larger towns, despite strict segregationist laws which restricted blacks to the townships at night. The expanding ghettoes of Johannesburg were to spawn this culture's most distinctive musical sound. Dubbed *marabi*, it consisted of a single phrase built around

shebeens (unregulated township drinking haunts), rather than the government-licensed and rigidly controlled beer halls.

The style quickly evolved. Legendary band leader Willard "Zuluboy" Cele introduced modern instrumentation. Later, idioms from American swing were blended in by popular bandleaders such as Zakes Nkosi. Later still, bebop was to prove a big influence, notably in the performances of reed virtuoso Kippie Moeketsi. Dorkay House became downtown Johannesburg's jazz haven, providing a platform for established players and a training ground for new ones.

In the 1960s, another new genre arose. White audiences had developed a taste for township *kwela* – simple saxophone-based jive tunes – and record companies accordingly started to put pressure on artists to record tracks in this style, along with lyrics. Purist jazz saxophonists disdainfully referred to this music as *mbaqanga* (meaning "just-add-water-and-stir") yet the vocal component of *mbaqanga* soon developed into a distinctive South African sound.

Also in the 1960s, many brilliant musicians – Hugh Masekela, Abdullah Ibrahim, Miriam Makeba and Jonas Gwanga among them – left to escape the pressures of apartheid, creating an enthusiastic following for South African jazz abroad. At home, the jazz scene mellowed,

marrabenta rhythms with a big-band format, the band Bayete, gospel singer Rebecca Malope, and young jazz-influenced vocalists such as Gloria Bosman and Busi Mhlongo.

Contemporary style

The most popular musical figure of the 1990s was undoubtedly disco diva Brenda Fassie, whose beats, brash sexuality and gift for attracting controversy prompted comparisons to Madonna. Fassie died in 2004, aged 39, after spending two weeks in a drug-related coma.

The pioneers of South African hop-hop, the Cape Town-based group Prophets of Da City,

absorbing fusion influences in the style of bands such as Weather Report. In Cape Town, musicians drew on an exotic range of influences from Latin sounds to the music of the local Cape Malay community to create a style which is now instantly recognisable as "Cape jazz".

During the 1990s, returning exiles achieved recognition at home as well as abroad, while a new generation drew on their South African heritage and world jazz trends. These included reedman Zim Ngqawana, Cape Town-based guitarist Jimmy Dludlu, who blended Shangaan guitar and

LEFT: a home band in Cape Town's Malay community.
ABOVE: Johnny Clegg and Savaka sing Zulu songs.

first recorded in 1988. Their highly politicised *Age of Truth* album, inspired by the likes of Public Enemy and released prior to the 1994 election, was the first classic in the genre and several songs were banned by the government.

The dominant music post-1994 is *kwaito* (derived from the Afrikaans *kwaai*, meaning "angry"), which draws on hip-hop, Chicago house and contemporary urban dance sounds, infused with African samples and lyrics in local languages. Popular *kwaito* artists include Boom Shaka, Bongo Maffin and Zola. This anti-establishment trend has been mirrored by a wave of mostly Afrikaans punk-influenced groups, such as *Fokofpolisiekar* ("Fuck Off Police Car"). ❑

THE MANY SOUNDS OF BLACK MUSIC

With its rich profusion of styles backed up by a highly developed recording industry, music is one of South Africa's most impressive endowments

In 1959, Black South African township music first exploded onto the international stage with the hit musical *King Kong*. With a score by Sowetan pianist-composer Todd Matshikiza, it told the story of South African heavyweight boxing champion, Ezekiel Dhlamini – "King Kong" – who murders his girlfriend and dies in prison. This slice of township life played to enthusiastic audiences not only in South Africa but in London and New York as well.

△ **KING OF REGGAE**
Hugely popular at home, where he has been dubbed "the natural successor to Bob Marley", Lucky Dube's status as an international star was cemented in 1996, when he received the World Music Award for Best-selling African Recording Artist.

EXILED BY APARTHEID

The show's remarkable line-up included Jonas Gwangwa, trumpeter Hugh Masekela, saxophonist Kippie Moeketsi and songstress Miriam Makeba, a one-time domestic servant who had paid her dues on the township scene in the 1950s with bands like The Cubans, The Manhattan Brothers and The Skylarks. At the very height of *King Kong*'s success, however, Makeba left South Africa for the United States, where she quickly re-established her career. Large numbers of the cast – including Hugh Masekela – also used the show's London run as an opportunity to flee apartheid and go into exile. The drain of artistic talent had begun.

◁ **AFRICAN SONGBIRD**
Turning her back on a successful career in the USA, Miriam Makeba made an emotional return in 1991 with a series of sell-out concerts.

◁ CROSSING THE BARRIERS
The Soweto String Quartet use the format of the classical string quartet to perform songs drawn from both traditional African music and contemporary pop. The result is an extraordinary hybrid of sounds that crosses every musical barrier imaginable. *Zebra Crossing*, their first album, went platinum in 1996.

▽ THE PRINCESS OF AFRICA
With a huge following across the African continent, Yvonne Chaka Chaka's sound epitomises the township pop known as "bubblegum" – a synthesised shebeen jive marrying modern technology and African rhythms. Her star has been somewhat eclipsed in the 1990s by newer forms, such as *kwaito* and hip-hop.

CLASSIC ALBUMS FOR COLLECTORS

● *King Kwela* by Spokes Mashiyane (Celluloid, France). A reissue of Mashiyane's classic 1958 album, featuring up-tempo rhythmic jives. You definitely get your money out of this pennywhistle.
● *The Lion Roars* by Mahlathini and the Mahotella Queens (Shanachie, USA). Culled from the glory days of the 1960s and 1970s, featuring *mbaqanga* king Simon Nkabinde *(pictured above)*.
● *The Best of Sipho Mabuse* by Sipho "Hotstix" Mabuse (Gallo, South Africa). Includes the soul luminary's greatest hits: *Jive Soweto* and *Burn Out*.
● *Verse One* by the Jazz Epistles (Celluloid, France), featuring Dollar Brand, Hugh Masekela, Kippie Moeketsi and Jonas Gwangwa.
● *Blues for a Hip King* by Dollar Brand (Kaz, UK). Dedicated to the groovy king of Swaziland.

◁ THE MUSICAL TRADITION
While most South African styles evolved against a backdrop of urban migration, rural music is an important part of the musical range as well. Best known for their "neo-traditional" styles of playing are the Pedi, Sotho, Zulu, Ndebele and the Shangaan. Here, a brightly costumed Ndebele woman sounds a traditional horn.

▽ THE BEAT GOES ON
It is now official policy in South Africa to support indigenous music, rather than look to the USA or Europe for inspiration. Not only are returning exiles achieving musical recognition at home, but a whole new generation is creating a rich mix of heritage and world musical trends.

▽ GODFATHER OF JAZZ
Forced into exile in the 1960s by the policies of apartheid, legendary trumpeter Hugh Masekela returned in 1990 and remains an active promoter of local jazz acts.

◁ ZULU HARMONIES
The brand of a cappella folk harmonies perfected by Ladysmith Black Mambazo – which means "the Black Axe of Ladysmith" – are instantly recognisable. Formed in 1970, their contribution to US musician Paul Simon's 1987 *Graceland* album first made them world-famous.

THE CHANGING FACE OF ART

The ending of the cultural boycott has finally exposed local talent to the rest of Africa – and the world

The art of southern Africa dates back to pre-history and, it has been argued, represents the human race's longest artistic tradition. San rock art developed from this time right up to the second half of the 19th century. The paintings and engravings of the San people are found mainly in the Drakensberg and its extension from the Eastern Cape to Lesotho and Swaziland, as well as in the mountains of Limpopo Province and sites on the inland plateau along the Vaal and Orange rivers. The sensitive depictions of animals and human figures painted and engraved in rock shelters are thought to be shamanistic and a link between the real world and the spirit world. There are over 15,000 documented sites in South Africa.

Woodcarving, beadwork, basket-making and pottery have for centuries been found here, serving both utilitarian and decorative purposes. You can still find carved headrests, initiation figures and decorative doors, stools and utensils.

Beadwork is produced throughout Africa but arguably most strikingly by the Zulu. This art, originally used as a symbol of status, is increasingly aimed at the tourist market. Highly original patterns, using traditional beads alone, have given way to the use of plastic, safety pins and other more modern materials, stitched on to decorative blankets.

Western influences

The influence of Western painters and art arrived alongside early explorers. The names of 19th-century chroniclers including Thomas Baines (1820–75), Fredrick I'Ons (1802–87) and Thomas Bowler (1812–69) are all synonymous with early South African painting; their works can be viewed in a number of museums and art galleries in the country.

Europe's influence remained strong as the Dutch tradition of landscape painting predominated, thanks to settlers such as Frans Oerder (1867–1944) and Pieter Wenning (1873–1921). They also helped establish

LEFT: interior design, Ndebele-style.
RIGHT: street art, Soweto.

South African-born painters J.E.A. Volschenk (1853–1936) and Hugo Naude (1869–1941), as well as artists who reflected the British and French Impressionist landscape tradition, such as Robert Gwelo Goodman (1871–1938).

Anton van Wouw (1892–1945) is commonly regarded as the father of modern Western sculp-

ture in South Africa. A Dutchman who arrived in 1890, van Wouw's work followed a descriptive realist tradition. Moses Kottler (1896–1977) and Lippy Lipshitz (1903–80) followed a carving tradition, as did later artists such as Elsa Dziomba (1902–70) and Lucas Sithole (born 1931).

The influence of Expressionism reached the country in the 1920s when Irma Stern (1904–66) and Maggie Laubscher (1886–1973) returned from studies in Germany. The 1930s saw the New Group set out to explore what they believed to be progressive ideals. Gregoire Boonzaier (b. 1909), Terence MacCaw (1913–76) and Walter Battiss (1906–82) led the break away from what they perceived to be amateurism in South African art.

Among the most prominent black artists of the early 1940s were Gerard Sekoto (b. 1913), who left to live in Paris in 1947; Ernest Mancoba (b. 1910); and George Pemba (b. 1920).

Township art

Post-war developments saw a move towards abstract art theories current in Europe and the United States, but also present was a growing body of black urban artists. Their subject matter of crowded townships and distorted expressive human figures became known as "township art".

Mslaba Dumile (b. 1939) is the best-known exponent of this type of art. Black sculptors

Tick
Time, Space and that River

such as Sydney Kumalo (1935–90) and Michael Zondi (b. 1926) became, together with Dumile, South Africa's first international black artists.

A further attempt to combine a European approach and African symbolism took place during the 1960s with artists such as Edoardo Villa (b. 1920), Giuseppe Cattaneo (b. 1929) and Cecil Skotnes (b. 1952) featuring prominently.

The 1970s saw the rise of protest art. Despite the country's enforced cultural isolation, black artists such as Leonard Matsoso (b. 1949) and Ezrom Legae (b. 1938) still achieved international recognition. Avant-garde artists tried to reflect the socio-political realities and challenge the social conscience.

A new generation of artists – including William Kentridge (b. 1955), Penny Siopis (b. 1953) and Keith Dietrich (b. 1950) – came to prominence in the mid-1980s and have used a figurative style in their interpretation of contemporary events. Personal iconography has been undertaken by artists like Karel Nel (b. 1955) and Paul Shelly (b. 1963).

The phenomenon of formally untrained rural artists finding their way into the mainstream of South African art can be traced to the 1985 BMW exhibition, *Tributaries*. Black sculptors from the Venda area in the northern Transvaal were introduced to the urban art world. Among the most original is Jackson Hlungwani (b. 1923), whose religious cosmology and world view are translated through innovative sculptures.

People's art

The 1980s saw the establishment of several collective projects which tried to teach art in the townships, providing skills, training and access to resources. The best-known of these were the Thupelo Arts Project in Johannesburg, which owed its origins to the Triangle Artists' Workshop in New York, and the Community Arts Project in Cape Town. The Thupelo Art Project saw the development of an abstract Expressionist style much criticised by some anti-apartheid artists, who felt a figurative socio-political style was more appropriate to the South African situation.

This era also witnessed the emergence of a spontaneous public art known as "people's parks". Here, symbols of work such as tools were juxtaposed in sculptures with common junk, maps of Africa and home-made wooden weapons.

The post-apartheid era has seen the introduction – for the first time in South Africa's history – of a ministry with an arts and culture portfolio. With the formation of national arts councils in 1997, and with more local artists being represented internationally in exhibitions focusing specifically on South African art, the place of the country's artists on the international art scene finally seems assured.

Sadly, despite much talk of an African cultural renaissance, radical cuts in subsidies have resulted in the deterioration of some of the country's best galleries, and the scrapping after only two years of the largest contemporary art event in Africa, the Africus Johannesburg Biennale. ❏

LEFT: modern art galleries showcase South Africa's contemporary artists.

The First Artists

South Africa is home to the largest collection of Stone Age art in the world. Scattered throughout the interior of the country are more than 150,000 rock paintings and engravings created by the San hunter-gatherers, who first made their mark in southern Africa about 40,000 years ago.

It is generally thought that this art has an occult significance, representing the San's strong identification with the animals they hunted and the rituals they used to obtain power over them. Some of the finest paintings depict eland hunts. The eland, largest of the African antelopes, was regarded as having supernatural powers and was the San's special link with the Godhead.

Another common theme is trance dancing, performed by the clan's shaman in order to activate a supernatural potency which would transform him and allow him to enter the spirit world. Paintings show women clapping and men dancing before an extraordinary half-animal, half-human figure – the shaman, merging with his animal power.

Shamans entering the spirit world experienced a variety of physical and visual hallucinations, a state depicted in their art by such metaphors as "being underwater". "Death" is another, because there were certain similarities between a shaman entering a trance and, for example, a dying eland – both bled at the nose, frothed at the mouth, stumbled about and eventually collapsed unconscious.

Once in the spirit world, it was the shaman's task to cure the sick, resolve social conflict and control the movement of herds of game, including the mysterious "rain animal" that brought rain. Such "work" guaranteed the continued existence of San society.

The paintings and engravings depicting trance dances and the symbols of supernatural power were a means by which the shamans tried to communicate what they had undergone to their peers. But they were also regarded as powerful things in themselves, storehouses of the very potency that made contact with the spirit world possible.

Historical events and observations of the newcomers who encroached on the San's living space were also recorded. Nguni warriors and cattle, Khoikhoian fat-tailed sheep, European settlers on horseback with rifles, ships and uniformed soldiers were all captured in surprising detail.

RIGHT: remote caves record the beginnings of mankind's artistic heritage.

Sadly, the San did not survive the arrival of the white man. When the diminutive hunter-gatherers who had lived in perfect ecological harmony with their environment for so many thousands of years saw the vast herds of game cut down by the settlers' guns, they launched fierce retaliatory raids. But their bows and arrows were no match for guns. The San were hunted from their lands like vermin; and today a few scattered artefacts and the rock-art sites are all that remain of their culture.

Carbon-dating has shown the rock-art sites range in age from about 20,000 years to about 100 years old. However, many prime works are at remote sites which are difficult to access.

Some of the most vivid and detailed paintings are in the uKhahlamba-Drakensberg mountain range. The Giant's Castle Game Reserve has a good site near the guest chalets, and another at the Sunday's Falls Christmas Cave in the Game Pass Valley, near the south end of the reserve. The Cavern and The Stream shelter in the Cathedral Peak area are also well-known and accessible.

In the Cape, the area around Queenstown has some excellent sites, as does Barkly East. There is a 105-ft (32-metre) long gallery of paintings on the Denorbin farm, between Elliot and Barkly East, which may be viewed. Driekopseiland, which lies on the banks of the Riet River near Kimberley, is one of the largest and best-known sites with over 3,500 engraved images. ❑

WHERE AFRICA AND EUROPE BLEND

From contemporary Western to distinctly African trends, from watercolours to wooden masks, artists draw on an eclectic range of styles and forms

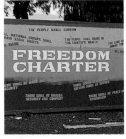

During the 1980s, the fight against apartheid reached its peak. For many artists, playwrights, writers and musicians the act of creation became a political one. This cultural struggle was symbolised by images of defiance, painted on walls, recited from stages and printed on T-shirts and badges. Art became a weapon of the struggle to make people aware of the realities of South African society under apartheid.

A NEW MEDIUM

What made this aspect of the cultural struggle so successful was its accessibility to a broader public, a public not used to seeing art unless it was hung upon gallery walls or displayed in highbrow journals. Coffee mugs, table placemats, badges and walls – even freight containers like the one pictured above – had become the new medium for the anti-apartheid message. A host of collectives (of which the best-known were Cape Town's Community Arts Project and Johannesburg's Thupelo Arts Project) were set up to provide the necessary skills. Today, with apartheid a thing of the past, these have become the cornerstone of a thriving independent crafts industry.

◁ **ZULU CRAFTS**
At Dumazulu Cultural Village at Hluhluwe, in the heart of KwaZulu-Natal, you can spend the night in a traditional kraal and watch demonstrations of basket-weaving, beadwork and clay-pot making.

◁ **SYMBOLS OF AFRICA**
Wooden ceremonial masks like these can be found at street markets in most big cities. Styles vary according to the tribal ritual for which the mask was devised.

▽ **"MADE IN SOUTH AFRICA"**
Oil by Gauteng artist David Koloane, who has exhibited worldwide with much success. In 1994 he was the winner of the prestigious 2nd Quarter FNB Vita Now award.

◁ **FINE LINES**
The cornerstone of both tribal dress and the curio market, you'll find beautiful beadwork like this wherever you go in South Africa. Traditionally, beads are used to denote the status of the wearer and to send messages – the Zulus wear blue for faithfulness and white for love, for example. These bracelets are made by the Ndebele people.

△ **TOY ART**
A good example of the cultural elevation of craft or folk art in South Africa, these Ndebele dolls can be found in museums and galleries as well as private collections.

ART COLLECTIONS AND GALLERIES

Innocence, by George Velaphi Mzimba. This Soweto-born artist made his mark in the 1980s with exhibitions in South Africa, Northern Ireland, Canada and the USA. His work is currently available through the **Everard Read Gallery** in Rosebank, Johannesburg (tel: 011-788 4805), one of the best commercial galleries in the country.

Other places to seek out the best in black art are:
● **The Gertrude Posel Gallery** in Senate House, University of the Witwatersrand (tel: 011-717 1365), which houses collections of both black contemporary art and a superb collection of tribal art, including Xhosa and Zulu beadwork.
● **The De Beers Centenary Art Gallery**, in the Centre for Cultural Studies at Fort Hare University (tel: 040-602 2277), spans works by pioneer painters such as George Pemba to more modern artists such as Sydney Khumalo. A collection with a strong emphasis on social realism.
● **Rupert Art Museum**, on Lower Dorp Street, Stellenbosch (tel: 021-888 3344), a collection assembled by the late Dr Anton Rupert and his wife Huberte, with artworks by artists such as Maggie Laubser, Irma Stern, Moses Kotler, Anton van Wouw and le Corbusier.

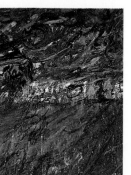

△ **A WAY OF LIFE**
The Ndebele people fill their lives with symbols of traditional culture, using dazzling colours to decorate their clothes, their homes and their household goods.

▷ **"THE SHEPHERD"**
Bronze by Ezrom Legae, 1995. One of a new generation of black artists whose works embody the synthesis of both Western and African traditions.

LITERATURE

Freed from the constraints of the apartheid years, fiction writers
are engaged in a search for compelling new themes

The first European literature to deal with the South African experience was the Portuguese. A significant part of Portugal's national epic, Luís de Camões' *The Lusiads* of 1572, deals with the early navigators' records of rounding the formidable Cape of Storms. Here the African landmass is portrayed as a

hostile and dark giant, threatening to all but the most heroic Christian adventurers. He is given a mythological name, Adamastor, and a part of his body is Table Mountain that guards the entry to the land.

After the settlement of the Dutch there in 1652, the written records of the Cape are mostly in diary form. During the 18th century, this small enclave had a considerable reputation in Europe as a botanical paradise, and several travellers' records portray its slave-holding milieu. Inland over the frontier was an explorer's playground, of which a boastful adventurer like François le Vaillant could in 1795 publish his highly exaggerated accounts.

Nevertheless, the travelogue of the Enlightenment included detailed records of the life and customs of indigenous peoples, together with colourful accounts of hunting big game.

British tradition

From the 1820s, with the British colonisation of southern Africa, a systematic literature began with the introduction of the press. On the Eastern frontier, the first Xhosa-language newspaper began in the 1840s, more or less at the time the emancipation of slaves became general. Missionary endeavour on many fronts, while translating the Bible, preserved the first accounts we have of the earliest oral literature in Xhosa, Zulu, Tswana and Sotho.

The even older poetry and folklore of the Khoisan peoples was first taken down and translated by the German philologist Wilhelm Bleek, whose collection for the South African Library in Cape Town has not yet been exhausted by scholars. The San and Khoikhoi – now practically extinct – provide us in their mythology and history with an absorbing account of the European conqueror from their respective side.

The British frontier produced two types of writing which persist even today. Thomas Pringle (1789–1834) introduced a high-flown, romantic style of poetry, starting a tradition which stays in touch with European models, while Andrew Geddes Bain (1797–1864) began a stream of popular songs and satires which used the far more earthy language of the marketplace. In Bain's polyglot work we find early forms of Afrikaans, the African language that was to develop from Dutch, as well as English, French and German (the languages of the early settlers), Malay and various African languages.

Continuing the Pringle line of high culture, we have by 1883 the publication of the novel *The Story of an African Farm*, which was really the first great work to be written in the far-flung colonies. It was greeted in the motherland with amazement and controversy, for it was the first work that gave a realistic and credible portrait of the conditions of daily life on an establishment in the Karoo and of the cruel and difficult society, with its educational, commercial and religious institutions, on which it depended. The author, Olive Schreiner (1855–1920), was the daughter of a German missionary and his English wife but considered herself one of the first South Africans, owing her inspiration to the modern nation she was so influential in building.

Adventure novels

The other popular stream of writing in the late 19th century was particularly productive and successful. With the appeal of British imperialism at its height, many earlier forms became concentrated in the adventure romance. In the hands of an exponent like H. Rider Haggard (1856–1925), this new genre created one of the first modern bestsellers: *King Solomon's Mines* (1885), which has been filmed at least five times.

What is so memorable about his original adventures is the skilful way Haggard wrote them. He used an endearing, self-effacing narrator, Allan Quatermain, who was a professional hunter, settled in Durban, always willing to guide newcomers into the interior of Africa. One must remember that it had not been so long since David Livingstone had set off from the Northern Cape to find the inland Okavango Swamps of Botswana and then the great Central Lakes of Africa, nor since Burton and Speke had located the source of the Nile. The imperial adventure romance has everything to do with glamorising these exploits for readers back home.

Directly in the Haggard line is Wilbur Smith, whose adventures (such as *Where the Lion Feeds*) are very widely translated.

The works of many South African writers have tended to dwell on the burning racial and political issues that have confronted the country. But in the works of Sir Laurens van der Post (1906–96), such debates, if they have arisen at all, have played only a subordinate role. The essence of *The Lost World of the Kalahari* (1958), his famous book and documentary film on the San, or his gripping adventure tales, such as *Flamingo Feather*, *A Story like the Wind* (1972) and its

LEFT: spreading the word.
RIGHT: taking cover: the work of Can Themba, the legendary chronicler of life in 1950s Soweto, is still very much worth reading.

sequel *A Far-Off Place* (1974), is far more the enduring culture of southern Africa's indigenous peoples (particularly the San) and the mysteries of the vast landscape in which they live.

The Black experience

Parts of this fiction-writing tradition are uniquely African. A Black writer, Sol T. Plaatjie (1876–1932), in *Mhudi* (1916), started to reformulate the Haggard-Schreiner heritage, making it sympathetic to a portrayal of Black history that white writers had tended to ignore or even destroy. In the same line, magical Bessie Head (1937–86), who lived the second half of

THE WORLD OF CAN THEMBA edited by Essop Patel

her life in Botswana, was able to recover whole areas of the Black experience from oral sources. These she converted into short stories that, while remaining African in spirit, are very familiar to white readers – *The Collector of Treasures* (1977) is a good example.

Those unfamiliar with South African writing should, however, beware of making simplistic distinctions between white and Black writing, as if these two categories existed far apart from one another. Throughout the 20th century, the great theme of South African fiction writers was precisely that relationship between Blacks and whites, so that every writer has, to some extent, been studying and presenting the country as one in which interrelationships are vitally important. The best example is Alan Paton's *Cry, the Beloved Country* (1948), which is still the widest-read South African work of all time.

Afrikaans writing

Poetry in modern South Africa has also proved a distinguished area of its literature, particularly in Afrikaans. Indeed, it is through their poetry that many Afrikaans-language artists have shaped their tongue as a written language. Eugene N. Marais (1871–1936), a founder of lyric verse in Afrikaans, was also a widely respected naturalist whose classic works such as *The Soul of the*

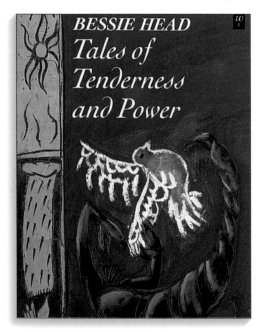

Ape (1969) helped to raised the science of zoological observation into an art form.

Another Afrikaans-language poet is C. Louis Leipoldt (1880–1947). Like Schreiner, he was born of German missionary stock. He wrote voluminously in several languages, particularly about Rhenish mission settlements which were such a feature of the Western Cape.

An overt form of political expression later matured in the work of poets such as N.P. van Wyk Louw and Dirk Opperman. In the 1960s a younger generation of writers – led by Breytenbach, Brink and Etienne Leroux – emerged, and their work represented a drastic departure from the conventional Afrikaans tradition.

Modern trends

During the apartheid era, when many artists were driven into exile in Europe and the USA, the form of autobiography became particularly rewarding among Black writers. Peter Abrahams in 1954 published *Tell Freedom,* the first of many such works to recount the life histories of Black people. *Down Second Avenue* (1959) by Es'kia Mphahlele is another important example of a Black man's story of climbing out of a disadvantaged world of poverty and illiteracy to be educated, and ultimately achieve the status of self-made writer.

Many contemporary novelists still concentrate on themes that explore the painfully oppressive past – for example, the bestselling *A Smell of Apples* (1993) by Mark Behr, the story of a white boy growing up in the militaristic 1960s and 1970s – but the enormous political changes that have swept South Africa since 1994 are also making their impact on the literary scene.

At the forefront of the new generation of post-apartheid writers is Zakes Mda, whose prize-winning novel about a professional mourner, *Ways of Dying* (1997) explores modern attitudes to traditional culture from a Black point of view. The same theme informs Mda's more recent novels *The Heart of Redness* (2001) and *The Madonna of Excelsior* (2003), which are set respectively in the former Transkei and in small-town Free State.

Other recent landmark novels include Patricia Schonstein's surreal *Time of Angels* (2003), set in present-day Cape Town, and Ivan Vladislavic's *The Restless Supermarket* (2002). The latter award-winning novel explores how the Johannesburg suburb of Hillbrow transformed from a chic café society populated by European immigrants in the 1970s to a modern-day melting pot for political and economic refugees from all over Africa

A writer can not write about South Africa without writing about life's great themes: oppression, adventure, conquest, defeat, struggle, pride and success. So it should be no surprise that the country's modern writers come well-feted with literary prizes, none more so than Nadine Gordimer and J.M. Coetzee, winners of the Nobel Prize for Literature in 1991 and 2003 respectively. ❏

LEFT: Bessie Head's work revealed apartheid's horrors.

Nobel Prize Winners

When Nadine Gordimer was awarded the Nobel Prize for Literature in 1991, approval reflected acclaim for her two lifelong preoccupations: the craft of writing, and the evil of apartheid.

Born in 1923 in the small mining town of Springs, east of Johannesburg, Gordimer had an atypical childhood. Her father was a Jewish watchmaker from Lithuania; her mother English. More significantly for her development as a writer, her mother took her out of school at the age of 11 on the pretext of a heart ailment, keeping her at home until she was 16.

The young Gordimer had private lessons at home, and developed a passion for reading and writing. She published her first short story at the age of 13, and her first novel, the autobiographical *The Lying Days*, in 1953. Subsequently, as well as building up a considerable reputation as a writer of fiction, Gordimer has become known as a tireless worker for, and advocate of, free expression in South Africa.

The Nobel Prize is the most illustrious of a series of awards dating back to 1961, when Gordimer won the W.H. Smith Literary Award for her short story collection, *Friday's Footprint* (1960). Others include the Benson Medal from the Royal Society of Literature and the French international award, the Grand Aigle d'Or. Her 1974 novel, *The Conservationist*, was joint winner of the Booker Prize in the UK.

Despite her formidable international reputation, Gordimer is somewhat underrated in her own country. Her refusal to submit her fiction to revolutionary sloganeering alienated her from many Black commentators, and in the 1960s and 1970s she was also criticised for choosing not to follow other intellectuals into exile. But while Gordimer has often explored the theme of commitment to political action, her own position is that she is first and foremost a novelist, not an activist or historian.

Post-apartheid, Gordimer continues to record and comment on the turbulent present with steely resolve. While much of her early fiction dealt with the impasse created by white supremacy, her more recent works deal with the complexities of a society in transition. Her 1994 novel, *None to Accompany Me*, explores with a ruthlessly honest eye the changes that occur within the individual – nothing less than an abandonment of the old self – along with the subtle hazards that characterise a transition to a new order.

RIGHT: Nadine Gordimer, now just one of South Africa's Nobel Prize winners.

What surprises many overseas visitors is Gordimer's relative lack of popularity among white South Africans. The chief reason for this is that readers satisfied with Wilbur Smith's bestselling blend of salacity, racial mastery and romance find Gordimer's work rather heavy going and – more trenchantly, perhaps – uncomfortable, even unpalatable reading.

Still, Gordimer's writing remains accessible by comparison to the dense, ascetic prose that characterises the novels of the enigmatic Afrikaans winner of the 2003 Nobel Prize for Literature. Cape Town-born J.M. Coetzee's early work, like that of Gordimer, explores the iniquities of apartheid, or a

system remarkably like it, albeit in a somewhat allegorical style that eschews overt political grandstanding. Published in 1983, the Booker-winning *Life & Times of Michael K* is arguably Coetzee's finest novel, though the older *Waiting For The Barbarians* is just as compelling.

Finally, if these two fine novelists do interest you, then don't miss out on Andre Brink, a prolific and insightful Afrikaans writer who might justifiably feel aggrieved at being overlooked by the Nobel committee in favour of his more self-consciously literary peers. More so than any other novelist, Brink at his finest – the historical *Chain of Voices* and *Rumours of Rain*, the more contemporary *Dry White Season* and *Act of Terror* – cuts to the complex core of what makes white South Africa tick. ❑

FOOD

*From hearty Dutch cooking to Indian curries and black "soul food",
the national cuisine is a delicious mix*

Remarkable yet true: the chief reason for South Africa's European colonisation was food and wine. Holland's domination of the East Indies' spice islands created heavy sea traffic past the Cape in the mid-1600s; after three months at sea, crews would stop in Table Bay to take on fresh water from Table Mountain. The vegetable garden started by Jan van Riebeeck, first commander of the Cape, still exists at the top of Adderley Street, although it is now a botanical park.

As the primitive settlement grew first into a seaside village, then into a town, hearty and wholesome Dutch cooking held sway. Gradually culinary ideas from the East Indies were introduced. Stews were enhanced by cloves, cinnamon, pimiento, turmeric, anise and tamarind, as were cakes and home-made sweets, confectionery and preserves.

It was not long before rice was a standard accompaniment to many dishes – a direct legacy of the Dutch/Indonesian *rijstafel* – as well as Oriental pickles and condiments. All still play a big role in the preparation of *boerekos* – traditional Afrikaner cuisine.

As well as being moulded by the passing spice trade, Cape food was influenced by East Indian slaves, political hostages and exiles, whose families transformed old Dutch recipes with the flavours of Bengal, Java, Malabar, Ceylon and Malaya. The Malay word *piesang* is Afrikaans for "banana"; small cubes of meat grilled on a short skewer are called *sosatie* (a corruption of Indonesia's *sate*).

A mouthwatering baked meat loaf, aromatic with mild curry and with a sweet/tart piquancy, is called *bobotie* after its Javanese original and enjoyed with a savoury fruit chutney *(blatjang)*.

A French influence arrived in 1688 with the Huguenots, who were fleeing the revocation of the Edict of Nantes. They settled in the beautiful Franschhoek valley, where they harvested fruit and made wine. Their technique of preserving

food by long slow simmering, *confit*, means that all fruits preserved in sugar syrup, including jam, are called *konfyt* in Afrikaans.

To the Huguenots, South Africa also owes a rich, succulent heritage of biscuits, tarts, cooking with wine, pastries and a bread roll called *mosbolletjies,* using fermenting wine as a raising

agent instead of yeast. Broken into pieces and dried in the oven, this fine-textured speciality is turned into rusks – the standard accompaniment to early-morning coffee all across the country.

Curry is another of South Africa's culinary signature dishes – a speciality of KwaZulu-Natal, where it was first popularised by the Asian community. Unlike the Cape's mild Malay curries, which work well with seafood, the curries of KwaZulu-Natal are hotter, and usually reserved for beef, lamb, chicken or vegetarian dishes. Rice, *sambals*, masala, crackly *poppadoms, roti* bread, fried *puri* dough, coconut and sliced banana are the signatures of curry restaurants throughout the province.

LEFT: mopani worms: crunchy, peppery, rich in protein.
RIGHT: adding zest to the national repertoire.

Indigenous cuisine

The dismantling of apartheid has sparked a new interest in the traditional cuisine of South Africa's black communities, with colourful "soul food" restaurants springing up in all the main centres.

A look at the menu at any of these establishments will reveal that the most basic foodstuff – although one introduced by the Europeans – is, maize. An enormous number of dishes are made with it, the most popular being ground-maize porridge *(pap)* and hominy grits *(samp)*. Sorghum is another staple, used in dishes such as *ting* (sour porridge) and for making beer.

Chicken, pork and mutton did not form part of the traditional diet (although that has now changed), and surprisingly fish is another recent addition. However, insects such as flying ants, along with mopani worms, are popular alternative sources of protein, roasted and eaten on their own or as a snack with porridge. Crunchy and faintly peppery, worms are much tastier than you'd think.

Gifts of the southern oceans

Fine-textured fish, mussels, oysters, crabs, baby squid and pilchards are all caught along the southern and eastern coastlines, but the finest

Beans are another key ingredient in the traditional diet, along with pumpkin, usually served stewed along with its fried flowers and seeds, or sometimes mixed with cereal as a porridge. Groundnuts or peanuts are used to enhance dishes such as *morogo,* a stew made with spinach or flavoursome wild leaves. Curd or *maas* (sour milk) is another favourite dish, either on its own or with *phutu pap* (crumbly porridge).

In traditional rural communities, meat and milk are the responsibility of the menfolk. Stock is usually slaughtered on a special occasion only; game and birds are more commonly hunted and eaten instead.

TOP OF THE POTS

Umngqusho is said to be Nelson Mandela's favourite dish. It is made with dried maize kernels, sugar beans, butter, onions, potatoes, chillies and lemons – all simmered until the ingredients are tender. And on Western Cape menus, the dish to look out for is *waterblommetjie bredie*. The *waterblommetjie*, a kind of pond weed, is indigenous to dams and marshes here. The time to enjoy it is July and August, when the buds are plump. Don't order it by using the pallid English translation ("waterlily stew") unless you wish to incur serious loss of face.

seafood is to be had between November and April: this is high season for the Cape's world-famous rock lobster (known locally as crayfish), a prized delicacy so sweet and tender that vast quantities are exported to top restaurants worldwide. Similar to North Sea lobster except that it has no claws, it is served in all the traditional ways, such as thermidor, grilled or cold with mayonnaise.

Other summer delicacies are the pelagic fish, found in large shoals along the east coast of the warm Indian Ocean. Barracuda, yellowtail, katonkel and shad are all fighting fish and therefore popular amongst anglers, but they are

and potatoes with browned snoek chunks, sometimes with a little stewed tomato, and always served with rice and tart chutney.

Satisfactions of the hunt

Since the first Dutch farmers cleared the Cape of lion, elephant, buffalo and buck, South Africans have relished the pleasures of meats and sausages grilled over wood coals, of enjoying air-dried venison called *biltong*, of savouring fresh-brewed coffee around a campfire under the Southern Cross. In countless gardens, weekend wood fires are lit for the family *braaivleis* (*braai* means to grill or roast, *vleis*

overshadowed by the Cape's pungently flavoured snoek. Named by the early Dutch settlers after the European freshwater pike, this long (measuring 1 metre/3 ft), silvery fighter is firm-fleshed and delicious.

Served fried, snoek is traditionally accompanied by sweet *korrelkonfyt*, a luscious jam made of honey-flavoured muscat grapes, which complements the bracing saltiness of the snoek. Visitors should also look out for *snoeksmoor*, a hot, savoury mix of fried onions

means meat in Afrikaans), while there is hardly a picnic spot, camp site or bungalow in the national parks that doesn't have a barbecue.

Lamb chops, curried *sosaties* and freshly picked corn on the cob are the foundations of this outdoor meal, but it can also include beef fillet, or cuts of springbok, kudu, bush-pig, eland or impala.

Then there's the coarse-minced sausage of spicy beef and pork fat called *boerewors* (*boer* means farmer, *wors* means sausage). The best specimens are usually purchased from rural butchers in the Free State and Limpopo Province, who make them using the same recipes as their grandmothers. ❑

LEFT: exotic road-side stall, KwaZulu-Natal.
ABOVE: inexpensive but sophisticated dining is one of South Africa's greatest pleasures.

WINE

With the advent of a post-apartheid democracy, the world has
rediscovered South Africa – and especially its wine

Cape wine underwent a revolution in the 1990s, borne of another revolution – the political kind. With the ascendancy of a man named Nelson Mandela and the advent of a non-racial democracy instead of apartheid, the world began to rediscover South Africa, and with it, its wine.

A NEW WORLD WINNER

Until the 1970s, South Africa's wine-making tradition was strongly influenced by Germanic styles, despite a latent French connection (way back in the late 17th century, when French Huguenot immigrants brought their expertise to bear on a viticulture established by Dutchman Jan van Riebeeck in the 1650s). Since the end of the apartheid era, however, wine-makers have been at pains to learn new skills; certainly, the country has all the ingredients to produce the ripe, fruity and accessible "New World" wines modern consumers find so appealing.

While South Africa is still largely a white wine-producing country in quantity, it's the classical red varieties that produce the finest quality. And the French influence remains strong, with well-travelled young local wine-makers constantly arguing the merits of "Old World" structure, elegance and longevity versus "New World" softness, fruitiness and immediate drinkability.

Although the Cape wine producers of the 1940s pioneered cellar techniques such as the cold fermentation of white wine, they subsequently fell behind in the vineyard, with old clones, poor material and bad management causing a dip in wine quality. They were severely shown up upon re-entry into world markets in the early 1990s, although inexpensive wines and the novelty factor wooed the world's pockets and palates. Booming exports have led to local wine shortages: from a target of just 1 million cases in the early 1990s, Cape wine exports now exceed 230 million litres per year (over 300 million bottles). While such success cannot hope to be maintained in an increasingly competitive wine market, this exposure has served to educate, temper and refine Cape wines and wine-makers alike.

The wine revival of the 1990s has drawn ambitious young wine-makers, monied businessmen and major corporations alike to seek out prime vineyard sites, build compact, hi-tech cellars and produce finely crafted wines. Boutique wineries are popping up all over.

There has also been a spate of international vineyard ventures. Burgundian Paul Bouchard has linked up with Pinot Noir and Chardonnay specialist Peter Finlayson to form Bouchard Finlayson, in Walker Bay. The Moueix family of Château Pétrus fame is developing a vineyard with Savanha Vineyards in Paarl. The French Cognac family of Cointreau has rejuvenated the historic Stellenbosch property of Morgenhof. Bordeaux's De Rothschilds and the Ruperts of Stellenbosch, billionaires both, have started a Paarl farm called Fredericksburg. Zelma Long of Napa's Simi Winery and Michael Back of

Backsberg are involved in a joint Cape venture. Needless to say, competition, export demand and the climb in quality has resulted in a steady rise in price. Good reds hover around R40 a bottle; whites are about R30.

While control over what's in the bottle remains strict, Cape wine producers are now at liberty to plant whatever they wish, wherever they choose. The "Wine of Origin" designation on Cape wine labels indicates the source of the grapes, the most standard being the traditional Cape wine regions of Stellenbosch, Paarl, Franschhoek, Constantia, Walker Bay, Wellington, Robertson and Worcester.

Serious wine-makers are bottling wines from selected vineyard sites, and specific areas within a designated region are being proclaimed, such as Helderberg and Devon Valley – both in Stellenbosch – and Elgin. And virgin territory is being identified as prime land for top-quality wines, including Noordhoek and Stanford along the southern coast of the peninsula.

Pick of the best? Cabernet Sauvignon is king, with Merlot on the upswing as both a blending partner and a strong, structured wine in its own right. Shiraz is probably the most underrated red, producing wines of consistency and charm, capable of both Rhône-like elegance and that Aussie fruit effrontery. But it's the Cape's home-grown variety, Pinotage, that has made a name for itself with international palates. Bred from Pinot Noir and Cinsaut – mistakenly called Hermitage – it can be sweet and simple, or robust and regal, depending on its treatment. And wine-makers are finally paying it the attention it deserves.

Chenin Blanc, a stalwart in the local brandy industry, still dominates in the vineyards. However, other more classic grape varieties are making inroads. Chardonnay is well-established, with styles that have evolved from the heavily wooded wines of the early 1990s to a more Burgundian elegance and complexity. Cool-climate sites are being sought out, producing Sauvignon Blancs combining Kiwi varietal character and Loire delicacy.

Pinot Noir continues to struggle as a red wine, although the Walker Bay and Franschhoek cellars make some fine Burgundian examples. But its use as an integral component of fine *méth-*

ode champenoise sparkling wine is putting the Cape's Cap Classiques on the map.

Stellenbosch and Paarl are the main, and probably the most versatile, wine regions of the Cape, offering the best of everything: rich reds, crisp whites, ports in true Portuguese style, Sauterne-like sweet Noble Late Harvest wines and some excellent value-for-money Cap Classiques.

Franschhoek, a valley of boutique wineries, offers mostly white wines, with a handful of red gems. Then there's Constantia, conveniently placed in the heart of Cape Town, with a select range of classical whites and reds nurtured in historic Cape Dutch cellars, in surroundings

equalled only by Stellenbosch for natural beauty. Walker Bay is the place for some of the Cape's benchmark Pinot Noirs and Chardonnays, and a taste of pioneering Pinotages.

Calitzdorp in the arid Klein Karoo, about 370 km (230 miles) from Cape Town, is the port capital of South Africa. The Douro-like environment here has encouraged several cellars to plant port varieties and adopt traditional Portuguese methods and styles. The Robertson and Worcester regions are traditionally known for fortified dessert wines such as Jerepigo, Muscadel and Sweet Hanepoot, but both regions also produce dry reds and whites that bear comparison to the Cape's finest'. ❑

LEFT: a sensual delight in a beautiful setting.
RIGHT: the Hex River Valley, classic Cape wine country.

SPORT

Since the end of apartheid, sportsmen and women have made
great strides in the international arena

With its rich sporting traditions and excellent facilities, South Africa is a sports fan's dream. The agreeable climate offers superb opportunities for golf, water sports, hiking and climbing – to name but a few outdoor activities – while avid spectators can catch world-class sporting action at stadiums like Johannesburg's Ellis Park, or Newlands in Cape Town.

Since South Africa's readmission to the international arena, local sportsmen and women have made great strides. In 1995, the national Springbok rugby team was crowned world champions at Ellis Park after defeating favourites New Zealand in the Rugby World Cup final, a triumph repeated in Paris, France in 2007 after thoroughly defeating England. The year 1996 saw the national football side defy the odds to lift the African Cup of Nations trophy. Nicknamed Bafana Bafana (a Zulu phrase meaning "the boys, the boys"), the South Africans also reached the 1998 and 2002 world cups, and have spent most of the past decade ranked among the top three sides in Africa.

The year 1996 was also when the Olympic Games were held in Atlanta. Here, swimmer Penny Heyns struck gold twice (in the 100 metres and 200 metres breaststroke), while marathon runner Josiah Thugwane stunned everyone by taking the gold medal in that most Olympian of events. In the 800 metres, track star Hezekiel Sepeng came from behind to snatch silver in breathtaking style.

Then there is golfer Ernie Els, who followed in the footsteps of legendary South African golfer Gary Player by winning the US Open in 1994 – a feat he repeated in 1997. Els, winner of the World Matchplay tournament for three years in succession, has of late been prevented from taking the world number one ranking only by the prodigious feats of Tiger Woods. Standing only a few rungs lower on the world rankings than Els

is another South African, Retief Goosen, who claimed his second US Open victory in 2004.

Other individual sports stars to achieve success since the moratorium on international contact came to an end are IBF World Junior Featherweight champion Vuyani Bungu; Junior Flyweight boxer Baby Jake Matlala, who has

won both the WBO and IBF world titles in his division; hurdler Llewellyn Herbert and javelin thrower Marius Corbett – silver and gold medallists respectively at the 1997 World Athletics Championships in Athens – and veteran tennis player Wayne Ferreira, whose appearance at Wimbledon in 2004 beat Stefan Edberg's long-standing record of 54 successive grand-slam appearances.

The challenge at home

While much has been made of South Africa's recent successes, the biggest sporting challenge has not been abroad, but at home. For years, only white players and the sports in which they

LEFT: sailing around Africa's cape is still a popular pursuit for the adventurous.
RIGHT: there will be no lack of support when South Africa hosts the football World Cup in 2010.

predominated (such as rugby, cricket and golf) received the necessary money and facilities for development. The vast majority of South Africans were given little opportunity to make an impact on the sporting scene.

All South African sporting bodies have made an effort to create a more equal sporting society, but none has been as successful as the United Cricket Board, whose impressive development programme in the townships and rural areas resulted in the game expanding both its player and fan base dramatically. Fast bowler Makhaya Ntini, whose tally of 300-plus test wickets had propelled him to second place in the ICC world

rankings in 2007, stands at the vanguard of a generation of black South African cricketers that also includes the talented youngster Monde Zondeki and his injury-prone fellow speedster Mfuneko Ngam. The success of the national cricket side was undermined by a match-fixing scandal centred on the dodgy activities of then-captain Hansie Cronje in 2001. Nevertheless, South Africa has retained its world number two ranking in one day international cricket under Graeme Smith, the pugnacious young batsman who succeeded all-rounder Shaun Pollock as captain following the side's dismal showing in the 2003 Cricket World Cup, the first such event to be held on home soil.

Football: the people's game

Soccer has always commanded the support of South Africa's black community, who are loyal to teams with names such as Kaizer Chiefs, Moroko Swallows and Orlando Pirates. Football has a showpiece stadium – Soccer City – halfway between Johannesburg and Soweto near the Expo Centre showgrounds. It is an eye-opener for any visitor with a passion for football.

While soccer has always attracted white fans too, they've tended to avoid local league action, deeming it inferior to the European game available on TV. But that perception began to change when Bafana Bafana reached the finals of the 1998 World Cup, storming into the top 20 of the FIFA world rankings in the process. The introduction of the fully professional Premier Soccer League has also led to better organisation and huge sponsorships in the sport.

Unfortunately, however, ongoing friction with regard to the selection of several key players signed to European clubs – notably striker Benni McCarthy, midfielder Quinton Fortune, and defenders Mark Fish and Lucas Radebe – has often had a negative impact on the result of important international fixtures. For all that, consistently strong showings in the African Cup of Nations and two successive World Cup appearances have helped cement the game as the number-one sport among all South Africans – a status that can only be boosted by the announcement that South Africa will host the 2010 World Cup.

Key events and venues

Apart from regular internationals in football, cricket, rugby and athletics, South Africa also hosts the Comrades Marathon. Held on 16 June every year, it is rated by some as one of the greatest ultra-marathons in the world – a 90-km (55-mile) pilgrimage made by more than 14,000 runners every year between the coastal city of Durban and Pietermaritzburg, provincial capital of KwaZulu-Natal. It's run "up" one year from Durban and "down" the next, from Pietermaritzburg. The Comrades made a hero of Bruce Fordyce, the world's most accomplished ultra-distance runner, who won it a record nine times.

If you're a cricket fan, the venues to head for are The Wanderers in Johannesburg (just off the M1 motorway at the Corlett Drive turn-off; graceful Newlands in Cape Town; historic St

George's Park in Port Elizabeth, overlooking the city centre; and Kingsmead in Durban, on the Old Fort Road heading for North Beach.

In Cape Town, Newlands rugby ground is just a block away from the cricket stadium, while Durban's King's Park stadium (which also hosts local soccer team, Amazulu) is a 3-km (1½-mile) drive up NMR Avenue from Kingsmead. In Johannesburg, rugby action happens at Ellis Park, the venue that staged the 1995 Rugby World Cup. Take the Harrow Road turn-off from the M1 South, and follow the signs – and the fans. The Ellis Park precinct is also home to the major tennis venue, the Stan-

Challenging courses

The course hacked out of the bush at Sun City is a challenge no golfing enthusiast can pass up; another equally demanding layout – designed by Gary Player – has now been built nearby for the Lost City leisure complex. The Sun City Million Dollar Golf Challenge, held here every December, offers 12 of the world's top golfers a chance to compete for the richest prize in international golf. Past winners include Seve Ballesteros, Bernhard Langer, Nicky Price and Nick Faldo. Durban's plush Country Club also has a fine course, rated among the top 100 courses in the world. ❏

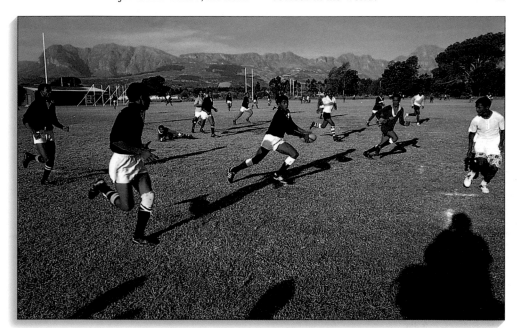

dard Bank Arena, as well as the country's premier athletics venue, Johannesburg Stadium (which, coincidentally, hosts the popular soccer team, Kaizer Chiefs).

A long coastline and plentiful inland dams and rivers mean that South Africa is the venue for some exciting and testing canoe races, the most challenging of which is the four-day, 228-km (142-mile) Berg River Marathon from Paarl to Veldrif, which includes stretches of "white water"; this is usually held in July.

LEFT: Ernie Els has inspired South African golfers.
ABOVE: after years of international isolation, South African rugby is back on track.

KEEPING UP WITH THE GAME

If you prefer the sedentary approach to your favourite sport – taking in the action in front of the television – South African broadcast networks between them offer one of the widest ranges of televised local and international sporting action you are likely to find anywhere in the world. Live football, tennis, golf, cricket and rugby are beamed in from local venues and across the globe, so you're not likely to miss any action from back home while you're away on holiday. In the big cities, you could also head for one of the numerous sports bars, often crowded with very vocal supporters.

ARCHITECTURE

The built environment reflects a rich cultural diversity –
as well as exposing the country's stark economic contrasts

South Africa's architecture reflects the country's distinctly different climatic zones, the cultural diversity of its people and, not least, the stark economic contrasts pervading every aspect of life.

The oldest surviving building in South Africa, the Castle of Good Hope in Cape Town, was built in 1666. Archaeological research in Limpopo Province and Mpumalanga, however, has uncovered several important stone ruins that predate white settlement at the Cape. Most notable is Mapungubwe Hill, which lies at the confluence of the Limpopo and Shashi rivers, and has been accorded both national park and UNESCO World Heritage Site status. Constructed *c.* AD 950, Mapungubwe was the capital of a gold-mining civilisation that entered into regular trade with coastal Swahili ports such as Sofala, and reached its architectural apex with the construction of Great Zimbabwe (in the country of the same name) in around AD 1300.

In response to local conditions of climate and availability of materials the 17th-century settlers of the Cape developed the Cape Dutch style, a truly vernacular architecture. Characterised by a pitched thatched roof, a decorative gable, white-washed walls and a symmetrical facade with shuttered rectangular windows, the early Cape Dutch houses were often built in the shape of a T; later, the larger H-plan design became more popular.

A fine example is Groot Constantia near Cape Town, the homestead and wine farm built for Dutch governor Simon van der Stel in 1685. The homestead's decorative pediment was added in 1778 by German sculptor, Anton Anreith.

Other important historic buildings in Cape Town are the Tuynhuys, built in 1700, and today used as the State President's office and residence, the Old Slave Lodge (now the South African Cultural History Museum), the Old Town House on Greenmarket Square, and the South African Library.

LEFT: a modern interior at V&A Waterfront, Cape Town.
RIGHT: brilliant colour subverts a soulless street in Khayelitsha township.

After a hugely destructive fire in 1736, thatching was strongly discouraged in Cape Town. As a result, a new house type featuring a flat roof and – sometimes – a decorative wavy parapet became common. The oldest surviving examples are now found in the city's Malay Quarter, the Bo-Kaap. These simple one-storey

buildings originally housed the fishermen, labourers and tradesmen who had come to the Cape as slaves. This district also houses the country's first official mosque, the Auwal, built in 1798. Only a few original walls survive.

As the frontiers of European settlement pressed northwards, a derivative of the Cape Dutch vernacular developed in the harsh, arid interior. The Karoo house is a flat-roofed yet pedimented building with a *stoep* (porch) and later a veranda. In the Northern Cape, early 18th-century Boer settlers responded to the scarcity of wood by building hut-like structures of corbelled stone, some of which survive in the towns of Williston and Carnarvon.

The British influence

In the 1820s, British settlers arrived in the Eastern Cape, an area previously occupied by Boer farmers. A vernacular architecture soon developed around Grahamstown, fusing the building traditions of the Cape with those of the settlers. Stone was more readily available here than in Cape Town, which led to Grahamstown's characteristic unplastered stone buildings with slate or shale roofs, some of which also have decorative open trelliswork. In Port Elizabeth, the British influence manifests itself architecturally in terraced houses with elegant Georgian and Regency verandas.

(now accommodating the post office), built in 1884 by Philip Dudgeon in a Classical style.

Yet the city's architectural uniqueness stems from the local Asian population. Well-preserved Hindu temples are scattered throughout the Asian districts, while the city centre boasts the gigantic Grey Street mosque.

Modernism, Gauteng-style

Just as the cities of Cape Town and Durban each have their own unique architectural character, the same is true for South Africa's third major urban centre: Gauteng. At its heart lies Johannesburg, a cosmopolitan industrial centre whose

KwaZulu-Natal: an exotic blend

The cities of Durban and Pietermaritzburg also have a pronounced British architectural character, even though the province was settled before 1839 by Voortrekkers. Trees for firing kilns were plentiful in this subtropical region, facilitating the making of bricks and consequently construction with face brick. Pietermaritzburg, in particular, is famous for its Victorian salmon-coloured brick buildings with corrugated-iron roofs and pretty filigreed verandas.

In the late 19th century, the economic impact of the growing mining industry resulted in a remarkable building boom, epitomised by the monumental structure of Durban's City Hall

growth and wealth were originally closely connected to the mining industry. Nearby is the smaller, much more provincial city of Pretoria, crowned by Herbert Baker's majestic Union Buildings (1912).

Both cities have some fine examples of the architecture of the Modernist movement. A new period in South African architectural history began when the International Style first took hold at the University of the Witwatersrand in Johannesburg, under the guidance of Rex Martienssen. In Pretoria, architects like Norman Eaton made significant contributions towards the development of a regional style, adapting Modernism to local conditions.

African vernacular

In the rural areas of KwaZulu-Natal, the original Zulu beehive hut of intricately woven grass has disappeared. In remote parts, a closely related type can still be found, consisting of a low wattle-and-daub cylinder with a dome-like beehive roof. Most common today, however, is the cone-on-cylinder type, often built with modern materials, or Western-influenced rectangular houses.

In rural Free State, beautifully decorated South Sotho homes are still frequent. Their rectangular shape with low mono-pitch roofs reveal Western influences, but construction methods and decoration are still traditionally African.

The legacy of apartheid

The 1960s and 1970s was when the bulk of municipal schemes to erect black townships around the cities were carried out. Endless rows of monotonous box-like structures with corrugated iron roofs are a sombre contrast to the much more elaborate homes in mostly white areas.

Providing affordable homes for South Africa's lowest-income population is the single greatest challenge facing local authorities, town planners, developers and architects today. Given the magnitude of the project, this issue will have a considerable effect on shaping the future of South Africa's cities.   ❏

The most splendid examples of African vernacular architecture are produced by the Ndebele people. These buildings have a complex system of courts and forecourts, reflecting the social hierarchy that structures both family and community.

However, the Ndebele are most famous for their ingenious way of assimilating influences from other cultures, creating a strong identity of their own in the process. This is particularly evident in the colourful decoration of their houses.

LEFT: Boschendal, near Stellenbosch, is one of the finest examples of the Cape Dutch style.
ABOVE: a covering of intricately woven thatch ensures these Zulu homes stay cool during the summer.

A GLARINGLY OBVIOUS STYLE

Apartheid's heyday, from the 1960s to the 1980s, saw an architectural attitude that defied South Africa's international isolation. Every major city centre proudly has a number of stark office tower blocks, epitomised by prestigious architect Helmut Jahn's tower in Johannesburg's Diagonal Street (1982), assertively competing with the architectural achievements of the rest of the world. And every town, whatever its size, has at least one Dutch Reformed church in a brutal brick and steel design, rearing a relentlessly modern spire against the bright blue sky.

MAMMALS

From the tiny shrew to the mighty African elephant, wildlife on the tip of the continent is simply spectacular

South Africa's richly varied mammal fauna, comprised of 230 land and 43 marine species, is linked to an ecological diversity that includes no less than six major terrestrial biotic zones, ranging from desert to montane forest. For those who go on safari, however, it is the classic African woodland savannah of the northeast that holds the greatest allure, harbouring as it does a wide range of favourites including the so-called Big Five of elephant, lion, leopard, buffalo and rhino. The Kruger National Park and bordering private reserves (now part of the Great Limpopo Trans-frontier Park) is South Africa's premier game-viewing destination, but hundreds of smaller reserves countrywide protect familiar safari species alongside regional specialities.

The list that follows describes over 50 of the more conspicuous large mammal species, but do look out also for some of the smaller mammals that account for more than 60 percent of the national checklist. These includes two dozen mole species, a variety of rabbits and hares, at least 75 bat species – often to be seen flying around rest camps at dusk – as well as the bizarre elephant-shrew, which can be distinguished by its twitchy elongated snout. For more detailed coverage, see the field guides listed under further reading *(see Travel Tips).*

PRECEDING PAGES: safety in numbers; or is it easy pickings? **LEFT:** the once endangered white rhino has made a dramatic comeback.

Lion *(Panthera leo)*

Tawny or fawn in colour, with manes ranging from gold to black on the male, the lion is the largest of Africa's three big cats, and also the most sociable. Prides consist of six to a dozen females and their cubs, with one or more dominant males. Most of the hunting is done by females, working as a team, usually at night, but males will usually be first to eat at a kill. Some prides specialise in hunting buffalo or giraffe, but most feed on impala, zebra or wildebeest, seizing the prey by the throat and suffocating it.

Leopard *(Panthera pardus)*

The leopard is bulkier than other spotted cats, from which it can be distinguished by its somewhat pugilistic build and elegant coat of black rosettes set against an off-white to russet background. It is a solitary animal, except when a pair come together to mate, or a mother is accompanied by cubs. Hunting mainly at night, the leopard steals up on its prey, then pounces from close range. A leopard will often carry a fresh kill (impala, baboons and monkeys are favoured) up a tree, safe from the reach of less dextrous carnivores.

Cheetah (*Acinonyx jubatus*)

Superficially similar to a leopard, the cheetah has a more greyhound-like build, with long legs, solid dark spots (as opposed to rosettes), and a small head with diagnostic black "tear-marks" below each eye. It inhabits open savannah, where it uses its impressive speed – up to 100 kph/60 mph over short distances – to run down medium-sized antelope such as impala or springbok. Cheetahs are usually seen singly, in pairs, or in small family groups consisting of a female and cubs. They normally hunt in the cool hours just after dawn.

Serval (*Felis serval*)

Another spotted cat, smaller than a cheetah but with a similar build, long legs and a short tail. Its black-on-gold spots give way to black streaks near the head. The serval is usually a solitary animal, but is sometimes seen in pairs or small family groups. It hunts mainly at night, and sometimes in the early morning or late afternoon, preying on small mammals, birds and reptiles. Although not uncommon, its favoured habitat of tall grass and reeds and its elusive habits mean that it is seldom seen

Caracal (*Felis caracal*)

Similar in appearance to a lynx, the caracal is a medium-sized cat, anything from pale fawn to chestnut in colour, with long, pointed, tufted ears. It is a solitary hunter, preying on mammals from mice to small antelopes, birds and reptiles. It stalks its prey as close as possible, then relies on a pounce or a short run. Its powerful hind legs enable it to leap vertically 3 metres (10 ft) to swat a bird. Caracal are widespread throughout Africa's drier regions, but are mainly nocturnal and rarely seen.

African wild cat (*Felis sylvestris*)

Ancestral to the domestic cat (with which it often interbreeds near human settlements), the African wild cat is similar but less variable in appearance. Typically its dark grey-buff coat is offset by striped legs and tail, and a ginger back to the ears. A solitary nocturnal hunter, it feeds on small mammals and birds. It occurs throughout South Africa, in western areas alongside the **black-footed cat** (*Felis nigripes*), an even smaller spotted cat endemic to Africa's arid southwest.

African wild dog *(Lycaon pictus)*

Unlikely to be mistaken for any other canid, the wild (or hunting) dog has long legs, huge ears, a white-tipped tail and a blotched black, white and tan torso. No two animals have exactly the same markings. It is a superb hunter – packs of 10 to 15 animals can maintain a chase over several kilometres and overwhelm much larger antelope by weight of numbers. Vulnerable to diseases carried by domestic dogs, the wild dog is listed as endangered, but the Kruger Park hosts one of the largest remaining wild breeding populations.

Black-backed jackal *(Canis mesomelas)*

Jackals are medium-sized dogs, usually seen singly or in pairs, with an omnivorous diet of small mammals, carrion and fruit. Primarily nocturnal (but also diurnally active in protected areas), their call – a scream followed by a few short yaps – is a characteristic sound of the African night. The widespread black-backed jackal is tawny-brown with a grizzled black back-saddle. Restricted to the extreme northeast, the **side-striped jackal** *(Canis adustus)* is smaller, paler and has an indistinct white stripe along its flank.

Bat-eared fox *(Otocyon megalotis)*

Small, grey and bushy-tailed, this fox-like insectivore is most easily identified by its black "robber mask". Its enormous ears and acute directional hearing are the key to its success, allowing it to locate harvester termites nests as far as 30 cm (1 ft) underground. Common in the arid Kalahari, the bat-eared fox forms permanent pairs, which den in burrows dug from scratch or modified from existing animal holes. It is typically nocturnal or crepuscular, but can be conspicuous by day during the winter.

Cape fox *(Vulpes chama)*

South Africa's only true fox is a regional endemic restricted to arid and semi-arid habitats from the Western Cape to southern Angola. The smallest of South Africa's canids, the Cape fox can be distinguished from all jackals by its grizzled grey back, russet underparts and very bushy tail, and from the bat-eared fox by its smaller ears and lack of a black mask. Its main food is invertebrates and small rodents, which it hunts by night. Although reasonably common and widespread in South Africa, it is seldom observed.

Spotted hyena *(Crocuta crocuta)*

Distinguished by its impressive bulk, sloping hindquarters, coarse spotted coat, round face, and powerful jaw, the spotted hyena, though often characterised as a pure scavenger, is also an efficient hunter. It was once thought to be hermaphroditic due to the false scrotum and penis covering the female genitalia. Clans of 10–100 individuals, led by a dominant female, are active mainly at night, when individuals maintain contact with an eerie whooping call that occasionally terminates in a demonic cackle.

Brown hyena *(Hyaena brunnea)*

This nocturnal scavenger is near-endemic to the semi-arid west of southern Africa, though its range extends into the northern Kruger Park. It is smaller, shaggier and more secretive than the spotted hyena, with a distinctive ruff-like mane of cream-coloured fur, and a similar repertoire of eerie, far-carrying whoops and chuckles. The remarkable **aardwolf** *(Protelus cristata)* is a small striped hyaenid whose distribution follows that of the few specific harvester termite genera on which it feeds exclusively.

Large-spotted genet *(Genetta tigrina)*

Similar in size and shape to a domestic cat, genets are streamlined nocturnal carnivores with short legs and an exceptionally long ringed tail. The large-spotted genet has dark blotched spots and a black tail-tip, while the **small-spotted genet** *(Genetta genetta)* has smaller spots and a white tail-tip. Both species prey on invertebrates and small mammals, and may be seen scavenging around lodges after dark. Within South Africa, the former is restricted to the eastern coastal belt while the latter ranges across the centre and west.

African civet *(Civettictis civetta)*

The size of a medium-sized dog, the civet is a stocky, powerful omnivore, its pale coat marked with dark blotches which merge into stripes nearer the head. It is a solitary hunter and may be seen at night (occasionally in the early evening) trotting with its head down in search of insects, rodents, reptiles – including venomous snakes – birds or carrion. It also eats fruit and can even digest poisonous plants. It is purely terrestrial, unlike its relative the forest-dwelling **tree civet** *(Nandinia binotata)*, which rarely comes to ground.

Ratel *(Mellivora capensis)*

A powerful, low-slung carnivore, mostly black but with a silver-grey mantle from head to tail, the ratel is the same size as a badger (its other name is honey badger, after its habit of breaking into beehives to eat honeycomb and larvae). Rather secretive, it hunts mainly at night, usually unaccompanied, using its massive claws to dig out scorpions, rodents and other burrowing animals. The ratel frequently scavenges round rubbish dumps and camps in parks and reserves, and will attack humans aggressively if it feels threatened.

White-tailed mongoose *(Ichneumia albicauda)*

The largest of South Africa's 10 mongoose species, this is also very distinctive due to its unique bushy white tail. Like most African mongooses, it is solitary and hunts mainly at night, feeding on invertebrates, small mammals and fruit. Quite common in the Kruger Park, it is often seen on night drives in neighbouring private reserves. More common in this part of the country, however, is the solitary but diurnal **slender mongoose** *(Galerella sanguinea)*, often seen darting across the road with diagnostic black tail-tip prominent.

Banded mongoose *(Mungos mungo)*

This diurnal and highly sociable predator – bands can be comprised of 50 individuals – is grey-brown with a dozen indistinct black stripes on its lower back. A true omnivore, it eats invertebrates, rodents, birds, eggs, fruit and berries. Almost as gregarious is the **dwarf mongoose** *(Helogale parvula)*, which is also one of Africa's smallest carnivores at 32 cm (1 ft) long including tail. Groups of 10–20 are often seen in or near the old termite mounds in which they den. Both are common in the Kruger Park.

Suricate *(Suricata suricatta)*

Also known as a meerkat, this pale grey mongoose, famed for its endearing habit of standing upright to survey the surroundings, lives colonially in old ground-squirrel burrows. Endemic to arid country from the Cape to southern Angola, it is restricted to the west of the country, where bands of up to 20 individuals are often seen on the roadside. Also common, the **yellow mongoose** *(Cynictis pencillata)* has a similar range and occasionally stands upright – but its woollier appearance and distinctive white-tipped tail should preclude confusion.

Elephant *(Loxodonta africana)*

The largest land mammal, the African elephant can reach 3.4 metres (11 ft) at the shoulder and weigh 6,300 kg (over 6 tons). Females live in loose-knit herds, in which the oldest cow plays matriarch. Males usually leave the family at around age 12, to drift between herds, roam singly or form bachelor groups. Elephants are active 16–20 hours a day, eating, drinking, bathing or travelling in search of food – they can eat up to 150 kg (330 lb) of vegetation in 24 hours. *For more information, see the feature on page 122.*

Hippopotamus *(Hippopotamus amphibius)*

This huge mammal (up to 2,000 kg/2 tons) is common in the waterways of the Kruger Park and Zululand, and has been reintroduced to Cape Town's Rondevlei Nature Reserve. Hippos live in groups of 10 or more, presided over by a dominant male, who defends his territory fiercely. The thin skin lacks sweat glands and can easily dehydrate, which is why hippos stay partially or fully submerged in daylight. After dark, hippos graze terrestrially, and they are often seen lumbering along well-worn trails at dusk or dawn.

Square-lipped rhino *(Ceratotherium simum)*

This bulky and peaceable grey-coated grazer is popularly called the white rhino, a name that derives from the Dutch *weit* (wide) and refers to the square lips that enable it to crop grass so efficiently. Once common throughout south-eastern Africa, the square-lipped rhino has been poached heavily in recent decades, mainly because its horn of compressed hair is valued highly as an aphrodisiac in Asia and as a dagger handle in Yemen. Zululand and the Kruger Park are the last major strongholds for this endangered species.

Hook-lipped rhino *(Diceros bicornis)*

Also known as the black rhino, the hook-lipped rhino is no darker than its square-lipped cousin, from which it can be distinguished by a muscular hooked upper lip designed for browsing from branches and leaves. It is smaller than the white rhino, and meaner-tempered, with a reputation for charging at any provocation. Poached to extinction in many areas where it was abundant in the 1970s, the black rhino remains common in many South African reserves, but relatively difficult to see due to its preference for dense vegetation.

Giraffe *(Giraffa camelopardalis)*

The world's tallest animal, a male giraffe can grow to 5.5 metres (18 ft); females are somewhat shorter. The giraffe prefers open country to woodland, although its main food is leaves, especially from the tops of acacia trees, which it grasps with its amazing 45-cm (18-in) tongue. Giraffes are non-territorial, roaming around in loose herds of up to 15, of both sexes. The subspecies found in South Africa is the **southern giraffe** *(G. c. giraffa)*, which has ragged edges to its blotchy markings.

Plains or Burchell's zebra *(Equus burchelli)*

As individual as human fingerprints, the zebra's trademark stripes are thought to confuse predators by breaking up the animal's outline. A typical zebra herd consists of one stallion and a few mares with their foals. The plains zebra mingles happily with other herbivores, but since it can eat coarse grass unpalatable to other grazers, it's often the first species in a grazing area. Common in the Kruger Park, the southern African race is distinguished from northern forms (and the mountain zebras) by its pale "shadow" stripes.

Mountain zebra *(Equus zebra)*

Endemic to southern Africa, both races of mountain zebra lack shadow striping and have a chestnut-tinged snout. **Hartmann's mountain zebra** *(E. z. hartmanni)* is centred on Namibia but a small number inhabits the extreme Northern Cape. One-third of the global population of 750 **Cape Mountain zebra** *(E. z. zebra)* lives in the eponymous national park founded in the 1950s – when, with fewer than 10 individuals remaining, the fate of the closely related **quagga**, (a dark-rumped zebra hunted to extinction by European settlers) beckoned.

Buffalo *(Syncerus caffer)*

Africa's only species of wild cattle, the buffalo is very heavily built (up to 150 cm/5 ft at the shoulder), with relatively short stocky legs. Large ears fringed with hair hang below massive curved horns which meet in a central boss. They are gregarious, living in herds from a few dozen to several thousand in number, though it is not unusual to encounter lone bulls (which can be dangerous). They most often graze at night, and drink in the early morning and late afternoon, spending the day resting or chewing the cud.

Blue Wildebeest *(Connochaetes taurinus)*

Africa's most abundant antelope, the blue wildebeest (or brindled gnu) is an ungainly grey-brown creature with a straggly black mane and small buffalo-like horns. Herds typically comprise about 30 animals, but larger numbers often congregate in the grassland around the Kruger Park's Satara Camp. Endemic to South Africa, the **black wildebeest** *(Connochaetes gnou)* is smaller, blacker and has a diagnostic white tail – some 10,000 are distributed across various small reserves and private ranches centred on Free State Province.

Tsessebe *(Damaliscus lunatus)*

The southern race of the East African topi, this distinctive antelope has shoulders higher (125 cm/49 inches) than its rump, a glossy tan coat with blackish upper and yellow lower legs, and stout ridged horns that curve backwards and upwards in both sexes. It is a grazer with a limited distribution in South Africa – small herds, controlled by a dominant bull, might be encountered in Ithala, Pilanesberg and the northeastern Kruger Park. The tsessebe is the fastest antelope in the region, and can outrun most predators.

Hartebeest *(Alcelaphus buselaphus)*

The hartebeest resembles the topi, but is paler, with a longer head and small curved horns whose exact shape varies greatly between a half-dozen regional races spread across Africa. The **red hartebeest** *(A. b. caama)* of southern Africa, darker and tanner than all other races, is common in the Kalahari Gemsbok and has been reintroduced into several other western reserves. The yellowish **Liechtenstein's hartebeest** *(A. (b.) lichtensteinii)* became extinct within South Africa in 1954 but was reintroduced to the Kruger Park in 1985.

Bontebok *(Damaliscus dorcas)*

This *fynbos* endemic has a similar silhouette to the topi, but is considerably smaller. Its sleek black-tan coat contrasts with bold white patches on the rump, lower-legs and snout. Both sexes have relatively long straight horns. Formerly endangered, the bontebok is now common in the likes of the eponymous national park near Swellendam and Cape of Good Hope. The similar **blesbok** *(D. d. phillipsi)* is a highveld endemic protected in several reserves and private farms in the Free State and Drakensberg regions.

Sable antelope (Hippotragus niger)

You could never confuse the sexes of this handsome large antelope: both have magnificent curved horns (particularly the male) and distinctive black-and-white faces, but the male's body is jet black and the female's chestnut brown. Predominantly a grazer, the sable favours dry open woodland such as characterises the Pretoriuskop and Letaba regions of the Kruger Park, where herds of 10–30 individuals are controlled by one dominant bull. The sable has been introduced to several small South African reserves outside its historical range.

Roan antelope (Hippotragus equinus)

Africa's second-largest antelope (150 cm/5 ft at the shoulder), the roan has a stocky equine build, a short neck, and a distinct erect mane. Both sexes have backward-curving, ringed horns and black-and-white face markings. The roan is a grazer that lives in herds of 6–12, defended by an adult bull but led by a dominant female, who selects feeding areas. Within South Africa, the roan occurs naturally only in the northern Kruger Park, where it is rather scarce, but introduced herds are found in several other reserves.

Common oryx (Oryx gazella)

Also known as the gemsbok, this statuesque grey desert-adapted antelope has a striking black-and-white face and long, straight horns in both sexes. Three races are recognised, of which the fringe-eared and **Beisa oryx** of East Africa regarded by some authorities as specifically distinct from the southern race (O.g. gazella). Predominantly a grazer, the oryx can survive for months without access to water. Small herds, led by a territorial bull, are common in the Kalahari Gemsbok and elsewhere in the Northern Cape.

Common waterbuck (Kobus ellipsiprymnus)

This large, robust antelope (up to 135 cm/53 inches at the shoulder) has a shaggy grey-brown coat and a pronounced white ring on its rump, as if it has sat on a freshly painted toilet seat. The male has long lyre-shaped horns, and both sexes are said to emit a smell that deters most predators. A dedicated grazer, the waterbuck is generally seen in small family groups in grassy areas near water. It is very common in the Kruger Park and some Zululand reserves, but is absent from most other parts of South Africa.

Eland *(Taurotragus oryx)*

Africa's largest antelope (up to 180 cm/6 ft at the shoulder), the eland has a somewhat bovine build, with a large dewlap and relatively short spiral horns, and a fawn coat with faint white vertical side stripes. Nomadic herds of 20 or more individuals are widespread in the Drakensberg and other grassland habitats countrywide, as well as in more arid regions, but they tend to be shy of humans. Active both diurnally and nocturnally, the eland is a prodigious jumper, able to clear 2 metres (6 ft) from a standing position.

Greater kudu *(Tragelaphus strepsiceros)*

This elegant antelope has slender legs, big ears, a greyish coat and 6–10 white stripes on each side of the body. It's most notable for the triple-spiralled horns of the fully grown male. Small herds of females and youngsters, as well as bachelor herds (often with half-grown horns), inhabit woodland or thicket habitats, where they browse on seeds, shoots and pods, also occasionally grazing. The greater kudu is common in the Kruger Park, and other suitable protected areas and private ranches in the north of the country.

Bushbuck *(Tragelaphus scriptus)*

This widespread medium-sized antelope appears in various hues. The sturdy-horned males are often dark brown and the hornless females paler chestnut, but there is much variation and either sex may or may not have white spots and/or stripes. Both browser and grazer, the bushbuck likes dense bush close to water, and is most active from late afternoon into early morning, but is generally shy and difficult to spot. Close-up sightings of habituated individuals can be had at the perimeter of some camps, for example Letaba in the Kruger Park.

Nyala *(Tragelaphus angasii)*

Intermediate in size between the closely related greater kudu and bushbuck, the nyala is a southern African endemic associated with thicket and riverine bush in Zululand and the northern Kruger Park. Both sexes are greyish in colour, with 10–12 vertical white side-stripes and a few spots. As with most other Tragelaphus antelope, the male is far larger and more cryptically marked than the female – and exceptionally handsome with its large spiralled horns, shaggy blue-black white-tipped mane and yellow lower legs.

Impala *(Aepyceros melampus)*

Particularly abundant in the Kruger Park, this slender, elegant, chestnut-coloured antelope is distinguished by unique black-and-white stripes on the rump and tail. Males have impressive lyre-shaped horns. Impala prefer wooded savannah, where they feed on fruits, seed pods, leaves and sometimes grass. They live in two kinds of groups: bachelor herds (all male) and harems of females and young. In the breeding season, a ram will take over a harem – and then battle with challenging males to preserve his breeding rights.

Springbok *(Antidorcas marsupialis)*

The springbok is the southern equivalent of the related East African "Tommy" (Thomson's gazelle). Both species have pale brown upperparts separated from a white belly by a broad black horizontal stripe, small upright near-parallel horns, and – when threatened – tend to bounce around stiff-legged, a type of behaviour known as pronking. The migrating herds of hundreds of thousands of springbok described by early European settlers are a thing of the past, but small herds remains common in the arid northwest of South Africa.

Southern reedbuck *(Redunca arundinum)*

This nondescript fawn antelope with small curved horns (male only) is distinguished by the bare patch found behind each ear. Pairs and family herds inhabit moist grassland, notably in the vicinity of Lake St Lucia. The **mountain reedbuck** *(Redunca fulvorufula)* has a black patch behind the ears, but is shaggier and darker, and favours grassy slopes. It often occurs alongside the rather similar **grey rhebok** *(Palea capreolus)* – which has no bare patch but does have strikingly elongated, almost hare-like ears.

Oribi *(Ourebia ourebi)*

This graceful fawn-brown small antelope has a long neck, black-tipped tail, black glandular spots below the ear, and (male only) short straight horns. It typically lives in small groups comprised of one vigorously territorial ram and up to three ewes. Mainly a grazer, it is most common in the rolling grassland of the KwaZulu-Natal/Eastern Cape border. When disturbed, the oribi emits a sharp whistle or sneeze and runs off with stiff-legged jumps. Alternatively (and unusually for antelopes), it might lie down to hide in long grass.

Steenbok *(Raphicerus campestris)*

Looking like a diminutive oribi, but without the black glandular spot and with shorter horns, the steenbok is South Africa's most widespread antelope, absent only from the northwest. It is common in the Kruger Park, where individuals and occasionally pairs freeze when disturbed, then suddenly bolt off. Similar, but with a darker and more grizzled coat, the **Cape grysbok** *(R. melanotus)* is endemic to the *fynbos* of the Western Cape, while **Sharpe's grysbok** *(R. sharpei)* is a tropical species whose range extends into the Kruger Park.

Klipspringer *(Oreotragus oreotragus)*

This alert-looking small antelope has a thick speckled grey coat, a unique white eye-ring punctuated by a black frontal "tear mark", and a rather stocky appearance belying its exceptional agility in its favoured habitat of cliffs and rocky slopes. Practically always seen in pairs, the klipspringer (an Afrikaans name meaning "rock-jumper") is a widespread but habitat-specific resident – it's common in the Drakensberg, and often seen near Augrabies Falls and on the cliffs around Olifants Camp in the Kruger Park.

Grey duiker *(Sylvicapra grimmia)*

Also known as the common or bush duiker, this small antelope is typically yellowish-grey in colour, and has a distinctive tuft of black hair between its ears. Rams have short, pointed horns. It is the most widespread of all the duiker species, and the only one associated with savannah woodland rather than forest interiors. Normally seen singly or in pairs, it has a remarkably varied diet, feeding on shoots, leaves, fruits and cultivated crops, digging for tubers and roots with its front hoofs, and even taking termites and other insects.

Red duiker *(Cephalophus natalensis)*

Also known as the Natal duiker, this tiny red-brown antelope, whose short horns are separated by a dark tuft of hair, inhabits forests along and below the eastern escarpment south to Durban. Solitary and timid, the red duiker is typically glimpsed bounding across a forest path into cover, but good sightings can be had at campsites in the vicinity of St Lucia. The **blue duiker** *(C. monticola)*, the region's smallest antelope (shoulder height 30 cm/1 ft) is a grey-blue resident of eastern forest and coastal scrub south to Knysna.

Chacma baboon *(Papio ursinus)*

Distributed throughout South Africa, the baboon is a large monkey that comes in varying shades of grey/brown, but can always be recognised by its dog-like muzzle and permanently kinked tail. Baboons are diurnal and largely terrestrial, but they will climb trees to gather fruit, evade predators, or sleep. Otherwise they are found on the ground in complex social groups of up to 100, foraging, fighting, playing, grooming, nursing or courting. They feed on all kinds of plants, including crops, as well as insects, eggs and small mammals.

Vervet monkey *(Cercopithecus aethiops)*

The vervet monkey is small and slender, with a long tail, grey fur, a white belly, and bare black face and hands. It is common in much of South Africa, living in troops of up to 30 individuals in savannah and woodland habitats rather than thick forest. The vervet is agile in trees, where it forages for fruit, leaves and flowers, but it is equally at home on the ground foraging for seeds and insects. Troops are very sociable, and communicate using a wide variety of calls, gestures and facial expressions.

Blue monkey *(Cecopithecus mitis)*

South Africa's one true forest primate, the blue or samango monkey is bulkier than the vervet, and its blue-grey back contrasts with pale yellow-brown underparts. Common elsewhere in Africa, the blue monkey is restricted to coastal forests within South Africa, and most likely to be seen in the vicinity of Sodwana Bay. Diurnal and arboreal troops of up to 30 individuals feed on leaves, fruits, seeds, gum and bark, and occasionally insects and birds. A wide range of calls includes a loud, far-carrying bark to warn of danger.

Greater galago *(Galago crassicaudatus)*

Galagos are small nocturnal primates, distant relatives of the lemurs of Madagascar. The greater or thick-tailed galago is by far the largest (80 cm/2 ft 6 inches overall), silver grey-brown with a darker bushy tail and large leathery ears. It is omnivorous but prefers fruit, especially figs. It has a loud screaming call, like a human baby in distress. The **bushbaby** *(G. senegalensis)* is the commonest of the smaller galagos. It has huge eyes and ears, and forages at night, usually alone, feeding on sap and insects.

Warthog *(Phacochoerus aethiopicus)*

The only African wild pig that's commonly seen by day, the warthog has a grey body sparsely covered with bristly hairs, a dark coarse mane and upward-curving tusks. It is named after the wart-like growths on its face (the male has four, the female two). Warthogs graze on a variety of grasses, and in the dry season also root for bulbs and tubers, kneeling down and digging with their tusks. They live in family groups of females and young with one dominant male, sleeping and hiding from predators in networks of burrows.

Bushpig *(Potamochoerus porcus)*

This hairy pig varies in colour from grey to reddish brown, and has a characteristic crest of hair along its spine, as well as tufted ears and a "beard". Males are larger than females (up to 170 cm/5 ft 6 inches long). The bushpig is probably more widespread than the warthog in South Africa, but is seldom seen because it prefers thick vegetation and is mainly active at night, snuffling around for roots, fruits and fungi. The bushpig is a favourite prey of the leopard and spotted hyena, and it is also hunted by humans for food.

Aardvark *(Orycteropus afer)*

An unmistakable creature, the aardvark is vaguely pig-like, but with a long tail, long tubular snout and huge ears. Digging is its speciality, as shown by its powerful forelegs and massive front claws, which it uses to excavate extensive burrows where it hides during the day. The aardvark is solitary and active only at night, when it may wander for several kilometres in search of termites, ants or larvae. When it finds a colony, it digs into it vigorously, lapping up insects with its long sticky tongue.

Rock hyrax *(Procavia capensis)*

Hyraxes look like large rodents, brown, round and short-legged, but are in fact distant relatives of the elephant. Rock hyraxes live in small colonies on rocky hillsides or kopjes, where they are often seen basking in the early morning. They feed on leaves, flowers and fruits, never moving far from the shelter of rock. They often become tame when accustomed to people, for instance around lodges. Their relative the **tree hyrax** *(Dendrohyax arboreus)* is a solitary, nocturnal forest animal with an eerie shrieking call.

Spring Hare *(Pedetes capensis)*

Despite its name, this is not a member of the rabbit family; and despite its appearance it is not related to the kangaroo. The spring hare is a true rodent, around 80 cm (2 ft 8 inches) long, yellowish-fawn above and paler below, with large ears and eyes, a long bushy tail and enormous hind legs. It propels itself with these, in a series of leaps or hops, and uses its tiny fore-legs solely for feeding or digging. It is a solitary animal, living alone in a burrow, and largely nocturnal, feeding on roots, grass and other plants.

Porcupine *(Hystrix spp.)*

Easily recognised by its covering of long black-and-white banded quills, the porcupine grows up to a metre (3 ft) in length. Two species are found in South Africa, both very similar in appearance and both sharing the same habits. They live in burrows (often several animals in the same network) in all types of habitat except thick forest, emerging only at night to forage for roots, bulbs, tubers and tree bark. A porcupine makes use of regular pathways: their quills are easily detached and often found along these trails.

Striped ground squirrel *(Xerus inauris)*

This endearing resident of plains west of the Drakensberg lives in sociable subterranean colonies of around 30 individuals. It is particularly common in the Kalahari, where semi-habituated colonies in national park's rest camps can be observed at close quarters as they scuffle around foraging and squabbling over scraps. Light grey-brown in colour with a pronounced side-stripe, and strictly terrestrial, the ground squirrel is replaced in the north and east by several more russet and arboreal species of **bush squirrel**.

Dolphins

Bottle-nosed dolphins are often seen off beaches as they relish playing in the surf. These creatures – one of 43 marine mammals occurring off the South African coastline – are believed to be highly intelligent, a claim easily accepted when their performances in Port Elizabeth and Durban aquariums are observed. In the wild, bottle-nosed dolphins may travel in groups of several hundred, which communicate by means of a highly sophisticated language of clicks and whistles. For details on whales, *see page 174.*

The Elephant Clan

African elephants display intriguingly complex social behaviour. Living in a matriarchal society, the herd consists of a core family group, led by the oldest female and her offspring (usually about four members). Even menopausal cows can retain their role as matriarch, suggesting that wisdom and the memory of watering holes, seasonal fruit, etc is more important than the ability to procreate.

The family group, including the matriarch's sisters and their young, and ranging to about ten elephants, in turn then expands to the bond groups of the extended family, with up to 30 elephants or more. Bond groups spend up to 50 percent of their time together. The large herds formed by 5–15 bond groups joining together are called clans, while unrelated elephants using the same area are known as a sub-population.

During the wet season, elephants can gather in herds of up to 500. Great excite-ment is displayed when two families meet. Trumpeting, growling, rumbling, defecating and urinating accompany the greeting ceremony. Trunks are entwined, with much touching and caressing as the elephants renew their acquaintance. As the water dries up and food resources shrink, the group splits up, but will stay in touch. Elephants can communicate over remarkably long distances using very low frequency infrasound, below the level of human hearing.

Research has shown that this low-frequency sound enables elephants to maintain contact for up to 10 km (6 miles) even through heavy vegetation. The deep rumble we hear from time to time is a contact vocalisation ("Here I am – where are you?") which just enters the range of human hearing. Elephants also roar and scream through the trunk to produce the classic trumpeting, either in anger or exultation, depending on the situation.

It is particularly moving to see the gentleness with which elephants nurture their young. Calves are born at night, weighing

BELOW: parading to the water hole.

about 100 kg (220 lbs), and can fit under their mother's bellies until they are six months old. A mother will use her trunk and feet to guide her baby under her tummy to shelter from the sun, or to her teats between her front legs. When on the move, she'll hold the baby's tail, guiding it forwards, crook her trunk around its rump to help it in steep places, lift it out of a wallow and spray it to keep it cool. As the baby grows, its older sisters help to look after it, preparing themselves for motherhood.

When a baby elephant is in trouble, its core family rallies around immediately, encircling the baby protectively. Similar concern is also seen if an elephant is injured, its companions using their tusks to support or lift it. When an elephant dies, it is mourned by family members who display evidence of distress, and will even sometimes cover the body with branches.

Adolescent males are driven from the matriarch's herd when they become too boisterous, and form often rowdy bachelor herds. These loosely knit bull groups can include up to 20 males who move together for a day, a week or a season, though its memberships is likely to continuously change. Larger bulls go off to mate while young bulls, newly ousted from their family unit, quickly find companionship, teachers and safety in numbers in bull groups.

When bond groups join in the rainy season (also the main breeding season), the matriarchal herds are often joined by a dominant breeding bull in musth, his readiness to mate recognised by a copious, pungent secretion from the temporal gland, the dribbling of urine and bouts of aggressive behaviour. Young bulls come into musth in their late teens for a few days; in a prime breeding bull, it can last four to five months.

Females come into oestrus for two to six days, every three to five years. The bull chases the cow briefly, lays his trunk along her back and rears up on his hind legs. Penetration only takes 45 seconds. Immediately after mating, the cow will scream, with her family group gathering around and trumpeting loudly, as if sounding their approval. ❑

BELOW: playtime for all the family.

AMPHIBIANS AND REPTILES

*South Africa has an incredible variety, as well as large numbers of
species exclusive to the subcontinent*

South Africa's ecological diversity guarantees a large number of amphibian and reptile species – most of them exclusive to the subcontinent.

As most amphibians are nocturnal, it can be hard to spot any of the 130 recorded species. However, during spring and early summer, visi-

At the other extreme is the little rain frog, which can live independently of water, even for reproductive purposes. It makes its nest underground, where the larval development takes place. Eleven species of rain frog can be found in South Africa; their Afrikaans name is *blaasop*, due to their ability to inflate their bodies with air when alarmed.

tors are often treated to the extraordinary range of night sounds made by amphibians, from the booming croak of the African bullfrog to the snoring rasp of the guttural toads and the ringing call of the reed frogs. Then there's the Karoo toad, whose shrill, squawking cry sounds like a baby.

Nonetheless, one of the most common indigenous frog species is rarely heard, for it lives, feeds and breeds under water. The aquatic platanna (a corruption of the Afrikaans phrase *plathander*, or flat-handed one) uses its agile fingers to cram food such as fish and dead animals into its mouth; it also has short claws on the inner toes of its webbed hind legs to help it dissect its prey before swallowing.

As for reptiles, the much-feared Nile crocodile is nowadays largely restricted to game reserves, while crocodile farming has become a popular and prosperous venture which helps to reduce the pressure on natural populations. The potential danger these reptiles pose to humans in the wild should never be underestimated – but if they are treated with respect, confrontation can be avoided.

The subcontinent has an exceptional variety of tortoises, including five marine turtles and five freshwater terrapins. The importation of the American red-eared terrapin for sale in pet shops has meant the growth of isolated colonies of discarded purchases.

Twelve species of land tortoise are found in South Africa, the highest number in any one country. The smallest species of all does not quite reach 10 cm (4 inches) in length, even when fully grown.

Among the lizards, the geckos predominate. Most are nocturnal; many have adhesive pads under their toes, enabling them to hang upside-down on a ceiling or walk up a window pane. They're usually welcome house guests thanks to their voracious appetite for insects. Visitors to the Kruger Park are quite likely to

> **ON THE LINE**
>
> The uniquely shelled geometric tortoise, which occurs on the Cape Flats, is currently South Africa's most threatened reptile species.

Girdled and plated lizards are also exclusively African. Most common are armadillo lizards, crag lizards and the brightly coloured flat rock lizards. If you're lucky, you may see the country's largest lizard species, the Nile monitor, or leguaan – a conspicuous creature which is usually found near water.

Snakes, which are represented by around 130 species on this subcontinent, hold a morbid fascination for many people. Yet only 14 species possess a potentially fatal bite, which means that the vast

spot the tropical house gecko on walls near lights after dark.

Sixteen species of chameleon are found in South Africa, of which 14 are endemic. Not only are these extraordinary, exclusively African creatures able to change colour in response to their environment, but they also have exceptionally long tongues with a sticky pad on the end, which they shoot out to snare their prey. Small wonder that they are venerated as sacred by some rural communities.

ABOVE and **LEFT:** the hunter and the hunted. Keep your distance from the cobra (above) – its poisonous venom can prove fatal if treatment is not administered.

majority of snakes are harmless or not seriously dangerous. Many species, such as the dwarf adders, the harmless egg-eating snakes and also the dangerous varieties of cobras, are in fair demand with snake-keepers. However, stringent measures aimed at curbing the commercial exploitation and illegal export of this slithery souvenir are now in place.

Cases of snakebite are rare; most result from clumsy handling. Adder bites (especially those of the Puff and Berg adders) can be lethal, but their venom acts slowly and allows time for treatment. Fortunately, the dangers of snakebite have been greatly reduced by the excellent quality of modern serum. ❏

BIRDS IN THE BUSH

As a result of the country's location at the tip of a mighty continent,
some unique forms of bird life have evolved

Visitors with an interest in bird-watching can look forward to spending hours in South Africa enjoying a rich variety of species – from the northeastern savannah where birds of prey soar effortlessly above herds of big game, through the arid interior where species have adapted to cope with semi-desert condi-

tions, to the Western Cape, which sustains so many beautiful birds with its floral wealth.

Thanks to South Africa's position at the southern end of one of the world's largest landmasses, its bird life has evolved plenty of unique forms – some of which can now be found on other continents too. Families endemic to South Africa include the hamerkop, the secretary bird, loeries, wood hoopoes, sugarbirds and whydahs.

The northeastern lowveld

About 60 percent of the African continent is savannah – or "bushveld" – so it's not surprising that most indigenous species (including the

birds of prey, the bustards and korhaans, kingfishers, bee-eaters, rollers, hornbills and bush shrikes) are found in this type of environment. Much of the Kruger National Park's vegetation is classic bushveld; almost half of the 718 bird species found in South Africa can be seen here, making it one of the most productive birding spots in the world.

As far as birds of prey are concerned, it is possible to see a good range of species in the course of a normal day's drive through the lowveld. One of the most striking is the bateleur, a snake eagle with a black body, white underwings and bright red face and legs. The best-known scavengers are the vultures, which can be seen wheeling high in the sky all day long, on the lookout for dying or dead game. However, contrary to what most people believe, lion kills make up only a fraction of vultures' food.

Other large birds of prey include the tawny eagle, generally found on the plains, and the smaller African hawk eagle, which lives in denser woodland along the rivers.

Riverine trees often include the giant fig, which attracts fruit-eating birds like the green pigeon, loeries, hornbills, barbets and bulbuls. Also keep a lookout here for the vivid, graceful bee-eaters, which usually perch conspicuously on top of leafless twigs of bushes or trees (or on telephone wires), and so are easy to photograph from a vehicle.

Surprisingly, most of Africa's kingfishers are woodland birds. Along the major rivers both giant and pied kingfishers are common, but in woodland areas you can see at least five species, including the grey-headed and the rare pygmy kingfisher.

Another essentially African group includes the rollers and hornbills. All five southern African roller species – easily recognised by their brilliant blue wings – occur in the Kruger Park. Like the bee-eaters, they perch conspicuously in the open. The exceptionally beautiful lilac-breasted roller is the most characteristic bird of the Kruger Park.

Hornbills are common over most of the park, especially the yellow-billed and red-billed varieties. One to watch out for is the extraordinary ground hornbill, a very large, black bird with white wings and a rather grotesque red-wattled face. These tend to stick together in solemn groups of around five to 10 birds, feeding on insects, reptiles and other small animals.

Another common sight at camp sites are the metallic-blue starlings with their glossy plumage and yellow button eyes, scavenging for hand-outs from visitors. The

> **LONG-HAUL TRAVEL**
>
> Every year, the ringed plover flies more than 10,000 km (6,000 miles) from Siberia to the Western Cape.

indeed – along with the bigger Kori bustard – is still sometimes hunted for its meat.

The magnificent, if somewhat ponderous, long-tailed widow, or sakabula, can often be seen sweeping across the grasslands, while the snow-white egret can be seen among grazing herds, picking at grasshoppers that the cattle disturb.

The secretary bird, which has long plumes resembling quill pens at the back of its head, is a splendid sight to behold. You may be lucky enough to witness the dramatic spectacle of a battle between a secre-

distinctive sound of the red-chested cuckoo, or *Piet-my-vrou*, can also be heard throughout the spring and summer.

The highveld

The beautiful blue korhaan is one of the most distinctive birds of the open grassland, which covers much of Mpumalanga and the Free State. One of the rarer members of the bustard family in Africa, it's quite common here, and

LEFT: you'll find the yellow-billed hornbill in northern KwaZulu-Natal and the Northern Province.
ABOVE: the flamboyantly crested African hoopoe is one of South Africa's best-loved birds.

tary bird and a snake, the bird using its long legs to try and stamp the reptile to death.

Quite a few highveld birds can also be found in the mountains to the east and in the Karoo to the west. Several of the chats fall into this distributional pattern and so does the endemic ground woodpecker, a curious bird that never perches in trees, feeding off ants on the ground. It nests in an earth burrow in a vertical bank or a steep hill side.

From mountains to sea

The eastern slopes of the uKhahlamba-Drakensberg range, and the dense evergreen forests and deep valleys at its foothills, provide a dramatic backdrop for some rich bird life. The forests harbour sunbirds, flycatchers and the shy bush blackcap, a species that may be found only in wooded valleys bordering clear mountain streams.

Orange-breasted rock-jumpers and Drakensberg siskins are endemic to the mountains of the eastern escarpment. On the grassy slopes here, you'll see grey-wing francolins, orange-breasted long-claws and cisticolas.

If there are protea bushes around, it is likely that you'll catch a glimpse of Gurney's sugarbird, whose squeaky song breaks the mountain silence. The brightly coloured forest weaver, emerald cuckoo and Knysna loerie are also found here, and in the Tsitsikamma Forest National Park.

South Africa's national bird, the blue crane, nests on the flatter tops of grassy spurs, laying two mottled eggs on the bare ground or rock. Overhead, the bearded vulture, black eagle and Cape vulture wheel about in search of food.

The crowned eagle in action is another extraordinary sight. After waiting in a tree to ambush an unsuspecting victim, it swoops down on its prey, carrying it off in its strong claws with the aid of its enormous wings.

The KwaZulu-Natal midlands are largely given over to farming but provide some excel-

FEEDING FRENZY

At Giant's Castle Game Reserve high in the uKhahlamba-Drakensberg, a unique "vulture restaurant" provides carrion for the endangered lammergeyer (bearded vulture) in winter. Bones are scattered on a high clifftop by the Parks Board, to protect the birds against accidental death from poisoned carcasses left out to kill jackals. Bird-watchers can photograph them from a comfortable hide fitted with one-way glass and specially cut ports for telephoto lenses – and, as there are only about 200 pairs of lammergeyer left in South Africa, this is not a sight to be missed.

lent birding spots. Close to Pietermaritzburg lies Game Valley, which has over 200 bird species, including water birds (kingfishers, wagtails and the hamerkop), grassland birds (long-claws, cisticolas and guinea fowl) and forest birds (trogons, robins, bush shrikes and many more). It is one of the best birding places in KwaZulu-Natal. Tracts of bushveld in the northern parts of the region are much like the Kruger Park in vegetation and avifauna. The reserves on the north coast are rich havens for waterfowl, pelicans, flamingos and the majestic fish eagle.

In Ndumo Game Reserve, on the border of Mozambique, you can find such subtropical specialities as the purple-banded sunbird, yellow-spotted nicator and Pel's fishing owl. Here, too, are tropical water birds, including the African finfoot and all kinds of storks, herons and bitterns. Reserves such as Hluhluwe-Imfolozi, uMkhuze *(see page 140)* and Lake St Lucia also boast prolific bird life.

The arid lands

Bird-watching is relatively easy in the dry, open Karoo and the arid western parts of the country. Perhaps the most eye-catching birds here are Ludwig's bustard and the Karoo korhaan. A road-side stop will almost certainly produce some arid-zone specialities like the rufous-eared warbler, Layard's titbabbler and chat flycatcher. Travelling westward, chances improve of seeing some of the endemic larks, such as Sclater's lark (around Vanwyksvlei and Brand-vlei) and the red lark (in the red sand dunes near Kenhardt and Aggenys).

At the Karoo National Park near Beaufort West, you can step out of the front door of your chalet and be greeted by white-backed mouse-birds, Karoo robins and the ubiquitous *bok-makierie*, a member of the endemic African family of bush shrikes.

The region's best-known inhabitant is the ostrich, the world's biggest bird. Males reach a height of about 2.5 metres (8 ft) and weigh up to 135 kg (300 lbs). Although the birds are gen-erally docile, the male – distinguished by its black plumage – can be temperamental during the mating season. Its skin may turn bright pink and it is likely to make a roaring sound – not unlike that of a lion – when approached by intruders. If all else fails, it may deliver a for-midable kick with deft accuracy.

Ostriches are known for their speed and can reach up to 50 km/h (30 mph) – which explains why "ostrich derbies" are such popular events at farms in the Oudtshoorn area. A major part of the local economy around here is dependent on the ostrich industry, in which every part of the bird has a use: the skin is used for leatherware such as handbags and shoes, the feathers for dusters, and the meat for dried *biltong* – and the massive eggshells are sold as curios.

LEFT: the secretary bird kills snakes – an important part of its diet – by stamping on them.
RIGHT: the white pelican is found all around the coast, and in huge numbers at St Lucia Bay.

The sandy Kalahari, dotted with low shrubs and bigger acacia bushes and trees, has an abundant supply of small and large mammals, which make birds of prey a significant feature of the avifauna.

Undoubtedly the most astonishing avian spec-tacle here is the sight of the huge nests of the sociable weaver bird, perched like untidy thatched roofs in the bigger camelthorn trees. These com-munally built structures can be up to 4 metres (12 ft) in diameter, and house anything up to 200 weavers. They live in these nests all year round, breeding there after suitably good rains. The dainty pygmy falcon, Africa's smallest raptor, makes its home here too. A pair of falcons may

take over one or two chambers in the weaver's nest, the two species living side-by-side.

The nests are dry and well-ventilated, but vul-nerable to attacks by predators such as snakes and honey badgers, who frequently raid them in search of eggs and young birds.

If you position yourself near a water hole shortly after sunrise, you may see huge flocks of sand grouse flying in to drink, sometimes in their hundreds or even thousands. Sand grouse are unique in their habit of carrying water in their belly feathers for their young to drink – the feathers are specially designed to take up large amounts of water in the manner of a sponge. The males wade into the water to soak before flying back to their thirsty chicks, which drink water from the feathers.

The *fynbos* region

Large tracts of land in the southern Cape hill sides and mountains are covered by a characteristic growth of low shrubs and bushes, known as *fynbos*. Many are pollinated by birds which come to the flowers to feed on the abundant nectar, especially of the proteas and heaths. Two of the endemic nectar-feeders are the Cape sugarbird and the orange-breasted sunbird. Also endemic are the protea canary, a seed-eater, and the insectivorous Victorin's warbler.

Further north, into Namaqualand (famous for its show of spring flowers), the *fynbos* assumes a more arid character. This is where one can find the cinnamon-breasted warbler and the fairy flycatcher, but bird-spotters must take a scramble into the dry, rocky hills for these special birds.

Coastal birds

The Benguela current along the southern and southwestern coastline supports a rich supply of fish, which in turn attracts large numbers of sea birds. Large flocks of cormorants can often be seen perching on rocks or flying in a characteristic V-formation in search of shoals. When one is spotted, the whole flock descends upon

it in a frenzy, diving into the water to gorge on their catch. Some garrulous and noisy gulls inhabit the shores, the most impressive being the kelp. These large birds often drop molluscs from great heights on to the rocks below, exposing the edible animals inside.

Large colonies of Cape gannets are found at Lambert's Bay and on small islets such as Bird Island and Malgas. This beautiful bird, with creamy plumage and distinctive black markings on the face, can often be seen swooping down on fish in the waves below. Arctic terns or sea swallows migrate from the Arctic to the Antarctic every year, using the South African coastline as a stopover. Other, smaller birds include the African black oystercatcher, the sanderling and the white-fronted plover.

Bird migration

Every summer more than 100 species of bird migrate from the northern hemisphere to the South African shores. The most common migrants are waders of the sandpiper family, but they also include other birds ranging in size from herons to shrikes.

The journey from South Africa to Europe may take a small bird five to seven weeks to complete. They travel at ground speeds of 40–75 km/h (25–45 mph) and often fly for up to 100 hours nonstop over inhospitable stretches of ocean and desert. Small birds must use flapping flight, but larger species, such as storks and eagles, can soar and glide. This is much slower, but this way they expend less energy – a useful method of travel for birds whose size does not allow them to store a great deal of fat. Travelling these vast distances, a bird may burn up to 40 percent of its body mass.

Big soaring birds migrate by day when the heat of the sun generates thermals from the ground below, and they can utilise the rising warm air for lift. Small birds usually migrate at night at heights of up to 2,000 metres (6,500 ft) above the ground. For navigation, they use the position of the sun and stars, assisted by other environmental factors such as magnetism, wind direction, smell and landmarks. This process remains one of nature's great mysteries: young birds instinctively know how to find the correct route, even in the absence of experienced adults. ❏

LEFT: the pretty little white-fronted bee-eater is confined to the Lowveld; look out for it near rivers.

Insects

With an estimated 80,000 species of insect, South Africa is a most exciting country for entomologists, collectors and photographers alike.

The subtropical bushveld savannah in the far north of the country is home to the largest variety of insects, from the giant termite and the huge baboon spider to the cleverly camouflaged stick insects and praying mantises; from the beautiful emperor moths and butterflies to the barely visible lice, ticks, fleas and aphids.

– some species so rare that they are known only from the fragments of a solitary dead beetle. The protea, South Africa's national flower, plays host to a variety of beautiful chafer beetles. Forests here are home to the velvet worm, the most primitive living arthropod, which has survived almost unchanged for the past 400 million years.

Arid Namaqualand is highly regarded among entomologists for its great wealth of insects and arthropods. Especially notable is the colourful bottlebrush beetle.

Wherever you are in South Africa, it's wise to give all small shiny, spherical spiders a wide berth in case they should turn out to be members of

Here you can see an astonishing variety of vividly coloured dung beetles push their dung balls along with their hind legs, while columns of matabele ants stage raiding parties on neighbouring termite nests before they themselves are waylaid by robber flies.

The tropical region of KwaZulu-Natal's east coast harbours an endemic fauna which takes some truly exotic forms. From web-throwing spiders and multi-coloured fruit chafers to glamorous butterflies, this narrow strip of coast supports an amazing range.

Down south, the Cape's unique floral kingdom supports some equally fascinating insect life. Wingless Colophon beetles inhabit the mountain peaks

the genus *Latrodectus* – the button spider. The poisonous black variety is most commonly found in the wheatfields of the Western Cape; you should be able to recognise it by a red stripe or spot on the tip of the abdomen.

Well over 100 species of mosquito are found in South Africa, including the genus *Anopheles* – some species of which are transmitters of malaria. They are confined to the northernmost parts of the Cape and KwaZulu-Natal as well as the lowveld.

Tick-bite fever may be transmitted by the bite of the red-legged tick as well as the common dog tick. The disease is most widespread during the summer, when humans spend most time outdoors in grassy or wooded areas. ❑

ABOVE: a colourful member of the leaf-eating fraternity.

FLOURISHING FLORA

*Thanks to its ecological diversity, South Africa is graced
with some of the richest and most varied flora in the world*

The flora of southern Africa is one of the richest, most beautiful and vulnerable in the world. Popular species include the red-hot poker, the bird of paradise flower, the arum lily, the gladiolus, agapanthus and sweet-scented freesias. Most of these were first introduced into European botanical gardens and private collections in the 18th century. More recently, plants such the richly coloured gazanias and the shy osteospermums, which open their petals only when the sun shines, have found favour abroad.

The Floral Kingdom

Located around Cape Town on the southwestern tip of the continent, the Cape Floral Kingdom or *fynbos* region covers about 70,000 sq. km (27,000 sq. miles) – an area the size of the Republic of Ireland – and is home to 8,600 kinds of flowering plants. On the Cape Peninsula alone, 2,600 indigenous species have been counted: more than in many considerably larger countries. Renowned for its proteas and heathers, this is also where you'll find South Africa's most famous orchid, the red disa, known as the "Pride of Table Mountain". This area receives most of its rain in the cold seasons of the year, between April and October. Kirstenbosch National Botanical Gardens in Cape Town is an excellent place to see *fynbos* in its natural habitat.

The semi-deserts

North of the winter rainfall zone lies the arid area known as Namaqualand, running parallel to the Cape's west coast as far as the lower Orange River Valley. This is a dry land which receives, on average, about 50–150 mm (2–6 inches) of rain a year. The correspondingly sparse vegetation is dominated by succulents, especially shrubs with fleshy leaves.

LEFT: cycad plants may live for hundreds or even thousands of years.
RIGHT: the orchid *Disa uniflora* flowers just below the cloud-line on the southwestern Cape's highest mountains.

Mesembryanthemums (*vygies* in Afrikaans), grow here in abundance. Other natives include the pebble plant *(Lithops)*, plants of the similar Conophytum families, and many species of daisies, which have adapted to their parched surroundings by germinating and flowering only after good spring rains. All

produce splendid blossoms of shimmering, metallic red-violet, yellow, white or copper-coloured petals, which appear in one burst in the spring.

Trees are, in general, rare in this region; but the tree-like *Aloe arborescens* (candelabra plant) can be found in large quantities in certain parts to the north. The Karoo National Botanical Garden, at the foot of the Brandwacht Mountains near Worcester, is an excellent introduction to the local flora.

Ranking a little higher on the vegetation scale is the Great Karoo, the vast semi-desert stretching up from the Northern Cape into the Free State and beyond. The rainfall here averages between 125–375 mm (5–15 inches) a year, and plant life is dominated by small shrubs, mainly members of the family Compositae, such as the camellia, the silk-cotton (kapok) bush and the quassia.

Great silvery plumes of feather grass and ostrich grass are a common sight here, while in the deeper valleys you will often encounter the sweet thistle, which produces a beautiful display of brightly coloured yellow blossoms in the summer months.

The savannah

Covering some 959,000 sq. km (374,000 sq. miles) from the Kalahari basin right across to the east coast, with a narrow strip reaching down into the Southern Cape, this is the subcontinent's largest floral region. Rainfall, which occurs primarily in summer, averages about 25 cm (10 inches) a year.

This is an area of mixed vegetation, consisting mainly of grassland, with scattered trees and drought-resistant undergrowth. Although isolated trees and shrubs are the norm, there are also large patches of savannah forest – the classic bushveld. The vegetation covering much of the Kruger National Park is a good example.

> ### FLOWER POWER
>
> 24,000 plant species – nearly 10 percent of all the flowering plants on earth – can be found here on 1 percent of the country's land area.

Thorny acacia trees, often with a distinctive umbrella crown, are characteristic in dry parts of the region. The bizarre baobab, with its mighty trunk which often attains a diameter of several metres, can be found in the extreme north, along with the marula, the fever-tree and the ubiquitous dark-green mopani.

Eye-catching grass varieties, such as red grass, pepper grass and ostrich grass, are all common. During the dry season – when many trees and bushes lose their leaves – these grasses take on a yellow or reddish colour, which has a corresponding effect on the overall landscape. Each year, large areas are burned off; but at the beginning of the rainy season, these bleak, blackened patches are covered virtually overnight with a colourful carpet of spring flowers and fresh green shoots. The Pretoria National Botanical Garden, located in an area where savannah gives way to grassland, has examples of the plant life of both regions – as well as over half of the country's tree species.

The grassland

Covering an area of some 343,000 sq. km (133,770 sq. miles), the grassland area encompasses Lesotho, western Swaziland, and large parts of the Free State and Northern Province. Rain falls virtually only in summer; frost occurs on most nights in winter. Even so, about one-tenth of the world's 10,000 species of grass are indigenous to the area.

The grasslands can be roughly divided into a western and an eastern region; of these, the

---

> ### ROOTED IN THE CAPE
>
> Many of Europe and America's favourite garden plants have their origins in South Africa's botanical treasure house. This is as a result of the endeavours of a number of 18th-century plant-collectors and explorers (many of them Dutch) who scoured the Cape for colourful flowers that would be suited to colder climates. One of the best-known plants introduced in this way was the pelargonium (commonly called geranium), first brought to Europe in 1690 and which now brightens gardens and window-boxes all over the world.

western receives less than 660 mm (26 inches) of rainfall annually, while the eastern receives more. The grasses of the west are generally designated "sweet" or "white", while the eastern, moister region produces "sour" or "purple" grasses. The descriptions are farming terms and refer to the grasses' value as fodder.

The forests

Forests are in short supply in South Africa; most of the relics (victims of man's depredations) are now protected by law. Only in the Southern Cape, in the vicinity of George, will you find extensive woodland.

extends northwards all the way from the Western Cape up into Limpopo Province, has many patches of what was once a larger forest in its deep gorges and on its more sheltered, humid slopes. Such areas are dominated by coniferous species, such as *Podocarpus*, known locally as yellowwood. These trees can grow into forest giants, reaching heights of up to 40 metres (130 ft) and with massive trunks. Species of the olive family also grow here, as does the stinkwood *(Ocotea bullata)*, so-called because it has an unpleasant odour when it has been freshly cut. Stinkwood furniture is a much sought-after feature of the Knysna area.

There are, however, small, generally isolated areas of forest in the coastal belt stretching between the sea and the mountain ranges on the continent's eastern edge, from the southwest Cape up the Garden Route and then north through KwaZulu-Natal and Mozambique.

Along KwaZulu-Natal's coastline you can still see isolated remnants of mangrove forest, growing in mud and sand. Further inland there are the remains of evergreen forests, where milkwood, ebony and wild bananas grow. The long chain of the Drakensberg Mountains, meanwhile, which

LEFT: the red-hot poker.
ABOVE: the protea, most famous *fynbos* plant of all.

The desert

The huge and desolate expanses of the Namib, a true desert, lie outside the republic's borders, stretching parallel to the coast of Namibia. In this region, almost entirely without rainfall, vegetation is scarce or entirely absent. When rain does fall, the soil comes alive with grasses whose seeds have lain dormant for years.

In places, you will see the Namib's most famous plant, the welwitschia, which resembles a giant carrot with two broad flat leathery leaves growing out of the top. It is an extremely long-lived plant, often surviving for centuries, and its appearance is all the more weird because of the way the desert wind erodes its leaves. ❑

THE CONSERVATION RECORD

Nature conservation has always been taken seriously here,

and the time of transition is proving no exception

A recent survey of overseas visitors to South Africa revealed that nine out of 10 came primarily to experience its wildlife and unspoiled natural areas. When one realises what a wide variety of wild plants, animals and ecosystems the country has to offer, this statistic is not at all surprising. However, although wildlife is extremely significant as a cornerstone of the rapidly growing tourist industry, the importance of conserving it does not rest on this consideration alone.

Why conserve?

Nature conservation is essential for the preservation of one of the world's richest centres of genetic diversity, and for the maintenance of natural resources on which many of the country's people depend for their livelihood. Nature conservation is accordingly taken very seriously and South Africans have much to be proud of, at least in recent times.

Not only is the area exceptionally rich in species, but many are found nowhere else. Thus about 80 percent of the plants are endemic to South Africa, 30 percent of the reptiles, 15 percent of the mammals and 6 percent of the 600 bird species breeding in the country. The plants that inhabit the southernmost tip of the continent are so different from those found anywhere else that the area has been defined as one of the six floral kingdoms of the world – the Cape Kingdom. This tiny area, only 46,000 sq. km (18,000 sq. miles) in extent, is thus considered equivalent, for example, to the Boreal Kingdom which includes all of Europe, North America and northern Asia, an area of more than 53 million sq. km (20 million sq. miles).

This high concentration of unique wild species places South Africa on a par with the much-discussed tropical rainforest areas, such as those of the Amazon Basin, as an area of international significance for conservation.

The conservation record

Africa, and thus South Africa, is most famous for its amazing variety of antelopes and other grazing mammals and the large carnivores that

GONE FOREVER

The huge herds of springbok and quagga (a now-extinct subspecies of the still-widespread plains zebra) that used to roam the Karoo plains soon disappeared before the guns of the European colonists eager to hunt game for food and especially sport. Those dark days before the dawning of the conservation ethic (which South Africa now proudly enforces) also saw the extinction of the endemic bluebuck, a relative of the sable antelope. This is the only endemic vertebrate animal known to have become extinct in South Africa.

LEFT: zebra are unique to Africa; South Africa has two species. Here, a Burchell's zebra crosses a river.
RIGHT: a rare shower in the Kalahari.

prey on them. These herds of antelope used to graze from the Cape Peninsula in the south to the Limpopo Valley on the northern border.

The conservation record is not so good for native plants: at least 60 species or subspecies have become extinct since their discovery.

As the herds of wild ungulates began to be reduced by hunters in the 17th and 18th centuries, they were replaced by flocks of sheep and herds of cattle. The larger carnivores – lions, spotted and brown hyenas, cheetahs and African wild dogs – came increasingly into conflict with livestock farmers. These species were soon restricted to the remaining unoccu-

pied or sparsely occupied portions of the country. Of all the larger carnivores, only the wily leopard has managed to persist in reasonable numbers outside the larger national parks and nature reserves, mainly in mountainous areas.

Today the large carnivores, the elephants, the rhinoceroses and the large herds of wild antelopes are restricted in main to the larger protected areas, particularly those in the country's northern savannahs. The greatest of these is the Kruger National Park, which since the end of 2002 has been part of the Great Limpopo Transfrontier Park. The new park, with an area

A COMMITMENT TO CONSERVE

It has been said that the way a nation preserves its heritage is also one way to gauge the level of its civilisation. Some 72,700 sq. km (28,000 sq. miles) are under formal protection for nature conservation in South Africa, in more than 580 game reserves, parks and wilderness areas. This amounts to some 5.8 percent of the total surface area – a figure which may sound generous, but falls somewhat short of the International Union for the Conservation of Nature's recommendations that at least 10 percent of a country's surface area should be conserved.

of 35,000 sq. km (13,500 sq. miles) links Kruger with Mozambique's Limpopo National Park and Zimbabwe's Gonarezhou National Park. The oldest park in Africa, Kruger has long been regarded as one of the world's finest examples of wildlife management.

Thanks to the range of different savannahs in the Kruger, well-prepared visitors can spend days exploring its vastness, its diversity and its unending series of wildlife interactions, without ever becoming bored. It is possible to see up to 147 native mammal species, over 500 species of birds, 104 reptile species and 1,771 plant species here, including 357 species of trees and shrubs. From your own vehicle, from a variety of hides or on an escorted bush walk with an armed game ranger you can view some of the finest spectacles of African game available to a visitor anywhere on the continent.

Kgalagadi Transfrontier Park

Kgalagadi Transfrontier Park is the country's first foray into the peace park initiative. Situated in the Northern Cape, the park combines the areas of what was South Africa's second-largest park, the Kalahari Gemsbok National Park (at 9,600 sq. km/3,700 sq. miles) and the even larger Botswana Gemsbok National Park

Their enormous communal nests not only provide accommodation for themselves but also harbour a whole community of "hangers-on", including the diminutive pygmy falcon, which appropriates and then nests in one of the many individual chambers that are built into the weavers' nests.

The tall acacia trees that grow in these riverbeds accommodate the larger birds of prey that abound in the open savannahs. There are few places in Africa where one can meet with such densities of large eagles, vultures, falcons, hawks and owls. Family parties of ostriches are frequently met with as they

(24,800 sq. km/9,500 sq. miles). The former border is along the normally dry bed of the Nossob River. The stark beauty of this semi-desert area is remarkable, with its red sand dunes dotted with low thorn trees, covered in good rainfall seasons with vast waving strands of sun-bleached grasses.

Here can be seen such dry-country specialists as the majestic gemsbok, the red hartebeest and the springbok. Among the birds, the sociable weavers are probably the most characteristic.

LEFT: preparing tranquilliser darts for elephants.
ABOVE: without man's help, the black rhino faces extinction in Africa.

slowly pick their way across the dunes or run energetically along a shimmering pan. In the dry heat of midday the pace of life slows right down in these silent savannahs. At this time Kori bustards, Africa's largest flying bird species, fly in from the surrounding dune veld to stand gasping in the shade of a gnarled old camelthorn tree.

Mammalian predators are also easily located along these sparsely vegetated river beds, and this is probably one of the best places in South Africa to observe the cheetah hunting. This is also the major sanctuary for the only large carnivore which is endemic to southern Africa: the brown hyena.

Jewels of the east

In the east of the country there are many smaller savannah reserves, including Africa's oldest surviving game reserve, Phongolo, proclaimed in 1894 just 12 years after Yellowstone National Park was established in the United States as the world's first. In 1895, nearby Hluhluwe-Imfolozi was proclaimed primarily to protect the last remaining populations of rhinoceros in Natal. These great parks have succeeded beyond their originators' wildest expectations.

The square-lipped rhinoceros (white rhino) found its last sanctuary in the Imfolozi Reserve individuals currently in the Kruger National Park all stem from individuals translocated from these two remarkable little reserves. This is one of the few instances worldwide where conservation measures have been so successful that it has been possible to remove a species from the IUCN Red Data Book of endangered species.

These two KwaZulu-Natal reserves have also played a significant role in the conservation of the South African population of the black or hooklipped rhinoceros. With the current deterioration of nature conservation programmes elsewhere in Africa, what was once the relatively insignificant

and this population was thought to have been reduced to fewer than 20 individuals early in the 20th century. By careful protection and through the development of methods to capture safely and transport these enormous creatures, the KZN Wildlife, which administers these reserves, has built up the world population of this species to its current total of more than 8,000 individuals. There are 1,800 to 2,000 of these rhinos inhabiting the Hluhluwe-Imfolozi Reserve.

More than 3,500 have been captured and safely transferred to other conservation areas in Africa and to zoos and parks throughout the world. The population of more than 900 population of about 600 black rhinos held by South Africa has suddenly become the only relatively secure wild population in existence. A massive conservation effort is continuing.

These reserves are not only famous for their rhinoceros populations. Other mammals abound, including the most attractive of the African antelopes, the nyala, found only in the dense thickets of the southeastern lowlands. The variety of bird life is astounding, and breathtaking hours spent in the hides at waterholes in these reserves during the winter dry season will be a memory never to be forgotten. The nearby uMkhuze Game Reserve is also renowned for its hides.

Maputaland

On the northeastern coastal plain of Maputaland there are a variety of different conservation areas to visit. Africa's largest estuary, Lake St Lucia, holds the country's most important hippopotamus and Nile crocodile populations. Waterbirds inhabit this enormous shallow lake, including large breeding colonies of white pelicans and the striking Caspian tern. If the water levels are low, vast flocks of flamingos can be seen. Rest camps are located at several points around the lake.

To the south of the estuary mouth, Maphelane Nature Reserve preserves a diverse dune forest

dreds of loggerhead and leatherback turtles haul themselves up these beaches to bury their clutches of eggs in these protected sands. After 25 years of strict protection by the KZN Wildlife, which each year monitors and safeguards their breeding activity, the populations are thriving.

To witness a huge turtle heave herself out of the surf and up the beach, the moonlight glistening off her wet carapace as its ancestors must have done each year for countless millennia, and then to silently watch her go about this age-old ritual of reproduction, is to experience something which cannot fail to confirm the importance of maintaining the full diver-

on what are said to be the world's highest forested sand dunes.

North of the estuary mouth stretches a series of coastal reserves, with a proclaimed marine reserve preserving the adjacent offshore wonders. Submerged coral reefs and the associated myriad tropical fish species and other sea life abound in the crystal-clear waters of the warm Mozambique Current that washes these golden beaches fringed by lush dune forests. Each summer, hun-

LEFT: leatherback turtle hatchlings getting acclimatised.
ABOVE: a black eagle being nursed back to health in a Lowveld wildlife clinic after injuring its wing.

sity of life on earth. There is something in the turtle's heroic exertions which drives home the message that this tenacious life force must not be summarily terminated through mankind's exploitation or pollution.

The coastal lakes of Sibayi and Kosi Bay lie close behind the forested dunes that back the turtle-nesting beaches of the Tongaland Marine Reserve. Small rest camps are located on the shores of these lakes as well as in Ndumo Game Reserve, located an hour's drive inland on the Usutu River, the country's border with Mozambique. This, the most tropical of the KwaZulu-Natal reserves, is probably the premier bird reserve in South Africa. A series of pans lined with yellow-barked fever trees are filled with an amazing variety of waterfowl, and provide sanctuary for many hippopotamuses and crocodiles.

The fig forests that fringe the rivers and pans and the thickets that cover most of this relatively small reserve (110 sq. km/42 sq. miles) hold a great variety of bird life. More than 400 species have been recorded from the reserve, and in the summer wet season (November to March) when migrant species are present, one may easily record upwards of 200 different species within a few days. Ndumo has the added advantage of allowing access to much of the reserve on foot under the supervision of

ning through tranquil forested gorges to fall tumbling over cascading waterfalls.

These mountains and grasslands are home to a fabulous variety of wild flowers and several of the country's endemic bird species, such as the yellow pipit and the Drakensberg siskin. The majestic lammergeyer is still secure here, too.

The arid interior

Further west one can visit the Mountain Zebra National Park or the Karoo National Park as well as several provincial reserves, such as the Goegap Nature Reserve or Rolfontein Nature

a trained game guard; many of these guards are expert fieldsmen and will much improve the visitor's ability to detect the often unobtrusive birds and mammals in the reserve's dense forests.

The high grasslands conservation areas have much else to offer. For instance, those of the uKhahlamba-Drakensberg mountain range that form KwaZulu-Natal's inland boundary with the mountainous kingdom of Lesotho are virtually all included in various reserves and wilderness areas. Here are found many of the country's most beautiful landscapes – huge, towering amphitheatres set above rolling grassy slopes, with numerous sparkling mountain streams run-

Reserve, to obtain a glimpse of the semi-arid Karoo ecosystem, now mainly used for sheep farming. The Karoo is probably the most characteristic of South Africa's ecosystems. For those who enjoy wide-open spaces and stark semi-desert landscapes, a trip through the Karoo, with planned stopovers at several of the relatively small reserves found here, will be well worthwhile.

The majority of the Karoo's animal and plant life is unique to this area. Those visiting the region shortly after good rains can witness levels of biological activity unsurpassed in any of the other ecosystems of South Africa. The fields of brightly coloured flowers, a host of insects and flocks of nomadic birds breeding in such an area provide an absolutely unforgettable spectacle.

Ironically, whereas in most other countries it is the semi-desert ecosystems which are best conserved in national parks, in South Africa the converse applies. This situation may soon be rectified, and the planned Richtersveld National Park (in the arid mountainous region just south of the Orange River border with Namibia) is one of the few large areas protected in the drier portions of the country.

The Augrabies Falls National Park, higher up the Orange River, is certainly worth a visit but it is not large enough to ensure the long-term survival of the rich semi-desert fauna and flora of the country's western arid zone.

Forests, lakes and *fynbos*

Further south still, is the well-watered coastal strip in the Eastern and Western Cape provinces. Here are found the country's largest evergreen forests. The Tsitsikamma Forest National Park, as well as the nearby Tsitsikamma Coastal National Park, allow the visitor a chance to see the region's dense temperate forests. The enormous yellowwood trees, their canopies often festooned with "old man's beard" lichens and the forest floor beneath them damp and mossy, are a far cry from the semi-desert Karoo ecosystems which are located only a few hours drive inland. The coastal park not only has a spectacular five-day hiking trail – called the Otter Trail after the Cape clawless otters which can sometimes be seen feeding along this coastline – but also has an underwater trail for snorkellers or scuba divers. The Knysna Lagoon and the Wilderness Lakes both fall within the major temperate rainforest areas of the Southern Cape; these verdant forest landscapes only add to the beauty of the area.

The mountains in these Southern Cape areas are almost all located within proclaimed and protected mountain catchment areas or state forest areas. Clad in the unique *fynbos* vegetation that holds the proteas, ericas and other renowned plants of the Cape Floral Kingdom, these mountains are traversed by a series of hiking trails. To take a four- or five-day hike along one of these is to get to know one of the most spectacular ecosystems of the world.

LEFT AND RIGHT: a feature of any stay in the bush is the distinctive character of the safari camps.

The future

Sitting on the top of Table Mountain and looking down on to the seemingly never-ending suburbs of Greater Cape Town, one cannot help feeling uneasy about the conservation future in South Africa. Within a single lifetime, the Cape Flats, which lie between the Cape Peninsula and the Hottentots-Holland Mountains to the east, have been engulfed by a spreading wave of humanity. What used to be an area of exceptional wetlands and a veritable garden of wild flowers is now virtually completely covered by factory land, suburbia and small agricultural holdings.

TABLE MOUNTAIN NATIONAL PARK

Most of the Cape Peninsula forms part of this 2,500-hectare (6,200-acre) park, which incorporates Boulders Beach, the Cape of Good Hope and the Silvermine Nature Reserve. Species are protected from agriculture, farming and urban sprawl, fire and marauding alien vegetation. World-famous Table Mountain, which forms the backdrop to the country's mother city, Cape Town, is the park's focal point. Visitors can take relatively easy day walks some way up the mountain (the easiest route starts in Kirstenbosch Botanical Gardens), or use a cable car to reach the summit.

Wattles introduced from Australia choke the native vegetation on the last remaining scraps of uncultivated land. Sadly, many of the plants and animals of this area and the adjacent Cape Peninsula are now threatened with extinction. Indeed, 39 plant species have already been lost from the Cape Peninsula; 15 of them peninsular endemics.

With a human population that is currently growing extremely rapidly (the population has burgeoned from approximately 18.3 million in 1960 to an estimated

PLANTS AT RISK

About 2,000 plant species are thought to be facing extinction unless trends in habitat destruction are halted.

Wildlife and Environment Society of South Africa, which first came into existence a century ago during the initial campaign to establish the Kruger National Park. It now has over 15,000 members, and runs a variety of high-profile conservation education programmes.

The major fund-raising organisation for the environment in South Africa is the local branch of the World Wide Fund for Nature, or the WWF *(for the latest local projects, check the website, www.panda.org.za).*

48 million in 2007), all the many pressures on South Africa's natural environment are now intensifying.

It is essential that conservation agencies continue to receive all of the necessary funds to carry out their important task of protecting the natural resources of South Africa for the benefit of all its peoples, including the generations still to be born.

A visitor who, having enjoyed the wonderful country and its superb national parks, wishes to do something constructive to assure the future of conservation might consider taking out membership in one of the many local conservation societies which work directly with local projects. The oldest and largest of these is the

The new South Africa

When the new government came to power following the historic April 1994 democratic elections, the environment was one of the causes that was set to benefit. The new South African Constitution, for example, contains a clause guaranteeing the "environmental rights" of every citizen; their rights to a clean and healthy environment, and the rights of both present and future generations to a well-conserved and cared-for natural environment.

With the country's readmittance to the international community has come the ratification by South Africa of several important international conventions, most important of which (from a nature conservation perspective) is the

Convention on Biological Diversity. Not only was this treaty ratified, but an extensive policy development process was carried out to support its local implementation, ending in the production of a Government White Paper on the topic. Another important treaty recently ratified was the World Heritage Convention, preparing the way for South Africa to nominate several of its important areas as World Heritage Sites.

The time of transition has also allowed several initiatives that have long been stalled to proceed: for example, the government has approved the creation of Table Mountain

cial conservation agencies losing the majority of their experienced conservation professionals as a result of an ill-conceived and poorly executed downsizing of the civil service.

Probably the single biggest environmental success story of the new South Africa has been the "Working for Water" programme of the National Water Conservation Campaign. Begun under the visionary guidance of the former Minister of Water Affairs and Forestry, Professor Kadar Asmal, this huge project ultimately aims to remove all alien trees from mountain catchment areas throughout the land, thus solving South Africa's single most serious

National Park, incorporating the mountain itself and the Cape Peninsula's remaining natural areas (an idea first mooted in the 1920s). Similarly, the long, drawn-out debate on the possibility of mining the dunes on the eastern shores of Lake St Lucia was ended when the Cabinet ruled that this mining would not be permitted. The long-awaited national park for the Highveld Grassland biome has also finally been created – in an area close to Potchefstroom.

Unfortunately, not all of the recent changes have been so positive, with many of the provin-

nature conservation problem. Involving an amazing number of different institutions, within just six months this campaign had mobilised more than 6,000 unemployed people, most of them women.

It has not only benefited streams and rivers, but also the native plants and animals that would otherwise have been replaced by rapidly spreading stands of invasive alien plants.

In many ways, the "Working for Water" programme epitomises the government's approach to conservation: doing everything it can to care for the environment, while at the same time taking into account the real needs of South Africa's predominantly poor population. ❑

Left: a relaxing end to a good day's walkabout.
Above: the pride of the "Big Five".

PLACES

*A detailed guide to the entire country, with principal sites
clearly cross-referenced by number to the maps*

With reliable sunshine, almost 3,200 km (2,000 miles) of sandy beaches, a mighty, wooded mountain escarpment criss-crossed with hiking trails and over 500 game farms, parks and reserves, South Africa is an extremely appealing destination for nature-lovers and outdoor enthusiasts alike.

By African standards, it's an easy country to negotiate, with good facilities that are well-organised and efficiently run. The internal infrastructure is excellent, too, all the way from the southern tip to brash Johannesburg, spinning on a hub of gold from the mines that provide so much of the country's wealth. And with a weak rand greatly increasing foreign visitors' spending power, South Africa is very good value for money.

South Africa is an enormous place; roughly five times the size of Britain and three times as large as California. Unless you plan to spend a few months in the country, it would be hard to take in the great variety of sights in a single visit. In order to help first-time visitors decide on a basic itinerary, we have therefore organised our descriptions of the country into a series of standard routes – not so much a prescriptive list of stops and sights as a basis for creative improvisation and overlap.

Classic sights? The Kruger National Park and the Kgalagadi Transfrontier Park are two of Africa's great game reserves, although the latter is extremely remote from other popular tourist centres. The Cape Peninsula must rank as one of the most beautiful and striking sights in the world, let alone the continent. But make time, too, to head off the beaten track: to explore the far reaches of Limpopo Province with its sacred lakes, home of the python-god; the Eastern Cape and its long, blond beaches, fringed with indigenous rainforest; and the majestic open expanse of the Great Karoo.

It is at last getting easier to cross the racial divide, which in the past meant so much of South Africa's cultural richness and energy was inaccessible to whites. Yet it is also impossible to ignore the statistics which show such worryingly high levels of violent crime. Although most instances occur in townships, visitors should be alert to muggings during the day as well as at night in tourist zones. And while it is not a good idea to visit townships as a lone wanderer, do try and visit with a guide or on an organised tour. Paranoia is not necessary; common sense is.

Lastly, while South Africa's public transport system is improving, it is still pretty limited, and won't take you into the country's most intriguing corners. To get the most out of your trip, it is strongly recommended that you hire a car. ❑

PRECEDING PAGES: golden arches in the Cederberg; a bushveld sunset; Cape Town at night.
LEFT: entering the Dutoits Kloof tunnel on the N1 motorway near Gauteng.

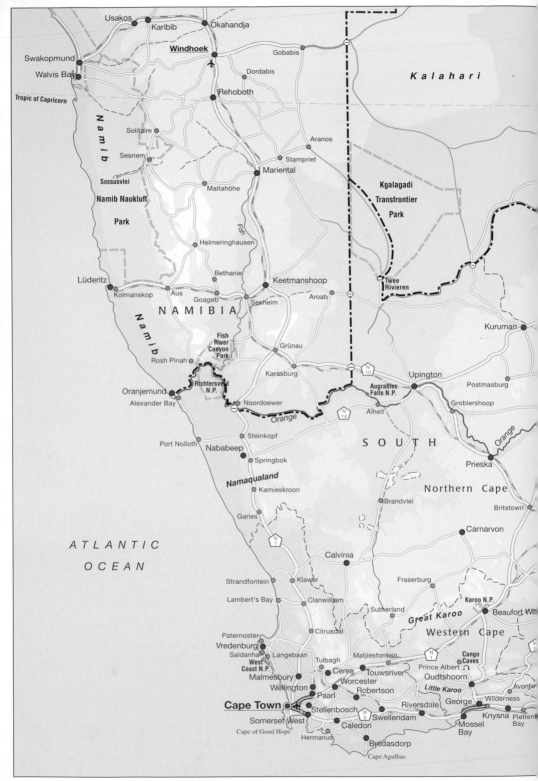

ATLANTIC OCEAN

Tropic of Capricorn

Kalahari

Usakos
Karibib
Okahandja
Gobabis

Windhoek

Swakopmund
Walvis Bay

Dordabis

Rehoboth

Namib

Solitaire

Sesriem

Aranos

Stampriet

Mariental

Sossusvlei

Namib Naukluft

Park

Maltahöhe

Kgalagadi
Transfrontier
Park

Fish

Helmeringhausen

Bethanie

Twee
Rivieren

Lüderitz
Kolmanskop
Aus
Goageb

Keetmanshoop

NAMIBIA

Seeheim

Aroab

Kuruman

Fish
River
Canyon
Park

Grünau

Rosh Pinah

Upington

Postmasburg

Karasburg

N 10

Augrabies
Falls N.P.

Groblershoop

Oranjemund
Alexander Bay

**Richtersveld
N.P.**

Noordoewer

N 14

Alheit

Orange

S O U T H

Orange

Steinkopf

Port Nolloth
Nababeep

Springbok

Prieska

Namaqualand

Northern Cape

Kamieskroon

Brandvlei

Britstown

Garies

Carnarvon

N 7

Calvinia

Fraserburg

Strandfontein
Klawer

Lambert's Bay
Clanwilliam

Sutherland

Great Karoo

Karoo N.P.

Beaufort We

Citrusdal

Prince Albert

Western Cape

Paternoster
Vredenburg
Saldanha
**West
Coast N.P.**

Langebaan

Tulbagh

Matjiesfontein

N 1

Cango
Caves

Oudtshoorn

Little Karoo

Avonto

Malmesbury
Wellington

Ceres
Worcester

Touwsriver

George

Wilderness

Paarl
Robertson

Cape Town
Stellenbosch

Riversdale

Knysna
Pletten
Bay

Somerset West

N 2

Swellendam

Mossel
Bay

Cape of Good Hope

Caledon

Hermanus

Bredasdorp

Cape Agulhas

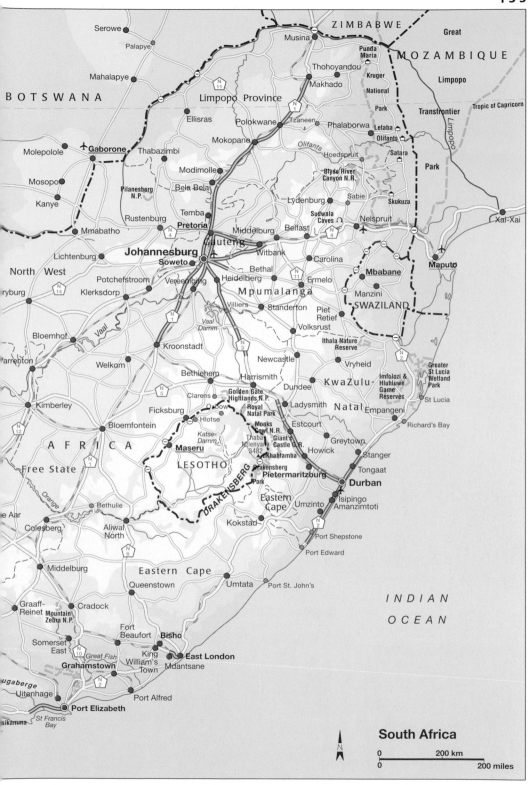

South Africa

0 — 200 km

0 — 200 miles

CAPE TOWN AND PENINSULA

A mountain plateau flanked by two oceans, graced with long, uncrowded beaches and some of the world's most unique vegetation

Maps on pages 158 & 168

When he sailed into Table Bay aboard the Golden Hind in 1580, Sir Francis Drake proclaimed it to be "The fairest Cape… in the whole circumference of the earth". To this day, the Cape Peninsula's combination of sea, spreading valleys and purple-headed mountains is still breathtakingly beautiful. All South Africans are proud of it, even Jo'burgers, who nevertheless spend quite a lot of time thinking up rude jokes about Capetonians to wipe the infuriating "we've got it all" smirks off their faces.

Through the centuries it has been called many names: the Cape of Good Hope, by those who survived the journey to enter into the calmer waters of False Bay; the Tavern of the Seas, when fresh produce was shipped in here to enable fleets to continue on their arduous journey to the East; the Cape of Storms, by the Portuguese soldiers who first navigated their way around the treacherous shores at Cape Point.

For most of the year the Cape experiences weather that wafts between pleasant and sublime, but it earned its sobriquet Cape of Storms not without reason. The southwestern Cape is the only section of Africa that falls within a temperate weather zone, and it enjoys a typically Mediterranean climate with long, hot summers and cool, wet winters. The howling southeaster is aptly called the Cape Doctor: it sweeps away every loose object in its path, cleansing the city of dust and pollution and making its atmosphere one of the healthiest.

The sense that this region is a fresh and fertile world apart is helped by the fact that **Cape Town ❶** is physically cut off from the rest of the country by a barrier of mountains, in places some 2,000 metres (6,500 ft) high. With their rich clay soils, the valleys they shelter are the nation's storehouse – the centre of its grape, wine, wheat and deciduous fruit industries.

The peninsula is South Africa's oldest European-settled region, and man-made attractions include some of the best shops, hotels and restaurants on the continent. But, like all South African cities, it is a Molotov cocktail of first and third worlds. Cape Town's British-built Georgian buildings, cobbled streets and ancient oaks may look familiar to Europeans, but the vast townships stretching across the plains east of the city could only be in Africa.

The historic city

If ever a landmass was designed to look like the punctuation mark at the end of a continent, it is the Cape Peninsula. That it is not actually located at the southern tip of Africa doesn't seem to deter the tour guides who unashamedly (and somewhat arbitrarily) point it out to their clients as the place where the Indian and Atlantic oceans meet. In fact, the most southerly point

LEFT: City Hall and Table Mountain.
BELOW: taking a dip at Long Street baths.

in Africa, and arguably the most meaningful dividing line between these oceans, is Cape Agulhas, some 200 km (120 miles) to the southeast.

Taking similar literary licence, most accounts of life at the Cape begin with the arrival of the first colonial governor, Jan van Riebeeck, in 1652. Others hoist their sails with stories of Portuguese navigators such as Bartolomeu Diaz and Vasco da Gama, who pioneered a sea route round the Cape to the East in the 15th century. In fact, Khoikhoi herders and San hunter-gatherers inhabited this corner of Africa long before the Portuguese showed up – indeed, archaeological evidence of human activity on the peninsula dates back some 40,000 years.

South African Museum

The best place to get a handle on this cultural puzzle – indeed, on the entire racial and cultural melting pot that is the Rainbow Nation – is at the **Iziko South African Museum** Ⓐ (daily 10am–5pm; entrance charge; tel: 021-481 3800) in Cape Town's Company's Gardens at the top of bustling Adderley Street. This is the

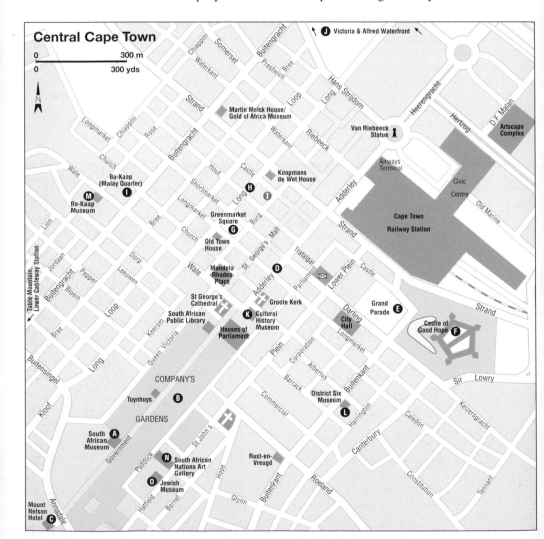

Central Cape Town

0   300 m
0   300 yds

Ⓙ Victoria & Alfred Waterfront

Martin Melck House/
Gold of Africa Museum

Van Riebeeck Statue

Artscape Complex

Koopmans de Wet House

Airways Terminal

Civic Centre

Bo-Kaap (Malay Quarter) Ⓘ

Ⓗ
ⓘ

Ⓜ
Bo-Kaap Museum

Greenmarket Square Ⓖ

Cape Town Railway Station

Old Town House

Table Mountain, Lower Cableway Station

Mandela Rhodes Place

Ⓓ

St George's Cathedral

South African Public Library

Ⓕ

Ⓚ Cultural History Museum

Groote Kerk

Grand Parade Ⓔ

Castle of Good Hope Ⓕ

Houses of Parliament

City Hall

COMPANY'S

Tuynhuys Ⓑ

District Six Museum

Ⓛ

GARDENS

South African Museum Ⓐ

Ⓝ South African National Art Gallery

Rust-en-Vreugd

Ⓞ Jewish Museum

Mount Nelson Hotel Ⓒ

oldest museum in the country, housing a wide variety of cultural and natural history displays, among them a superb selection of rock-art panels that were removed from their natural homes and a set of 2,500-year-old ceramic works unearthed in present-day Mpumalanga. Don't miss the extraordinary Whale Well – a multi-sensual, multimedia display dedicated to these immense marine mammals. The neighbouring **Planetarium** (tel: 021-481 3900) hosts regular shows introducing visitors to the main features of the southern hemisphere night sky.

The **Company's Gardens** ❸ were first laid out under the instruction of the Dutch East India Company, who wanted to provide a midway victualling station for its ships on the way to the East. Van Riebeeck duly planted patches of cabbages, potatoes, turnips and grains. As a doctor, he knew how valuable wine and brandy could be in staving off the sailors' curse of scurvy, so he planted grapes as well. The first vintages probably tasted like tar, but this far from home, a drink was a drink.

Tucked into other secluded, leafy corners of the gardens are grand buildings housing various museums, as well as the Anglican **St George's Cathedral**, former diocese of Nobel Laureate Desmond Tutu. Dominating the area, however, are the **Houses of Parliament** (guided tours Mon–Fri; free), built in High Victorian style and facing on to Government Avenue. Close by is **Tuynhuys**, the office of South Africa's State President, done out in grand Colonial Regency style. And at the southernmost tip of Government Avenue, in the shadow of Table Mountain, you'll find the city's best-known hotel, the **Mount Nelson** ❸. After over a century of service, the pale-pink "Nellie" prides itself on retaining a grand colonial atmosphere, exemplified by the sumptuous afternoon tea.

Walking up **Adderley Street** ❸ towards the harbour, take a left at Wale Street and at the corner of Wale and Burg streets is **Mandela Rhodes Place**, a

Map on page 158

BELOW: the newly revitalised Victoria and Alfred Waterfront.

complex with a hotel, restaurant and shopping outlets, which takes up a city block. Back on Adderley Street you'll pass the historic **Groote Kerk**, the oldest church in South Africa, containing an elaborately carved pulpit. At the top end of the street is a statue of Jan van Riebeeck and his wife, Maria, which stands close to the City Hall with its Victorian baroque embellishments and honeymarble facade. It faces the **Grand Parade** , originally marked out as a place to train military troops but now a thriving open-air market.

On the eastern side of the Parade, the sturdy stone **Castle of Good Hope** (daily 9am–4pm except Christmas and New Year's Day; entrance charge; tel: 021-787 1249; www.castleofgoodhope.co.za) was completed in 1697, making it the oldest surviving intact structure in South Africa. With its 10-metre (30-ft) thick walls and five corner bastions, each named after one of the various titles of the Prince of Orange, the castle is today a military headquarters; it also houses a military and maritime museum and the **William Fehr Collection** (9.30am–4pm) of paintings, Cape silver and furniture and Asian porcelain. Cutting across the courtyard of the castle is the Kat balcony, fronting the large reception room which was once a focal point of the colonial governor's official residence and the city aristocracy's social life. For contrast, peek into the dungeons, or "Black Holes", where criminals – and those who had simply fallen out of favour with the colonial authorities – were locked away

Greenmarket

The heart of the old city is **Greenmarket Square** , abuzz with flea-market stalls (Tues–Sun), buskers, shoppers and cultural voyeurs. Facing it is the **Old Town House** (Mon–Fri 10am–5pm, Sat 10am–4pm; free), a grand baroque

TIP

Raise a glass to Table Mountain and the strains of live jazz while cruising the harbour. Jazz cruises, such as the *Seahorse*, depart from Quay 6 at the V&A Waterfront; drinks and dinner served. For details, tel: 021-419 3122.

BELOW:
plenty of options at Greenmarket Square.

building dating from 1761 that holds the Michaelis Collection of Dutch and Flemish art, including a treasured Frans Hals portrait. Two blocks west, find buzzing **Long Street** ⊕ that's lined with fine Victorian buildings, most of them restored to their former glory, which house pawn shops, vintage clothing boutiques, funky bars and restaurants, knick-knack outlets and second-hand book shops specialising in Africana and first editions.

West of the city centre, beyond Buitengracht Street, is one of Cape Town's most exotic districts – the **Bo-Kaap** ❶ (Upper Cape), or Malay Quarter. Here, winding, narrow streets are flanked by restored early 18th- and 19th-century cottages painted in pastels – originally slave quarters, stables and a military barracks. This was where many of the Muslim Batavian slaves imported by the 17th-century Dutch colonists settled, alongside powerful imams exiled from Indonesia where they had challenged Dutch colonial rule. Their descendants still live here, and they have, by and large, kept the community's Cape Malay identity intact. This part of town is also the centre of the Cape Minstrel's Carnival, which takes place in January.

For the best part of 50 years, the oldest part of the harbour, the **Victoria & Alfred (V&A) Waterfront** ❶ (daily; tel: 021-408 7600; www.waterfront.co.za) lay in a state of disrepair. Then in the 1980s it was given a thorough face-lift, emerging as a multifaceted playground crammed with shops, crafts markets, upmarket hotels, and quay-to-quay pubs and restaurants, all below the spectacular backdrop of Table Mountain. Despite being somewhat artificial, the V&A Waterfront is easily the most successful tourist development of its kind in South Africa. For a seal's-eye perspective on all this, you can join a short boat trip around the harbour – several kiosks along the waterfront offer departures every hour or so.

Map
on page
158

A sunset cruise on the bay: a beautiful way to end the day.

BELOW: one of the colourful buildings of Bo-Kaap.

A vacant Robben Island watchtower stands as a monument to freedom. The infamous prison was declared a World Heritage Site by UNESCO in 1999.

BELOW: street vendors rely on the tourist trade.

Recently incorporated into the waterfront complex, the **Clock Tower Centre** housed in a bright red clock tower built *c*.1880, offers a 360-degree view of the harbour and surrounds, and brings South African crafts together in one centre. Situated within the complex, the head office of **Cape Tourism** (daily 9am–9pm; tel: 021-405 4500; www.tourismcapetown.com) is an excellent source of local and national tourist information, with an internet café attached, as well as an exclusive wine shop that specialises in international deliveries.

The clock tower is also home to a number of historical sites, including the Nelson Mandela Gateway to **Robben Island** (daily; tel: 021-413 4200; www.robben-island.org.za). Originally a penal colony for errant slaves, Robben Island became one of the most notorious prisons in the world. Many of the top officials in South Africa's first post-apartheid government were held here at some point – most famously, former President Nelson Mandela, who spent nearly 20 years in Section B. Recently proclaimed a World Heritage Site, Robben Island is today protected as a nature reserve, though penguins – which re-colonised the island in 1983 after an absence of 180 years and now number 4,000 pairs – are more likely to be seen than the seals from which its name derives *(see box below)*. More significantly, the island and its old jail buildings now function as a museum dedicated to the struggle against apartheid. The island is visible from across the bay on a clear day, and boat tours there depart from the Gateway daily at regular intervals. The crossing and tour takes 3–4 hours.

A highlight of a visit to the waterfront is the **Two Oceans Aquarium** (daily 9.30am–6pm; entrance charge; tel: 021-418 3823; www.aquarium.co.za), which brims with marine life of all shapes and dimensions, from delicate seahorses and spiky sea urchins to colourful reef fish and rapacious great white sharks. Among

ROBBEN ISLAND

World-famous as the place where Nelson Mandela was condemned to life imprisonment, this little kidney-shaped island 11 km (7 miles) off the shores of Green Point was named by the Dutch for the large numbers of seals *(rob)* they encountered here. It has a grim history: this was where Jan van Riebeeck kept rebellious Khoikhoi leaders captive; later, the British used it as a general dumping-ground for lepers, paupers and lunatics. In the second half of the 19th century, the small village known as Irishtown was built next to the jetty. A military base during World War II, it was finally taken over by the Department of Prisons in 1960, quickly acquiring a reputation as South Africa's most notorious penal colony. Today, South Africa's own Alcatraz has been turned into a national monument and museum, run by the Ministry for Arts and Culture. Ferries and charter boats bound for the island leave Cape Town's V&A Waterfront several times a day, but not all of them are allowed to land. In order to protect the environment (Robben Island is a haven for wildlife, especially sea birds and African penguins), visitor numbers are limited to 300 a day. Many boats simply circle the island, giving passengers a view from about 1 km (⅔ mile) out at sea.

several innovative displays is a transparent tank that allows you to watch the submarine manoeuvres of a delightful group of Cape fur seals (non-captive specimens of which are also often to be seen sunning themselves in the V&A Waterfront) and a rocky walk-in aviary inhabited by black oystercatchers, African penguins, and rockhopper penguins – the latter rather comical in appearance thanks to its foppish yellow eyebrows.

Cutting across the foreshore is Table Bay Boulevard – the start of the major N1 Highway that bisects the country 2,000 km (1,200 miles) from the south to the northernmost boundary point at Beitbridge in Limpopo Province.

Museums and galleries

Cape Town has numerous museums relating to various aspects of its colourful past; most now operate under the umbrella of Iziko Museums of Cape Town. The **Slave Lodge** (Mon–Sat 10am–5pm; tel: 021-460 8242), at the top of Adderley Street, opposite the gardens, is a beautiful 17th-century building which was at different times a lodge for slaves as well as the Cape Supreme Court. Today, it houses some fine collections of Cape silverware and furniture. The tombs of van Riebeeck and his wife lie in the cobbled courtyard.

Associated with this museum is a collection of other old city houses that have been restored and preserved as outstanding examples of different architectural periods and lifestyles. These include the **Koopmans-De Wet House** (Tues–Thur 9am–4pm; entrance charge; tel: 021-481 3935) with an impressive neo-classical façade, at 35 Strand Street and **Rust-en-Vreugd** (Tues–Thur 8.30am–4.30pm; entrance charge; tel: 021-465 3628) at 78 Buitenkant Street.

The **District Six Museum** (Mon 9am–3pm, Tues–Sat until 4pm; entrance charge; tel: 021-466 7200), a little further along at 25a Buitenkant Street, presents the other side of the coin: relics of a vibrant inner-city community destroyed during the apartheid era in the name of racial purity. At 71 Wale Street, the **Bo-Kaap Museum** (Mon–Sat 9am–4pm; entrance charge; tel: 021-424 3846) portrays in meticulous detail the lifestyle of a wealthy 19th-century Muslim family, complete with prayer room.

The Company's Gardens is the peaceful setting for the **Iziko South African National Gallery** (Tues–Sun 10am–5pm; free on Sat; tel: 021-467 4660), which during the apartheid era built up an impressive collection of mainly Western art, including works by Gainsborough, Reynolds and Rodin. The current acquisitions policy is now biased towards indigenous art. Nearby is the **South African Jewish Museum and Synagogue** (Sun–Thur 8am–5pm, Fri 10am–2pm; entrance charge; tel: 021-465 1546; www.sajewishmuseum.co.za), housing a rich collection of items depicting the history of the Cape Town Hebrew Congregation and other Cape congregations.

Table Mountain

Locals simply call it "the mountain", for this famous flat-topped block of horizontally bedded sandstone dominating Table Bay is a lodestone to all who live there. **Table Mountain** is a compass, an anchor, a

Maps on pages 158 & 168

TIP

Drinking alcohol is forbidden on Llandudno beach. Apply for a special charge permit from the local police station if you wish to toast the sunset with champagne.

LEFT: the queen of Cape Town's alternative attractions.

You're bound to spot dassies (rock hyraxes) on the top of Table Mountain. Also known as the rock rabbit, the dassie is, in fact, more closely related to the elephant.

wilderness in the heart of the Mother City. No visit to Cape Town is complete without gaining a view from the top. The journey up takes about six minutes by cable car, though long queues are a possibility in the peak summer holiday season, when the cableway ferries, on average, 1,500 people a day up to the 1,086-metre (3,585-ft) summit. To reach **Lower Cableway Station** (open daily, weather permitting; entrance charge; tel: 021-424 8181; www.tablemountain.net) from Kloof Nek Road, turn left into Tafelberg Road and follow the signs.

For those with enough determination there is another way – actually, around 500 ways – of getting to the top on foot. One of the easier hiking routes starts from the botanical gardens at Kirstenbosch, and takes about three hours. Be aware, though, that a chill wind often blows across the summit, making a sweater or windcheater necessary, and that the fickle weather conditions means you should also take suitable protection in case it rains. If you ascend on foot, be prepared to turn back at the first hint of the mist that frequently blankets the upper reaches of the mountain.

However you get there, the relatively flat section of the mountain above the cableway is serviced by a busy little restaurant and coffee shop, and criss crossed with several walking trails through a montane *fynbos* (scrub land) community of 1,500 plant species, 50 of which are endemic or endangered. A highlight of the mountain in season is the flowering protea shrubs, which often attract *fynbos* endemics such as Cape sugarbirds, protea canaries and orange-breasted sunbirds.

As for wildlife, you're unlikely to miss the habituated and docile rock hyraxes that live around the coffee shop, and can also expect to encounter parties of equally tame but rather more boisterous chacma baboons – the latter not to be fed or approached closely under any circumstances. Other resident mammals, though

not so likely to be seen on a casual visit, include the eland, Cape grysbok and grey mongoose. More controversially, the mountain hosts a small population of the tahr, a goat-like antelope that was introduced to the country from Asia in the 19th century – the official SANParks policy of hunting out the tahr, whilst ecologically sound, is subject to passionate criticism from many locals at the time of writing.

On the slopes

Table Mountain naturally forms the centrepiece of the Table Mountain National Park (tel: 021-701 8692), which incorporates a number of former nature reserves and other protected areas, such as Boulders Beach, the Cape of Good Hope Nature Reserve, and the magnificent 560-hectare (1,380-acre) **Kirstenbosch National Botanical Gardens ❸** (Sept–May daily 8am–7pm; June–Aug daily 8am–6pm; entrance charge; tel: 021-799 8783; www.nbi.ac.za) gracing the mountain's eastern slopes. The formally laid-out beds of Kirstenbosch display some of South Africa's showiest flora before blending into the natural protea *fynbos* and yellowwood forests on the mountain slopes. In total, more than 5,000 plant species are found in the gardens, along with a varied selection of birds.

Flanking Table Mountain are the imposing peaks of **Lion's Head** and Devil's Peak. It was on the slopes of the latter, according to legend, that a retired soldier named Van Hunk was challenged by the devil to a pipe-smoking contest. The result of their showdown can best be judged in the summertime, when a seemingly motionless sheet of cloud (popularly known as the "tablecloth") often hovers over the mountain top.

Devil's Peak is also the site of the **Groote Schuur Estate ❹**, once owned by Cecil Rhodes. Bequeathed to the nation on his death in 1902, it now includes a

Map on page 168

TIP

If the Peninsula's troops of chacma baboons become dependent on tourist handouts, they can become annoyingly persistent. Please don't feed them.

BELOW: beautiful Kirstenbosch National Botanical Gardens.

CAPE TOWN'S KARAMATS

A magic circle of *karamats* – the tombs of holy men who once lived and worked within Cape Town's Muslim community – graces the city, forming an important part of local Islamic lore. Muslims believe the circle provides Cape Town with a protective spiritual barrier, helping to prevent natural disasters. Before making a pilgrimage to the Holy City of Mecca (as is required of every Muslim, if he can afford it), local believers will visit each *karamat* in turn. There is a shrine to Sayed Abdurahman Matura, Prince of Ternate, on Robben Island and one to Nureel Mobeen at Oudekraal near Bakoven beach. The tomb of Abdumaah Shah lies by the gate to Klein Constantia farm in the Constantia valley. Of the two shrines on the slopes of Signal Hill, one contains the remains of Tuan Guru, the Cape's first imam and founder of the country's first mosque.

Most revered of all is the tomb of Sheik Yusuf, near Eerste River in the township of Macassar (take the Firgrove turning on the N2 from Cape Town to Stellenbosch). Yusuf was a 17th-century nobleman who, having rebelled against the high-handed authority of the Dutch East India Company in his native Indonesia, was exiled to the Cape for his pains. His tomb was erected as recently as 1925 by Hadji Sullaiman Shah.

number of ministerial residences as well as the campus of the University of Cape Town. The Groote Schuur Hospital and Medical School here was the scene for the world's first heart transplant, performed by Professor Chris Barnard in 1967.

Best beaches

Given Cape Town's seductive summer climate, visitors are often surprised by the near-freezing temperatures at the bathing beaches of **Clifton**, **Camps Bay** and **Llandudno**, to say nothing of the nudist beach at **Sandy Bay**.

For those who enjoy swimming in the sea, **Muizenberg** and **Fish Hoek** on the warmer Indian Ocean coastline provide the best spots. The secret is to choose a beach according to the wind direction: if there is a cloud-cloth on Table Mountain it means the southeaster is blowing and you should head straight for Clifton or Llandudno; but if there is a northwesterly sea fog brewing, go to Muizenberg and environs.

The reason for the Atlantic's chilly waters is more complex than most people realise. It has a lot to do with the whims of the southeasterly wind. When this wind pushes the warm surface water away from the western shore, the water is replaced from underneath. This phenomenon is called upwelling, bringing with it the cold Antarctic water of the Benguela Current. Small wonder water temperature can be as low as 12° or even 10°C (54–56°F) after a strong "blow". Ironically, it is in the winter (June–Aug) – when the southeaster abates – that the Atlantic beaches experience their warmest sea temperatures.

The Cape's grape

Head out on the Eastern Boulevard or De Waal Drive, both of which become the M3 route. Continue along this road, leaving the city behind you, and climb Wynberg Hill (where Jan van Riebeeck first extended his vineyards), before dropping down into leafy Constantia Valley. This is one of Cape Town's most beautiful suburbs, and certainly its most exclusive.

Here, you can visit the site first developed by early Dutch governor Simon van der Stel in 1685 as his private estate. As well as building a modest homestead here which he named **Groot Constantia ❺** (May–Oct daily 9am–5pm, Nov–Apr daily 10am–6pm; wine-tasting charge; tel: 021-794 5128; www.grootconstantia.co.za), van der Stel planted vines. A century later, the farm had become world-famous for its wines (a drop of "the finest old Constantia that ever was tasted" soothes Elinor Dashwood's broken heart in *Sense and Sensibility*), and the homestead enlarged and converted into a splendid manor house. Bought by the Cape government in 1885, Groot Constantia is now run as a model wine farm. The house and old wine cellar are now a museum.

Van der Stel's original farm was later divided into a number of smaller plots. **Klein Constantia** (open for tastings and sales Mon–Fri 9am–5pm, Sat 9am–1pm; tel: 021-794 5188), with its magnificent maturation cellars set inside a mountain, is one of the Cape's most rewarding wineries. So, too, is nearby **Buitenverwachting** (open for tastings and sales Mon–Fri

It is off Cape Point that the Flying Dutchman, *a phantom ship with tattered sails and a broken mast, is doomed to sail until the end of time – a legend which inspired an opera by Wagner.*

BELOW: windsurfing is just one of many ways to end up tasting the salty Atlantic.

9am–5pm, Sat 9am–1pm; tel: 021-794 5190; restaurant: 021-794 3522), whose name translates as beyond expectation – a fair description of this gracious old manor house in its lovely setting of spreading vineyards and oak-dotted hill sides. The restaurant it contains is excellent, too.

Also centred on a lovely old manor house, but a relative newcomer to the wine industry, is the **Steenberg Estate** (Mon–Fri 9am–4.30pm, Sat and public holidays 9.30am–1.30pm; tastings free; tel: 021-713 2211), whose superb sauvignon blanc, despite being made from vines planted in the 1990s, scored second place in the best white wine category in *Wine* magazine's 2004 readers poll. The restaurant here is another gem, while the attached golf course is regarded to be one of the best in the Cape.

Nightlife and entertainment

Cape Town's culinary speciality is Cape-Malay cooking – spicy and fruity, but seldom hot. Fruit and chutney-enhanced *boboties* (mince-based casseroles), skewered-meat *sosaties* (kebabs), *frikkadel* patties and tomato-based *bredie* with *blatjang* (meat stew with chutney) – you will find all these delicacies at the Cape Malay Restaurant at the Cellars-Hohenort Hotel in Constantia.

As far as seafood is concerned, restaurants can offer fresh catches of crayfish (rock lobster) and *perlemoen* (abalone), black mussels and oysters, prawns and linefish. Blues on The Promenade at Camps Bay is an institution on this lively beach strip and serves up fresh seafood dishes with an Italian twist; the restaurant also overlooks a pristinely beautiful beach.

There are literally hundreds of restaurants to choose from, catering to all tastes and budgets. The best for authentic African cooking, however, are The

Map on page 168

Check the wind direction before heading out: if a southeasterly is blowing it will bring the chilly waters of the Antarctic along with it.

BELOW: lifeguards receive hours of training – not just distinctive hats.

The Minstrel Festival is one of Cape Town's biggest annual parties.

Africa Café in suburban Observatory, and the stylishly ethnic Mama Africa Restaurant and Bar in downtown Long Street – the latter is also well-known for its lively music.

Cape Town has a vibrant late-night café society, the hub of which is "restaurant mile" in Kloof Street, in the Gardens area. Also reliably busy and bustling is the Victoria and Alfred Waterfront *(see page 161)*, packed with bars, restaurants and cafés. **Theatre @ The Pavilion** (tel: 021-419 7661; www.thepavilion.co.za) is situated on the quieter side of the V&A complex and rocks with high-volume musical tribute shows where the audience are usually singing along to familiar tunes by the interval.

As for the performing arts, the city's chief venue is the enormous **Artscape Complex** (formerly the Nico Malan Theatre) on the Foreshore, which houses an opera house and several theatres. High-quality productions are also put on at Rondebosch's **Baxter Theatre**, which stages a three-week local comedy festival every October. Also noteworthy is the University of Cape Town's **Little**

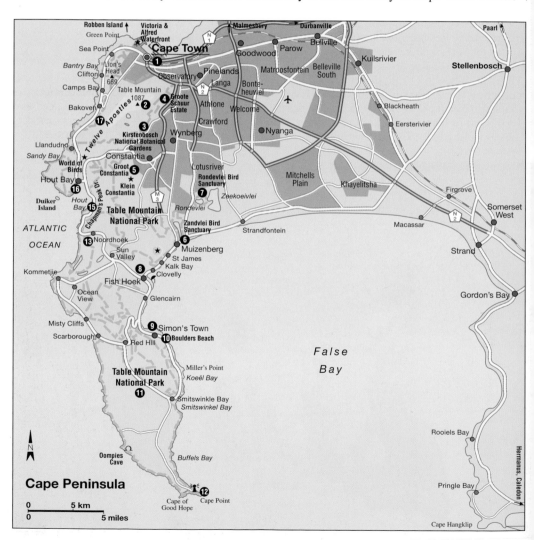

Cape Peninsula

Theatre (student plays; tel: 021-480 7129) and **Theatre on the Bay** (tel: 021-438 3301) in Camp's Bay (contemporary plays).

Night-crawlers looking for late, loud action will find a thriving club scene centred around Loop Street and Long Street in the city centre. There are plenty of clubs and bars here, notably **Joburg** (R&B) and **The Waiting Room** (funky lounge music), as well as dozens of bars. The **Drum Café** in Gardens is a great place to catch live music and/or join informal drumming workshops, while popular jazz venues include the **Green Dolphin** on the V&A Waterfront (live music every night).

The self-proclaimed gay capital of South Africa, Cape Town is the most amenable city in Africa for gay visitors. Certainly, there must be few other cities anywhere in the world whose tourist department produces an official "pink map" listing gay and lesbian orientated guesthouses, night venues and facilities. Many of these are clustered in Greenpoint's so-called "gay village" (in and around Somerset Road). Important events on the local gay calendar include a pink parade, Cape Town Pride, which takes place in February, and the Mother City Queer Project held in early December every year, while the new year is ushered in with the South African Gay & Lesbian Film Festival, held at the end of January.

The Peninsula

Cape Town's urban areas spread across the extreme northern end of a 100-km (60-mile) sliver of land – much of it now protected in Table Mountain National Park – terminating at the Cape of Good Hope. Here, precipitous mountain passes link up innumerable coves and sandy beaches, villages and fishing communities

Map on page 168

Cape Town is one of few African cities with an out and about gay scene.

BELOW: with so many cultures mixing, the musical varieties seem endless.

Picturesque lighthouses still protect the Cape's busy shipping trade.

like beads on a necklace. To make the most of a drive round the peninsula, you should set out early – ideally, just as the sun breaches the jagged Hottentots-Holland Mountains and dapples the surface of False Bay. Following the sun, the journey begins at **Muizenberg** ❻ on the east coast, about 20 km (12 miles) from the city centre. This bustling seaside town was a popular resort in Victorian times; it was in a cottage here (now a small museum) that Cecil Rhodes spent his last years when his health prematurely failed him. The beachfront here has become rather tacky, but the surf is still splendid.

The nearby **Rondevlei Bird Sanctuary** ❼ (daily except Christmas Day 7.30am–5pm, until 7pm Dec–Feb; entrance charge; tel: 021-706 2404; www. rondevlei.co.za) is mainly of interest to bird-watchers, with 230 species recorded including a resident population of the uncommon great crested grebe, but visitors are also likely to see the hippos that were reintroduced a few years back to help thin out the aquatic vegetation.

Down the False Bay coast, narrow Main Road follows closely alongside the railway line, with Muizenberg Mountain crowding in on the left; it passes the pretty villages of **St James**, **Kalk Bay** with its old fishing harbour, and **Clovelly**, until you come to what is arguably the peninsula's safest swimming beach at **Fish Hoek** ❽. From here, fork left on to the M4, and follow the winding road through Glencairn to the historic port settlement of **Simon's Town** ❾. Named after Simon van der Stel, who first recommended it as a safe winter anchorage, it was a Royal Navy base from the time of the second British occupation of the Cape in 1806 until it was handed over to the South African Navy in 1957.

At the southern end of town you'll find **Boulders Beach** ❿ (Oct–Nov daily 8am–6.30pm; Dec–Jan daily 7am–7.30pm; Feb–May daily 8am–6.30pm; June–

BELOW: colourful beach huts lining St James Bay.

Sept daily 8am–5pm; entrance charge; tel: 021-786 2329), a smaller but more secluded swimming beach than that at Fish Hoek. In 1985, for the first time in recorded history, the giant granite rocks for which this beach is named were used as a breeding site by a few pairs of African penguins. Today, several thousand of these remarkably fearless birds are resident at what is one of just three mainland breeding colonies (open daily; entrance charge) and you can swim among them at the southerly end of the beach – an unforgettable experience.

Map on page 168

Cape of Good Hope

Leaving Simon's Town, the M4 winds up past **Miller's Point** and **Smitswinkel Bay** with wonderful views down to the sea far below. A 12-km (8-mile) turn-off to the left takes you to the **Table Mountain National Park ⑪** (Oct–Mar daily 6am–6pm, Apr–Sept daily 7am–5pm; entrance charge; tel: 021-780 9010), which was formerly protected in a modest 7,750-hectare (19,000-acre) provincial nature reserve, but is now part of the Cape Peninsula National Park – the second most-visited reserve in the country after the Kruger National Park.

At this most southerly point on the peninsula, a stiff uphill walk or short funicular train ride leads to the old cliff-top lighthouse at **Cape Point ⑫**. Peering out across the great curve of ocean, you could almost imagine seeing South America to the right, Australia to the left and, yes, far to the south, the thin white sliver of the Antarctic. The reserve was first proclaimed in 1936 to preserve a chunk of indigenous *fynbos* (scrub land) close to the city and to protect some rare plant species here. There are over 2,700 different kinds. It also serves as a breeding ground for rare antelope and you might well see some Cape mountain zebra, bontebok and eland on the sandy plateau.

BELOW: the African penguin – one of the country's more humorous-looking inhabitants.

Return to the city along the western seaboard, the cold side. Turn left as you leave the reserve, then left again where the road forks, 8 km (5 miles) later. This will take you past the hamlets of **Misty Cliffs** and **Scarborough**, and the fishing village of **Kommetjie**. Turn left onto the M6 at the next intersection (if you go straight on it will take you through the Fish Hoek Gap), then left again after 900 metres (½ mile) and you will reach **Noordhoek ⑬**. This is where Cape Town residents head if they want to be alone at the beach; it's 7 km (4 miles) long and it is wildly scenic – breathtaking, even.

Worth a detour if you're looking for a picnic spot is the **Silvermine Nature Reserve ⑭** (Sept–Apr daily 7am–6pm, May–Aug daily 8am–6pm; entrance charge; tel: 021-780 9002), situated on either side of the scenic Ou Kaapse Weg (Old Cape Road); the turn-off is signposted between Kommetjie and Noordhoek. Somewhat overshadowed by its proximity to the Cape of Good Hope, this sector of Table Mountain National Park is nonetheless crisscrossed with good hiking trails through beautiful *fynbos*. The walk to the heights above the reservoir leads to spectacular views across Hout Bay.

Back on the M6, the road snakes steeply upwards on a nerve-racking 7-km (4-mile) journey around **Chapman's Peak ⑮**. Arguably one of the world's most spectacular scenic drives, this route re-opened as

Unsurprisingly, township street art celebrates the country's new generation of political leaders such as Thabo Mbeki.

BELOW: colourful interior of a Khayelitsha home.

a toll road in early 2004, after having been closed for several years due to rock falls. It would be something of a challenge to steer around this road's abundant curves while also admiring the view – but fortunately there are several parking spots at which you can stop and enjoy the scenery.

You should now return to Ou Kaapse Weg then follow the M5 to Constantia and past the entrance to Groot Constantia, continuing over Constantia Nek to **Hout Bay** ⓰, another fishing village turned satellite suburb. Not only is it the headquarters of the peninsula's rock-lobster fleet, but freshly caught fish of all description are sold daily off the quayside – so it's hardly surprising that the village has some fine seafood restaurants. A popular excursion from Hout Bay is a boat trip to nearby **Duiker Island**, site of a major breeding colony and sanctuary to thousands of Cape fur seals. Meanwhile, the giant walk-in aviary at the **World Of Birds** (daily 9am–5pm; tel: 021-790 2730) is Africa's largest bird park and offers the opportunity of nose-to-beak encounters with a wide selection of exotic and indigenous species.

Heading north from here over Suikerbossie Hill, you'll be able to peer down into posh Llandudno with its perfect sickle-shaped beach and rocky points. This is near the journey's end, but some of the best is still to come. After Llandudno, the grand profiles of the **Twelve Apostles** ⓱ (Table Mountain's western buttresses) come into view, jutting out like the prows of gigantic ships at anchor along the shore. When the southeaster whips its tablecloth over the crags, the clouds look like sea swells frothing around their tightly berthed hulls.

The M6 now winds through some of the most sought-after and exclusive residential addresses in the country: Camps Bay, Clifton and Bantry Bay. The first two also have popular beaches, the sort where high society sun-lovers go more to see and be seen than to frolic in the (very cold) sea. From Bantry Bay, the road passes the busy seaside suburbs of Sea Point and Green Point before leading back to City Bowl.

Cape Town active

Cape Town's post-apartheid resurrection as an international tourist hub has been mirrored by a veritable mushrooming of worthwhile day trips and adventure activities, for which further information can be obtained from the tourist office in the Clock Tower Centre or its website (www.tourismcapetown.co.za). Offering a similar insight into contemporary black South Africa as Johannesburg's Soweto Tours, township tours to **Khayelitsha** *(see feature page 191)*, **Langa** (the country's oldest township) and **Imizamu Yethu** (near Hout Bay) also focus on the hardships and discriminatory laws that permeated township life during the apartheid era. Musical tours of the townships, featuring drumming and other traditional instruments, are available too.

Other popular and relatively sedate day tours visit the **Stellenbosch Wine Routes** and whale-watching in the seaside fishing village of **Hermanus** *(the Western Cape chapter, see pages 183 and 189)*. Every year around July, locals eagerly await the arrival of the Southern Right Whales. More energetically, various local tour companies offer the opportunity to abseil down a 100-metre (328-ft) cliff on Table Mountain; kloofing (leaping from a cliff into the water below) on the Steenbras River Gorge near Gordon's Bay; white-water rafting at various sites depending on the current water level; sandboarding on the dunes to the north of the city centre; as well as canoeing, paragliding, water-skiing, caving, rock-climbing and game fishing. Roughly 50 established dive sites are dotted around the waters off the peninsula, offering access to rocky reefs, submarine caverns and swaying forests of kelp inhabited by a varied menagerie of marine creatures – including sharks *(see Travel Tips page 363)*.

The underpublicised **Durbanville Wine Route** (tel: 083-310 1228; www.durbanvillewine.co.za), about 20 km (12 miles) north of the city centre, is worth exploring, especially if you want to get away from the crowds. It was one of the first parts of the country to be planted with vines, yet its estates remain rather low-key and well-priced by comparison to their counterparts in Stellenbosch and Constantia. Six estates are open to the public for tasting, including **Durbanville Hills** (tastings Mon–Fri 9.30am–4.30pm, Sat 9.30am–2.30pm, Sun 11am–3pm; tel: 021-558 1300; www.durbanvillehills.co.za), which is known for its good restaurant and excellent sauvignon blanc, and the historical **Meerendal Estate** (tastings daily 8am–5pm; tel: 021-975 1655), whose flagship Cabochon is a classic Bordeaux-style blended red. Best explored before hitting the vineyard trail, the tiny **Tygerberg Nature Reserve** outside Durbanville protects a type of coastal *fynbos* known as *renosterbos* (rhinoceros bush) that's regarded to be one of the most endangered plant communities in the world.

En route back from Durbanville to Cape Town, it's worth diverting to Blou-bergstrand, which – as its name (Blue Mountain Beach) suggests – offers superb picture-postcard views of Table Mountain across the bay. ❑

Map on page 168

The Cape's unique flora makes it an exceptional destination for migrating birds and the tourists who follow them.

BELOW: on the loose at Camp's Bay.

THE WESTERN CAPE'S COAST OF WHALES

Whale populations are on the increase, and the Cape is one of the best places in the world to see the southern right whale in coastal waters

No fewer than 29 species of toothed whale *(Odontoceti),* including the killer whale, are found off the South African coast, along with eight species of baleen whale (suborder *Mysticeti).* But by far the most commonly spotted are the southern right whales, pods of which seek out sheltered bays along the Cape coastline every year for breeding. Between June and December, there is a good chance of seeing them all the way round the peninsula from Elands Bay on the west coast to Mossel Bay on the Garden Route. On a good day, you might see them spyhopping (standing on their tails with their heads out of water), lobtailing (slapping their flukes on the water's surface) or breaching – leaping out of the sea like a trout.

THE RIGHT WHALES TO CATCH?

The southern right *(Balaena glacialis)* is distinguished by its V-shaped "blow" – the cloud of vapour produced when the whale exhales a large volume of air through its pair of blowholes. They are thought to live for up to 100 years; an adult can reach 16 metres (53 ft) in length. They are called right whales because 18th-century whalers regarded them as the "right" whales to catch: the carcass was oil-rich, and the whalers' task of collecting their booty was made more easy by the fact that the whale floats on the water after slaughter. They were valued for their blubber, which was reduced to oil for use in margarine, soap and linoleum, and for their bones, used to make glue, gelatine and fertiliser. International legislation was introduced to protect the species in 1935, but the southern right has subsequently shown only a slight increase in numbers.

▷ **ENDANGERED GIANTS**
As many as 80 southern right whales (out of an estimated world population of about 6,000) have been recorded seeking regular refuge in Hermanus's Walker Bay to court, mate and calve. A South African law bans the use of any vessels for whale-watching (anyone caught within 305 metres/ 1,000 ft of a whale is liable to a hefty fine), and whales now seem unafraid to come close to the shore.

◁ **SLAUGHTER AT SEA**
South Africa has some of the strictest whale conservation legislation in the world, so sights like this traditional harpooner are thankfully now a thing of the past. As a result, the numbers of southern right whales spotted along the Cape coast has steadily increased – at a rate of 7 percent per year during the 1990s.

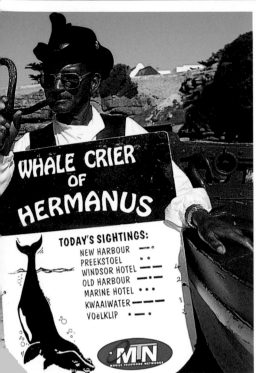

◁ WELCOME BLAST

The Cape village of Hermanus has the world's only official whale-crier, who, during the peak whale season in September and October, parades through the streets announcing new arrivals in Walker Bay with a blast on his kelp-horn. During this period, visitors can also telephone a special Whale Hotline (083-910 1028) for updates on all the latest sightings. The service covers the coast from Gansbaai to Betty's Bay.

▽ CLOSE ENCOUNTERS

With a unequalled combination of low cliff-tops and clear water at the base of the cliffs, Hermanus offers some of the world's best land-based whale-watching. In season, visitors are practically guaranteed a whale sighting – and living here is about as close as you can get to having them in your back garden.

WHERE TO HEAR WHALES SING

Hermanus's Old Harbour – replaced in the 1940s after nearly a century – now houses a museum in a row of beautifully restored fishermen's cottages *(above)*. As tourism has replaced fishing as the primary industry, so the museum has become a focal point for visitors to the town.

One of the museum's most interesting features is an underwater microphone, attached to a sonar buoy in Walker Bay. The eerie, sing-song sound of whales chatting to one another deep underwater is picked up and transmitted back to a public audio room in the museum. There is also a telescope for watching whales far out in the bay.

The new harbour, to the west of the old one, in Westcliff, is a bustling little fishing port, where fresh seafood – including mussels and crayfish – is sold from the docks. Boats can be hired here for deep-sea tuna and marlin expeditions.

Also in Westcliff is the start of Hermanus's famous cliff path, which follows the shore round Walker Bay to the lagoon at Grotto Beach, allowing unrivalled views of whale activity out at sea. The walk takes at least a morning; bench seats are provided along the way and many people take a picnic. There are even grander views along the Rotary Mountain Way, a scenic drive. The tasting rooms of Hamilton Russell vineyards face the Hermanus marketplace.

▷ THE WHALING DAYS

A relic of the bad old days. The wholesale slaughter of whales has been so great that by the 1960s, the world's blue whale population had dropped to an estimated 6 percent of its numbers before whaling began. The last South African whaling station closed in 1975.

THE WESTERN CAPE

Deserted beaches, rugged mountain ranges, colourful wildflower displays, bountiful vineyards and whale watching – all within day-tripping distance of the Mother City.

Map on page 178

T he hinterland within a 200-km (124-mile) radius of Cape Town is an area of outstanding natural beauty, and it wouldn't be difficult to devote a fortnight to exploring its beaches, mountains, nature reserves and vineyards – and still be left with a long list of outstanding places to visit and things to do.

The Western Cape can be broken up into three broad regions – the West Coast, the Winelands and the Overberg – each of which has a distinct character and is treated as a self-contained travel circuit in this chapter. Given sufficient time, however, it is possible to plan a loop that takes in any two of these regions, or all three – you could, for instance, follow the R27 along the West Coast as far as Saldanha, then cut east along the R45 to Paarl, Stellenbosch and Franschhoek in the Winelands, then follow the R43 through Caledon to Hermanus and the Overberg.

THE WEST COAST

The roughly 200 km (124 miles) of Atlantic coastline between Cape Town and Lambert's Bay offers a tantalising smorgasbord of unspoilt beaches, sleepy fishing harbours, magnificent spring wildflower displays and superb marine bird life. So why, then, hasn't this picturesque stretch of coast ever caught on as a tourist destination? The answer, in a nutshell, is that swimming conditions here tend to be chillier and rougher than along the Indian Ocean coastline, making it a poor bet for a straightforward beach holiday. Equally, the relatively low-key nature of tourist development along the West Coast does make it that much more alluring to anybody interested in a bit of off-the-beaten-track exploration.

The main road servicing this region is the N7, which runs about 50 km (30 miles) inland for most of its length, and forms the springboard for the little-used route between Cape Town and Johannesburg via the Northern Cape *(see page 299)*. For sightseeing purposes, however, a more scenic option would be to leave Cape Town along the coastal R27, through the somewhat industrialised suburb of Milnerton, towards **Saldanha** then (assuming you have a night or two to spare) on to Lambert's Bay, before returning on the nippier N7 via **Malmesbury**.

The first of several worthwhile stops along the R27, the former fishing village of **Bloubergstrand ❶** is now little more than a suburb of the city whose centre lies less than 15 km (9 miles) further south. Its main claim to fame is as the site of that classic view of Cape Town with Table Mountain in the background (the one so beloved of postcard manufacturers). Bloubergstrand also has a long sandy beach, studded with rocky outcrops in the north, and its large breakers are very popular with surfers. Quieter Melkbosstrand, 11 km (7 miles) further north, has a similar view of Cape Town.

LEFT: the dramatic setting of a Stellenbosch vineyard.
BELOW: the town's *Moederkerk* was founded in 1710.

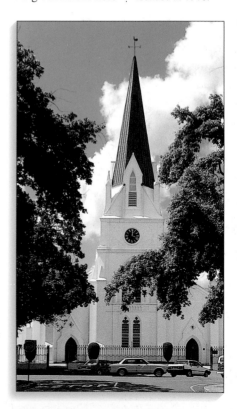

It takes the male crayfish between seven to 10 years to reach a size at which he may legally be caught for human consumption; it takes the female 20 years.

After another 40 km (24 miles), a short sideroad runs west to **Yzerfontein**, a scenic fishing village set on the remote southern border of the West Coast National Park. Some 15 km (9 miles) inland of this, the presciently named small town of **Darling ❷** leapt from obscurity in 1996 when gay icon and satirist Pieter Dirk Uys converted one of its railway buildings into a delightfully kitsch cabaret theatre called Evita se Perron. Uys named the theatre after his Dame Edna-esque alter ego Evita Bezuidenhout – *perron* is Afrikaans for railway platform – and his one-man show (tel: 022-492 2851) forms a lively and irreverent introduction to contemporary South African politics.

West Coast National Park to Lambert's Bay

About 20 km (12 miles) further north along the R27, the **West Coast National Park ❸** (open daily; entrance charge; tel: 022-772 2144; www.sanparks.org) protects a 30-km (18-mile) stretch of coast dominated by the **Langebaan Lagoon**. This magnificent wetland is one of the world's most important conservation areas for migrant birds, and its islands host significant breeding colonies of Cape cormorant, Hartlaub's gull, Cape gannet and seven other species. But most people who visit this park do so to marvel at another natural phenomenon – the glorious eruption of spring wildflowers that generally takes place in August.

The Postberg area of Langebaan is a favourite stopover for wildflower enthusiasts – during the spring season, you're permitted to walk across any private land or track here – and it also harbours large mammals such as springbok, bontebok and gemsbok. En route to Postberg, you'll pass Church Haven, a traditional Cape fishing village hugging the salt-marsh shoreline of Langebaan Lagoon. The resort village of **Langebaan ❹**, on the lagoon's eastern

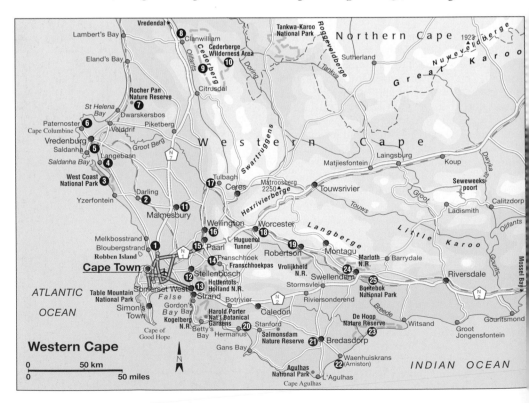

shore, caters for a good range of water sports, including angling, yachting, water-skiing and sail-boarding.

Map on page 178

To the north, the lagoon flows into Saldanha Bay, the deepest natural harbour in South Africa. Unsurprisingly, there is a large naval presence at **Saldanha ❺**, and it's also a key railway link, where enormous quantities of iron ore are deposited after being shuttled across the Kalahari from the mines at Sishen. One might wonder at the effect of all the battleship and freighter traffic on the vulnerable ecosystem of the lagoon, but the mussels that have been farmed here since 1984 remain delicious. So, too, are crayfish from **Paternoster ❻**, an unspoilt fishing village some 30 km (18 miles) further north – both can be sampled at local restaurants.

The rocks off Cape Columbine, which lies just 3 km (2 miles) south of Paternoster, once posed a real threat to sailors; several ships came to grief here before the lighthouse was built. Today, the cape and surrounding *fynbos*-covered dunes are protected within the scenic Columbine Nature Reserve, which forms an excellent retreat for self-sufficient campers. The reserve is a breeding ground for gulls, cormorants and ibises among others, and is at its most attractive in spring-time, when the wildflowers bloom.

Found around the coastline, the indigenous Cape fur seal especially likes Lambet's Bay.

Situated near the one-resort town of **Dwarskersbors** about 35 km (21 miles) north of Saldanha, the **Rocherpan Nature Reserve ❼** (Sept–Apr daily 7am–6pm, May–Aug daily 8am–5pm; tel: 022-931 2900 for reservations; www.cape nature.co.za) is home to thousands of wading birds, including seasonal concentrations of flamingos, as well as a variety of small antelope. The bird life is even more abundant around the picturesque lagoon at **Eland's Bay**. The town itself is not all that interesting, but the beach is excellent, and has become a popular weekend destination for "surfies" from Cape Town.

BELOW: a good day's work.

TAKE ONE CRAYFISH...

Until the beginning of the 20th century, crayfish were so plentiful in Cape waters that they were viewed with disdain by the upper classes, and used instead as fodder for the inmates of the penal colony on Robben Island. Today, however, crayfish are regarded as a delicacy, commanding top billing and high prices on seafood menus in the most elegant restaurants. Indeed, so valuable has the rock lobster fishing industry become in South Africa that they are often referred to as the "red gold from the sea". The species *Jasus lalandi* is the one most commonly found on the West Coast, and in smaller numbers from Cape Point to East London. To cook them yourself, bring a large saucepan of salted water to the boil. Plunge the live crayfish (one per person) firmly into the saucepan, head end first; this kills them instantly. Cover the pan and boil for about 20 minutes until the crayfish turn bright red. Now place in a pan of cold water and when cool, chop off the pincers and split each body lengthways. Remove the small sac at the back of the head (the stomach), the large intestine running from the stomach to the base of the tail, the liver and the lungs on either side of the body. Serve as simply as possible – lemon wedges, a pot of mayonnaise, brown bread and a bottle of chilled white wine are really all you need.

On the way to the small fishing town of **Lambert's Bay**, 16 km (10 miles) further north (Bartholomeu Diaz was the first European to arrive here in 1487), the coast grows increasingly lonely and deserted. If you don't mind the smell and the noise, walk across the stone dam to **Bird Island** (open daily; entrance charge; tel: 022-931 2900; www.lambertsbay.info), with its nesting colony of around 14,000 Cape gannets. Most of the island is closed to public access, but an observation tower provides a fine view not only of the gannets but also of the African penguins who breed here. Cape fur seals are often present in the town's picturesque harbour.

The Cederberg

Time to head some 67 km (42 miles) inland of Lambert's Bay for a change of scene. Here, just off the N7, in the heart of the irrigated Olifants River Valley, lies **Clanwilliam ❽** – an orchard town founded at the beginning of the 18th century and still in possession of some fine historic buildings. One of them, the Old Jail (1808), now houses the municipal museum and tourist office (open daily). The famous beverage known as *rooibos* (red bush) tea is grown around here.

North of Clanwilliam, the stretch of the Olifants River Valley around **Vredendal** is an emergent centre of wine production. Tastings are available at half a dozen estates, most of which traditionally specialise in cheap 'n' cheerful whites, though some 25 percent of the local plantation now consists of red cultivars. A popular starting point is the vast Vredendal Estate, which recently amalgamated with nearby Spruitdrift to form the largest single wine producer in the southern hemisphere, and whose iconic Gôiya export range – stylised bushman painting on the label – might be familiar to UK wine buffs.

BELOW: life here can be as rugged as the coastline.

Clanwilliam is also the springboard for excursions into the craggy **Cederberg Mountains ❾** – the highest of which, the Sneeuberg (2,000 metres/6,500 ft), does indeed get covered with snow each winter. The mountains are named after a species of cedar indigenous to the area, *Widdringtonia cederbergensis*; deforestation has destroyed almost all the trees, a few survive on the more inaccessible slopes. Several short walks on the lower slopes are possible to day visitors; one of the most worthwhile leads to a well-preserved rock-art panel depicting an elephant herd.

Permits for overnight hikes and climbs in the **Cederberg Wilderness Area ❿** can be obtained through Cape Nature Conservation at the Citrusdal Tourism Bureau (tel: 022-921 3210). To protect the environment, a limited number of permits is issued, so if you plan to visit during the busy summer holidays, you should book permits (and accommodation) a few months in advance. It's definitely worth the trouble. You'll encounter bizarre sandstone formations such as the dramatic Wolfsberg Arch and the weird Maltese Cross, caves decorated with ancient rock paintings, and crystal-clear rivers to swim in. Lucky hikers might come across spoor of the mountains' secretive leopard population, but are considerably more likely to see klipspringer, baboon and rock hyrax. The Cederberg is particularly attractive and colourful during the spring wildflower season.

Back down in the Olifants River Valley, you can take a leisurely canoe trip 50 km (30 miles) south to **Citrusdal**, which – as its name (literally Citrus Valley) suggests – exports thousands of tonnes of fruit annually. The private reserve known as **Kagga Kamma** (tel: 021-872 4343) can be reached from both Citrusdal and Ceres. As well as such game as kudu and springbok, you can admire some old San rock paintings, and visit a reconstructed San village, founded in 1989 with the aim of preserving the traditional lifestyle of this ancient people – or rather, with the

Map on page 178

These unique spiral horns only occur on fully grown male kudus.

BELOW: a couple among the crowd.

French settlers refused to leave certain luxuries behind.

aim of showing tourists how they live. Even though the anthropologists who set up the village have done so with the best of intentions, the place still seems very much like an open-air zoo in which the humans take the place of animals.

The drive south from Citrusdal along the N7 passes through a region that's been known as the Swartland (Black Land) since the earliest days of European settlement, most probably in reference to the *renosterbos* (rhinoceros bush) that once grew there prolifically and turns black seasonally. Today, it might more accurately known as the *geel* (yellow) land, since it produces about 15 percent of the national wheat crop – as well as being a burgeoning centre of wine production. The Swartland Cellar (open for tastings Mon–Sat), which lies some 50 km (30 miles) before Cape Town on the outskirts of **Malmesbury ⓫**, is the country's third-largest co-op, using grapes grown on almost 100 different farms to produce a popular range of 20-plus everyday wines (the Shiraz and Columbard deserve singling out) and a more limited selection of reserve reds in good years.

THE WINELANDS

The traditional centre of Cape viniculture, and home to its highest concentration of vineyards today, is the mountainous region situated immediately east of Cape Town itself. Known as the *Boland* (Highland), this region – studded as it is with literally hundreds of wineries, and distinguished by some beautiful montane landscapes and elegant Cape Dutch architecture – begs extended exploration over a few days. Indeed, it would require a full week of dedicated effort to cover each of the dozen or so wine routes comprehensively.

A more normal strategy is to pick one or two routes, depending on your main interests. If you're after classic Cape Dutch architecture and memorable mountain scenery, then concentrate on the venerable estates that grace the footslopes of the Hottentots Holland Mountains around Somerset West, Stellenbosch and Franschhoek – all of which can easily be visited as a day trip from Cape Town. On the other hand, serious wine-tasters looking to ship home a few bargains might prefer to head for the relatively remote and untouristed routes centred on Wellington, Worcester or Robertson.

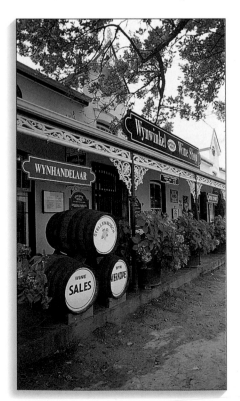

Most estates open from around 9am–4pm daily for tasting and the more popular ones generally charge a nominal fee, but some have abbreviated opening hours or close altogether on Saturday or Sunday – full details are provided in free booklets at the tourist offices in Stellenbosch or Cape Town, or you can ring the estate to confirm. At tasting sessions, it is customary to deposit the tasted wine in a spittoon, but few people do so; unless a driver designates him or herself, there's a strong case for even the most independent-minded of travellers hooking up with one of the many organised wine-tasting tours that run out of Cape Town daily and generally take in up to five different estates.

Stellenbosch

An obvious first port of call in the Boland is **Stellenbosch ⓬**, which lies about 30 km (18 miles) east of Cape Town as the crow flies, and is connected to it by regular passenger trains and several different road routes (the quickest being the N2 and M12). Founded in 1679 by the Dutch Governor Simon van der Stel, this architectural jewel is the second-oldest town in South Africa, and lies at the heart of the winelands. It's known for its university, the first Afrikaans-language institution of higher education to have been established anywhere in the country, and for having the largest number of Cape Dutch houses of any town in the region. The most harmonious examples are to be found on Dorp, Church and Drostdy streets.

Map on page 178

On and facing Die Braak commonage are the Rhenish Church, the VOC Kruithuis or munitions magazine, and the neoclassical **Cape Dutch Burgerhuis Museum** (Mon–Fri 8am–4.30pm, Sat 10am–1pm and 2–5pm). Heading up Dorp Street, you'll pass the **Stellenryck Wine Museum** (Mon–Fri 9am–12.45pm, Sat 10am–1pm and 2–5pm), the **Rembrandt van Rijn Art Gallery** (Mon–Sat 9am–1pm and 2–5pm; tel: 021-886 4340), the old Drostdy, **Oom Samie se Winkel** (Uncle Samie's Store – an old-fashioned shop), the Lutheran church, and, finally, the four period houses forming the **Dorp (Village) Museum** (Mon–Sat 9am–5pm, Sun 10am–4pm; entrance charge; tel: 021-887 2902). These are the rather primitive Schreuderhuis cottage (1709), the elegant Cape Dutch Blettermanhuis (1789), Georgian-styled Grosvenor House (1803) and mid-Victorian Murray House (1850).

The Cape Dutch architecture of the winelands is as rich as the grapes on offer.

Stellenbosch's wine route, the oldest in the country, now consists of five different routes embracing almost 100 estates that are open to the public. Making a choice is correspondingly difficult. Should you try the dry Rieslings at **Neethlingshof** (tel: 021-883 8988) or the remarkable Pinotage produced by **Kanonkop** (tel: 021-884 4656)? What about the outstanding Pinot Noir and Merlot on offer at **Meerlust** (tel: 021-843 3587), or perhaps the excellent Cabernet Sauvignon made at **Thelema** (tel: 021-885 1924), the latter served complete with a panoramic view of the Groot Drakenstein Mountains? For variety, **Simonsig** (tel: 021-888 4900) produces 15 varieties of red and white wine, while the winery on the **Morgenhof Estate** (tel: 021-889 5510) offers just as large a selection, as well as picnic-basket lunches in summer. Finally, don't leave without visiting the **Rustenberg Estate** (tel: 021-809 1200), which, with its orchards and gabled dairy on the outskirts of the town, is one of the most beautiful in the Cape.

BELOW: catering to tourists has helped many vineyards thrive.

Many would argue, however, that this accolade belongs to **Vergelegen** (daily 9.30am–4.30pm; entrance charge; tel: 021-847 1334; www.vergelegen.co.za), which attained the dual distinction of heading up both the top winery and the most beautiful winery lists in a readers' poll published in the June 2004 issue of South Africa's *Wine* magazine. Situated on the lower-slopes of the Helderberg above **Somerset West ⓭**, some 20 km (12 miles) south of Stellenbosch, Vergelegen – which means far away – was granted to William van der Stel (son of Simon) in 1700 and the first vines were planted there shortly afterwards. The old manor house, now a private museum decorated in period style and set in tranquil gardens, is a fine example of Cape Dutch architecture, and its setting is equally superlative. There's a great little coffee shop on the estate, and the wine itself – the multi award-winning red blend in particular – ain't exactly plonk.

The Western Cape serves as a vital home for birds which migrate between the Northern and Southern hemispheres.

BELOW:
grapes need
careful handling.

The small but picturesque **Helderberg Nature Reserve** (daily 7.30am–7pm; tel: 021-851 4060), which stands guard over Somerset West, offers the opportunity to ramble along well-maintained footpaths across mountain sides strewn with ericas and proteas. Its best-known feature is Disa Gorge, where you can see the exquisite "flower-of-the-gods", the red disa orchid, growing on inaccessible rock faces from January to March. A remarkable variety of birds also inhabit this reserve, while seven trails range from 15 minutes to three hours in duration.

Franschhoek

From Stellenbosch, the R45 leads in a northeasterly direction for 28 km (17 miles) to **Franschhoek** ⓔ, or "French Corner", a reference to the Huguenots who settled here in the 18th century. The **Huguenot Memorial Museum** (Mon–Sat 9am–5pm, Sun 2–5pm; entrance charge; tel: 021-876 2532) and the Huguenot Monument, completed in 1943, recall the history of these Protestant refugees, persecuted by Louis XIV because of their religious beliefs. Blessed with perhaps the most perfect setting of any Boland town, Franschhoek is an ideal place to settle in for an alfresco lunch at one of eight restaurants listed in the top 100 countrywide.

The wine route leading through the **Franschhoek Valley**, framed as it is by lofty mountain peaks, is spectacular too – and not only from a scenic point of view. For one thing, it includes the beautiful 300-year-old **Boschendal Estate** (Nov–April Mon–Sat 8.30am–4.30pm, Sun 9.30am–12.30pm; free entrance, tasting fee; tel: 021-870 4200; www.boschendal.com), which is best known perhaps for its popular Blanc de Noir, an off-dry white made from red grapes. It's definitely worth giving in to temptation and sampling the splendid Boschendal Brut, a champagne in all but name, or the estate's highly rated Shiraz, depending on your taste.

The estate's restaurant is not at all bad; between November and April you can also indulge in a garden "Pique Nique" before heading off to the cellars.

The Optima Reserve produced by the nearby **L'Ormarins Cellars** (tel: 021-874 9000) is a fine blend of Cabernet Sauvignon and Merlot with a hint of Cabernet Franc – a full-bodied wine that can profitably be stored for 10–15 years. The Cape Dutch-style manor house on this estate is quite lovely, with the dramatic peaks of the Simonsberg and the Groot Drakenstein rising up in the background. The cellars of **La Motte Estate** (tel: 021-876 3119) offer an excellent Shiraz, while the vintners at **Haute Cabrière** (tel: 021-876 3688) will ply you with no fewer than five different sparkling wines – or you can just drop into the Franschhoek Vineyards Co-op cellar in the town centre and sample any of perhaps 100 wines produced by the above and other local estates.

Paarl

Some 30–45 minutes drive north of either Stellenbosch or Franschhoek, and a similar distance from Cape Town along the N1 highway, **Paarl** ⑮ (Afrikaans for Pearl) is named for the polished granite domed mountain that rises behind it. Despite its inviting name and relative antiquity (it was founded in 1720), Paarl feels rather dour and unattractive by Boland standards, and the sprawling town centre can take ages to drive through. On the southern slope of Paarl Mountain, you'll notice the slender granite needle of the **Afrikaans Taal (Language) Monument**, erected in 1975 to commemorate the centenary of a movement started in Paarl that eventually led to the recognition of Afrikaans as an official language.

Paarl's wine route was established in 1984 and, as with Franschhoek or Stellenbosch, it offers not only fine wines, but also a whole series of first-class restaurants. A good place to begin a tasting tour is in the central **KWV Cellars** (tel: 021-807 3900) or at the vast **Nederburg Estate** (tel: 021-862 3104) on the outskirts of town. Probably the best known of all South Africa's wineries, Nederburg has received countless awards for its reserve range, while its everyday drinking wines are a ubiquitous feature on the wine lists of less adventurous restaurants. The Nederburg Auction, held in March or April, is when the best South African wines are sold to the highest bidders.

Other prominent cellars in the area include **Avondale** (tel: 021-863 1976), **Landskroon** (tel: 021-863 1039) and **Glen Carlou** (tel: 021-875 5528), while the **Simonsvlei Co-op** (tel: 021-863 3040) has a wide range of well-priced wines for everyday sipping. When it comes to value for money, however, the **Du Toitskloof Winery** (tel: 023-349 1601), with its fantastic situation at the northern base of the eponymous mountain pass about 16 km (10 miles) east of Paarl, takes some beating. Formerly best known for its multiple award-winning dessert fare, Du Toitskloof now also produces some excellent dry wines – the Shiraz, Ruby Cabernet/Pinotage blend, and Sauvignon Blanc all stand out.

Situated on the R44 about 12 km (7 miles) north of Paarl, the small town of **Wellington** ⑯ is notable for its Dutch Reformed Moederkerk built in 1838 (with an interesting spire added in 1891) and imposing Town Hall. Particularly recommended among the

Map on page 178

The Huguenot Memorial remembers the trials of the Cape's first vintners.

BELOW: grapes are delicately aged before being sold.

vintners whose properties border this town's small wine route are the **Diemersfontein Wine & Country Estate** (tel: 021-864 5050) and the **Onverwacht Wine Estate**, which both have a Cape Dutch manor house dating from the 18th century, and a restaurant.

Tulbagh

North of Wellington, the R301/46 passes through the wheat-golden and vine-red Land van Waveren Valley and crosses the Slanghoek Mountains over the most magnificent of all mountain passes, Bain's Kloof, until after 50 km (30 miles) it emerges at the miniature historical gem and small wine-production centre of **Tulbagh ⑰**. Following a series of earthquakes that virtually demolished the town in 1968, Tulbagh's historic Church Street was rebuilt in Cape Dutch style. The restoration work was extremely thorough – perhaps even a little too thorough. Church Street now looks like a huge open-air museum. Nor does the village church serve its original purpose; it has been transformed into the **Oude Kerk Folk Museum** (open daily; entrance charge). On display is a noteworthy collection of Victorian furniture and other household objects.

The gracious **De Oude Drostdy** (daily, Sun pm only; entrance charge), 4 km (2 miles) outside the village, was designed in 1804 by the French architect Louis Michel Thibault. Prisoners once languished in the cellar, which today serves as a storeroom for vintages from the nearby Drostdy vineyards, which you can taste and buy. Tulbagh also has its own wine route to offer visitors. The **Theuniskraal Estate** (tel: 023-230 0687), which has been in the possession of the Jordaan family since 1927, produces some excellent white wines including an iconic dry Riesling.

Worcester

Back on the N1, some 50 km (30 miles) southeast of Tulbagh and 100 km (60 miles) northeast of Cape Town, **Worcester** ⑱ is cupped in the lush Breede River valley at the foot of the Hex River Mountains (the highest peaks in the Western Cape and snow-dusted in winter). This small town offers a typical Boland blend of elegant Cape Dutch architecture, a beautiful setting, and vineyards on all sides.

Founded in 1820, Worcester possesses a number of neoclassical buildings, including the elegant Drostdy, probably the finest example of Cape Regency architecture in the country. So-called Worcester gables add an individual architectural accent. Many Cape Dutch gabled houses later acquired Victorian verandas with wrought-iron railings; the one at No. 132 Church Street, built in 1832, is a fine example. The town's most prominent building is the Dutch Reformed Moederkerk, built in 1824 in the neo-Gothic style.

The Worcester Winelands Association has signposted a wine route for visitors to follow. Here, even the oldest wine producer, **De Wet Wine Cellar** (tel: 023-341 2710), 8 km (5 miles) north of the town, was not founded until 1946, so although the wines are good, you may find both architecture and landscape more attractive around Stellenbosch or Paarl. Do not leave Worcester without visiting the lovely **Karoo National Botanical Garden** (daily 8am–5pm; entrance charge), behind the golf club north of town. Following rainy spells in spring, the landscape bursts into bloom, sprinkling the gardens with a bright carpet of flowering succulents – but it has plenty of other non-seasonal attractions, too.

Situated roughly halfway along the 100-km (62-mile) road connecting Worcester to Swellendam, **Robertson** ⑲ lies at the centre of South Africa's second-largest wine route, with almost 40 estates open to the public. Robertson is largely

Map on page 178

BELOW: vines stretch to the horizon.

If you want to indulge in the many free tastings at the vineyards, leave the car behind and board an organised tour.

BELOW: Overberg farms raise their glass to sheep.

overlooked by tourists, partly due to its relative remoteness from Cape Town and partly because it is historically associated with dessert wines and brandies. These days, however, the area also produces some excellent dry reds and whites. Prominent estates include **De Wetshof** (excellent Chardonnays; tel: 023-615 1853), **Excelsior** (good-value Cabernet Sauvignon and Merlot; tel: 023-615 1980), **Graham Beck** (several good reds; tel: 023-626 1214), **Zandvliet** (well-known for Shiraz; tel: 023-615 1146) and attractively priced all-rounders such as **Robertson Winery** (tel: 023-626 3059) and **Van Loveren Estate** (tel: 023-615 1505).

THE OVERBERG

This route follows the N2 southeast from Cape Town over the Hottentots-Holland Mountains and into the isolated Overberg region. The quickest way to Hermanus – which offers the best land-based whale-watching in the world – leads along a well-surfaced road to Botrivier, and from there along the R43 down to the coast. The coastal road, however, is much more exciting. After **Somerset West**, follow signs to **Gordon's Bay**, an attractive resort on the shores of False Bay. Whales can often be seen frolicking offshore here during October and November. After Gordon's Bay, the R44 hugs the coastline around Koeëlbaai, with some fantastic sea views. Some 7 km (4 miles) to the east, not far away from the old whaling station of Betty's Bay and dramatically situated between the Kogelberg Range and the Atlantic coast, are the **Harold Porter National Botanical Gardens** (daily; entrance charge; tel: 028-272 9311), which are definitely worth a visit. Waterfalls and small streams splash through a *fynbos*-sprinkled landscape, inhabited by numerous colonies of baboons. Twelve km (7 miles) after the little town of Kleinmond, turn right on to the R43, which leads on to Hermanus.

A MASTER ENGINEER

Many of the first roads in the Cape were not built, but followed the trails worn into the earth over the centuries by herds of migrating game. Sir Lowry's Pass across the Hottentots-Holland Mountains, for example, was opened in 1830 and for a good deal of its length followed the track used by migrating eland. This meant that right up until the mid-19th century, Cape Town – surrounded as it is by a series of towering mountain ranges – remained virtually sealed off from the rest of the country. Villages which were only 30 km (18 miles) apart, as the crow flies, took over a month to reach over the winding animal trails. In 1848, desperate for access to the interior, the Cape colonial government appointed the Scottish-born Inspector of Roads, Andrew Geddes Bain, to solve the problem. Over the next 45 years, Bain – followed by his son, Thomas – supervised the construction of ten mountain passes into the interior, using only hand-held rock drills, picks, shovels and gunpowder. In terms of scale and logistics, these roads are extraordinary feats of engineering; many (the Swartberg Pass, the Montagu Pass, Bain's Kloof Pass, Prince Alfred's Pass) are still in daily use today. But Bain achieved something else, too; he always insisted on choosing the most beautiful routes. They make very rewarding driving.

Hermanus is the largest coastal town in the Overberg and can get pretty crowded, especially at Christmas time. The best time to visit is spring, when the biggest visitors of all arrive in Walker Bay: the whales *(see page 174)*. The municipality hires a special whale crier during September and October who not only keeps tourists up to date on whale activity but can even be reached by mobile phone (the Whale Hotline, tel: 083-910 1028). If you take the 11-km (7-mile) cliff walk at this time of year you're almost sure to see whales; sometimes far away on the other side of the bay, sometimes only 30 metres (100 ft) away and very clearly visible in the crystal-clear water. An underwater microphone transmits their strange songs live back to a room in the **Old Harbour Museum** (Mon–Sat 9am–4pm, Sun 11am–4pm; entrance charge; tel: 028-312 1474).

The route back towards the N2 is a particular treat for wine fans, because the R320 goes past the **Hamilton Russell Vineyards** (Mon–Fri, Sat am only; tel: 028-312 3595) in the Hemel-en-Aarde Valley, where you can sample some of South Africa's best Pinot Noir. Situated near Stanford some 45 km (28 miles) west of Hermanus, the often overlooked **Salmonsdam Nature Reserve** (open daily; entrance charge; tel: 028-425 5020) protects a mountainous area coloured by a variety of protea species and inhabited by bontebok, klipspringer and numerous birds. It is excellent walking country.

From **Caledon**, continue along the N2 via **Riviersonderend** to Swellendam. If you're keen on seeing South Africa's southernmost tip, however, you should turn off onto the R316. This road leads through the sleepy town of **Bredasdorp** ㉑; the **Shipwreck Museum** (Mon–Fri, Sat and Sun am only; entrance charge) here contains a fascinating exhibition of treasures taken from ships wrecked off the stormy coast. The route continues across gently undulating farmland as far as

Map
on page
178

BELOW:
Swellendam is
the third-oldest
city in the country.

Map on page 178

In 1795, Swellendam rejected Dutch authority and formed an independent government. Just 91 days later, the British occupied the Cape and Swellendam's short-lived independence was over.

BELOW: taking a break at Bontebok National Park.

Cape Agulhas which officially separates the Indian and Atlantic oceans. This is where Africa comes to an end – definitively. Portuguese sailors gave it the name Agulhas, meaning "needles", because it is at this point that the needle of a compass points due north, with no deviation. If you're expecting the sort of dramatic landscape you see at Cape Point you'll be somewhat disappointed; apart from a flat, rocky peninsula and a lighthouse (the second-oldest in South Africa, built in 1848) there is very little else to look at. But you can climb the **Lighthouse** (Mon–Sat, Sun am only; entrance charge), and the magnificent beach at nearby Struisbaai is unforgettable, with its turquoise-blue sea and colourful fishing boats.

Just as rewarding is a detour from Bredasdorp to **Waenhuiskrans**, which is also known as **Arniston ㉒**. This fishing village with its thatched, whitewashed houses has been declared a national monument. White sand dunes form a contrast with the bright-blue sea behind, but the southeast wind can blow a little too harshly for comfort.

Running for some 50 km (30 mile) along the coast east of Arniston, the **De Hoop Nature Reserve & Marine Protected Area ㉓** (open daily; entrance charge; tel: 028-425 5020; www.capenature.co.za) protects what is probably the Cape's largest remaining contiguous *fynbos* habitat, together with significant populations of the endangered Cape mountain zebra and bontebok, and various other antelope and small predators. Several walking routes run through the reserve, ranging from the two-hour Klipspringer Trail to the 55-km (34-mile), five-day Whale Trail. Large flocks of water birds frequent the extensive lake and wetlands formed where the mouth of the Sout ("Salt") River is blocked by dunes, while the offshore marine reserve offers great snorkelling and forms a breeding ground for an estimated 120 southern right whales between June and November.

The route rejoins the N2 some 60 km (37 miles) north of Bredasdorp, near Stormsvlei. From there it's only another 12 km (8 miles) to **Swellendam ㉔**, the third-oldest town in South Africa, and a Cape Dutch architectural jewel. Founded in 1743, the town's Cape Dutch buildings include a particularly fine **Drostdy** (open daily; entrance charge). Built in 1746, it contains a select assortment of Cape furniture and paintings. An old prison and two Victorian buildings, **Mayville** (1853) and **Auld House**, also form part of the same complex. Even more popular with photographers is the magnificent **Dutch Reformed Church** (Voortrek Street), which dates from 1911; it's a wedding-cake of a building, combining neo-Gothic, neo-Renaissance and neo-baroque elements with the Cape Dutch style to form an astonishingly harmonious ensemble. The Town Hall, also on Voortrek Street, is another imposing Cape-style Victorian building.

Just 6 km (4 miles) south of Swellendam is the entrance to the **Bontebok National Park ㉕** (daily 7am–7pm; entrance charge; tel: 028-514 2735), the smallest national park in South Africa with a surface area of just 28 sq. km (11 sq. miles). You won't see elephant, lion or rhinoceros here – just plenty of graceful little bontebok, a species of antelope hunted almost to extinction during the early part of the 20th century. Springbok and the rare Cape mountain zebra are also found here. ❑

Township Life

The street lamps lighting Cape Town's white suburbs at night are still shining when Khayelitsha starts waking up. Cape Town's biggest township is well over an hour's journey by overloaded minibus taxi from the city centre and industrial areas. The name means new home in Xhosa, but for the one million people who live here, it could just as well mean early start.

As dawn breaks, low mists mask the woodsmoke still rising from last night's cooking fires. The light reveals the extraordinary array of building materials used in Khayelitshan homes, from broken bits of advertising hoarding to bin liners and flattened tin cans.

Some houses have TV sets resourcefully powered by car batteries; on others, the flimsy roofs are pinned down by rusty upturned wheelbarrows – small protection against the summer southeaster which drives sand into every corner (in winter, by contrast, the roads seldom dry out, and there is mud everywhere). "The rich get richer," goes the popular catchphrase, "the poor get Khayelitsha".

Three-quarters of Khayelitsha's residents live in informal housing, or squatter shacks. After the apartheid legislation which created South Africa's townships was repealed, this was the first community in the Western Cape to be earmarked for upgrading – but while there's now a core of formal, serviced houses, electricity and running water remain a rare luxury. People wash at communal taps (one per street), and attend the small corrugated-iron toilets nearby.

Many of Khayelitsha's residents first came to the city because they found it increasingly difficult to survive in the former homelands, areas ravaged by overcrowding, soil erosion and a grim shortage of opportunity. Their presence here – and it is a similar story in all South Africa's townships – underlines an urgent and ongoing need for more houses, roads, schools, clinics and other services.

Crime statistics – especially for violent crimes such as murder and rape – are frighteningly high. Yet strangers are greeted warmly, neighbours help each other. At night, the *shebeens* (taverns) are crowded with merrymakers; on weekends, the churches resound to gospel choirs. Community halls host jazz concerts, ballroom-dancing contests and beauty pageants; dusty streets double up as bumpy soccer pitches.

Unemployment here is about 60 percent, but the sidewalks are crowded with hawkers; a parked minibus acts as a shop, with cabbages lined up on the roof. Fires line the roadside, roasting "smileys" (half a sheep's head), along with offal and sausages. Thriving *spaza* stores (the name means "hidden" in township slang – a reference to the days when blacks were not permitted to run their own businesses) operate from private homes, offering an amazing range of services from groceries to hairdressing and shoe repairs.

The great majority of South Africans are township-dwellers. They take their feisty, inventive local culture for granted; yet it is a side to the country that few visitors (and indeed, few white South Africans, either) ever explore. ❑

RIGHT: interior, Khayelitsha shack, with walls decorated with soap labels.

THE GARDEN ROUTE

*Wild forests and unspoilt beaches lead past hidden valleys
and majestic mountains to the forested shores of
Tsitsikamma National Park*

Map
on page
194

L ush and bountiful, the relatively short stretch of coastline between Mossel
Bay and Tsitsikamma is popularly referred to as the Garden Route, and its
timeless appeal both to foreign travellers and to South African holidaymakers is reflected in a booming guesthouse and hotel industry, not to mention
the region's ever escalating real-estate prices. This, however, is a distinctly
African garden – not the manicured lawns of Europe with their neat and formal
layouts, but an exhilaratingly rugged coastline flanked by indigenous rainforests, blue lagoons, parallel rows of serrated mountain peaks, and fields bright
with *fynbos*.

Mossel Bay and George

Coming from Cape Town, the eastbound N2 runs inland through **Swellendam** *(see page 190)* and **Riversdale** to finally reconnect with the seaside
after almost 400 km (240 miles) at **Mossel Bay ❶**. Generally regarded to
mark the beginning of the Garden Route, Mossel Bay also boasts the distinction of being where the Portuguese navigator Bartholomeu Diaz set anchor in
1488 to become the first European to touch South African soil. The
Bartholomeu Diaz Museum Complex (Mon–Fri 9am–5pm, Sat and Sun
9am–4pm; entrance charge; tel: 044-691 1067),
housed inside a converted granary, is dedicated to
his memory. Displays include exhibitions of shells
and shipping; best of all is the full-scale replica of
Diaz's surprisingly small caravel.

The first permanent settlement at Mossel Bay did-
n't begin until about 300 years later, though passing
ships often stopped for water and to trade with the
local Hottentots. The town is still a popular holiday
resort thanks to its many beaches and calm swimming
pools between rocks. It has also become a sprawling
industrial centre due to the discovery of oil and natural
gas reserves off its coast. Write postcards, nevertheless, because the local mail system has a long tradition: in 1500, a Portuguese sailor named Pedro
d'Ataide placed a letter inside an old boot and hung it
beneath a milkwood tree.

A year later, another sailor found the letter and was
kind enough to forward it. The tradition continued as
the tree became a message board for passing sailors.
Today the tree is part of the Diaz museum, and if you
post your cards in the boot-shaped letterbox provided,
the "oldest post office in South Africa" will process
them promptly – naturally, with a suitable stamp.

If Mossel Bay has sacrificed something of its former charm to industrial development, there's no doubt
that it also offers some of the most alluring marine
activities in the region, full details of which can be

LEFT: a riot of
flowers bloom
between coast
and desert.
BELOW: relaxing
at the evening's
braaivleis.

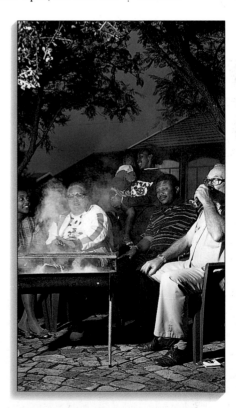

obtained from the tourist office next to the old post office. Most popular, and relatively inexpensive, is a boat excursion to nearby **Seal Island** (hourly departures Mon–Sat 10am–4pm, Sun 11am–4pm; tel: 044-690 3101), where hundreds of Cape fur seals can be seen basking on the rocks and foraging in the surrounding waters. Somewhat more daunting (and not just financially) are the **caged shark dives** arranged by **Shark Africa** (tel: 044-691 3796; www.sharkafrica. co.za) to view predatory great whites in their natural habitat. More conventional dives can be arranged out of Mossel Bay, as can kayaking expeditions, while back on terra firma – or, more accurately, suspended above it – the **Gouritz Bridge** bungee-jump from the N2, 35 km (22 miles) back towards Swellendam, is popular with adrenaline junkies.

Posting a letter in Mossel Bay's unique boot-shaped postbox.

Leaving Mossel Bay, the scenery grows increasingly wild as the N2 continues east towards the former lumber village of **George ❷**, founded in 1811 at the base of the Outeniqua Mountains (Outeniekwaberge) and described a few decades later by Anthony Trollope as "the prettiest village on the face of the earth." Situated a few kilometres inland, George today is anything but a village – indeed, its population of 150,000 is twice that of any other town on the Garden Route – and few would regard it to be especially pretty. On the credit side, George does offer a good range of tourist facilities at lower prices than you'll find elsewhere in this popular area, and it's well placed as a base for numerous day trips along the Garden Route or the Little Karoo.

Within George's historic town centre stand several fine buildings. These include the **Dutch Reformed Moederkerk** with its magnificent carved stinkwood pulpit, and the elegant **Public Library** (1840) – although the latter's books have, unfortunately, all been moved to Cape Town. Outside the library is the mighty **Slave Tree**, one of the broadest oak trees in the southern hemisphere, beneath which a slave market was once held. And since we're touching on a dark chapter of South African history, the **George Museum** (Mon–Fri 9am–4pm; entrance charge; tel: 044-873 5343) on Courtenay Street has an exhibition devoted to the years of apartheid rule under President P.W. Botha, the last of the hard-liners – he retired here in 1989.

Rather jollier times are to be had on the local **Outeniqua Choo Tjoe** (tel: 044-801 8288), a popular narrow-gauge railway. Here, a steam locomotive dating from 1928 transports passengers from George through several attractive, wooded ravines along the coastline to Knysna. The trip takes 2½ hours each way, and can be linked to a return shuttle-bus service. Around 115,000 passengers travel the line annually. The Outeniekwa Mountains to the north of George offer some excellent hiking possibilities, while motorists can explore

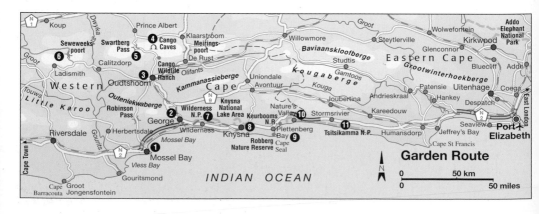

Garden Route

the *fynbos* and forest-covered slopes along a road loop via the sensational Outeniqua and Montagu passes to Oudtshoorn.

The Little Karoo

Situated roughly 60 km (36 miles) north of George via the N12 and Outeniqua Pass, **Oudtshoorn ❸** is an increasingly popular day or overnight trip out of the Garden Route proper. It is the principal town of the Little Karoo, a somewhat arid region whose name derives from a Khoi word meaning dry. It can get blisteringly hot in summer, but Little Karoo also has an austere beauty that comes in many different guises – the serenity of far horizons, a black eagle soaring high above a silent plain, a cool breeze after a stifling day, or just a donkey cart crunching slowly along an old farm road.

Oudtshoorn was once a celebrated ostrich-feather centre: between 1880 and 1910 a number of Jewish traders from eastern Europe emigrated to South Africa, set up ostrich farms and made a small fortune exporting the feathers back to fashion-conscious Europe. The trade generated vast riches – 1 kg (2 lbs) of tail-feathers could fetch up to R200. The **C.P. Nel Museum** (open daily; entrance charge; tel: 044-272 7306) on Baron van Rheede Street has displays on the history of the ostrich boom. All this revenue pouring into what had hitherto been nothing more than a remote hamlet helped build a number of "feather palaces", several of which have survived the decline in the market – one such being the **Le Roux Townhouse** (entrance included in museum ticket), which stands on the corner of Loop and High streets, complete with period fittings and furnishings.

Today, the ostrich industry still thrives, but the feathers are used more for dusters than for the hats and boas of high fashion. But while the feather market

The moods of an ostrich are as unpredictable as its bites are painful.

BELOW: family life on the Karoo.

At speeds of up to 78 km/h (48 mph), the ostrich can outrun most of its enemies.

BELOW: the dramatic interior of Cango Caves.

took a dip the skins of this strange bird have become part and parcel of the world of high fashion. Ostrich skins used in the manufacturing of expensive shoes, handbags and purses now command prices comparable to the highly prized skins of baby crocodiles. And the farms where the ostriches are bred also form the lynchpin of an increasingly lucrative tourist industry. Why Oudtshoorn? It seems ostriches are happiest in a hot, dry climate; they like the type of alfalfa grown here and the availability of their favourite dietary supplements: sand, stones and insects.

Several such farms are open to the public, including the **Safari Ostrich Show Farm** (daily 7.30am–5pm; entrance charge; tel: 044-272 7311; www.safari ostrich.co.za), which lies just outside town on the Mossel Bay road. The homestead here boasts teak from Burma, roof tiles from Belgium and marble floors. Lunch time at an ostrich farm usually means an opportunity to dine on an ostrich steak; you can also try your riding skills on the back of the world's largest bird or watch jockeys spur on their mounts in a mock Ostrich Derby. Similar entertainment is offered at other ostrich farms such as **Highgate** (tel: 044-272 7115) and **Cango** (tel: 044-272 4623), the latter situated 15–20 km (9–12 miles) from town along the R328 towards the Cango Caves *(see below)*.

Situated about 2 km (1½ miles) from the town centre along the R328, **Cango Wildlife Ranch** (open daily; entrance charge; tel: 044-272 5593) was established in the 1980s as a breeding centre for endangered wildlife. One of the world's most productive breeding centres for cheetah, it has also successfully bred serval, aardwolf, African wild dog and pygmy hippo (the latter a West African rainforest species). This aside, the ranch essentially comes across as a zoo – albeit a very good one – offering the opportunity to hold hand-reared

cheetahs and to see a variety of indigenous and exotic animals, including white Bengal tigers, pumas, jaguars and a colony of meerkats. A snake park, curio shop and restaurant are attached.

Map on page 194

The fascinating **Cango Caves** ➍ (open daily, hourly guided tours; entrance charge; tel: 044-272 7410; www.cangocaves.co.za), 32 km (20 miles) north of Oudtshoorn, are part of a massive system of limestone caverns that extends into the Swartberg Mountains. The caves once sheltered San bushmen whose paintings can be found on the walls. An hour-long guided tour introduces you to three of the biggest caves, after which you can either turn back or continue on a more adventurous route, which involves squeezing your way along a series of narrow, hot, damp and stifling shafts. The seat of your trousers gets just as much exercise as your shoes during this operation.

Past the caves, the R328 continues on towards the whitewashed village of **Prince Albert** over one of the most beautiful of all South Africa's mountain passes – the **Swartberg Pass** ➎ (1,436 metres/4,700 ft). Built between 1881 and 1888 and now a national monument, this gravel road climbs 1,000 metres (3,281 ft) in 12 km (7 miles) over the mighty Swartberg Range, with very sharp, blind hairpin bends. The views are magnificent, but this is not a drive for vertigo sufferers.

The native aloe plant has renowned medicinal properties.

If that's not challenging enough, you could take an alternative route across the mountains via the main road (the R29) through Meiringspoort, or by the **Seweweekspoort Pass** ➏. First opened in 1857, this pass crosses the River Groot some 30 times along its 17-km (11-mile) length, snaking through bare walls of vertical rock which at times stretch hundreds of metres high. Twisted bands of red sandstone and milky quartz loom above the road, their yellow-lichened crags glowing in the sun. Check the status of the road before you set out to drive through the gorge, though; it's often closed after heavy rains.

Most visitors approach Oudtshoorn via the N12 from George, either returning the way they came or using the R328 to Mossel Bay via the **Robinson Pass** (859 metres/2,818 ft), or the rougher **Montagu Pass** to the east. Coming to or from Cape Town, however, a rewarding alternative is to travel between Swellendam and Oudtshoorn using the R324 through Tradouw Pass to **Barrydale**, then to follow the R62 through the series of fertile valleys and pretty orchard villages such as **Ladysmith** and **Calitzdorp**.

BELOW: a walkway along Wilderness National Park.

Wilderness National Park

Heading east from George, the railway and the N2 both pass through **Wilderness**, a bustling little resort town fringed on one side by a magnificent, 8-km (5-mile) long sandy beach and on the other by the Wilderness National Park. Shortly before the N2 enters Wilderness, it offers a superb view over a photogenic riverine gorge spanned by the Outeniqua Choo-Tjoe's railway bridge. Immediately after this, you can pull up at a viewpoint from where dolphins are regularly observed playing in the surf below.

Wilderness National Park ➐ (daily; tel: 044-877 1197; www.sanparks.org) protects a series of freshwater pans – the largest being Swartvlei, Langvlei,

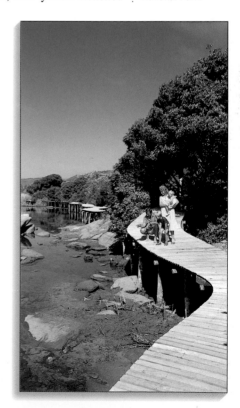

Groenvlei and Rondevlei – connected by various tributaries of the Touws River, which empties into the ocean in the town itself. It's a beautiful park, and the combination of open waterways, reed beds and marshes provides a rich source of food and varied habitats for a wide array of bird life, as does the surrounding bush and forest. Most attractive of all are the large wading birds that scour the shallows for food; pockets of pink flamingos, drifting across the shimmering water, straining the surface for tiny algae and crustaceans; and African spoonbills that rake the mud with their broad, wide beaks. Of the 95 water-bird species recorded in South Africa, 75 have been seen bobbing about on the lakes here.

Understandably popular with bird-watchers, Wilderness National Park also offers some great rambling opportunities in the form of a network of non-strenuous day trails, each of which is named for one of the park's six kingfisher species. A good starting point is the Half-collared Kingfisher Trail, an 8-km (5-mile) circular ramble that leads through riparian woodland fringing the Touws River to an attractive waterfall that tumbles over a group of gigantic round boulders. Forest birds such as the beautiful Knysna loerie and yellow-throated warbler are likely to be seen here, and bushbuck and duiker are present as well. A similar route can be followed on the water by renting a canoe from the main rest camp and punting gently upstream to the base of the falls.

A short distance east of Wilderness lies the busiest resort on the Garden Route: **Knysna ❽**, founded at the beginning of the 19th century by George Rex, rumoured to be an illegitimate son of George III. Wooded hills, dotted with holiday homes, surround pretty **Knysna Lagoon**, connected to the ocean by a narrow waterway. The mouth of this canal is flanked by two huge sandstone

BELOW:
nature's bounty
sold for a song.

KNYSNA'S ELEPHANTS

Two hundred years ago, great herds of elephants roamed the southern Cape. Today, due to ruthless hunting, there is thought to be only one left, hidden in the secretive dark-green depths of the forests around Knysna. The lone beast – a cow – has adapted successfully to forest conditions. Although she belongs to the same species as the savannah elephants, her habits and lifestyle are now thought to be more similar to the elephants found in the equatorial forests of Central Africa. Attempts have been made to build up the herd again, most recently in 1994, when three young elephants from the Kruger National Park were introduced into the forest. Unfortunately, the Knysna elephant fled in fear, only to be pursued by the newcomers in a chase which went on for several days and resulted in the death of one of the youngsters from pneumonia brought on by stress. The other two were eventually relocated to Shamwari Game Reserve outside Port Elizabeth after ravaging local farmland. Although it's unlikely that you'll catch a glimpse of the lone ranger herself, the Elephant Walk from Diepwalle Forestry Station (off the R339; open daily; entrance charge) offers the chance to spot another forest giant – a 46-metre (150-ft) high yellowwood known as the King Edward VII tree, which has a 9.5-metre (30-ft) circumference.

Map on page 194

cliffs known as **The Heads**, and it is thanks to them that Knysna never became an important harbour town: access by sea was simply too dangerous. The eastern cliff is the only one open to cars (along George Rex Drive), and the view from the top is fantastic. The western cliff can only be reached by taking a ferry excursion across the lagoon mouth to the private **Featherbed Nature Reserve** (daily excursions; tel: 044-382 1693/7; www.knysnafeatherbed.com), home to the shy blue duiker, various birds, and the endangered Knysna seahorse.

A good place for crafts, pottery and woven fabrics is **Thesen House**, a historic town house named after one of Knysna's oldest and most influential families. However, the area is chiefly known for its natural wood products, and especially hardwood furniture. The best-quality products are manufactured by hand by master craftsmen, using yellowwood, dark stinkwood and ironwood judiciously culled from the surrounding forests. A popular photo opportunity – although it's rather surreal for Africa – is the **Holy Trinity Church** in the leafy settlement of Belvidere, which looks very much like an 11th-century Norman implant. By way of contrast, the last week of May is when Knysna hosts a four-day gay, lesbian, transsexual and transgender carnival called the Pink Loerie Mardi Gras, the only celebration of this sort in the African continent.

Like Mossel Bay, Knysna is a popular base for a wide range of marine and other adventure activities, including scuba diving, sailing, hiking, mountain biking, canoe trips upriver, whale and dolphin safaris, and abseiling down the Knysna Heads. The excellent **tourism office** on Main Road (tel: 044-382 5510) can provide up-to-date details of costs and booking contacts. There are also several excellent overnight hikes through the surrounding

BELOW: the Holy Trinity Church at Belvidere, Knysna.

The strong cheek teeth of the Cape clawless otter make short work of bones and crab shells.

hills, details of which can be obtained from the Department of Forestry office, also on Main Road. More sedately, don't leave Knysna without sampling the frothy produce of the legendary **Mitchell's Brewery** on Arend Street (Mon–Fri 8am–5pm, Sat 9am–1pm; tel: 044-382 4685; www.mitchellsknysna brewery.com) or the sumptuous oysters that are served fresh from the lagoon at several dock-side restaurants.

Thus fortified, you'll be ready to visit **Plettenberg Bay ❾**, South Africa's most up-market seaside resort, 32 km (20 miles) east of Knysna. Although the town lacks Knysna's charm, the perfectly rounded Baia Formosa (Beautiful Bay) with its golden beaches has long been a favourite with holidaymakers. Sadly, a hideous multistorey hotel, the Beacon Isle, now dominates Plettenberg Bay's beach front from its rocky promontory. A better option for those who like their beaches relatively unspoilt is the lengthy **Keurboomstrand**, which is ten minutes' drive to the east near the Keurbooms River mouth. During the Christmas holidays, "Plett" is extremely popular, but out of season the place is often surprisingly quiet.

Nature reserves

A bracing day hike leads through the **Robberg Nature Reserve** (daily 7am–6pm; entrance charge) some 9 km (5 miles) south of Plettenberg Bay. The centrepiece of the reserve is the Robberg Peninsula, whose dramatic windswept cliffs rise almost vertically from the choppy blue sea, interspersed by several small sandy coves. The full circle around the peninsula covers about 11 decidedly undulating kilometres (7 miles), but shorter variations are available. As the peninsula's name suggests (Robberg translates as Seal Mountain), it hosts an impressive colony of

Cape fur seals – along with marine birds such as the African black oyster-catcher. Look out, too, for the whales and dolphins that pass by seasonally.

Another scenic gem is the **Keurbooms River Nature Reserve** (open daily; entrance charge; tel: 044-533 2125; www.plettenbergbay.co.za), the entrance to which lies along the N2 some 7 km (4 miles) east of Plettenberg Bay's town centre, immediately before it crosses a bridge across the forest-fringed Keurbooms River. Ferry cruises run along the river three times daily, and it's also possible to follow a hiking trail into the spectacular wooded gorge that rises from its banks. But for those with the time and energy, there is no more satisfying way to explore this reserve than on the overnight canoe trail that terminates at a rustic river-side hut set deep in the forested gorge. The tourist office in the town centre can provide full details of this and other local attractions.

About 10 km (6 miles) west of Plettenberg Bay on the Knysna Road, the **Knysna Elephant Park** does not – as might be expected – protect the few survivors of the wild herds that once roamed these coastal forests *(see box Knysna's Elephants, page 198)*, but instead offers the opportunity to touch and feed a few semi-domesticated tuskers relocated from elsewhere in the country (scheduled tours daily 8.30am–4.30pm; entrance charge; tel: 044-532 7732).

Equally contrived, but great fun all the same, is the private primate sanctuary called **Monkeyland** (daily 8am–5pm; guided tours available hourly; tel: 044-534 8906; www.monkeyland.co.za), which lies 16 km (10 miles) east of Plettenberg Bay shortly before the turn-off to **Nature's Valley** ❿. The forested sanctuary hosts about 200 monkeys belonging to a dozen species, ranging from the South American spider monkey to various Madagascan lemurs, which were rescued from domestic captivity. A visit can be combined with the neighbour-

Map on page 194

BELOW AND LEFT:
the coastline along
the Garden Route
has many moods.

ing **Birds of Eden**, where a 1-km (⅗-mile) walkway and suspension bridge leads through a huge free-flight aviary. All these places are open daily, offer guided tours, and have an entrance charge.

Tsitsikamma National Park

From Plettenberg Bay you can take either the N2 toll road that cuts a fairly straight path through forests and across the high coastal plain, or the byway (the R102) winding downwards past the Grootrivier and Bloukrans gorges and through sleepy Nature's Valley on the western boundary of the **Tsitsikamma National Park ⓫** (daily; entrance charge). One of the Garden Route's best-kept secrets, Nature's Valley is a tiny forested village overlooking a wonderfully isolated beach that remains practically undeveloped for tourism – as a result, there are few more attractive places to pitch a tent than at the magical national park camp site on the edge of town.

Those who take the back road will be rewarded by the experience of sinking deep down into the forest's cool microclimate. Beneath the giant yellowwoods, the shaded floor is thick with proteas, arum lilies and watsonia; vividly coloured loerie birds dart through the dense forest canopy, while shy duiker and bushbuck hide in the undergrowth below. Back on the N2, the single-span arch concrete bridges over the Storms, Groot and Bloukrans rivers had the distinction – when they were each newly completed – of being the biggest such structures in the world. The **Bloukrans Bridge**, suspended 215 metres (710 ft) above the river for which it is named, is also the site of the world's highest bungee jump.

Either option – the N2 or the R102 – will bring you to the turn-off to **Storms River Mouth**, with its forests and unspoilt, rocky shore, its log cabins and

BELOW: fishing at Tsitsikamma.

intimidating suspension bridge at the eastern border of the beautiful Tsitsikamma National Park. Stretching for about 35 km (20 miles) between Nature's Valley and Stormsrivier, this scenic park protects a varied ecosystem of coastal lagoons, dunes, cliffs, beaches and coral reefs, complemented by an interior of steep wooded ravines thick with ancient yellowwood trees that grow up to 50 metres (164 ft) high.

Map on page 194

Storms River

The well-run **Storms River Rest Camp**, which lies within the national park 1.5 km (1 mile) west of the river mouth, has chalet accommodation and camp sites, and forms a good base for swimming, snorkelling and hiking. The short walk from the rest camp to the suspension bridge across the river mouth is a must-do – look out for seals below the bridge – and if you're feeling ambitious you could ascend from there to a viewpoint high on the surrounding cliffs. Another justifiably popular day hike effectively follows what would be the first day of the longer Otter Trail along the rocky coast for about 4 km (2½ miles) to the base of a small waterfall.

For dedicated hikers, the **Otter Trail**, which follows the coast all the way from Stormsrivier to Nature's Valley, is renowned as one the most scenic and challenging hikes in South Africa. The 42.5-km (27-mile) trek takes five days (with one night at each of four overnight huts positioned along the way) and there's a lot to do and see – 11 rivers to cross, for example, and sometimes you will need to swim rather than just wade. Only 12 people are allowed to start the trail daily, and because it is so popular it should be booked through SANParks up to 13 months in advance (tel: 012-426 5111). ❑

BELOW: the beach offers more relaxed pleasures.

MARVELS OF THE FLORAL KINGDOM

Home to more than 24,000 species – one-tenth of all known flowering plants – South Africa's flora is amongst the richest and most varied in the world

From the weird succulents of the dry Kalahari to the brilliantly coloured blossoms which transform Namaqualand's semi-desert plains in the spring, South Africa is impressively endowed with some spectacular plant life. Most enticing of all for botanists, gardeners and walkers alike is the slender strip of Cape coastline stretching inland in the west as far as Clanwilliam, around the peninsula and then east as far as Port Elizabeth. Dominated by a unique heathland vegetation known as *fynbos* (Afrikaans for "fine bush"), this area enjoys special status as the smallest of the world's six "Floral Kingdoms", and the one with the richest species diversity.

A THREATENED KINGDOM

Characterised by very small or leathery leaves often protected by hairs, the three most common *fynbos* families are Proteaceae (including the national flower, *Protea cynaroides,* or king protea), Erica-ceae and the reedy Restionaceae. *Fynbos* grows in some extremely diverse habitats – from arid salt marshes and sand dunes to mountain slopes and crags up in the cloud zone – but the best time to see it is the spring (September and October), when the veld blooms into kaleidoscopic colour. Sadly, as many as 1,326 *fynbos* species are on the endangered list, including the lovely snow protea, which only grows above the snow line in the Cederberg and defies cultivation.

◁ **DELICATE BEAUTY**
The Common Watsonia *(Watsonia densiflora)* is one of the jewels of the *fynbos* region. You can see it in flower in late spring (October–November) throughout the southwestern Cape.

◁ **KING OF THE HILLS**
Clusters of majestic *Protea cynaroides* growing wild in the world-famous Botanical Garden at Kirstenbosch, Cape Town. In a lovely setting on the eastern slopes of Table Mountain, Kirstenbosch nurtures over 5,600 indigenous plant species. It's one of the best places in the country to see Cape *fynbos* displayed in its dramatic wild mountain habitat.

▽ **SOUTHERN SHRUBS**
The Cape Floral Kingdom is particularly rich in indigenous heathers – over 600 species, compared to Britain's handful. Characterised by needle-like leaves and pendent, bell-shaped flowers, they make popular garden and pot plants. Look out for this pretty specimen *(Erica versicolor)* on the Robinson Pass, heading over the Outeniqua Mountains from George.

◁ **SACRED CYCADS**
Sacred to the Rain Queen, ruler of the Lobedu people who live near Duiwelskloof in the Northern Province, the Modjadji cycad (*Encephalartos transvenosus*) is a striking feature of the lowveld landscape. These rare plants may reach a height of 13 metres (43 ft), which makes them one of the largest cycad species in the world. Modjadji Nature Reserve has some particularly fine specimens.

◁ **FOREST GIANTS**
Outeniqua yellowwoods *(Podocarpus falcatus)* are the giants of the Knynsa and Tsitsikamma forests, reaching heights of 60 metres (200 ft). All yellowwood species are now protected by law.

STAR ATTRACTION▷
Now exported all over the world (it is, for example, Los Angeles' floral emblem), the spectacular Crane Flower *(Strelitzia reginae)* is indigenous to the Eastern Cape and KwaZulu-Natal.

GREAT BOTANICAL GARDENS

Kirstenbosch *(above and left)* is probably South Africa's most famous garden. Equally rewarding, however, are the seven other national botanical gardens ("NBGs"), strategically located in each of the country's major floral zones.

● Founded in 1946, the plantings in Pretoria's sprawling NBG represent every major type of southern African vegetation. The Garden was declared a National Monument in 1979.

● In the Witwatersrand NBG near Roodepoort, a dramatic waterfall provides a backdrop for more than 500 species of highveld aloes, trees and shrubs.

● The Lowveld NBG on the outskirts of Nelspruit has a spectacular series of waterfalls and river gorges, as well as the country's best outdoor collection of indigenous trees, ferns and rare cycads.

● The tranquil Natal NBG in Pietermaritzburg was originally founded in 1872, and features some superb specimens of imported trees.

● The Karoo NBG near Worcester concentrates on plants from the arid semi-desert areas of the country.

● On the outskirts of Bloemfontein, the Free State NBG specialises in frost and drought-hardy plants.

● The beautiful, secluded Harold Porter NBG at Betty's Bay boasts one of the densest concentrations of *fynbos* in the country.

THE EASTERN CAPE

*Sandy shores and lazy lagoons give way to high, green hills
dotted with thatched huts, sweeping down to jagged
cliffs – this is the traditional land of the Xhosa*

Map
on page
208

An amalgamation of the eastern part of the former Cape Province and the apartheid-era homelands of the Transkei and Ciskei, the Eastern Cape is a large and ecologically diverse province whose habitats range from subtropical beaches to the arid scrub of the Karoo Nature Reserve and breezy montane grassland near the Lesotho border. It is the main population centre of the Xhosa people and produced several prominent anti-apartheid leaders, including president Thabo Mbeki and his predecessor Nelson Mandela. In 1820, Algoa Bay, the site of present-day Port Elizabeth, became the first main focal point for English settlement in the Cape, an influence that still permeates nearby towns such as Grahamstown and Port Alfred.

PORT ELIZABETH AND SURROUNDS

Coming from the west, the 160-km (100-mile) trip along the N1 from Storms River to Port Elizabeth is fairly unremarkable and seldom ventures within eyeshot of the coast. That said, no self-respecting surfer would pass up on the short diversion south to the legendary **Jeffrey's Bay**, an otherwise unremarkable resort town regarded by some as possessing the world's most perfect waves. Also of interest is the **Shell Museum** (Mon–Sat 9am–4pm; donation expected; tel: 042-293 2923) next to the tourist information office, and the relatively unspoilt coastline protected within the more southerly **Cape St Francis Nature Reserve**, connected to Jeffrey's Bay by a dirt road and a walking trail from where dolphins are quite often observed.

The fifth-largest city in the country, **Port Elizabeth ❶** is an important harbour town and industrial centre, long associated with the country's motor industry, the modern decline of which is mirrored by the city's general aura of having seen better days. Somewhat confusingly, greater Port Elizabeth, which also embraces the smaller towns of Uitenhage and Despatch immediately inland, is now known officially as Nelson Mandela Bay, but locals still refer to the three towns – which have quite separate identities – by their individual names.

Few would go out of their way to visit Port Elizabeth – or PE, as it's more often called – but those who do generally find that it lives up to its epithet of "the friendly city" and offers plenty of worthwhile sites and activities. In the city centre, the 5-km (3-mile) long **Donkin Heritage Trail** begins at the Market Place and imposing City Hall (1858), and leads to several other historic buildings including Fort Frederick (1799) and a restored and authentically furnished settlers cottage (1827) at the 7 Castle Hill Museum.

About 2 km (1½ miles) south of the city centre, in the suburb of Humewood, **Kings Beach** is popular with swimmers and surfers alike, while the nearby

LEFT: a Xhosa woman surveys the scene.
BELOW: Addo Elephant National Park.

Bayworld complex (daily 9am–4.30pm; dolphin presentations 11am and 3pm; entrance charge; tel: 041-584 0650) combines an excellent anthropological and natural history museum with an aquarium and snake park. Recommended for train enthusiasts is the **Apple Express** (Saturdays only; tel: 041-583 2030), a recreational steam-train excursion to Thornhill along a track that was built in 1906 and crosses the world's highest narrow-gauge bridge.

Port Elizabeth began life as a military outpost to guard the first British settlers arriving in 1820. The then Cape governor, Sir Rufane Donkin, named it after his wife.

Addo Elephant National Park

You may have failed to spot elephants in Knysna, but you'll not miss the **Addo Elephant National Park ❷** (daily 7am–7pm; entrance charge; tel: 042-233 8600), which lies about 50 km (30 miles) northeast of PE on the R335. Elephants used to be plentiful around here, but ivory hunters and farmers had shot out most of the herds by 1918, when World War I veteran Major P.J. Pretorius – nicknamed Jungle Man – killed more than 100 individuals at the invitation of Uitenhage Town Council. In 1931, the surviving 11 animals were rounded up into the newly gazetted national park, but they still made regular forays onto surrounding farms to supplement their leafy diet with oranges and other crops until 1954, when a fence of steel ropes was constructed to pen them in.

By 1968, the number of elephants in Addo had increased to 50, and ten years later it topped the century mark. Today, more than 450 remarkably relaxed pachyderms roam the park, which must surely rank as one of Africa's great elephant-watching destinations. Eight bull tuskers were recently relocated from the Kruger Park to broaden a gene pool that bottlenecked through a mere six sexually active individuals in the 1930s. Addo also contains substantial numbers of rhinoceros, buffalo, kudu, jackal, ground squirrel and

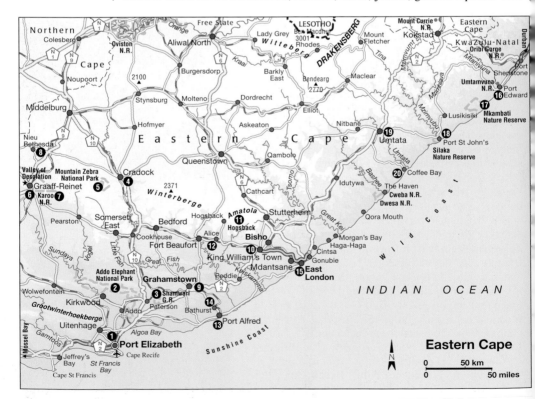

Map
on page
208

endemic birds such as the colourful bokmakierie and handsome jackal buzzard – not to mention lions, which were reintroduced in 2003.

In 1997, SANParks announced a proposal to create the Greater Addo Elephant National Park linking the arid Karoo to the Indian Ocean coastline east of Port Elizabeth. In only seven years, the core 200-sq. km (78-sq. mile) national park had been extended to cover 12,500 sq. km (4,880 sq. miles) and includes five of South Africa's seven terrestrial biomes, an ecological diversity which possibly exceeds that of any other African conservation area. From the visitor's perspective, Greater Addo remains something of a work in progress – the offshore islands with their immense bird and seal colonies are currently inaccessible to tourists, while the former **Zuurberg National Park** and **Woody Cape Nature Reserve** can only be explored on hiking trails – but this space is well worth watching.

Several private reserves in this region offer game viewing, most famously the private – and pricey – **Shamwari Game Reserve ❸** (access to overnight guests only; tel: 042-203 1111), 72 km (45 miles) northeast of Port Elizabeth. More than 26 species of game have been reintroduced here, including elephant, rhino, lion, leopard, buffalo, giraffe and zebra. Don't expect a classic safari amid thorny bushveld, however: these green hills and valleys with their streams and rivers seem almost too idyllic for a safari park, and the accommodation – especially in the most elegant of the four lodges, an Edwardian manor house – is actually very reminiscent of England.

CRADOCK AND GRAAFF-REINET

About 150 km (90 miles) inland of Addo lies the town of **Cradock ❹**, founded in 1813 on the upper reaches of the Great Fish River as a frontier post to defend

BELOW:
Port Elizabeth.

the region against Xhosa attacks. Like most other rural towns in South Africa, the stark monumental steeples of the Dutch Reformed church buildings are among its most notable features. Often, these were built as imitations of European churches – in Cradock, the model for the Moederkerk was St Martin-in-the-Fields in London's Trafalgar Square.

The little town was first made famous by the writer Olive Schreiner (1855–1920), whose controversial 1883 novel *The Story of an African Farm*, was a powerful attack on the arrogant and racist attitudes of her fellow whites – during the Boer War she was interned for her views. The house in Cross Street in which she lived between 1867 and 1870 has since been turned into a museum (open Mon–Fri; entrance charge). Also of interest are the **Dutch Reformed Church** built in 1868, the series of 14 restored Victorian houses in **Market Street**, and the local history museum housed in a former parsonage that dates to 1849.

With the mountain zebra dismissed by one cabinet minister as just "donkeys in football jerseys", it took a fight by conservationists before they were granted sanctuary in their own park.

Mountain Zebra National Park

The region's main attraction, the **Mountain Zebra National Park ❺** (sunrise to sunset daily; entrance charge; tel: 048-881 2427), lies 15 km (9 miles) west of town. Some 6,600 hectares (16,300 acres) in size, the park was established in 1937 to protect the Cape mountain zebra – it was feared that it might go the way of its half-horse, half-zebra cousin the quagga, which became extinct when the last individual died in a zoo in 1883. Through a careful programme of conservation and breeding the park now accommodates about 200 mountain zebras, and smaller herds have been transferred to other parks in the province. It is also home to springbok, bontebok, kudu, caracal, jackal and baboon. A checklist of 200 bird species includes endemics such as orange-breasted rockjumper, Layard's titbabbler and ground woodpecker, while the majestic black eagle can sometimes be seen soaring in the sky above. Finally, don't be too surprised if you do happen to see something resembling a quagga here – in 1987, DNA studies on museum specimens determined that the quagga had been a race of plains zebra, and a project is currently underway to recreate it through selective breeding of an introduced herd of individuals with unstriped hindquarters.

BELOW:
the now protected mountain zebra.

The choice of accommodation on offer includes the Victorian **Doornhoek Guest House**, built in 1836 and today a national monument. Roaring fires are an added attraction here – winters in this part of the Karoo are sometimes cold enough for snow to fall. Walkers with three days to spare can follow the 31-km (19-mile) **Mountain Zebra Trail**, leading through the Fonteinkloof and Grootkloof gorges and then up Banks Mountain, from where there is a magnificent view of Compass Mountain, the highest peak in the Sneeuberg.

Graaf-Reinet

Continue another 120 km (75 miles) west of Cradock, and you'll reach **Graaff-Reinet ❻**, the gem of the Karoo, enclosed by a bend in the Sundays River. Founded in 1786 (making it the fourth-oldest town in the country), it soon became a hub of political turbulence. In 1795, fed up with colonial rule and inspired by the example of the French Revolution, the inhabitants chased the government representative from town and declared an independent – albeit short-lived – republic. Despite all this, Graaff-Reinet looks today like the very model of good order, and differs markedly from the many other provincial towns which clearly grew up without any overall plan.

With the possible exception of Stellenbosch, no other town in South Africa has retained Graaff-Reinet's pervasive Cape Dutch architectural character. More than 200 of its buildings have been declared national monuments, including an entire street – **Stretch's Court** – now restored to its original 18th-century splendour. The splendid **Dutch Reformed Church**, reputedly modelled on Salisbury Cathedral in England, and the old parsonage – once occupied by one of the country's most noted churchmen, Dr Andrew Murray – have both been converted into museums. In the gardens of the parsonage, now called **Reinet House** (daily 9am–noon, Mon–Fri 2–5pm also; entrance charge; tel: 049-892 3801), grows the largest living grapevine in the world. With a girth of 2.4 metres (8 ft) and a height of 1.5 metres (5 ft), it covers an area of 124 sq. metres (1,335 sq. ft) – and still bears fruit. **The Drostdy** in Church Street, completed in 1806, originally served as the seat of the local magistrate, but at the end of the 19th century it was converted into a hotel. You can no longer spend the night in the Drostdy itself, but you can stay in one of the cottages behind it.

Palaeontologists consider the Karoo basin and its unbroken fossil record one of the world's great natural wonders. An extensive private collection of fossils – some exposed after an entombment of up to 230 million years – can be seen in the **Old Library** (daily 8am–12.30pm, Mon–Fri 2–5pm also; entrance charge; tel: 049-892 3801), situated on the corner of Church and Somerset streets. Just outside town is a statue of Andries Pretorius, the Voortrekker leader who lived

Map on page 208

BELOW:
mailing a letter
from Graaf-Reinet.

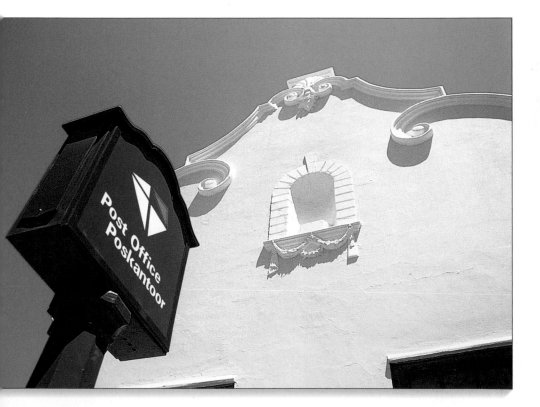

in Graaff-Reinet before joining the Great Trek and leading his people to victory against the Zulus in the Battle of Blood River *(see pages 32 and 248)*.

About 14 km (9 miles) west of town and definitely worth the detour is the **Valley of Desolation**, part of the **Karoo Nature Reserve** ❼ (open sunrise to sunset daily; free) and known for its bizarre rock formations of domes and pinnacles, or dolerites, with heights reaching more than 120 metres (393 ft). On the outskirts of town there's a walking trail around the **Van Ryneveld Dam**, from which kudu and other typical Karoo antelope are often seen. Back in the town centre, the **Obesa Nursery**, named after a euphorbia species endemic to the vicinity of Graaff-Reinet, hosts a world-class succulent collection that includes several rare and endangered species.

From Graaff-Reinet, take the northbound N9 for Middelburg, then turn off after some 27 km (17 miles) for the village of **Nieu-Bethesda** ❽. In River Street here you will find the eerie, extraordinary **Owl House** (daily 9am–5pm; entrance charge; tel: 049-841 1603; www.owlhouse.co.za), which until quite recently was the private home of a reclusive and enigmatic artist, Helen Martins. Working chiefly at night, away from the prying eyes of the neighbours, she covered almost the whole interior of her house – walls, ceilings and some of the furniture – in crushed glass, mixed with cement. Flamboyant murals of suns, moons and stars are emblazoned on the ceilings, while enormous mirrors in all the rooms reflect the glittering whole. Outside, in the vegetable garden, a haphazard jumble of over 300 cement sculptures (camels, peackocks, sun-worshippers and hooded shepherds) turn their faces to the east, while cement guardian owls glare balefully from the garden fence and from perches on the veranda. It's an extraordinary piece of Outsider Art, although sadly Miss Martins didn't live to see it recognised as such – she committed suicide by drinking caustic soda in 1976.

BELOW: the devil fire fish, an exotic import to South African shores.

PORT ELIZABETH TO EAST LONDON

Two roughly equidistant road routes connect Port Elizabeth to the Eastern Cape's other major city, the oceanic port of East London, which lies 250 km (150 miles) to the northeast as the crow flies. The quicker of these roads is the N2 through historic Grahamstown and King William's Town, while the more scenic option is the coastal R72 via Port Alfred – and those who want the best of both worlds can cut between Grahamstown and Port Alfred using the R67 through Bathurst.

Grahamstown

The university town of **Grahamstown** ❾, located some 130 km (80 miles) east of Port Elizabeth, is certainly worth a visit. Founded in 1812 by a British soldier, Colonel John Graham, the town is steeped in British colonial history, with whitewashed Georgian and Victorian buildings in plentiful supply – **Merriman House** on Market Street, the home of a former bishop of Grahamstown (and where the ill-fated General Gordon of Khartoum spent some nights) is typical. A total of 40 churches are dotted around the town, leading to one of its nicknames: City of the Saints.

Other sightseeing includes the **Observatory Museum** (Mon–Sat 9.30am–1pm, Mon–Fri 2–5pm; entrance charge; tel: 046-622 2312) with its bizarre camera obscura, the **Albany Museum** (good rock-art displays) and the **History Museum** (both open Mon–Fri 9am–1pm, daily 2–5pm; entrance charge; tel: 046-622 2312). From the 1820 Settlers National Monument on Gunfire Hill, there is a magnificent view down over Grahamstown's flock of steeples. But the town is best known for the National Arts Festival, the largest and most diverse event of its type in South Africa, starting in early July to coincide with campus holidays.

Map on page 208

King William's Town

After Grahamstown, **King William's Town ⑩**, 110 km (66 miles) further east along the N2, comes across as somewhat undistinguished. The centre of a thriving agricultural area, "King" – as it is commonly known among its residents – was founded by the London Missionary Society in 1825 and later became the capital of the colony of British Kaffraria. A stopover should include a visit to the **Amathole Museum** (Mon–Fri 9am–1pm, 1.45–4.30pm, Sat 10am–12.30pm; entrance charge; tel: 043-642 4506). Here, you can view displays devoted to the region's British and German settlers and the culture of the Xhosa and Khoisan people.

An abakwetha. According to Xhosa tribal custom, teenage boys must undergo a circumcision ritual to attain manhood. During this period, the youth's face and body is daubed with clay.

The museum's most famous exhibit is undoubtedly Huberta the stuffed hippo. Huberta first captured the country's imagination in 1928, when she took off from Zululand on a 2,000-km (1,200-mile) journey southwards. On her way, she became the most fêted hippo in history, pursued by photographers, journalists and adoring crowds alike. She popped up in cities and towns, wandering through the busy streets of Durban and gatecrashing plush parties. Tragically, three years later, she was shot by hunters while taking a dip in the Keiskamma River near King William's Town. Her remains were recovered and today take pride of place in the museum.

BELOW: traditional Xhosa village.

King William's Town lies at the junction of several roads running northward into the thickly forested **Amathole Mountains**, a popular destination with ramblers. If you're serious about your hiking, and have the time, the tough but rewarding six-day, 105-km (65-mile) **Amathole Hiking Trail** begins in **Stutterheim**, on the N6 some 40 km (24 miles) north of King William's Town, and terminates at the idyllic village of Hogsback. (For more information and to book accommodation in the overnight huts, contact the Keiskamma Ecotourism Network in King William's Town, tel: 043-642 2571.)

The Katberg escarpment is the highest point on the Amatola Range, and in winter its peaks are often capped with snow. But it is the **Hogsback ⑪** that makes the Amatola really memorable. Here, ferns cling to the lichened trunks of ancient yellowwoods and line the banks of rushing streams; blackberries, other wild berries and vines clamber over the forest flora. It's a popular birding site, too, with more than 220 species recorded, including forest specialists such as the crowned eagle, black sparrowhawk, emerald cuckoo, Knysna woodpecker and Cape parrot. Blue monkey and bushbuck are the most frequently seen wild mammals. Booklets outlining marked trails through the forests are available from local hotels.

Immediately to the west of the Hogsback (about 25 km/15 miles) lies **Alice ⓬**, named after the daughter of Queen Victoria. Scarcely more than a village, Alice looks distinctly down on its luck these days, although the **University of Fort Hare** on the outskirts of town is definitely worth a stop. Established in 1916 as the country's first tertiary educational institution for blacks, it counts among its alumni some of the country's most influential political and intellectual leaders, including Nelson Mandela. The main reason to visit, however, is the **De Beers Art Gallery** (Cultural Studies Centre; open daily in theory, but ring to confirm an appointment; tel: 040-602 2269), which houses one of the country's best collections of contemporary art.

Back in Stutterheim, take the R61 – which branches off outside the town and leads back onto the N2 at Umtata – for a rewarding detour towards the Lesotho border and the southern extension of the Drakensberg that's known locally as the **Witteberg** (White Mountains) because it receives snowfall with reasonable regularity.

Steam-train enthusiasts should not miss the ride between **Barkly East** and **Lady Grey**; at one point in the 64-km (39-mile) journey the train climbs a breathtakingly steep gradient in just eight loops. A short drive east of Barkly East, the remote but pretty montane settlement of **Rhodes** lies close to the 3,001-metre (9,990-ft) **Mount Ben Macdhui** – it's also South Africa's one and only ski resort, albeit active only in midwinter. Many of the caves up in the mountains here are also bright with San paintings, some of which are thought to be as much as 2,000 years old; a good spot for rock art is **Maclear**, which also lies close to an amazing set of fossilised dinosaur footprints. There are numerous walks, sparkling streams and waterfalls in the **Malekgonyane Nature Reserve** on the Lesotho

BELOW: the vintage steam train from Barkly East.

Map
on page
208

border, an area that's most beautiful in spring, when the montane grassland is covered in fire lilies, gladioli, red-hot pokers and other wildflowers.

Back on the coast, the small settler town of **Port Alfred** ⑬ sprawls attractively either side of the Kowie River mouth almost exactly halfway between Port Elizabeth and East London. The beach here offers good swimming and surfing conditions, while other local attractions include scuba diving along a nearby reef, a superb golf course, mountain-bike trails and the wonderful overnight canoe trail along the Kowie River. Further afield, some 53 km (33 miles) back towards Port Elizabeth, the former **Woody Cape Forest Reserve** – now incorporated into the Addo Elephant National Park *(see page 208)*– is the site of a wonderful two-day hiking trail passing through an extensive dune field as well as lush coastal forest.

If you're thinking of cutting between the R72 and N2, the main settlement along the R67 is **Bathurst** ⑭, a sleepy 1820 settler village whose oh-so-English atmosphere – the only hotel is called the Pig & Whistle – is subverted somewhat by the decidedly tropical nature of the pineapples that form the main local crop. There are some great walks in the area, in particular one that leads 5 km (3 miles) out of town into the **Waters Meeting Nature Reserve** and to a magnificent view over a horseshoe bend in the Kowie River.

EAST LONDON

Well-tended golf courses, hospitable people and some fine 19th-century architecture make the city of **East London** ⑮ a pleasant enough place to visit. Situated at the mouth of Buffalo River, it is the only river port in the country. The two most popular bathing spots are **Orient** and **Eastern** beaches – both

BELOW: the rock art here dates back over 2,000 years.

suitable for children – while Nahoon Beach is an excellent surfing spot with vast areas of sanded wilderness. The harbour here has a miniature version of Cape Town's V&A Waterfront – **Latimers Landing**, complete with shops, restaurants, bars, theatres and even a weekend flea market.

Sadly, many of East London's fine Victorian buildings are being systematically demolished; one honourable survivor is the imposing **City Hall**, built in honour of Queen Victoria's diamond jubilee. Its whitewashed oriel windows and gables still contrast appealingly with its red-brick walls and bell tower. Equally attractive is the Edwardian **Anne Bryant Art Gallery** (Mon–Fri 9.30am–5pm, Sat 9.30am–noon; free; tel: 043-722 4044), a former private residence that today houses a collection of South African art dating from 1880 to the present.

One of the quirkiest natural-history collections in South Africa is housed in the **East London Museum** (319 Oxford Street; Mon–Fri 9.30am–5pm, Sat 2.30–5pm, Sun 11am–4pm; entrance charge; tel: 043-743 0686). It's strong on the tribal histories of the Xhosa, but the real highlight is a stuffed and mounted coelacanth, an extraordinary-looking fish with fins like short, stumpy legs. It was thought to have been extinct for 80 million years. This specimen was netted in the nearby Chalumna River in 1938 – a world first.

Gately House (Tues–Thur 10am–5pm, Fri 10am–1pm, Sat and Sun 3–5pm; entrance charge; tel: 043-722 2141), built in 1878 for the mayor of the same name, is an interesting town-house museum furnished with Victorian antiques. And down on the Esplanade, you really can't avoid the monumental **German Settlers Memorial** – it's quite astonishingly ugly. It commemorates the thousands of German-born settlers who arrived here in the second half of the 19th century; several local place names (Hamburg, Potsdam, Berlin) also make it clear how strong their influence was in the region.

BELOW: dramatic rock formations are typical of the Wild Coast.

Also located on the Esplanade, between Orient and Eastern beaches, the **East London Aquarium** (daily 9am–5pm; feeding times 10.30am and 3pm; shows at 11.30am and 3.30pm; entrance charge; tel: 043-705 2637) harbours more than 400 kinds of sea and freshwater creatures, including intricately patterned subtropical fish, sea anemones, squid, sharks, sea turtles, penguins and seals.

The **Queens Park Botanic Garden and Zoo** (daily 9am–5pm; tel: 043-722 1171) lies on a hill between the city centre and the Buffalo River. In the middle of the beautifully laid-out garden with native plants and trees, the zoo has a special children's section. At 2pm, you can accompany the zoo-keepers on their feeding rounds.

The attractive 93-km (57-mile) stretch of coast between East London and the Kei River – formerly the border with the defunct Transkei homeland – is dotted with small low-key resorts but otherwise remains remarkably undeveloped by comparison to, say, the Garden Route. The most accessible resort here is **Gonubie**, whose bush-fringed beach and prolific water birds seem at odds with its location only 10 km (6 miles) east of East London (but quite a bit longer by road due to the intervention of the Buffalo River). Even more remote in feel is the lovely small resort of **Cintsa**, 25 km (15 miles) further east.

THE WILD COAST

Map on page 208

The beautiful Wild Coast was once part of the Transkei, a nominally independent Xhosa homeland under apartheid. In the rural areas here, rolling grass hills are dotted with mud-and-grass huts; women walk around with ochre-painted faces, smoking long-stemmed pipes; old men and children urge on teams of oxen to plough the hill-side fields.

As you drive through the region, you may also spot the occasional teenage boy standing by the roadside naked but for a patterned blanket, his face covered in white clay. He is an *abakwetha*, an initiate, and with a group of his peers he will be spending up to three weeks at a secluded bush lodge while clan elders tutor him in traditional customs *(see page 213, margin tip)*. The process culminates in a circumcision ceremony, after which the youths cleanse themselves in a river and burn all their old possessions. Then they are presented with a new set of clothes in which to return to their villages for a celebratory feast accompanied by traditional dancing. Now begins a year-long intermediary period during which the boys must keep their faces daubed with ochre clay, for according to Xhosa lore, "a boy is merely a dog", and the attainment of manhood is a serious matter. Only when that ends can they step forth into the world of men.

The Wild Coast lies between **Port Edward ⑯** in the north and **Morgan's Bay** in the south, and its wildness is apparent from the moment its deep ravines, steep cliffs and waterfalls come into view. Properly speaking, however, the coast was named after the reefs and rocks that lie some distance offshore which in the past have posed a great danger to shipping. Many of the wrecks submerged around here have still not been thoroughly explored; the vessels issue quite a challenge to divers.

BELOW: it takes two weeks to hike the Wild Coast trail.

Diving and dolphins

The best-known wreck is the **Grosvenor**, a fully laden British treasure ship which came to grief on a stormy night in 1782 off the Pondoland coast. Rumours that the cargo included the glorious Peacock Throne looted from the kings of Persia have sparked off numerous attempts to recover the cargo – all of which have so far come to naught in the restless Wild Coast sea. Ironically, apart from eight cannons salvaged in 1952, the richest haul taken from the ship was its iron ballast, recovered by the ship's blacksmith, who chose to remain on the coast and settle down with two Mpondo wives.

Between May and November, whales with their newborn calves can often be seen offshore, while dolphins are a year-round attraction. This coast also offers some excellent angling opportunities, from fishing the Indian Ocean for enormous reef fish such as musselcracker, to trying your luck in the rivers and lakes, many of which are full of trout.

Unfortunately, the Wild Coast gained something of a reputation as a crime hotspot following several nasty attacks on tourists during the 1990s. This crime wave seems to have abated, and it's now probably as safe as anywhere in South Africa, though it's best not to camp on lonely beaches, travel at night, or make a conspicuous display of cameras and other valuables. Visitors might also want to check the current situation with the local tourist office before setting off.

On the nature trail

Port Edward marks the start of the splendid **Wild Coast Hiking Trail**, one of South Africa's best. It takes a full two weeks to hike the 200-km (160-mile) long route as far as Coffee Bay, though the trip can of course be split up into shorter

The little resort of Coffee Bay received its name when a large cargo of coffee beans was washed up at the mouth of the Nenga River after a shipwreck.

BELOW:
mangrove swamps.

Map
on page
208

sections. The southern stretch is the more easy-going and relaxing, thanks to its miles of sandy beaches, while the northern part with its steep cliffs, rivers and ravines is distinctly rugged and difficult. Here, you can walk for days without seeing another human being. To book permits and accommodation in the basic huts spaced at 12-km (8-mile) intervals along the trail, contact the Cape Nature Conservation office in Umtata (tel: 047-531 5290).

Largest and finest of the nature reserves scattered along this coast is the 8,000-hectare (19,750-acre) **Mkambati Nature Reserve** ⓱ (open daily; entrance charge; tel: 037-727 3124), created on the site of an old leper colony about 40 km (25 miles) north of Port St John's. There are two wide estuaries for canoeing; long stretches of deserted, rocky beach; and accommodation in comfortable bungalows between tall shady trees, or in self-catering rondavels right on the seashore. The flora is wonderfully diverse, too, from mangrove swamps to rare species of palm tree growing in a ravine amphitheatre, and numerous species of wild orchid.

If you'd prefer a smaller retreat, there's **Dwesa Nature Reserve** between The Haven and Qora Mouth, a good place to see wildebeest, eland, monkeys and – if you're very lucky – the Cape clawless otter. Stock up before you travel and plan on being totally self-sufficient during your stay, as there are no shops for miles. To book accommodation in either place, contact the Eastern Cape Parks offices in East London (tel: 043-742 4450; www.ecparks.co.za).

After so much rural tranquillity, arriving in **Port St John's** ⓲ is like entering a major metropolis. Here, the mighty Mzimvubu River – the only navigable river on the Wild Coast – has gouged out an impressive portal for itself as it reaches the sea. The town itself, once a thriving colonial-style outpost, saw an exodus of its white population after Transkei independence. Today, it survives in

BELOW: Hole in the Wall, near Coffee Bay.

Map on page 208

somnambulent idleness and indifference. Most of its charm lies in this state of semi-decay, the grand old houses having been abandoned or taken over by new tenants. Not surprisingly, perhaps, it is also home to a flourishing artists' colony.

The R61 now leads back inland for 90 km (56 miles) to **Umtata** ⑲, the dusty, nondescript capital of the former Transkei, which today seems to be little more than a large construction site. Still there – but only just, it seems – are a few historic buildings dating from 1879, the year the town was founded, namely the Bunga (old Parliament) and the Town Hall.

Between Umtata and East London, several sideroads wind their way from the N2 down to the coast. Some of the small resorts they lead to – Cintsa, Cefane and Double Mouth among them – are frequented mainly by local farmers, while **Haga-Haga** and **Morgan's Bay** have grown into sizeable resorts with hotels and holiday homes. Their common factors are their small size and situation off the highways. The locals like it this way; it frees some of the pristine lagoons, sun-drenched beaches, and abundant bird life and fishing resources for their personal enjoyment.

The only surfaced road that branches off this route leads to **Coffee Bay** ⑳ where another dream beach awaits. An 8-km (5-mile) walk south down the beach brings you to the giant rock formation known as Hole in the Wall. In Xhosa, this whaleback island with its huge wave- and river-bored tunnel is known as esiKhaleni, or the place of sound – for reasons obvious to anyone who stands on the pebbly beach and listens to the booming echo funnelling through the 20-metre (65-ft) hole. But visitors should be forewarned: the rock and the pounding seas that surround it are treacherous and many lives have been lost here by the foolhardy. ❑

BELOW: sailors named the Wild Coast for its reputation of wrecking ships.

The Southern Skies

South Africa stretches down from the tropics to about 35 degrees south. Visitors from the northern hemisphere will find all the familiar constellations look upside down here; even the Man in the Moon seems to be standing on his head!

The most easily recognised constellation is Crucis, or the Southern Cross. Astronomers have determined that, thousands of years ago, this bright constellation was visible from most of Europe. Today, it is visible from just south of 30 degrees north latitude. On a clear night, it is a simple matter to find south by using the Southern Cross and two stars called the Pointers, which are nearly always visible from anywhere in South Africa – bearing in mind that although the stars change their position during the night, the pattern always remains the same. In your imagination, draw a line in the sky linking the two stars on the main axis of the Cross, and another at right angles to the Pointers. The point where they intersect is directly above due south.

Take care to distinguish the Southern Cross from the "Diamond Cross" and the "False Cross", lying slightly to the northeast.

The Pointers are the two brightest stars in the constellation of Centaurus. Alpha Centauri, the brighter of the two, is the fourth brightest star of all, and also – at 4.3 light years – the Sun's closest neighbour. Viewed with a small telescope, it resolves rather startlingly into two separate pinpoints of light; viewed with a larger telescope it reveals a third, fainter, companion.

Conveniently, the five brightest stars of the Southern Cross are arranged clockwise in order of apparent brightness: Alpha, Beta, Gamma, Delta and finally Epsilon.

The Cross is also a convenient reference point for the Milky Way's two satellite galaxies, the Large and Small Magellanic Clouds. Again, extend the long axis of the Cross by about seven times. On either side of this line, you'll see what resembles two small clouds,

except that they do not move or change shape. At roughly 200,000 light years away, they are two of our galaxy's closest neighbours, linked to it not only gravitationally, but via a tenuous bridge of hydrogen gas.

The Large Magellanic Cloud (LMC) came into prominence in 1987 as a result of the massive explosion known as Supernova 1987a. A very bright object, known as S Doradus, is prominent in the LMC and is associated with a gaseous nebula known as the Tarantula Nebula, a remnant of a much earlier supernova event.

Near to the Small Magellanic Cloud, you can spot a hazy white patch with the naked eye. With binoculars it is more prominent; a small telescope resolves it into thousands of stars. This is one of two great globular clusters, consisting of 100,000 stars or more, seen clearly only from the Southern Hemisphere. This one is called 47 Tucanae, and its fellow cluster is Omega Centauri.

The Astronomical Observatory at Sutherland in the Karoo is South Africa's best-known astronomical research facility. ❑

RIGHT: to northern visitors, all the familiar constellations look upside down.

KwaZulu-Natal Coast

*East meets west in Durban – a cosmopolitan, holiday
city set in sugar country and on the edge
of a lush subtropical coast*

Maps
on pages
226 & 230

Durban is traditionally South Africa's most popular holiday resort town, thanks to the combination of a seductive subtropical climate (summer temperatures regularly reach 32°C/90°F), alluring beaches, year-round warm seas and excellent facilities – not to mention its relative proximity (about five hours' drive on the nippy N3) to landlocked Gauteng. Durban's bustling beachfront probably hosts South Africa's largest concentration of hotels – unfortunately, many of them of the soulless high-rise variety so beloved of architects in the 1960s and 1970s. As the "Whites Only" signs came down from the beaches in the 1990s, the fan-base of these hotels started to change: Durban is now as popular with black holidaymakers as with its established clientele of white middle-class families from Gauteng.

DURBAN

The site of **Durban ❶** – eThekwini in the local Zulu tongue, meaning place of the sea – was one of the first parts of South Africa to appear on European maps, after the Portuguese navigator Vasco da Gama landed there on Christmas Day 1497 and christened it Terra do Natal. The name Port Natal was still in use in 1823, when a party of British traders led by Henry Fynn founded a trading post close to where the city hall stands today, but 12 years later the fledgling city was renamed in honour of the then Governor of the British Cape Colony, Sir Benjamin D'Urban.

With a population of more than 3 million, Durban is South Africa's third-largest city, yet it has never been afforded so much as the status of provincial capital. It is also the biggest and busiest port anywhere on the continent, despite its early development having been hampered by a shallow, narrow entrance that caused some 65 shipwrecks prior to 1895, when dredgers were imported from Europe to remove almost 10 million tonnes of sand.

A distinctive feature of Durban is its large community of Indian people – around one million strong, of which 70 percent are Hindu, 20 percent Muslim, and the remainder mostly Christian. Descendants of the indentured labourers who arrived in the 1860s to work in the local sugar-cane industry, the Indians of KwaZulu-Natal have largely resisted assimilation into the wider South African society, and they enthusiastically maintain their languages, religions, dress codes and even caste system.

Metropolitan playground

The Durban metropolitan area has the highest population density in the country – a fact that becomes apparent during the peak holiday season, when day-

PRECEDING PAGES:
a lonely stretch of
Eastern Cape coast.
LEFT AND BELOW:
Durban's biggest
attraction is its
outdoor life.

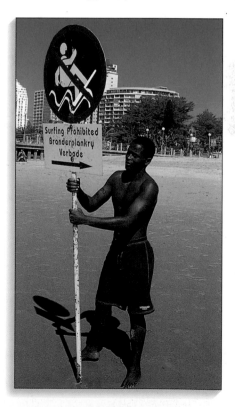

The ornate wrought-iron curlicues of Da Gama Clock, on Victoria Embankment.

trippers from miles around flock to the bathing beaches stretching in a long golden line north from the harbour entrance. **South Beach** is the most densely packed beach in South Africa; **North Beach** and the adjacent **Bay of Plenty** are also crowded but slightly trendier, lined with bars, cafes and restaurants for surfers and posers. All the beaches are protected by shark nets and patrolled by lifeguards.

The heart of the resort area is the pedestrianised **Marine Parade Ⓐ** – a brash, busy playground of pools, fountains, amusement arcades and fast-food kiosks, flanked by innumerable luxurious (and not so luxurious) high-rise hotels and apartment blocks. Most of the major tourist attractions are found here, clustered along the strip known as the **Golden Mile Ⓑ**, which actually extends for about 6 sandy kilometres (4 miles) along the coastline running south from the Umgeni River mouth to the main harbour.

Although perfect for swimming, sunbathing, surfing and other typical beach activities, the Golden Mile is also dotted with several more manufactured places of interest. Children and adults alike will enjoy **Fitzsimons Snake Park Ⓒ** (open daily; entrance charge; tel: 031-337 6456) on North Beach, slithering with 80 species of indigenous snake – venom-milking sessions take place several times daily – as well as crocodiles and iguanas. Also very popular, mystifyingly, is **Mini Town** (Tues–Sun; entrance charge; tel: 031-337 7892), with its miniature replicas of major city landmarks. **Waterworld** (daily 9am–5pm; entrance charge; tel: 031-337 6336), opposite the Country Club Beach, is always packed with thrill-seekers braving the kamikaze water slides and rides. A short walk away at Bay of Plenty beach are the **Amphitheatre Gardens**, a tranquil collection of sunken pools, gardens, lawns and fountains.

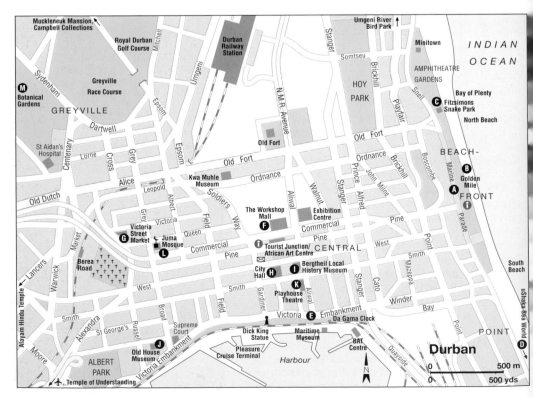

Map on page 226

For anybody with an interest in marine wildlife, a certain highlight of Durban's seafront will be **uShaka Marine World** ❿ (open daily; entrance charge; tel: 031-328 8000; www.ushakamarineworld.co.za), founded opposite New Pier in the 1950s, but reopened in new premises on uShaka Beach, near The Point, in 2004. Claiming to be the fifth-largest aquarium in the world, its Sea World is known for its comprehensive collection of live sharks, and it also puts on daily shows featuring performing dolphins, seals and penguins – the truly bold can hire wetsuits and dive in the tank with them.

Victoria Embankment

Situated at The Point, on the harbour end of the Golden Mile, **Victoria Embankment** ❿ is graced with a number of interesting historical features, including **Da Gama Clock** – erected by the Portuguese Government to mark the 400th anniversary of Da Gama's discovery of Port Natal. To the west of this, also overlooking the harbour, the Dick King Statue commemorates its namesake's heroic 1,000-km (600-mile) 10-day horseback ride to Grahamstown, undertaken in 1842 to fetch reinforcements to relieve the Voortrekker-besieged British fort at Durban.

For a less crowded experience, head further afield, to **The Bluff**, the 4-km (2½-mile) long ridge that hems in the southern shore of the harbour – known in Zulu as *isiBubulungu*, which translates as long bulky thing. Here, **Brighton Beach** is good for body surfing, while at nearby **Treasure Beach** you can explore an unspoilt stretch of tidal pools, with rare corals and marine life. The Wildlife and Conservation Society conducts tours here for a small fee. Otherwise, it's a brief 15-km (10-mile) trip north of the city to the up-market resort of Umhlanga Rocks *(see page 237)*, which has a particularly fine stretch of sand.

Durban forms a good base for adventure activities, which can be arranged with ease through any hotel or hostel, or through tourist kiosks along the Golden Mile. Popular with adrenaline seekers are the white-water rafting day trips that run on a lively stretch of the Tugela River during the rainy season (typically November–April). A number of scuba-diving schools offer one-off dives, as well as PADI and/or NAUI courses that run over several days. As for surfing, the options are endless, but the readily accessible South Beach offers conditions suitable to novices, while the more experienced might want to head to Dairy Beach on the Golden Mile or Cave Rock on The Bluff.

Craft markets and malls

Situated on Gillespie Street, a vast and rather fancifully designed complex called **The Wheel** (daily 9am–5pm; tel: 031-332 4324) contains an excellent selection of shops, as well as cinemas, banks, restaurants and bars, and it's the most convenient of Durban's shopping malls, at least if you're based on the Golden Mile. Larger still, but less accessible for most visitors, **The Pavilion** (open daily; tel: 031-265 0558) lies just off the N3 in the district of Westville. But the most interesting mall is **The**

Dick King's epic 10-day ride to Grahamstown in 1842 – to get help for the British garrison besieged by Boers at Durban's Old Fort – is marked by a statue of him on Victoria Embankment.

BELOW: living it up in one of Durban's many clubs and bars.

TIP

Take an unusual ride along Marine Parade on one of Durban's famous rickshaws, pulled by a flamboyantly costumed Zulu driver.

Workshop **F** located in downtown Commercial Street – this consists of 120 upmarket shops in a converted 1890s railway shed. All these malls offer a few good craft shops along with standard mall-type fare. Of particular note, however, is the **African Art Centre** (Mon–Fri 8.30am–5pm, Sat 9am–1pm; tel: 031-304 7915), a non-profit gallery situated in the old railway station building (an impressive example of Victorian architecture) on Commercial Street opposite The Workshop. **Tourist Junction** – the official tourist information office – is in the same building and can arrange a variety of guided tours and other activities in and around Durban.

By far the most exotic place to shop for curios is **Victoria Street Market G** (open daily; tel: 031-306 4021), west of the city centre near Warwick Avenue, where both Indian and African craft markets jostle for space alongside fresh produce stalls. Here, you can spend a morning haggling for Zulu *assegais* (spears) and carved masks, or Indian silver jewellery and leather-work, as well as stocking up on spices (try the potent Mother-in-Law Masala). If you'd prefer to visit with a guide, numerous companies offer city tours which include this market.

A good bet for quality handicrafts and souvenirs is **Essenwood Park** in Berea, which hosts a busy craft market every Saturday (9am–2pm). Then there's the **Heritage Market** (open daily), with an eclectic range of crafts, antiques and tat housed in a picturesque Victorian building in Hillcrest, 20 minutes' drive from the city centre. Finally, with more than 750 stalls, the **South Plaza Market** (Sun 9am–4pm; tel: 031-301 9900) near The Workshop in the city centre is one of the largest flea markets in the country selling crafts, plants and food.

BELOW: the Durban area is home to the largest Muslim community in the country.

Mosques and museums

Durban has surprisingly few museums; although each sheds some light on the city's social and natural history, few are exceptional. Make time, nonetheless, for the **Natural Science Museum** (Mon–Sat 8.30am–4pm, Sun 11am–4pm; entrance charge; tel: 031-311 2256), which not only has some interesting wildlife displays (it's especially good on local birds), but is housed in the splendidly neo-baroque **City Hall** ⓗ in downtown Smith Street – built in 1910, it's a near-exact copy of Belfast's City Hall. This is also where you'll find the **Durban Art Gallery** (Mon–Sat 8.30am–4pm, Sun 11am–4pm; free; tel: 031-311 2264), which is worth a visit for its excellent collection of Zulu handicrafts.

A few minutes' walk from the City Hall in Aliwal Street is Durban's original Victorian courthouse, now the **Bergtheil Local History Museum** ⓘ (Mon–Fri 8.30am–4.45pm, Sat 8am–noon; free; tel: 031-203 7107); it tells the story of Port Natal's colonial past.

From here, a short drive west along the Old Fort Road brings you to the leafy suburb of **Berea**, which is set on a ridge, and whose Victorian showpieces include the gracious Muckleneuk Mansion. It houses the worthwhile **Campbell Collections** (Tues and Thur am by appointment only; tel: 031-260 1722), a museum of rare and valuable Africana which includes books, maps and manuscripts as well as the Mashu Collection of indigenous Zulu art. Also interesting is the **Old House Museum** ⓙ (Mon–Sat 8.30am–4pm, Sun 11am–4pm; entrance charge; tel: 031-311 2261) at 31 St Andrews Street – a detailed replica of a settler home.

Near the City Hall on the corner of Smith and Acutt streets, the **Playhouse Theatre** ⓚ (tel: 031-369 9555) is the city's major arts venue. It's the place to come for symphony concerts by the now-privatised Natal Philharmonic, as well

BELOW: Zulu basketry is a popular souvenir.

as performances of ballet, drama and opera. Down on Victoria Embankment just a short walk away, the **BAT Centre** arts complex has a concert hall, dance and drama studios, and a particularly nice café overlooking Durban's small crafts harbour. Visit on Friday evenings for the free sundowner jazz concerts.

One of Durban's best-known landmarks is the **Islamic Juma Mosque** , on Grey Street, close to Victoria Street Market. It is the largest place of worship for Muslims in southern Africa, and famous for its enormous golden domes. Further from the city centre, on Somtseu Road, the **Alayam Hindu Temple** (open daily; free) is the largest – and the oldest – building of its type in the country.

Parks and gardens

Durban's lush climate supports a healthy number of green spaces and parks. One of the best is the **Umgeni River Bird Park** (daily 9am–5pm; bird show Tues–Sun 11am and 2pm; entrance charge; tel: 031-579 4600), on Riverside Road on the north bank of the Umgeni River. It contains a marvellous collection of over 1,000 mostly exotic birds, including the rhino hornbill, which sports a 30-cm (1-ft) long multicoloured beak. The adjacent **Beachwood Mangroves Nature Reserve** (entrance through north gate daily; access by appointment only; tel: 031-205 1271) offers the opportunity to explore a mangrove environment from a wooden boardwalk. Look out for the peculiar mudskipper (a type of fish that "walks" on uniquely adapted fins), as well as some interesting indigenous birds such as woolly necked stork, mangrove kingfisher, purple-banded sunbird, both African species of pelican, and various terns, gulls and waders.

Another attractive retreat from the city centre is the 253-hectare (625-acre) **Kenneth Stainbank Nature Reserve** (daily 6.30am–6pm; nominal entrance

BELOW: Orchid House in Durban's Botanical Garden.

KwaZulu-Natal Coast

charge; tel: 031-469 2807), situated in the suburb of Yellowwood Park, where several walking trails lead through a mixture of coastal forest and grassland inhabited by zebra, bushbuck, impala, all three duiker species, vervet monkey and various mongooses. Popular with local bird-watchers is the **Bluff Nature Reserve** (daily 7am–5pm; nominal entrance charge; tel: 031-469 2807), where, a short distance south of the city centre, two strategically located hides overlook a reed-lined pan inhabited by the likes of the striking purple gallinule and malachite kingfisher.

The futuristic marble **Hare Krishna Temple of Understanding** (open daily; free) just south of the city centre in the suburb of Chatsworth, is the largest of its kind in the southern hemisphere, yet its lush ornamental gardens are a tranquil oasis. It also supports a very good vegetarian restaurant, serving snacks as well as large curries. The **Botanical Garden**  (daily 7.30am–5.15pm; free; tel: 031-309 1271) in Berea is a more conventional escape from city heat and dust, but it's worth visiting for the collection of rare cycads and the splendid orchid hothouse – to say nothing of the delicious cream teas.

Guards keep swimmers safe from an unpredictable tide.

Durbs after dark

Nightlife in "Durbs", as it's fondly known, traditionally revolved around the hotels, discos and clubs lining the beach front. More recently, a clutch of trendy bars and restaurants have sprung up in the Florida Road area in the suburb of Morningside, and around Musgrave Road in Berea.

Seafood lovers in search of local specialities like crayfish and tiger prawns should head for the harbour and the King's Battery Development at New Point Waterfront, where a line of derelict warehouses has been revamped as a lively bar-and-restaurant strip. For a taste of hot and spicy Indian fare, head for downtown Smith Street and the five-star Royal Hotel; the swish Ulundi Grill here has long been regarded as one of the best curry houses in town. Aangans in Queen Street, serving authentic, delicious South Indian vegetarian food, is a cheaper alternative.

BELOW: the sunshine coast.

THE SUNSHINE COAST

The Sunshine Coast is the lyrical name given to the lush subtropical coastline that runs parallel to the N2 for about 150 km (90 miles) south of Durban, passing through a string of popular seaside resorts – Umzumbe, Banana Beach, Sea Park and Umtentweni among them – before veering sharply inland near Port Shepstone. Some of the country's loveliest beaches grace this stretch of coast, and the associated resorts – which cater mostly to local holidaymakers as opposed to international tourists – tend to be relatively uncrowded except during school holidays, and to offer better value for money than their counterparts on the more publicised Garden Route.

Some of the best scuba diving in South Africa can be had just 22 km (14 miles) south of Durban, at **Amanzimtoti** ❷. Here, regular boats depart for the **Aliwal Shoal**, a sandbank roughly 5 km (3 miles) from the coast, overgrown with hard and soft coral. At very low tides, passage out to the Shoal may be blocked by a large natural breakwater – but get past

Maps on pages 226 & 230

The wild hibiscus that grows profusely along the road sides between Hibberdene and Port Edward has given the area its name: Hibiscus Coast.

that and you can look forward to exploring natural tunnels, caves and reefs up to 43 metres (140 ft) below the surface. Two wrecks – the *Nebo* and the *Produce* – lie just north of the northernmost tip of the Shoal, known as the Pinnacles. Around the seaward section nicknamed the Outside Edge you could see ragged-tooth shark, along with manta rays and moray eels. Only experienced divers should attempt the Shoal's dive sites, however, as currents can be very strong; beginners would do better to dive at nearby **Umkomaas**, a further 19 km (12 miles) down the coast.

The south coast boasts several excellent golf courses – indeed Selbourne Park and San Lameer are rated among the top 12 in the country. A game at Selbourne Park course can be great fun, thanks to the water obstacles; the fairways at **Scottburgh** also take some getting used to. For a pleasant day trip from Scottburgh, take the R612 heading inland towards Ixopo through sugar and eucalyptus plantations to reach the **Vernon Crookes Nature Reserve ❸** (Oct–Mar daily 6am–6pm, Apr–Sept daily 6am–5pm; entrance charge; tel: 039-974 2222), which has a good range of scenery from river valleys and coastal forest to swampland. This range of habitats supports plenty of wildlife – over 300 species of bird, including the rare African broadbill – as well as zebra, blue wildebeest, eland, impala, reedbuck and nyala. If you're visiting in mid-January, there's a good chance of spotting the beautiful snake lily in flower in the reserve's swamp forest.

THE HIBISCUS COAST

Known collectively as the Hibiscus Coast, the resorts that lie between Hibberdene and Port Edward – notably Margate, Ramsgate and Southbroom – are hugely popular with South Africans looking for a good-value alternative to the likes of Port Elizabeth, Plettenberg Bay and Knysna in the Cape. Accordingly, in December and January, this stretch of coast can get very crowded indeed, but it's usually pretty quiet at other times of year.

Port Shepstone ❹, the largest town on the Hibiscus Coast, retains a pleasant provincial air. There are several very good (and unbelievably cheap) seafood restaurants here – some specialising in oysters – while the local craft shops are a good bet for high-quality Zulu basketware, handcrafted beadwork and pottery. Golfers should definitely try out the local course, high above the rocky coast, while train fans will enjoy a trip on the **Banana Express**, a narrow-gauge railway line with trains that steam their way through banana and sugar-cane plantations on 90-minute journeys to Izotsha, and day trips to **Paddock** four times a week (tel: 039-682 4821).

Scuba divers, meanwhile, should head down to the bustling seaside resort of **Shelley Beach ❺**, about 5 km (3 miles) south of Port Shepstone, where you can arrange to be taken by launch to some excellent shallow-water reef sites – those at Deep Salmon and Bo Boyi reefs are recommended. To see the corals and tropical fish at their best, avoid the summer months – visibility is poor after the seasonal rains. If you're a thrill-seeking diver and fancy getting close to hammerhead and great white sharks, Shelley Beach is also the place to join trips to the deeper waters of Protea Banks, some 9 km (6 miles) offshore.

About 12 km (8 miles) south of Shelley Beach, **Margate ❻** is a sleepy small resort whose idyllic white-sand beach, which stretches for 1.5 km (1 mile) in front of the town centre, is widely regarded to offer the best swimming conditions in the region. Only 3 km (2 miles) north of Margate, a circular two-hour walking trail runs through the **Uvongo Nature Reserve** (open daily; free), which protects a near pristine patch of coastal forest and a diversity of tree, orchid and coastal bird species.

Map
on page
230

Oribi Gorge Nature Reserve

A highlight of this region is the **Oribi Gorge Nature Reserve ❼** (daily 6.30am–7.30pm; entrance charge; tel: 039-679 1644), which lies some 21 km (13 miles) inland of Port Shepstone just off the N2. Here, numerous short hiking trails radiate from an inexpensive cliff-top rest camp into the spectacular euphorbia-studded canyon carved by the Mzimkulwana River, which is also accessible via a steep but surfaced road. The canyon supports a fair bit of wildlife, too – bushbuck and the localised blue monkey lurk in the forested base, black and crowned eagles nest on the cliffs, and gaudy agama lizards scuttle around the rocky rim. The part of the gorge outside of the reserve has recently caught on with adventure-sport enthusiasts; activities on offer include white-water rafting and abseiling alongside a waterfall.

From Oribi Gorge, the N2 continues inland, running roughly parallel to the Eastern Cape border for about 120 km (70 miles) until it eventually crosses into that province near **Kokstad**. Although somewhat unremarkable in itself, Kokstad has an attractive location amid the rolling green southern Drakensberg foothills. The nearby **Mount Currie Nature Reserve ❽** (daily 6am–6pm; entrance charge; tel: 039-727 3844) is a low-key, pedestrian-friendly retreat where ramblers can expect to encounter a bafflement of small grassland antelope (grey rhebok, oribi, common duiker, and mountain and southern reedbuck are all present) as well as crowned, wattled and blue cranes. By contrast, a network of hiking trails in the **Weza Forest Reserve** – which flanks the N2 between Harding and Kokstad – passes through dense indigenous forest inhabited by bushbuck, duiker and a wide variety of forest birds.

Back on the coast, situated south of **Port Edward ❾**, lies a jagged series of steep cliffs and deep bays, most of which can only be reached along tiny unsurfaced footpaths such as those that meander through the remote **Umtamvuna Nature Reserve ❿** (daily 6.30am–5.30pm; entrance charge; tel: 039-313 2383) on the Eastern Cape border. Named after the Umtamvuna River and its wild, forested gorge, this little-known reserve is renowned for its stunning coastal scenery and spring wildflower displays, but it also harbours several rare or endemic plant species, as well as a breeding colony of the endangered Cape vulture and smallish mammals such as bushbuck, red and blue duiker and rock hyrax. ❑

BELOW:
Umzimkulu River.

ZULULAND

*From St Lucia's wild waterways to historical Anglo-Zulu
battlefields, this compelling region lies at the very heart
of the legendary kingdom founded by Shaka Zulu*

Informally but ubiquitously referred to as Zululand, the northern part of KwaZulu-Natal (KZN) Province, with its distinct wilderness flavour, numerous fine game reserves and seemingly endless succession of untrammelled beaches, makes for an immensely rewarding day to self-drive visitors with an interest in natural history. The main road through the region is the N2 running north from Richard's Bay/Empangeni to Pongola, which forms part of the most popular and straightforward route between Durban and the Kruger National Park, as well as a slower but more scenic alternative to the N3 highway connecting Durban to Gauteng.

The Dolphin Coast

Heading from **Durban ❶** towards Zululand, the N2 first follows the so-called Dolphin Coast for roughly 140 km (87 miles) between Umhlanga Rocks and **Richard's Bay**. Like the beaches south of Durban, this stretch of the north coast is studded with seaside resorts, though these are generally more upmarket than their southern counterparts, and the area is less heavily developed. Many resorts here are prettily situated on river estuaries, and despite their popularity with holidaymakers it's still possible to find wide, unspoilt beaches along with sheltered coves fringed with tropical palms, bougainvillea and hibiscus.

As the epithet suggests, bottle-nosed dolphins are plentiful along this stretch of coast, and can be spotted from the beaches all year round. Sharks are also very common; the KZN Sharks Board in Umhlanga Rocks puts on a fascinating audiovisual display on these extraordinary creatures and their importance in the ecological chain in an effort to remove some of the prejudices felt against them (Mon–Thur, five times daily; small charge; tel: 031-566 0400). **Umhlanga Rocks ❷** itself is a middling-sized resort with good shopping, magnificent sandy beaches and great watersports facilities – all very conducive to a long stay. The Zulu trails running along the coast make for excellent hiking, too.

More remote sections of coast can easily be explored by car. Clearly signposted sideroads branching off the N2 lead to a host of pleasant little resorts such as **Tongaat Beach**, **Ballito** and **Shaka's Rock** with its splendid tidal pools – an idyll only briefly interrupted by the unprepossessing industrial sprawl of **Stanger ❸** on the N2. This sizeable sugar-cane processing centre was the site of the Zulu king Shaka's royal kraal and the place where he was murdered in 1828 by his brothers and arch rivals, Umhlangana and Dingane. There's a small park and **Shaka Monument** in Couper Street in the centre of town which commemorates his death *(see page 31)*.

Beyond Stanger the N2 continues to hug the coast, with good swimming and particularly picturesque

PRECEDING PAGES:
heading home.
LEFT:
neck and neck.
BELOW:
Inkatha Freedom
Party members on
the march,
KwaZulu-Natal.

scenery at **Blythdale**, 8 km (5 miles) away, and little Zinkwazi. Some 24 km (16 miles) north of Stanger, Tugela Mouth marked the southern boundary of Zululand prior to the era of expansionism initiated by Shaka and his successors. These days, the southern bank of the Tugela Mouth is protected within the **Harold Johnson Nature Reserve** ❹ (daily 6am–6pm ; entrance charge; tel: 032-486 1574). With its forested dunes and cliffs overlooking the sea, this is a nice place for a picnic; trails lead off from the main car park to the reserve's various historical sites, most of which are connected to the Anglo–Zulu war of 1879.

At Umgungundhlovu just across the river, the R68 leads off to Vryheid, the start of the Battlefield Route *(see page 247)*. For now, we continue along the N2 through the industrial centre of **Empangeni** and then on to the equally ugly **Richard's Bay** ❺, some 20 km (12 miles) further east down a clearly marked turn-off. Set at the mouth of the Mhlatuze River, this busy port shifts vast quantities of coal mined in the highveld town of Witbank, and transported here on a seemingly endless series of trains. There's not much to see in either of these towns, but their tourist facilities are good and as such they are useful jumping-off points for exploring the game parks and resorts further north.

For a break from the grime and grit, head for the **Umlalazi Nature Reserve** ❻ (daily 5am–10pm; entrance charge; tel: 035-340 1836) bordering the small resort town of Mtunzini some 50 km (30 miles) south of Richard's Bay. Set on a near-perfect beach, this suburban reserve protects a remarkable habitat diversity within its small area, attested to by a checklist of more than 300 bird species. The avian highlight of Umlalazi is the country's only breeding population of the striking palmnut vulture, which inhabits a raffia palm swamp that can be explored on a boardwalk. A trio of walking trails twist

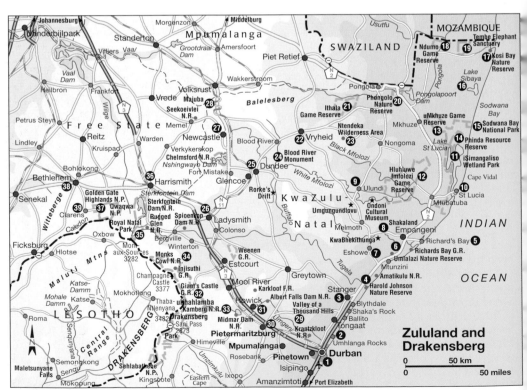

Map on page 238

along the banks of a lagoon, across dunes, and into a mangrove swamp where mudskippers and hermit crabs scuttle around the mud and the localised mangrove kingfisher reveals its presence with a trademark high trilling call.

Eshowe and the Zulu heartland

Offering some respite from the coastal humidity in midsummer, the cosy small town of **Eshowe** ❼ is set at an altitude of 500 metres (1,650 ft) among lushly forested hills along the R66, just 25 km (15 miles) inland of the N2. Bordering the town centre, the lovely **Dhlinza Forest Reserve** (daily; free) is probably the most accessible patch of mistbelt forest in the country, and the quiet paths that run through it are often crossed by the shy blue duiker. The Dhlinza Aerial Boardwalk runs for 125 metres (415 ft) through the canopy, culminating in a 29-metre (96-ft) high tower that affords a grandstand view over the forest to the Indian Ocean, and provides a great opportunity to see localised forest birds such as Delegorgue's pigeon, spotted thrush, grey cuckoo-shrike and olive woodpecker. Easily visited on foot in combination with the forest, the informative little **Zululand Historical Museum** (open daily; nominal charge) is housed in Fort Nongqai, built by the British in 1883.

Coming from the coastal N2, Eshowe also forms the gateway to a series of cultural lodges and historical sites dotted along or close to the R66 in what was the heart of the Zulu Kingdom during its mid-19th century peak. The best known of the lodges – and for many visitors a highlight of their tour through southern Africa – is **Shakaland** ❽ (daily 7am–8.30pm; main cultural programme 11am–2pm for day visitors, 4–8.30pm and 9–10am for overnight guests; entrance charge; tel: 035-460 0912), which lies on the R66 just 15 km

BELOW: fever trees on the edge of a pan.

(9 miles) north of Eshowe, on the site of Shaka's original kraal, which was reconstructed in the 1980s as the set for the television series Shaka Zulu. Activities at Shakaland, designed to give visitors genuine insight into traditional Zulu culture, include a visit to an *inyanga* (traditional healer), spear-throwing demonstrations, and – utterly spellbinding – an exuberant drumming and dancing performance set in a traditional dome-shaped auditorium.

Shakaland, it could be argued, has become a victim of its own success, insofar as the sheer volume of tourists that pass through daily has robbed the cultural programmes of some of their immediacy and intimacy. It's a fabulous set-up, but those who prefer a more low-key and personalised approach might prefer to try one of two smaller lodges offering a broadly similar experience. The first of these is **KwaBhekithunga**, a small family-run lodge founded some 25 years ago as a craft centre for the disabled on a private farm 10 km (6 miles) east of the R66 along the R34 to Empangeni. Cultural programmes here are by prior arrangement only (tel: 035-460 0929), and cater to one group at a time, which means that a personal touch is ensured.

A yet more authentic experience is offered by **Simunye** (overnight visitors only; tel: 035-450 3111), another small, intimate lodge, to which you'll be transported by traditional ox-wagon from a meeting point on the R66 about 10 km (6 miles) south of Melmoth. Simunye takes a singularly integrated approach to cultural tourism, giving visitors the choice of sleeping in a traditional beehive hut situated within a functioning Zulu homestead – your wake-up call here might well amount to having a goat lick your feet – or in more conventional rooms built into a cliff overlooking the Mfule River. Day visitors are not permitted, and the lodge's isolation is underscored by the absence of electricity

BELOW: don't be fooled by the tubby hippo's benign appearance – when threatened it can be formidable.

(communal areas are lit by paraffin lamps) and the dense nocturnal chirruping of frogs and insects from the nearby river.

Sticking to the R66, about 35 km (21 miles) past Melmoth you'll reach **Ulundi** , a somewhat nondescript medium-sized town that – rather improbably – served as the capital of the patchwork KwaZulu homeland during the apartheid era. An important site in the vicinity of Ulundi is **Umgungundlovu**, the former capital of King Dingane and burial place of the Voortrekker Piet Retief. Situated at the end of a short side road that runs west from the R34 about 5 km (3 miles) north of the intersection with the R66 between Melmoth and Ulundi, Umgungundlovu underwent partial restoration in the 1990s and a small but interesting site museum is attached.

The **KwaZulu Cultural Museum** (open daily; entrance charge; tel: 035-870 2051) lies 5 km (3 miles) from Ulundi at Ondoni, the site of the capital founded by King Cetshwayo in 1873 and razed by British troops six years later in what was effectively the last battle of the Anglo-Zulu War. The hill-top kraal (Ondoni literally means elevated place) was left untouched for almost a century after that defeat, due to a traditional law preventing the re-use of royal land, but partial restoration began in 1981 and the museum now offers what might be termed a low-budget version of the Shakaland experience – complete with affordable accommodation in traditional beehive huts.

St Lucia estuary

Back on the coast, the N2 continues north from Empangeni via Matubatuba and the R618 to the village of **St Lucia** ⑩, which overlooks the mouth of the vast St Lucia Estuary. This is the largest estuarine system in Africa, extending over an area of 325 sq. km (125 sq. miles), and its shores are protected within a network of small reserves that collectively form the **iSimangaliso Wetland Park** ⑪ (with the exception of public areas, open Oct–Mar daily 5am–7pm, Apr–Sept daily 6am–6pm; entrance charge; tel: 035-590 1340), a UNESCO World Heritage Site since 1999.

Almost 60 km (37 miles) long, up to 10 km (6 miles) wide and with a maximum depth of just 1.5 metres (5 ft), this extraordinary freshwater estuary is fed by the Hluhluwe, uMkhuze and Imfolozi rivers. It harbours an estimated 800 hippos (the largest population in the country) and a similarly impressive crocodile population. The delta is a breeding ground for rare loggerhead and giant leatherback turtles, while an incredible 500 species of bird are known to breed in the vicinity, including pink-backed pelicans, flamingos, spoonbills, fish eagles and Caspian terns.

Hikers have a superb network of routes at their disposal, crisscrossing right across the park along the promontory between the lake and the Indian Ocean through a stunning, lushly forested sand-dune landscape (some of the dunes are as much as 150 metres/ 500 ft high, among the highest in the world). Divers shouldn't miss the coral reefs and the myriads of colourful fish in the St Lucia Marine Reserve; away from the protected area, the coastline is also hugely popular with anglers. If you hire a powerboat for some

Map on page 238

Horse rides are a popular way of exploring the estuary.

BELOW: flamingos thrive in St Lucia's environs.

This Nile crocodile is one of an estimated 1,500 which inhabit Lake St Lucia; needless to say, swimming in the lake is forbidden.

lake fishing, however, keep a sharp eye out for hippos; these portly creatures have fixed underwater routes and can become extremely aggressive if their progress is disturbed in any way. One of the best and safest ways to observe them is to join a guided tour of the estuary aboard an 80-seater launch.

There's plenty of self-catering and hotel accommodation in St Lucia village, which makes for an excellent base for exploring the immediate vicinity as well as for day trips to some of the other reserves in the area. The village is also one of the few urban areas in South Africa where you can still see wildlife – hippos occasionally wander through town, while a great little walking trail through the bordering reserve offers the opportunity to see zebras and various antelope on foot. A more rustic option, however, is to stay at one of the several overnight camps operated by KZN Wildlife, which include huts and camp sites at Charter's Creek, Fanie's Island, Mapelane and Cape Vidal, as well as campgrounds at the St Lucia Estuary. For keen walkers, the trails at Charter's Creek are particularly recommended – warthog, vervet monkeys and nyala are common, and you might also catch a glimpse of the shy red duiker on a forest clearing.

Hluhluwe-Imfolozi Game Reserve

Just 25 km (18 miles) west of St Lucia lies another important conservation area – the **Hluhluwe-Imfolozi Game Reserve** ⓬ (Oct–Mar daily 5am–7pm, Apr–Sept daily 6am–6pm; entrance charge; tel: 035-562 0848 for Hluhluwe, tel: 035-550 8476 for Imfolozi). Originally proclaimed in 1897, making them the second-oldest game reserves in Africa after Phongolo, Hluhluwe (pronounced *shloo-shloo-ee*) and Imfolozi (formerly Umfolozi) were originally discrete entities, but they are now linked by a corridor of state-owned land to create a combined area of roughly 1,000 sq. km (390 sq. miles) that is jointly administered by KZN Wildlife. A public link road (the R618) passes through the central section of the reserve and leads north as far as Nongoma. The animals seem to have become quite accustomed to this arrangement, and happily cross the asphalt all the time.

BELOW: looking for spoor is one way to track animals.

Hluhluwe is best known for the success it achieved in saving the white (or wide-lipped) rhino from extinction. By the early 1930s, only about 150 white rhinos were left in southern Africa, having been shot almost to extinction. A breeding programme here has succeeded in raising the population to more than 1,000, while a further 4,000 of these magnificent animals have been exported to parks around the world. Today, a similar battle is underway to save its cousin, the black rhino – distinguishable only by its narrow upper lip. A total of 81 mammal species occur in the reserve, with several of the larger species having been reintroduced relatively recently. Elephant, giraffe, warthog, impala and the localised nyala are all common, and lion, leopard, cheetah, hyena and hunting dog are also present.

Imfolozi's celebrated **Wilderness Trail** was established in 1957, the first of its kind in South Africa, and it is still one of the best ways of exploring the region. Accompanied by experienced armed rangers who act as guides, these bush walks can last between three and five days. To minimise the ecological impact of visitors to this unspoilt area, numbers are strictly controlled, so booking ahead through KZN wildlife is essential, particularly during the busy holiday periods. In addition to mouth-drying encounters with rhino – and possibly elephant or lion – the wilderness trails offer a good opportunity to see a wide range of the 380 bird species recorded in the area.

Map
on page
238

uMkhuze Game Reserve

Elephant, rhino, leopard, giraffe and nyala are among the game that can be spotted in KZN Wildlife's **uMkhuze** (formerly Mkuzi) **Game Reserve** ⑬ (Oct–Mar daily 5am–7pm, Apr–Sept daily 6am–6pm; entrance charge; tel: 035-573 9001), which borders the iSimangaliso Wetland Park to the east and covers some 36,000 hectares (89,000 acres). uMkhuze is best known for its tropical bird life, which includes such rarities as Neergard's sunbird and the African broadbill. Because the bush vegetation is so thick, the best place to spot game is from one of the several hides that overlook the park's waterholes, which can also be highly rewarding for wildlife photography. Another draw at uMkhuze, situated on the eastern edge of the reserve, is Nsumo Pan, whose shores are attractively encircled by yellow-fever trees and low hills, and support a good range of water-associated birds including pelicans. Sadly, the 3-km (2-mile) trail through the fig-tree forest bordering the pan had to be closed after elephants were reintroduced to the reserve. The three-night wilderness trail, which must be booked in advance, is a good option if you really want to get back to nature.

Mother's milk is best for the nyala calf.

Better still for spotting big game are private reserves such as the 17,000-hectare (42,000-acre) **Phinda Resource Reserve** ⑭ (access to overnight visitors only; tel: 011-809 4300), which is owned and managed by CCA

BELOW: rhino are one of Africa's most aggressive animals.

(Conservation Corporation Africa) and supported by a number of wealthy trusts. Part neglected farmland, part hunting concession before the land was bought up by CCA in 1991, the newly created reserve was immediately subjected to a massive clean-up operation in which 15,000 kg (15 tons) of scrap metal was removed, followed by an even more ambitious programme of reintroductions to boost the then-skittish resident populations of leopard, nyala and other antelope. Small, exclusive, luxurious and definitely not cheap, Phinda today provides an upmarket safari experience to compare with anywhere in Africa; it's particularly good for cheetah and rhino, but lion, leopard, and elephant are also regularly observed. A less luxurious but more affordable alternative, harbouring a similar range of wildlife, is the neighbouring Zulu Nyala Lodge.

Northern Maputaland

North of the St Lucia Estuary, the iSimangaliso Wetland Park protects a narrow belt of pristine coastline that runs north to the Mozambican border, where it is dotted with remote beach-front camps, most of which are accessible by dirt road only. The best-known and busiest of these, serviced by a small resort-like village of the same name, is **Sodwana Bay** ⑮ (daily 24 hrs; entrance charge; tel: 035-571 0115). The offshore coral reefs at Sodwana are widely regarded to provide the best snorkelling and scuba diving anywhere in South Africa (for which reason it can become rather crowded during South African school holidays), while endangered turtles regularly land on the beaches to lay eggs. The terrestrial part of the reserve consists of swamp and dense jungle where fig and milkwood trees can grow as high as 40 metres (130 ft). The rest camp and camp site are in a reliable location for the lovely blue monkey, as well as various small forest antelope, and birdwatching is excellent. Beware of snakes in this park, by the way, and make sure you bring mosquito nets and repellent for the nights. It's important that you begin a course of anti-malaria tablets several weeks before visiting the area, too.

BELOW:
a purple gallinule.

Further north still, **Lake Sibaya** ⑯, separated from the ocean by a thin strip of wooded dunes, is South Africa's largest freshwater body at 77 sq. km (30 sq. miles) and home to prodigious numbers of hippo and crocodile, as well as a varied avifauna that includes the highly localised pink-throated longclaw and Woodward's batis, along with various herons and storks. Somewhat remote from the N2, Sibaya – like Sodwana Bay – only forms a realistic destinaton if you plan to overnight at KZN Wildlife's **Baya Camp** (closed at the time of writing), or one of a handful of pricier lodges in the vicinity. Sibaya and Sodwana Bay are both reached via the R22, a surfaced road that branches northeast from the N2 at the town of Hluhluwe.

About 50 km (30 miles) north of Hluhluwe, just past the town of Mkuze, a surfaced road running northeast from the N2 leads to three of South Africa's wildest, most remote parks – Kosi Bay Nature Reserve, Tembe Elephant Sanctuary and Ndumo Game Reserve – all of which are nestled up against the border with Mozambique.

Set on a dramatic stretch of pristine Indian Ocean beach front, **Kosi Bay Nature Reserve** ⑰ (daily 6am–6pm; entrance charge; tel: 035-592 0234) consists of a network of lakes which are home to hippos and crocodiles as well as an extraordinary variety of aquatic birds, including black egret, fish eagle and jacana. As far as accommodation goes, various comfortable thatched cottages, bungalows and huts accommodate house visitors; there are also caravan and camp sites. While the camp area is accessible to all vehicles, sandy terrain makes a four-wheel-drive essential to reach The Mouth, 5 km (3 miles) from the camp site; visitors who don't have such a vehicle can book a guided tour.

The 10,000-hectare (25,000-acre) **Ndumo Game Reserve** ⑱ (Oct–Mar daily 5am–7pm, Apr–Sept daily 6am–6pm; entrance charge; tel: 035-591 0058) was established in 1924 to protect a lush section of the Pongola River floodplain and an associated network of seasonal waterways and fever tree-lined perennial pans. Black rhino and white rhino are often seen here, along with giraffe, nyala and other antelope. But the reserve is best known for its bird life – indeed, many dedicated birdwatchers regard it to be the single most alluring destination in the country – which includes several species rare elsewhere in South Africa. Boat trips through the swamp offer the chance to seek out the localised Pel's fishing owl, lesser jacana and pygmy goose, interrupted by close encounters with crocs and hippos. A long list of "specials" associated with terrestrial thickets includes African broadbill, Narina trogon, Neergard's sunbird, pink-throated twinspot and grey waxbill.

A more recent creation, proclaimed in 1983 and opened to the public seven years later, the **Tembe Elephant Sanctuary** ⑲ (Oct–Mar daily 5am–7pm, Apr–Sept daily 6am–6pm; 4x4 only; tel: 035-592 0001) protects a herd of roughly 180 elephant that once ranged freely between this part of South Africa

Map on page 238

BELOW: blue wildebeest.

and neighbouring Mozambique. Managed by KZN Wildlife in conjunction with the local Tembe people, this sanctuary operates much like a private reserve – the only accommodation consists of an upmarket private lodge that runs guided 4x4 drives to seek out the region's legendarily large elephants. Other wildlife at Tembe includes buffalo, rhino, lion, leopard, nyala and the tiny suni antelope, and the bird life is almost the equal of Ndumo's.

From the junction with the road to Kosi Bay, the N2 leads northwards through the Lebombo Mountains along the border with Swaziland, following the Pongola River to the eponymous dam and nature reserve. It comes as a surprise to learn that **Phongolo Nature Reserve ⑳** (Oct–Mar daily 5am–7pm, Apr–Sept daily 6am–6pm; entrance charge; tel: 034-435 1012) – developed for tourism but still a somewhat obscure destination – has the distinction of being the oldest game reserve in Africa and second-oldest in the world, proclaimed in 1894 by Paul Kruger to curb the activities of commercial hunters. Wildlife includes white rhino, giraffe, kudu, blue wildebeest and a recently introduced herd of tsessebe, as well as some 300 bird species. The dam, overlooked by a small camp site, is popular with game fishermen for its combative tigerfish – indeed an annual tigerfish competition is held here every September.

From Phongolo, it is just 50 km (31 miles) to the **Ithala Game Reserve ㉑**, (Oct–Mar daily 5am–7pm, Apr–Sept 6am–6pm; entrance charge; tel: 034-893 2540), yet another fine reserve run by KZN Wildlife. The scenery in this 30,000-hectare (75,000-acre) reserve is breathtaking, with dramatic granite cliffs, rolling hills, open savannah, dense forests and romantic rivers all blending together to form a fabulous game-viewing environment. Nor does the wildlife disappoint: it includes elephant, white and black rhino, giraffe, leopard, cheetah and eland.

BELOW: the rolling mountains on the Swaziland border make splendid riding country.

A wide range of accommodation is available, from luxury lodges and fully equipped self-catering chalets, to simple rondavels and bush camps. There is also a small camp site located beside the Thalu River.

Map on page 238

The Battlefield Route

From northern Zululand, visitors heading for Mpumalanga and the Kruger Park have the choice either of travelling directly through Swaziland or else taking a slightly more circuitous route through Piet Retief and Barberton, while Gauteng-bound travellers normally follow the R29 through Piet Retief, Ermelo and Bethal.

Whichever route you choose, it's also possible to divert to the small town of **Vryheid** ㉒, which lies 100 km (60 miles) southwest of Ithala in the heart of KwaZulu-Natal's historic battlefield area. Plenty of blood was shed round here in the 19th century, first due to conflicts between the British and the Zulus (1879) and then between the British and the Boers (1880 and 1881). Vryheid was also briefly the capital of the short-lived Boer New Republic (1884–88), a small piece of land granted to a band of 500 Voortrekkers by the Zulu king, Dinizulu. You can learn more at the **New Republic Museum** (Mon–Fri 7.30am–4pm; entrance charge), which is housed in the old Raadsaal (parliament building).

On the northern outskirts of Vryheid, the tiny **Vryheid Nature Reserve** (open daily) is a pleasant place to take a stroll among zebras and various antelope, while the combination of protea bush, grassland and montane forest provides suitable habitats for 175 bird species.

Situated about 60 km (35 miles) along the R618 east of Vryheid, the pristine indigenous forest protected within the underrated **Ntendeka Wilderness Area** ㉓ (open daily; nominal entrance charge) is where King Cetshwayo laid

BELOW:
traditional dancers.

A small memorial on the banks of the Jojosi River marks the spot where Napoleon III's son, the Prince Imperial, died under a hail of Zulu spears in 1879.

low for seven weeks after his capital at Ondoni was razed by the British. Some 40 km (25 miles) of hiking trails offer the opportunity to see some of the forest's impressive strangler figs, as well as giant tree ferns, various epiphytic orchids (more than half of South Africa's species are present), troops of blue monkey, porcupine quills and many colourful butterflies. Accommodation is limited to one rustic camp site near the entrance gate.

From Vryheid it is 27 km (16 miles) to Blood River – and a 20-km (12-mile) turn-off to the dour **Blood River Monument ㉔** (open daily; entrance charge). It was here in 1838 that a troop of 468 Boers, armed with rifles and cannons, defeated a 10,000-strong Zulu army. The Zulu short spear proved no match for such firepower and more than 3,000 warriors were killed, many of them shot while fleeing across the Ncome River *(see page 32)*.

The coal-mining town of **Dundee ㉕** lies a further 48 km (30 miles) southwest along the R33. On the northern outskirts of town, the **Talana Museum** (Mon–Fri 8am–4.30pm, Sat–Sun 10am–4.30pm; entrance charge; tel: 034-212 2654) has interesting displays on the key skirmishes that took place around here, laid out in a series of historic cottages; the area's industrial heritage (mainly coal mining and glass-making) is also documented. In the grounds are graves of British soldiers who died in the battles. Military history buffs can drive a further 50 km (31 miles) south to visit the evocative battlefield of **Rorke's Drift** *(see box, opposite)*.

Our route now continues past meadows and fields towards **Ladysmith ㉖**, a pretty place which has preserved many of its 19th-century buildings and which makes a handy starting point for trips into the Drakensberg. Originally established by the Voortrekkers in 1847, Ladysmith soon came under British control. Some 50 years later, in October 1899, the British were besieged here by Boer forces.

BELOW:
monument to the Battle of Blood River, near Dundee.

Shelled and starved almost to the brink of defeat, the inhabitants were only relieved by British troops after 118 days. The **Siege Museum** (Mon–Fri 9am–4pm, Sat 9am–1pm; entrance charge; tel: 036-637 2992) documents life during the Boer War and displays artefacts dating from the siege. Nearby battle sites such as Lombard's Kop, Wagon Hill and Caesar's Camp can all be reached from town along signposted trails.

Map on page 238

Coal country

Eighty km (50 miles) further north on the N11 is gritty **Newcastle ㉗**, one of South Africa's major producers of coal and steel. It was founded in 1864, and its chimneys and smoke are a reminder that the Gauteng, the country's industrial nerve-centre, is not far away. A welcome scenic diversion lies 16 km (10 miles) to the west of Newcastle on the Muller's Pass road: the Ncandu River waterfall is set amid good hiking territory in a fold of mountains.

Another major battlefield site on our route lies 43 km (27 miles) north of Newcastle on the N11 towards Volksrust. **Majuba ㉘** was the site of a humiliating defeat for the British by the Boers in 1881, when 285 British troops died in the battle, compared to just two Boers. Today, Majuba Hill, the high ground which was of such strategic importance during the fighting, offers superb views over the surrounding countryside.

In **Volksrust**, a road off the N11 leads through further historic battlefields to Piet Retief, an unremarkable little place named after a leader of the Great Trek whom Zulu Dingane had murdered. Back on the main route, the town of **Standerton** and the Grootdraai Dam come into view. The dam has pleasant hiking possibilities and is a good place to relax before heading to Johannesburg. ❏

BELOW: Zulu warrior in traditional dress.

THE BATTLE OF RORKE'S DRIFT

In 1879, with the centre column of the British Army engaged in attacks on the Zululand border, troops under Lieutenant John Chard of the Royal Engineers were left to guard the post at Rorke's Drift, a tiny Swedish mission church, storehouse and hospital. On 22 January, news of the disastrous defeat of the 24th Regiment at Isandlwana reached the garrison. Even more alarming was the report that a large Zulu force was approaching at speed. Lieutenant Chard gave orders that Rorke's Drift would stand and defend itself, and arranged for a barricade to be constructed, although biscuit tins and mealie bags were the only materials to hand. Just 139 men were present on 23 January (of whom 35 were sick) when, soon after 4pm, a force of some 4,000 Zulu warriors appeared. One furious charge after another was launched, often resulting in hand-to-hand combat against the barricades, in an attack which continued until dawn. The Zulu forces were supremely confident – yet incredibly, Rorke's Drift proved unassailable, the British defending their position with immense bravery. That terrible late afternoon and night left 17 British dead, while Zulu losses were estimated at a minimum of 500. Eleven Victoria Crosses were awarded to the defenders. Today, a memorial and small museum mark the site.

CROSSING THE DRAKENSBERG

Map on page 238

A route winding up from the KwaZulu-Natal midlands to an eagle's view of the Drakensberg – then through the rolling Free-State highveld to Gauteng

After the hustle and bustle of Durban, the trip northwest along the N3 is initially rather a comedown – chiefly because it leads through **Pinetown**, a large and depressing slum. However, all that changes as soon as you get beyond the satellite towns of Hillcrest and New Germany: a signposted turn-off at Kloof leads to the **Krantzkloof Nature Reserve** (sunrise to sunset daily; tel: 031-764 3515) and the **Inanda Dam**, a lushly forested area noted for its cycads and other rare plants, as well as 200 bird species including the imposing crowned eagle. There are some fine walking trails, too, the most spectacular of which brings you to a cliff edge with panoramic views of the Kloof Falls.

Travellers with time on their hands should also explore the romantically named **Valley of a Thousand Hills ②**, a deeply eroded valley cut through by the Umgeni River on its way to the sea. It's known to the Zulus as emKhabathini, the place of the giraffe thorn tree, and according to Zulu legend, this was where God grabbed the world and scrunched it up in his hand, on the point of throwing it away – a story that's easy to believe when you look out over hills stretching towards the horizon like a vast piece of crumpled green velvet.

To get there from Durban, take the N3 through Pinetown and turn right at the Hillcrest/Old Main Road turn-off onto the R103; this will take you through the valley. After some 20 km (12 miles), you'll see a turn-off to the Nagle Dam, 4 km (2 miles) before Cato Ridge, leading to the foot of KwaZulu-Natal's very own 1,000-metre (3,200-ft) high Table Mountain standing sentinel at the head of the Valley of a Thousand Hills. It's definitely worth a climb to the summit; the view is breathtaking.

Pietermaritzburg

The journey picks up pace as you rejoin the N3 and before long **Pietermaritzburg ③** comes into view, its English settler roots evident in the white picket fences, precisely manicured lawns, red-brick paths and neatly trimmed azalea bushes that characterise the leafy suburbia. "Maritzburg" promotes itself as one of the world's best-preserved Victorian cities, and visitors can follow a self-guided trail through its historic heart, starting from the elaborately decorated **City Hall** (the largest all-brick building in the southern hemisphere), built in 1893 on the site of the old Voortrekker Parliament. Facing the City Hall on Commercial Street are two other important buildings: the Legislative Assembly and the old Supreme Court with its striking portico. The latter building now houses the **Tatham Art Gallery** (Mon–Fri 8am–5pm; free; tel: 033-392 2801), where an impressive collection of paintings by European artists (Matisse, Picasso, Hockney) is exhibited alongside works by South Africans.

LEFT: spectacular view, Royal Natal National Park.
BELOW: Zulu *nyanga*, traditional healer.

Giant insects adorn a neo-classical frieze on the façade of Pietermaritzburg's Natal Museum.

BELOW: the lush botanical gardens of Pietermaritzburg.

The **Voortrekker Museum** (Mon–Fri 9am–4pm, Sat 9am–1pm; entrance charge; tel: 033-394 6834) is situated in the Church of the Vow, a small, white-gabled building erected in 1841 to commemorate the Boer's victory over the Zulus at Blood River in 1838 *(see pages 32 and 248)*. The museum offers some interesting insights into frontier life in the mid-19th century. Next door is the restored home of the Voortrekker hero, Andries Pretorius. Not far away at 237 Loop Street, the **Natal Museum** (Mon–Fri 9am–4.30pm, Sat 10am–4pm, Sun 11am–3pm; entrance charge; tel: 033–345 1404, www.nmsa.org.za) has displays devoted to natural history, palaeontology and ethnology, along with an excellent reconstruction of a Victorian street.

Another building of note is the **Victorian Railway Station**, which you'll find – unsurprisingly – on Railway Street. This was where the Indian lawyer Mohandas Gandhi (later known as Mahatma, the man who became world-famous for his policy of non-violence, *see page 41*) was forcibly thrown off a train in 1893, simply because he had dared to take a seat in a whites-only carriage. The incident sparked Gandhi's desire to fight for human rights, a purpose which he pursued until his death in 1948. A statue to his memory was erected opposite the Old Colonial Building as recently as 1993.

Boshoff Street leads out of town to **Queen Elizabeth Park** (open daily; free), where some magnificent old trees and flowerbeds provide a fitting setting for the headquarters and booking office of KwaZulu-Natal (KZN) Wildlife, the authority responsible for 66 protected areas within the province. Situated some 8 km (5 miles) from the town centre, the park is an attractive place for a gentle stroll through gardens inhabited by zebra, impala, bushbuck and a variety of small mammals and birds. There are several picnic areas. Also of interest is the collection of endangered cycads in the Douglas Mitchell Centre.

A further 28 km (15 miles) along the N3, **Howick** ❸ is a small but pretty town distinguished by the Howick Falls, which crash 110 metres (360 ft) down a vertical rock face right next to the town centre. Only 5 km (3 miles) west of Howick, KZN Wildlife's **Midmar Dam Nature Reserve** (Oct–Mar daily 5am–7pm, Apr–Sept daily 6am–6pm; entrance charge; tel: 033-330 2067/8) boasts a pleasant waterfront resort, good watersport facilities, and a small game reserve stocked with rhino, zebra and various antelope species. Also of interest, about 10 km (6 miles) north of town, the **Karkloof Forest Reserve** (open daily; tel: 033-330 3415) is notable for the attractive Karkloof Falls, a wide range of forest birds and small mammals, and – for adrenaline junkies – a three-hour canopy tour that involves the horizontal equivalent of abseiling between a series of seven platforms set high in the treetops. The **Albert Falls Dam Nature Reserve** (open daily; entrance charge; tel: 033-569 1202) to the southeast offers endless scope to keen anglers, canoeing enthusiasts and wildlife lovers, though the waterfall itself didn't survive the construction of the dam wall.

The area around Howick, often referred to as the Natal midlands, is a relatively cool and moist part of South Africa, and its neatly fenced green meadows often draw comparisons to the English countryside. This English connection is reinforced as you explore the so-called Midlands Meander, a loosely defined route that runs southeast from Howick to Hilton and northwest to **Mooi River**, and is dotted with dozens of interesting sites from potteries and art studios to dairies and herb gardens selling fresh produce. The midlands is also where you'll find some of South Africa's finest English country house hotels – a free map with details of all the sites is available from local publicity offices along the route.

Map on page 238

uKhahlamba-Drakensberg Park

The Drakensberg – Afrikaans for Dragon's Mountain – is South Africa's highest and most extensive range, running for 1,000 km (620 miles) from Hoedspruit west of the Kruger National Park all the way south to Rhodes in the Eastern Cape, interrupted by just one valley between Harrismith and Barberton. Not only does this gargantuan range span four different provinces, it also extends into the western half of Swaziland and lies at the core of the Kingdom of Lesotho, reputedly the only state in the world to lie entirely above the 1,000-metre (3,300-ft) contour.

When South Africans talk about "The Berg", however, they are almost certainly referring to its most spectacular section: the sequence of jagged cliffs and towering peaks that rises from the KwaZulu-Natal midlands to run for 200 km (120 miles) along the eastern border with Lesotho. The Zulu people who live in the shadow of this impenetrable sequence of peaks know it as uKhahlamba – The Barrier of Spears – and even today just one solitary road pass, navigable by four-wheel-drive vehicles only, crosses the formidable crags that divide KwaZulu-Natal from Lesotho.

Today, this central Drakensberg region is protected within a patchwork of reserves, all of which now fall under KZN Wildlife, and is referred to collectively as the **uKhahlamba-Drakensberg Park**. The area as a whole has an agreeably temperate climate, but temperatures can drop sharply with altitude, and winter nights are often very chilly. Be prepared, too, for unexpected snowfalls during winter (May–Sept), while sudden thunderstorms or blinding mists can make hiking hazardous at any time of year.

One of the most attractive parts of the uKhahlamba-Drakensberg Park is **Giant's Castle Game Reserve** ㉜ (Oct–Mar daily 5am–7pm, Apr–Sept daily 6am–6pm; entrance charge; tel: 036-353 3718), the main camp of which lies 50 km (30 miles) by road from the N3 near **Estcourt**. Originally established to provide sanctuary to the eland, the largest species of antelope, Giant's Castle is now considered the best place in the country to spot the endangered lammergeyer (or bearded vulture), which occurs here alongside other raptors such as the majestic black eagle, Cape vulture and lanner falcon. A special lammergeyer hide, to which these massive birds are lured by carrion, is open from May to September, and advance booking is required; tel: 036-353 3718.

Scenically dominated by the 3,377-metre (11,076-ft) **Champagne Castle** and 3,315-metre (10,873-ft) **Giant's Castle** mountains, this reserve is ideal for

BELOW: traditional dancing in a rural village.

climbers, and it also has an extensive network of hiking routes, the most demanding of which is the 40-km (25-mile) trail leading in a series of bends to the very top of Giant's Castle. Hikers may come across numerous animals including jackal, caracal and baboon. Keen anglers will already have heard about the enormous rainbow trout in Little Tugela and Bushman's River.

As recently as the mid-19th century, the Drakensberg was inhabited by San (or bushman) hunter-gatherers whose vivid rock paintings, executed anything from 150 to more than 3,000 years ago, still decorate numerous shelters and caves throughout the range. At least 500 sites containing a total of 40–50,000 paintings are known to exist within the uKhahlamba-Drakensberg Park alone – quite possibly the richest collection of rock art anywhere in the world.

One of the finest panels can be visited at **Main Cave**, just 30 minutes' walk from Giant's Castle's rest camp, on an inexpensive guided tour that leaves hourly from 9am–3pm daily. This superb panel is dominated by two 60-cm (2-ft) tall humanlike creatures with animal's heads (a type of figure known as a therianthrope), but there are also paintings of a snake, a lion, and a procession of cloaked figures. Another high-quality panel that's reasonably accessible is Battle Cave in the **Injisuthi Game Reserve** (Oct–Mar daily 5am–7pm, Apr–Sept daily 6am–6pm; entrance charge; tel: 036-431 7848) to the north of Giant's Castle (about three hours on foot from the rest camp), which depicts a clash between two groups of archers, as well as portraits of bushpig, leopard and grey rhebok.

Kamberg and Monks Cowl nature reserves

BELOW:
Devil's Tooth.

South of Giant's Castle, the **Kamberg Nature Reserve** ㉝ (Oct–Mar daily 5am–7pm, Apr–Sept daily 6am–6pm; entrance charge; tel: 033-267 7312) pro-

tects another thrillingly scenic stretch of the uKhahlamba-Drakensberg known for its hiking opportunities and trout fishing. Kamberg is also host to an innovative new **Rock Art Centre** where a fascinating DVD presentation on rock-art interpretation is supplemented by a guided visit to the Game Pass Shelter, a panel of such quality and significance it has been described as the Rosetta Stone of ancient rock art. The main frieze here is dominated by some superbly executed portraits of eland superimposed on humans and therianthropes, while other scenes depict what appears to be a dying antelope held by a shaman. Further south still, the Sani Pass is the only route leading from the east to the independent state of Lesotho – poor road conditions and treacherous hairpin bends make a four-wheel-drive vehicle essential.

North of Giant's Castle, and accessed via Winterton, the area bordering the **Monks Cowl Nature Reserve** ❹ (Oct–Mar daily 6am–7pm, Apr–Sept daily 6am–6pm; entrance charge; tel: 036-468 1103) is serviced by a selection of perhaps two dozen resorts catering to all budgets, from four-star luxury hotels and family-orientated self-catering chalets, down to no-frills camping. Hikes and walks in this part of the uKhahlamba-Drakensberg, which is dominated by the peak of Champagne Castle, range from moderately easy to seriously strenuous, while free-standing peaks such as the Bell, the Inner and Outer Horn, and the very demanding Cathkin Peak offer the experienced climber some interesting challenges. It's also here that you'll find the **Ardmore Ceramic Art Studio** (daily 9am–5pm; tel: 036-468 1314; www.ardmore.co.za), whose bold ceramic artefacts – a fusion of traditional African icons with modern-day functionalism – have achieved international recognition and are displayed next to the workshop in a small gallery.

Map on page 238

Limerick County Library

BELOW:
Giant's Castle.

The crested guineafowl is a common sight in the Royal Natal National Park.

Possibly the most scenic part of the uKhahlamba-Drakensberg, however, is the far north, protected in the Royal Natal Park and adjoining **Rugged Glen Nature Reserve** (both open daily 6am–10pm; entrance charge; tel: 036-438 6310), which lie about 60 km (37 miles) from Harrismith and the N3 via the spectacular Oliviershoek Pass. This region's dramatic mountain landscape is dominated by the Amphitheatre, an 8-km (5-mile) crescent-shaped stretch of sandstone escarpment providing magnificent views.

Royal Natal Park ㉟ is where you will find the country's highest peak, the 3,282-metre (10,760-ft) high **Mont-aux-Sources** (Mountain of Springs), so named because three of the country's major river systems – the Elands, the Western Khubedu (which eventually becomes the Orange) and the Tugela – all have their sources here. A steep two-hour walk, with sturdy chain ladders to ease the ascent, brings you to the summit. For experienced, well-equipped mountaineers there are longer and more challenging routes available.

Within a few kilometres of its source, the Tugela plunges for almost 2 km (1 mile) in a dramatic series of cascades down to the valley floor below. The combined drop of the **Thukela Falls** (949 metres/3,114 ft, over five stages) makes it the second-highest waterfall in the world. Other attractions of Royal Natal and surrounds include several rock-art sites (none quite so impressive as Game Pass Shelter or Giant's Castle's Main Cave), the attractive Woodstock and Sterkfontein dams, and wildlife such as grey rhebok, mountain reedbuck, bushbuck and the exquisite malachite sunbird, often seen feeding on blooming aloes.

Situated in the lower-lying country to the east of Royal Natal, the **Spioenkop Dam Nature Reserve** (Oct–Mar daily 6am–7pm, Apr–Sept daily 6am–6pm;

BELOW: a demonstration of how the springbok acquired its name.

entrance charge; tel: 036-488 1578) supports a cover of dense acacia bush offering lovely views across the dam to the towering peaks of the uKhahlamba-Drakensberg. Wild mammals and birds occur here in abundance, but the dam and public resort on its shores also offer a variety of watersport facilities, and canoes can be hired. Conducted tours of the Anglo-Boer War site at Spioenkop – the plug-like hill overlooking the dam – illustrate the ins and outs of this battle in graphic and somewhat depressing detail.

Map on page 238

Harrismith and on...

Harrismith **36**, which lies just across the provincial border in the southern Free State, is the main town in this part of the country and something of a route focus, but otherwise difficult to get excited about. If you're heading to Gauteng, the drive from Harrismith to Johannesburg takes about three hours on the N3 (dual carriageway most of the way), and there's very little to distract you en route. The only real exception (and then only in a generous mood) is the vast Vaal Dam, which is signposted just north of Villiers. The Vaal River, which feeds the dam, is one of the country's largest, forming the natural border between Free State Province and Gauteng. Apart from supplying water to the Witwatersrand, the dam also caters to the recreational needs of local watersport enthusiasts, but otherwise it's of limited scenic interest.

Alternatively, follow the N5 and R74 west out of Harrismith for about 60 km (35 miles) until you reach the splendid **Golden Gate Highlands National Park 37** (open daily; entrance charge; tel: 058-255 0012). Over the centuries, wind, rain and sunshine have carved the sandstone hills here into bizarre formations that glow golden at dusk to give the area its unique appeal. Located on

BELOW:
heading home.

the border of the Free State and Lesotho, the park is named after its "gate" entrance, composed of two massive sections of sandstone. Hikers are in their element here, as are horse riders: the small Basotho ponies bred in nearby Lesotho have no problems negotiating this terrain. To book accommodation and arrange hiking permits, contact the National Parks Board.

Heading west from Harrismith on the N5, there are three places worth stopping en route to Winburg – where you connect with the N1 between Cape Town, Bloemfontein and Johannesburg. **Bethlehem 38**, dotted with distinctive Voortrekker sandstone cottages, was founded in 1864 beside the Jordan River. Today, it's a modern town with restaurants and all the usual tourist amenities, but they jar with the pleasingly simple original architecture. A 30-km (19-mile) diversion south on the R711 brings you to pretty **Clarens 39**, another Voortrekker village set on the western edge of the Golden Gate Highlands National Park. Named after the Swiss village where Paul Kruger lived until his death in 1904, it's now a thriving artists' colony. Finally, hugging the Lesotho border southwest of Clarens (along the R26 to the Basotho capital of Maseru), sleepy little **Ficksburg** – notable for its old sandstone buildings, Drakensberg backdrop, and ubiquitous cherry trees – is definitely worth a diversion in the second week of November when it hosts a popular cherry festival. ❏

JOURNEYING BY STEAM TRAIN

If travel by steam-hauled train in romantic turn-of-the-20th century style is the sort of journey that sparks your imagination, South Africa will not disappoint

Electrification of the railways came slowly to South Africa. Because coal was cheap and readily available, the authorities were reluctant to relinquish steam – indeed, by the early 1960s, the South African Railways were still operating a record 2,682 steam trains. The end of main-line steam traction was only officially announced in June 1991.

ALL ABOARD

All this, of course, is very good news for steam-train enthusiasts, who can look forward to travelling on a remarkable number of vintage trains which have been preserved as tourist attractions. One of the best-known – and certainly the most opulent – is Rovos Rail's *Pride of Africa,* which plies a route from Cape Town to Pretoria and on to the Victoria Falls and back. These up-market steam safaris in immaculately restored 1920s and '30s rolling stock evoke the Edwardian era of luxury rail travel.

A little easier on the pocket are the Union Limited steam tours managed by Transnet, South Africa's privatised railway network. Options include a six-day Garden Route trip as well as day excursions from Cape Town. Transnet also manage South Africa's last scheduled mixed steam-train service, the *Outeniqua Choo Tjoe,* which originally worked the spectacular lake and mountain route between George and Knysna. The current service operates between George and Mossel Bay only (for more details about steam train trips, *see Travel Tips, page 360*).

▽ **TRAINSPOTTERS' DELIGHT**
A brightly polished number plate from one of the steam locomotives which still regularly ply the Garden Route.

▽ **ONE TO PICK**
As one of the last countries to operate steam trains commercially, South Africa attracts railway romantics from all over the world. The Eastern Cape's historic 24-inch gauge *Apple Express* does daily runs from Port Elizabeth to the village of Thornhill, a distance of some 53 km (30 miles). Booking offices can be found in town, at the Greenacres Shopping Centre.

▷ **A FINE OLD BOILER**
The Greytown Museum's fine collection of railway memorabilia, including this veteran steam engine, reflects the pioneering role played by KwaZulu-Natal in South Africa's railway history.

A ROUTE FROM THE CAPE TO CAIRO

THE RHODES COLOSSUS

It was Cecil Rhodes' most cherished ambition to have a railway line built from Cape Town to Cairo, passing only through British colonies. That way, Britain – rather than her European rivals – would be able to gain possession of Africa's riches. The groundwork for this scheme was laid in 1885, when the first railway trunk routes in South Africa were constructed, linking Cape Town to the Kimberley diamond fields – in which Rhodes' De Beers Consolidated Company just happened to have a very large stake.

Having achieved the wealth that he craved, Rhodes turned his attention to politics, becoming prime minister of the Cape Colony in 1890. But the discovery of huge deposits of gold on the Witwatersrand – right in the middle of the Boer South African Republic – was to prove something of a stumbling block. A strong SAR, Rhodes reasoned, would constitute a severe threat to British supremacy. The subsequent struggle for control of the gold fields was a long and bloody one, culminating in the Anglo-Boer War of 1899–1902. Needless to say, Rhodes' Cape-to-Cairo British line never materialised.

◁ STAYING ON TRACK

The railway age first came to South Africa in 1860, when on 26 June, the country's first steam train made its first official journey from Durban to the Point – a distance of some 3 km (2 miles). Today, the railways extend over some 36,000 km (22,000 miles) of largely electrified track, on which nearly 5,000 locomotives are in operation.

△ SURF AND STEAM

The most photographed section of track from South Africa's most famous steam-train journey – the *Outeniqua Choo Tjoe*, thundering out onto the long bridge across the mouth of the Kaaiman's River. With daily departures from George, the train arrives in Wilderness after a memorable journey of some two hours, past beaches, lakes and forest.

FULL STEAM AHEAD ▷

Known to steam enthusiasts worldwide, the Garden Route's *Outeniqua Choo Tjoe* gets ready to huff and puff its way out of George station in a blaze of summer sunshine – a sight guaranteed to delight.

GAUTENG

This industrial powerhouse contains Johannesburg, Pretoria and some of the country's best museums and galleries – plus a surprising number of parks

Maps on pages 262 & 270

The province of Gauteng – a seSotho name meaning Place of Gold – accounts for less than 1.5 percent of South Africa's surface area, yet its estimated 12 million residents represent more than a quarter of the country's population and their collective enterprises account for 40 percent of the national GDP. Somewhat bizarrely, these impressive statistics are attributable to one single factor: the precious metal for which the province is named. Certainly, without gold, the vast urban sprawl that we know as Johannesburg – significantly, the largest city in the world not to be built on a major river – would still be open grassland or farmland. More speculatively, had it not been for the gold boom 50 km (31 miles) to its south, Pretoria would most likely be a quaint backwater remembered as the former headquarters of Kruger's 19th-century Zuid-Afrikaansche Republiek *(see page 37)* rather than the capital city of modern South Africa.

Populous and wealthy as it is, Gauteng doesn't top many peoples' list of must-see places in South Africa. Unsurprisingly, business travellers generate some 70 percent of tourism to the province, which boasts more conference facilities than the rest of the country put together, while its combination of well-stocked shops and affordability by international standards has made it a popular shopping destination for wealthy residents of other African countries. Much of the remainder of Gauteng's tourism is comprised of incidental transients (Johannesburg International Airport remains the regional transport hub) or family visits. And frankly, if your time in South Africa is limited, it would be difficult to make a strong case for dedicating more of it than is necessary to this least scenic and most industrialised part of the country – no less so because of its unenviable crime rate.

That said, should you spend time in Gauteng, there's no reason to feel downhearted. Boasting more than 60 theatres and 100 museums, not to mention a superb selection of musical venues, restaurants, bars and markets, Gauteng vies with Cape Town as the cultural capital of South Africa. For wildlife enthusiasts, several small sanctuaries are dotted around the province, while only slightly further afield, in the otherwise seldom-visited North West Province, the larger and wilder Pilanesberg National Park and Madikwe Game Reserve both support the full quota of Big Five species. Also popular are tours to the vast, modern township of Soweto, while the out-of-town Kromdraai Conservancy was proclaimed a World Heritage Site in recognition of its wealth of ancient hominid fossils and artefacts.

JOHANNESBURG

E'Goli, it is called by the locals – the City of Gold. **Johannesburg ❶** is the heart of South Africa's industrial and commercial life, where more than a mile below bustling city traffic, miners dig for the world's most pre-

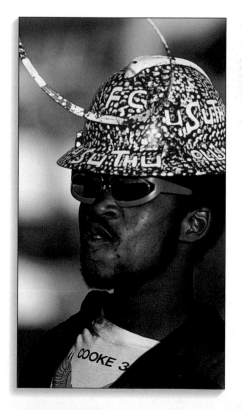

LEFT: a mosque reflected in a Johannesburg skyscraper.
BELOW: Gauteng's street style is the country's slickest.

cious metal. At street level, stockbrokers and company directors rub shoulders with street vendors and traditional healers. Ultra-modern corporate towers dwarf noisy pavement stalls. It's the official capital of Gauteng Province, and many residents of Jo'burg or Jozi – as it's known informally – regard it to be the ipso-facto capital of South Africa, and will fervently defend it against the more obvious charms of places like that sleepy *visdorpie* – fishing village – Cape Town.

Ever since a fateful day in 1886 when George Harrison, a humble prospector, stumbled upon an outcrop of gold-bearing rock, the region's economy and life have been driven by the pulsating rhythm of the mining industry. The effects are inescapable. Stand on the top floor of the **Carlton Centre Ⓐ**, the city's highest building, and you see tawny mine dumps and shaft headgears dotting the skyline. Walk the streets of downtown Johannesburg, and you find road and building names vividly evoking the gold-rush days.

Harrison's discovery sparked a gold fever never experienced before or since, anywhere in the world. Prospectors and fortune seekers descended on the area

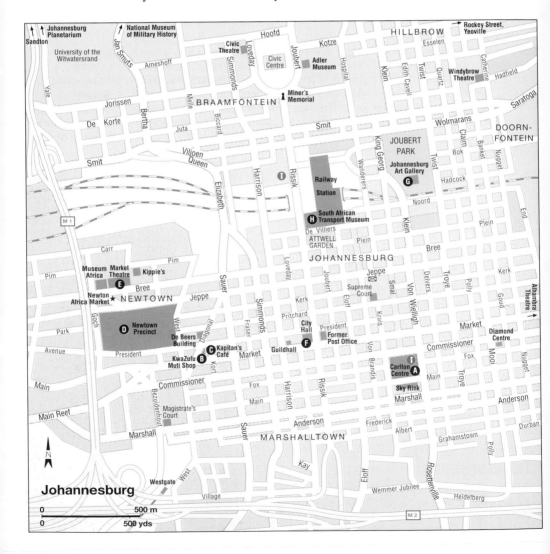

in search of instant wealth. Makeshift shelters and tents mushroomed all over the tranquil veldt. A sprawling, rough and raucous shanty town sprang up almost overnight. Within three years, Johannesburg was the largest town in South Africa. A rudimentary stock exchange was established. Men outnumbered women three to one. Hotels and canteens, brothels and music halls were erected throughout the town to satisfy the needs of this boisterous new community. But it wasn't long before fledgling mining corporations moved in to take control of the industry and swallow up individual claims. "Randlords" like Cecil John Rhodes, Barney Barnato and Alfred Beit quickly accumulated huge fortunes, imposing a semblance of order on the unruly mining town in their wake.

Today, Johannesburg forms the hub of a sprawling metropolis called the Witwatersrand (Ridge of White Waters), stretching more than 120 km (75 miles) from Springs in the east to Randfontein in the west, with a rapidly growing population of almost 5 million. The Witwatersrand is the core of Gauteng, and the place where all the country's major industries are based – making this the undisputed powerhouse of sub-Saharan Africa, if not the entire continent.

A diverse and divided city

By global standards, Johannesburg is a medium-sized city, at least in terms of population, though it must rank as one of the world's most spread-out urban centres, due to a tendency towards lateral rather than vertical growth. And in the African context, it is a giant, offering some of the continent's best nightlife, hotels and shopping opportunities. Yet nowhere are the contrasts that typify the place so forcefully experienced as in the busy downtown area. Just eleven blocks west along Commissioner Street from the modern Carlton Centre mall

Huge cockroaches known as Parktown prawns are a familiar sight in Jo'burg gardens (and living rooms). They can grow up to 7.5 cm (3 inches) long.

BELOW: Johannesburg is southern Africa's commercial centre.

Johannesburg's famous Market Theatre complex is housed in an old produce market.

you'll find the traditional charms of Diagonal Street. Here, dimly lit herbalists such as the **KwaZulu Muti Shop** Ⓑ (Mon–Sat 9am–5pm; tel: 011-836 4470) sell skins, dried plants and the "magic" bones thrown by *sangomas* (traditional healers) during divination, alongside tiny stores crammed with household goods and cheap African art with a kitsch appeal.

Where the road meets Kort Street lies one of Johannesburg's best-loved Indian restaurants, **Kapitan's Café** Ⓒ. This was once a favourite haunt of young attorneys Nelson Mandela and Oliver Tambo, and it's still serving up some of the finest curries this side of Asia (open lunch time only). North along West Street you reach one of the city's chief cultural centres, the enormous **Newtown Precinct** Ⓓ. Here, a conglomeration of warehouses stretching several blocks has been converted into venues for experimental theatre, live music performances, exhibitions and workshop courses for students. It also contains an entire complex of museums.

Next door to the Precinct complex, the **Market Theatre** Ⓔ (tel: 011-832 1641; www.markettheatre.co.za) was the home of protest theatre in the 1970s and '80s, and a renowned cornerstone of the intellectual revolution against apartheid. Today, it is an arts complex in its own right, housing art and photographic galleries, a jazz venue and a restaurant. The Oriental Plaza lies a few blocks further west from Newtown Precinct, sandwiched in between Bree Street and Central Avenue. Here, shoppers can bargain for the best prices on everything from silks and spices to herbs and haberdashery, or simply settle down to a leisurely curry. Heading back towards the Carlton Centre, the elegant **City Hall** Ⓕ on Rissik Street offers a rare glimpse of how this area must once have looked, before the office blocks and concrete flyovers sprang up.

In the 1990s, violent crime became such a problem in downtown Johannesburg that many local businesses moved out to safer northern suburbs such as Rosebank and Sandton, and most of the upmarket hotels that once graced its streets were forced to close or to convert to low-rental apartment blocks. Many residents feel that crime in the city centre is now on the decrease, and there's been much talk of urban rejuvenation in recent years, but still the safest way to see the city centre is on an organised tour. It's probably inadvisable to walk around the city centre without a local companion who knows the ropes, especially after dark, and – as in any city centre, only more so – it would be inviting trouble to carry a camera, or wear expensive jewellery, or flash a loaded wallet. If you drive into central Jo'burg, it's a good idea to keep your car doors locked at all times.

Shopping: markets and malls

Johannesburg's flea markets attract a large informal sector of traders from as far afield as Nigeria, Congo and the Ivory Coast, so pickings are rich as far as tribal crafts are concerned. In the downtown area, **Newtown Africa Market** (open Sat; tel: 011-832 1641) in the square opposite the Market Theatre, is home to the city's original – and most bohemian – "flea". It has around 350 stalls, selling everything from street fashion to arty tat. Producing work on-site for some of Johannesburg's most original artisans is the **Mai Mai Market** (open Mon–Fri), popular with migrant workers looking for fancy keepsakes (wooden chests inlaid with illustrated panels; hand-made stools) to take back home after completing their stint on the mines. It's tucked away at the bottom of Anderson Street, and well worth the trouble it takes to find.

A 15-minute drive from the city centre northeast on the airport road brings you to **Bruma Lake Flea Market World** (Tues–Sun 9.30am–5pm; small entrance charge; tel: 011-622 9248), on the corner of Ernest Oppenheimer and Marcia streets. There are more than 600 stalls and the quality is generally good, particularly the carved wooden masks and sticks, and the printed fabric. Free entertainment is laid on, too, from buskers to Zulu dancers. On Thursdays and Saturdays, there are children's activities such as face-painting and bouncy castles.

The **Rosebank Mall Rooftop Market** (open Sun and public holidays 9.30am–5pm; tel: 011-442 4488) is a 30-minute drive from the city centre in the smart northern suburb of Rosebank, on the top floor of the mall's car park. Bargain hunters will find their patience rewarded; there are over 500 stalls, some selling high-quality antique fetishes, spears and carvings. Haggling is expected.

Golden City culture

If you're interested in African art, don't miss the **Johannesburg Art Gallery G** (open Tues–Sun; free; tel: 011-725 3130) in Joubert Park. During apartheid, the acquisitions policy was virtually to ignore black talent; today, however, all that has changed, and works by South African painters, craftspeople and sculptors add shape and colour to the gracious display rooms in a building designed by Sir Edwin Lutyens. The collection also includes Pre-Raphaelite and Impressionist

BELOW: fine wines and sleek decor – just an average meal out in Johannesburg.

works. Bear in mind, however, that the surrounding area is one of Johannesburg's most crime-ridden quarters, and not a place to linger.

Displays of tribal art are on show at the **Gertrude Posel Gallery** (Tues–Fri 10am–4pm, Sat by appointment only; closed public holidays; free; tel: 011-717 1365) in Senate House at the University of the Witwatersrand, a 10-minute drive west of the city centre. It's a superb collection, containing many valuable examples of vanishing art forms from masks and headdresses to drums.

Johannesburg's commercial galleries are the best in the country, and the **Everard Read Gallery** (Mon–Sat; closed public holidays; free) in Rosebank is definitely worth a visit – a huge variety of artists are represented here, from landscape painters to wildlife sculptors and cutting-edge township whizz-kids.

The innovative displays at **Museum Africa** (Tues–Sun 9am–5pm; entrance charge; tel: 011-833 5624) in Newtown Precinct depict scenes from Johannesburg's brief but turbulent history. You'll find, for example, a cluster of squatter shacks brought from Alexandra township and painstakingly reconstructed; displays focusing on the Rivonia Treason Trial, which sentenced Nelson Mandela to life imprisonment on Robben Island; even a fearsome assortment of home-made weapons confiscated from a miners' hostel.

In the same building are the **Geological Museum**, displaying some of the country's unique mineral wealth; the **Photographic Library and Museum**, and the fascinating **South African Rock Art Museum**, giving an idea of the wide scope of styles and subjects which influenced the San rock artists.

Steam-train enthusiasts will enjoy the **South African Transport Museum** Ⓗ (Mon–Fri 7.30am–4pm; free), on the old concourse of the main railway station

The mine dumps, such a common feature of Jo'burg's cityscape, are fast disappearing – they're being reworked to recover the last traces of gold.

BELOW: dancers at Bruma's Lake Flea Market World.

in downtown De Villiers Street, which houses the best collection of vintage steam engines in the country, as well as ox wagons and vintage cars.

Located in the grounds of the University of the Witwatersrand, which lies in Braamfontein, immediately northwest of the city centre, the Johannesburg Planetarium is a good place to view the southern skies from a fresh angle. Here, audiovisual shows and multimedia displays take visitors on an astronomical journey to distant galaxies (shows Fri, Sat, Sun; entrance charge; tel: 011-717 1390). At the **South African National Museum of Military History** (daily 9am–4.30pm; entrance charge; tel: 011-646 5513) near the zoo in the Herman Eckstein Park in Saxonwold, 12 aircraft and a military submarine vie for your attention with armoured flight vehicles, artillery, small arms and uniforms.

Map on page 262

On the wild side

Although the city centre is filled with high-rise buildings and space is at a premium, this crowded area soon gives way to the interminable sprawl of leafy suburbia that characterises Greater Johannesburg. The city council also administers more than 600 parks and open spaces, most of which are dotted around the suburbs. One of the biggest is the 100-hectare (250-acre) Delta Park, between Blairgowrie and Victory Park, which contains the lovely **Florence Bloom Bird Sanctuary** (open daily; free). Both of the dams here are rich with bird life; you can watch from several specially constructed hides.

One of the nicest of Jo'burg's green patches is the **Melville Koppies Nature Reserve** (daily from dawn to dusk; free; tel: 011-782 7064), just north of Melville suburb; it even has Stone- and Iron-Age ruins for added interest. It

BELOW: the musical fountain of Randburg Waterfront.

One of Gauteng's celebrated Zola Budd minibus taxis, which provide transport for the majority of local commuters.

forms the southernmost section of the much larger Jan Riebeeck Park, where you will also find the **Johannesburg Botanical Garden** (open daily; free; tel: 011-782 7064) in Roosevelt Park Extension, half-an-hour's drive from the city centre on the banks of the Emmarentia Dam. This tranquil spot covers 148 hectares (365 acres), and contains a rose garden, a bonsai garden, pools, fountains and oaks; the dam itself is a pleasant stretch of water, popular with rowers, windsurfers and sailors.

The **Melrose Bird Sanctuary** (open daily; free) in the suburb of Melrose includes a dam surrounded by extensive reed beds, providing nests for a large variety of weaver birds. It's part of the James and Ethel Gray Park, a 10-minute drive from the centre of town.

More than 3,000 mammals, birds and reptiles – 30 of them on the endangered list – are housed at the **Johannesburg Zoological Gardens** (daily 8.30am–5.30pm; entrance charge; tel: 011-646 2000) inside the Herman Eckstein Park in Saxonwold. There are enclosures for big cats, elephants, giraffes and large apes, guarded only by moats and free of iron bars. Popular night tours are conducted on Wednesday and Friday (6.30–9.30pm). Across Jan Smuts Avenue at popular Zoo Lake, also in the park, there are rowing boats for hire, a restaurant and children's playgrounds.

One of the best places to admire Johannesburg's Manhattan-esque skyline is **Pioneer Park** (open daily; free), on the banks of Wemmer Pan in Rosettenville. On the northern bank is **Santarama Miniland**, a contrived but nonetheless very popular miniature city built to a scale of 1:25, depicting all sorts of South African landmarks, including Kimberley's Big Hole.

BELOW:
ready to please
at Melrose Arch.

Visitors can also explore Greater Johannesburg's remaining streams and ridges on a number of self-guided walking trails (detailed brochures marking sites of historical, archaeological and ecological interest are available from the tourist information office). Hikes include the Bloubos Trail and the Sandspruit Trail; closer to the centre of town, you can admire some of the grand Edwardian homes built for the original gold-rush mining barons – led by appropriately costumed guides – on the Parktown Heritage Tour. Contact the Parktown and Westcliff Heritage Trust, tel: 011-482 3349.

Nightlife and entertainment

As far as clubs and bars are concerned, Johannesburg's best venues are in and around the trendy northern suburbs of Melville and to a lesser extent Rosebank. Probably the greatest concentration of such hangouts is along **Melville's Fourth Street** – try Xai-Xai at the northern end for a glass of wine and typical Mozambican selection of seafood and spicy peri-peri dishes, or Cool Runnings at the other end of the road for a relaxed outdoor beer, or Ratz and the Tokyo Star in-between for trendy (sometimes live) music.

The seedy (but infinitely more colourful) **Rockey Street** in Yeoville, just east of the city centre, was one of the hippest districts in the country during the 1980s and home to a flourishing multiracial culture long before apartheid collapsed. Since then, Rockey Street's gone distinctly downmarket and sports a

Map on page 262

disreputable, even dangerous, air. That, according to a diminishing band of aficionados, only adds to the appeal – but do be warned that violent crime is a real risk here, particularly if you carry valuables on your person.

Thanks to Johannesburg's position at the centre of the South African music industry, most of the country's top bands are based in the city. At any one time, expect to choose from a rich cross-section of acts, from standard rock, pop and dance music to the snappy sounds of township jive, Afro-jazz, kwaito and bubblegum pop. **Kippies**, relocated from the Market Theatre complex to Carr Street in Newton, is named for legendary 1950s sax player Kippie Moeketsi, and specialises in township jazz.

Rockey Street is a good place to hear music from all over the African continent. It's not unusual to find artists from as far afield as Ghana, the Congo, Zimbabwe and Kenya performing here at assorted venues, of which the **House of Tandoor** is one of the safest and longest serving. Another excellent and well-established venue is **Melville's Roxy Rhythm Bar**, which hosts a wide variety of local bands playing internationally influenced alternative rock as well as more distinctively African sounds. Popular with clubbers and ravers, by contrast, is **Carfax** in the more central suburb of Newtown, which often hosts local and visiting dance acts.

Local theatre is to a high standard, both in terms of production and theatre facilities. Well-established venues include the Market Theatre *(see page 264)* and the Newtown Precinct; the cavernous modern Civic Theatre in Loveday Street, Braamfontein, stages opera and ballet as well as theatre.

When it comes to eating out, Johannesburg caters to every taste and pocket. Northern suburbs foodies go into raptures over Linger Longer in Sandton and Bistro 277 in Bryanston, while at the other end of the scale, the city's large

BELOW: the man-made oasis of Sun City.

SUN CITY

South Africa's answer to Las Vegas lies 90 minutes' drive west of Jo'burg, on the fringes of the Kalahari. This glitzy resort – the most luxurious in southern Africa – contains casinos, cinemas, restaurants, a world-class golf course and numerous hotels. Most over-the-top of all is the Lost City complex, in which a spectacular five-star hotel – a fantasy African palace – rises from an imported tropical jungle setting, complete with artificial beach and wave pool. Special effects such as the Bridge of Time – scheduled to shudder and shake every now and again, hypoallergenic smoke seeping out of its man-made fissures to simulate an earthquake – complete the picture. The brains behind it all? Step forward, Sol Kerzner, the flamboyant boxer-turned-businessman whose hugely successful company, Sun International, operates hotels and gaming resorts around the world. Part of Kerzner's financial genius was in recognising the potential of building resorts in the so-called homelands, which were granted independence during the days of apartheid. While South Africa's Calvinist white rulers forbade gambling, you could do pretty much anything in the homelands'. Sun City – itself established in the former homeland of Bophutatswana. It is complemented by the nearby Pilanesberg Game Reserve.

A contender in one of the weekly Best-Dressed Man competitions, a regular feature of township life in Soweto.

Portuguese and Italian communities support a range of unpretentious Mediterranean-style cafés. There are plenty of mostly mid-priced restaurants along Melville's Fourth Street, though this has been eclipsed of late by two-dozen or so eateries (collectively representing pretty much every conceivable cuisine, from Japan to France, India to Morocco, and Italy to Mozambique) that line Grant Avenue in the suburb of Norwood, not far east of Rosebank.

As for indigenous African cuisine, Gramadoelas at the Market Theatre Precinct serves up succulent versions of the rib-sticking Cape Dutch cuisine, including *potjiekos* (stew cooked in a three-legged iron pot) and *melktert*, a creamy custard tart.

FURTHER AFIELD

It may seem bizarre to treat the townships as a tourist attraction, but to truly appreciate both sides to life in what is still largely a segregated society, they should be visited. One of the few ways to do this safely is on a guided tour. The Soweto City Council runs bus tours on Monday to Friday morning to **Soweto ❷** (SOuth WEstern TOwnships), the sprawling city near Johannesburg with close on 2 million inhabitants. They must be booked in advance via the Gauteng Tourist Authority (tel: 011-639 1600). A number of private companies also run trips; most collect guests from their hotels and include stops at such places as Winnie Mandela's security-camera-covered house and a *shebeen* (local tavern).

Wherever you go in downtown Johannesburg, street names reflect the pioneer days – Claim, Prospect, Nugget, Main Reef. A visit to a working gold mine outside the city can be arranged through the **Chamber of Mines** (daily tours; advance booking essential; no-one under 16 years or over 60 years of age admitted; tel: 011-

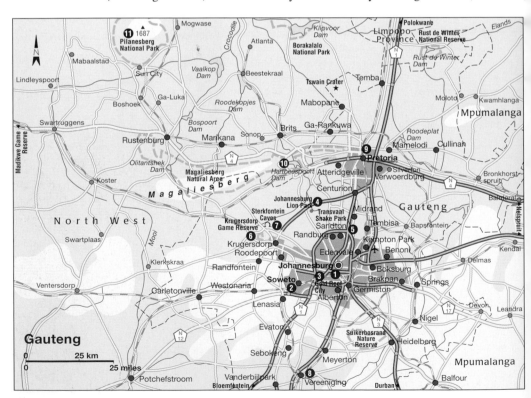

498 7100). But be warned, it's a sweltering journey 1 km (⅔ mile) underground, deep into the earth's crust.

An easier way to get to grips with the industry is to visit **Gold Reef City** ❸ (Tues–Sun 9.30am–5pm; entrance charge; tel: 011-248 6800) at Crown Mines, south of Crown Interchange off the M1 highway, 6 km (4 miles) from the city centre. A lift takes visitors 200 metres (650 ft) down the No. 14 Shaft – once the richest in the world – as part of a reconstruction of the mining process, from the extraction of the ore to the pouring of the molten gold into ingot moulds. Above ground, an attempt has been made to recreate the rumbustious atmosphere of gold-rush Johannesburg in the form of a Victorian-style theme park, featuring a funfair and old-style shops and restaurants. Contrived and commercialised it may be, but there are interesting touches, such as the energetic daily demonstrations of *isicathulo* (gumboot dancing) first popularised by migrant workers in the mine hostels.

Next to Gold Reef City is the new **Museum of Apartheid** (Tues–Sun 10am–5pm; not suitable for children under 12; tel: 011-496 1822), which illustrates the grim story of apartheid. This is done through graphic photographs, film footage and imaginative installations, including an armoured police casspir once used to patrol the townships.

While they cannot compare with the real thing, Johannesburg offers a few scaled-down versions of big-game parks close to the city centre. Up to 60 lions live in an enclosure at the **Johannesburg Lion Park** ❹ (daily 8.30am–5pm winter, 8.30am–6pm summer; entrance charge per car; tel: 011-460 1814), about 12 km (7 miles) northwest of Sandton off the Witkoppen Road. You can also see impala, gemsbok, blesbok and ostrich.

Maps on pages 262 & 270

BELOW: good-humoured banter in a Soweto shebeen.

TIP

Bullfrog Pan in President Steyn Street, Benoni, makes an unusual outing. It's the second-largest bullfrog reserve in the southern hemisphere. Tel: 011-849 5466.

The **Transvaal Snake Park ❺** (open daily; entrance charge; tel: 011-805 3116) on the R101 at Halfway House is home to the world's largest collection of predominantly African snakes. Here, poisonous vipers are milked daily for visitors; you can also see crocodiles, alligators and terrapins, in their purpose-built pools. The 1,400-hectare (3,400-acre) **Krugersdorp Game Reserve ❻** (open daily; entrance charge per car; tel: 011-950 9900) is also worth a visit; less than half-an-hour's drive from Roodepoort on the R24, about 7 km (4 miles) outside Krugersdorp, it has white rhino, giraffe, blue wildebeest and several species of antelope. As well as a guest lodge, there's a camp site and a caravan park.

About 22 km (14 miles) west of the reserve, off the R563, **Sterkfontein Caves ❼** (Tues–Sun; guided tours every 30 minutes; small charge; tel: 011-956 6342), the most renowned of the archaeological sites situated within the Cradle of Humankind, is one of seven World Heritage Sites in South Africa. The caves were exposed in the late 19th century by lime-quarry blasting, and consist of six chambers and an underground lake that's said to have healing powers. Of more than 500 hominid fossils unearthed in the area, the most famous is a 2.5 million year old skull discovered by Dr Robert Broom in 1936 and nicknamed Mrs Ples (short for Plesianthropus transvaalensus, though the skull is now assigned to the species Australopithecus Africanus – and thought to be male). More recent discoveries include a 3.3 million year old male skeleton nicknamed Little Foot, while a near-complete skeleton dating back 3.5 million years, unearthed in 1998, is the oldest hominid fossil known from southern Africa.

Sterkfontein is best visited in conjunction with a two-hour self-guided tour of the **Maropeng Visitors Centre** (daily 9am–5pm; entrance charge; tel: 014-577 9000), where innovative multimedia displays provide background to the discoveries.

BELOW: a novel way to ski: down a mine-dump.

South of Johannesburg, grimly industrial **Vereeniging ❽**, on the shores of the Vaal, is where the peace terms that brought the Boer War to an end were concluded in 1902 – if you're in the area, you might like to visit the **Vereeniging Museum** (Mon–Fri; entrance charge) on Leslie Street. A more compelling attraction south of Johannesburg, **Marievale Bird Sanctuary** (sunrise to sunset; free; tel: 011-734 3661) consists of a Ramsar Convention wetland set between the old mine dumps near the dreary little town of Nigel. Although worth a visit at any time of year, Marievale is best in summer, when its resident birds (herons and waterfowl are particularly well represented) are joined by a host of migrants including rarities such as yellow wagtail, European marsh harrier and black-tailed godwit. Nearby, several walking and hiking trails, as well as a road network, run through the **Suikerbosrand Nature Reserve** (open daily; entrance charge; tel: 011-904 3930), which protects typical Highveld flora and fauna.

Johannesburg's public transport system is not very good. There's no underground train system or light-railway network and buses follow limited routes at limited times. The range of conventional taxis isn't extensive, either, although enquiries about reputable firms can be made at hotel desks. As for the city's celebrated Zola Budds, the minibus taxis used mostly by black South Africans, not only do the operators' driving skills often leave a lot to be desired, but territorial disputes between rival firms mean taxi ranks have been the site of random shootings. It is best to avoid them.

PRETORIA (TSHWANE)

Only 50 km (30 miles) north of Johannesburg, **Pretoria's ❾** relatively small size disguises its influence as the centre of political decision-making. All state departments and parastatal bodies have their head offices here in South Africa's administrative capital; money may do the talking in the Golden City, but it is in Pretoria where the strings of power are manipulated. In the past, this gave Pretoria a bit of an image problem; most black South Africans saw it as a place where apartheid's most insular strictures were upheld to the letter and a spirit of killjoy puritanism prevailed.

Today, however, Pretoria supports a sophisticated international colony of diplomats, politicians and businessmen, and this refreshing exposure to cosmopolitan influences has inspired something of a local cultural renaissance – including the emergence of a thriving gay scene. The Greater Pretoria area recently adopted the name Tshwane, but the city itself is still known by its established name – or as the Jacaranda City for reasons that become obvious if you visit in October, when its 50,000-plus jacaranda trees come into bright mauve blossoms.

Historic Pretoria

Many of Pretoria's historic sites commemorate the late 19th-century heyday of Paul Kruger's Zuid-Afrikaansche Republiek *(see page 37)*. In the heart of the city lies **Church Square 🅐**, skirted by the Old Raadsaal (seat of the old Republican government); the Palace of Justice and the original South African Reserve Bank. But the chief landmark is a large

BELOW: Voortrekker monument.

The blue crane,
South Africa's
elegant national bird,
can be seen
in Pretoria's
Austin Roberts
Bird Sanctuary.

statue of Kruger himself, flanked by burgher sentries. A short walk down Church Street brings you to Strijdom Square, dominated by a giant bust of a more recent leader of the Volk, former Prime Minister, J.G. Strijdom. This was created by South African artist, Coert Steynberg.

The **Paul Kruger House ❸** (daily 9am–4pm; entrance charge; tel: 012-326 9172) on Church Street West, the unpretentious home occupied by Kruger and his wife between 1884 and 1901, has been immaculately restored. Some of the dour old Calvinist's personal belongings are on display, as well as his private railway carriage and official state coach. Kruger's grave lies nearby at Heroes' Acre.

A 15-minute walk to the southeast brings you to gracious **Melrose House ❹** (Tues–Sun 10am–5pm; entrance charge; tel: 012-322 2805), in Jacob Maré Street opposite **Burgers Park**. Designed and built in 1886, the mansion is one of South Africa's finest surviving examples of Victorian architecture; it is also where the treaty ending the Anglo–Boer War was signed.

Guarding the southern entrance to the city is the **Voortrekker Monument ❺** (May–Aug daily 8am–5pm, Sept–Apr daily 8am–6pm; entrance charge; tel: 012-326 6770), a looming granite structure built to celebrate the centenary of the Great Trek (1834–40), which opened up the country's interior for white occupation *(see picture page 273)*. Also easily visible from here is the headquarters of the University of South Africa (UNISA), one of the largest correspondence universities in the world, with more than 100,000 students globally.

The government's administrative headquarters are situated in the **Union Buildings ❻** (tours of the gardens only, by appointment; Mon–Fri; entrance charge; tel: 012-300 2000) on Meintjieskop Ridge, overlooking the city to the east. The image of this stately red sandstone building, designed by Sir Herbert

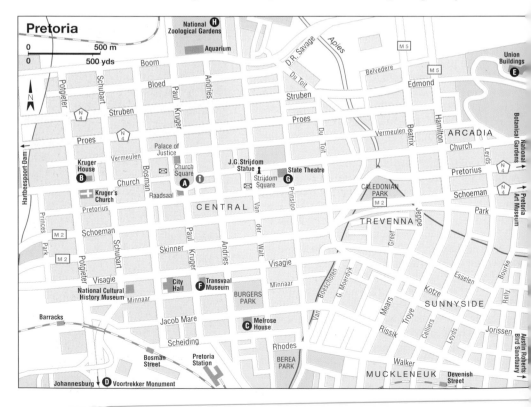

Pretoria

Baker and completed in 1913, adorns souvenir tray cloths, coffee mugs and biscuit tins nationwide – it was also the setting for Nelson Mandela's historic inauguration on 10 May 1994.

Map on page 274

Culture and entertainment

The **Pretoria Art Museum** (Tues–Sat 10am–5pm, Sun 2–6pm; entrance charge; tel: 012-344 1807/8) in the eastern suburb of Arcadia Park houses an impressive collection of work by white South African artists, including such local talent as Frans Oerder, Maggie Laubscher and Walter Battiss. At 218 Vermeulen Street in the city centre you'll find the **Pierneef Museum** (Mon–Fri; closed public holidays; entrance charge), devoted to the work of another well-known local painter with a distinctive, if rather sentimental, style.

Celebrating the history of the Great Trek at the Voortrekker's Monument

The renowned **Transvaal Museum** ❺ (Mon–Sat 9am–5pm, Sun 11am–5pm; entrance charge; tel: 012-322 7632), a 10-minute walk away in Paul Kruger Street, opposite the City Hall, specialises in natural history and houses a collection of fossils, as well as one of the country's largest collections of San rock art. Situated 40 km (25 miles) northwest of Pretoria, the **Tswaing Crater Museum** (daily 9am–4pm; entrance charge; tel: 012-790 2302) protects a 1-km (⅔-mile) wide meteorite crater and the brackish lake on its floor, while a neighbouring cultural village is a good place to see the colourful geometric house painting for which the Ndebele people are renowned.

The **State Theatre** ❻ (tel: 083-915 8000) on Church Street is the centre of cultural life in Pretoria. A grand total of six separate auditoriums in the complex provide facilities for opera, drama, ballet and symphony concerts. As far as more informal entertainment is concerned, some of the liveliest nightlife centres around the suburbs of Hatfield and Sunnyside. The Oeverzicht Art Village in Gerhard Moerdyk Street here houses a lively strip of restaurants, bars and arts and crafts shops; the Provençal cuisine at nearby La Madeleine restaurant is much-vaunted by the local élite. At Gerhard Moerdyk's restaurant in Arcadia, diplomats and politicians wheel and deal over springbok pie and other hearty dishes from a strictly South African menu in an incongruously chintzy setting, complete with crystal chandeliers.

BELOW:
Paul Kruger monument.

The outdoor life

A short drive north of the city centre on Boom Street brings you to the **National Zoological Gardens** ❼ (daily 8am–5pm; entrance charge; tel: 012-328 3265), regarded as one of the largest and best of its kind in the world. It is home to about 3,500 southern African and exotic animals; an overhead cableway provides the visitor with a panoramic view of the zoo and the surrounding city. A market at the entrance sells arts and crafts. Also worthwhile is the **Austin Roberts Bird Sanctuary** (May–Aug daily 7am–6pm, Sept– Apr daily 7am–5pm; free; tel: 012-440 8316) in the southeastern district of Muckleneuk, where more than 100 indigenous bird species such as blue cranes, herons, ostriches and water birds can be viewed.

Pretoria's magnificent **National Botanical Gardens** (daily 6am–6pm; entrance charge; tel: 012-804

Map on page 270

3200) lie 8 km (5 miles) east of the city centre and contain every major type of southern African vegetation. Conducted tours include a slide show and visit to the nursery. The **Hartbeespoort Dam** , 35 km (22 miles) west of Pretoria, in a beautiful location against the backdrop of the Magaliesberg Mountain Range, is the setting for numerous small holiday resorts – popular weekend retreats for locals – as well as a good snake park. The **De Wildt Cheetah Research Station**, off the R513 near Hartebeespoort Dam (Tues, Thur, Sat and Sun 8.30am–1.30pm; three-hour tours by advance booking only, tel: 012-504 1921) is the first place where the cheetah was successfully bred in captivity and it's also where researchers discovered that the rare king cheetah, whose spots meld together into stripes, is not a separate species, but the result of a recessive gene in both parents.

Further afield, the road across Hartebeespoort Dam Wall leads after another 60–90 minutes to the 500-sq. km (195-sq. mile) **Pilanesberg Game Reserve** (daily sunrise to sunset; entrance charge; tel: 014-555 5354), which is set in a collapsed volcanic crater where reintroduced lion, elephant and rhino roam freely alongside various antelope and a remarkable 350 bird species. Serviced by good internal roads and the full gamut of accommodation options – from camp sites to the luxury Sun City complex *(see box on page 269)* – Pilanesberg is the perfect destination for a one- or two-night self-drive safari out of Gauteng. For those seeking a more exclusive game-viewing experience, **Madikwe Game Reserve** (access to overnight visitors only) lies along the Great Marico River on the Botswana border, and a similar range of species can be seen on guided game drives out of a few small and relatively costly lodges. Both reserves have the advantage of being free of malaria. ❏

BELOW:
Union Buildings.

The Lure of Gold

The gold-mining industry has for a long time been the flywheel of South Africa's economy. Of the metal estimated to have been mined in the world to date, around a half of it has come from the African continent, the bulk of it from South Africa. It is the largest producer of gold in the world.

Johannesburg grew from the rough-and-ready diggers' camps that mushroomed here when gold was first discovered in 1886. Today's visitors to Gold Reef City *(see page 271)* – a popular theme park depicting Johannesburg at the dawn of the 20th century – can take a cage some 200 metres (650 ft) underground, to see just how the precious metal is wrested from the rock. But gold has little to do with nostalgia or romance for South Africa's 500,000-odd mine workers.

"The wealth of our gold-mining industry is not so much due to the richness of gold as it is to the poorness of Black wages," wrote Alan Paton in the 1960s. Today in the "new" South Africa, despite the minimum wage levels negotiated by the trade unions, the mineworker's life is a tough one.

Most miners begin their day by climbing into the giant metal cages that will take them deep into the belly of the earth for their working shift. Already, South Africa's gold mines probe deeper than their counterparts around the world. In the mid-1980s, for example, the Witwatersrand's Western Deep Levels was mining 3,447 metres (10,300 ft) below the earth's surface – a world record. Working conditions are intensely hot and humid, and despite stringent safety measures, often hazardous. Many of the gold-bearing underground seams are narrow, and the shafts or "stopes" in which the miners work little more than 1 metre (3 ft) high. Rock temperatures can reach 55°C (131°F), and even though refrigerated air is constantly being pumped through the networks, air temperatures often exceed 32°C (90°F).

Because of the narrowness of the seams, drilling and blasting are usually manual operations. The raw rock is hoisted onto carts which are whisked up to ground level to undergo a series of gold extraction processes – but there is the ever-present danger of rockbursts or earth tremors.

The mining industry has long relied on contract labour as the backbone of its workforce. Johannesburg's bleak hostels and mining compounds were first built to house the thousands of men forced off the land in the early part of the 20th century, who came seeking work in eGoli – the city of gold. Mineworkers' traditional songs bear testament to the loneliness and boredom of the mining life, to the harsh, crowded conditions in the single-sex hostels, and to their longings for home life and faraway families.

Inevitably, perhaps, hostels became flashpoints for political violence in the 1980s and 1990s, fuelled by alienation, bitterness and despair. Today, mining companies have been forced to reconsider ways of housing their workers. Behind the glittering images of South Africa's golden treasure, the reality remains: an industry built on back-breaking work and sub-standard conditions. ❏

RIGHT: molten millions.

MPUMALANGA AND LIMPOPO

North and east of Gauteng, the highveld rolls on to a vast escarpment, where wooded cliffs plunge down to the bushveld wilderness of the vast Kruger National Park

Map on page 282

E xtending northeast from Gauteng to the borders with Zimbabwe and Mozambique, the provinces of Limpopo and Mpumalanga are dominated by the charismatic wilderness of Kruger National Park that runs for a full 350 km (190 miles) along their eastern borders. This game-rich area is larger than Wales or Massachusetts, and abutted by private sanctuaries to the west, and by the Zimbabwean and Mozambican components of the Great Limpopo Trans-Frontier Park to the north and east.

Most Kruger safaris stick to the southern fifth of the park. In part, this is because the southern Kruger has better facilities than the north, and offers better game viewing, but another factor is relative proximity to Gauteng and ease of onward road travel to Swaziland and KwaZulu-Natal. Similarly, Mpumalanga's southerly Panorama Route can become rather crowded in season, yet comparably scenic parts of Limpopo Province in the north feel decidedly remote. Logistically, sticking to the south makes sense within the time frame of a standard holiday, certainly if you also intend to visit Cape Town. Nevertheless, with sufficient time – ten days, say – you could travel the full loop out of Gauteng described in this chapter, heading east to Mpumalanga, then driving right through the Kruger Park to the far north, and returning via off-the-beaten-track Limpopo Province.

PRECEDING PAGES: Oryx follow the water as seasons change.
LEFT: *Panthera pardus*, the leopard.
BELOW: scene from an Ndebele village.

The highveld: eastern grasslands

Leaving **Pretoria ❶** on the N4, or Johannesburg on the N12, the road east rolls steadily on through sun-bleached grassland. Initially, the journey shows little promise of the beautiful eastern escarpment that lies ahead, yet these undulating plains once teemed with herds of wildlife, particularly black wildebeest, zebra and antelope. Today, the indigenous wildlife has been displaced by cattle and sheep farming, as well as intensive maize and sunflower monoculture. Occasionally, domesticated blesbok can be seen grazing in game-fenced ranches along the roadside.

The N12 and N4 converge outside of **Witbank ❷**, where the country's largest coal deposits provide fuel for several nearby power stations. Depressingly, mining here has given rise to growing environmental problems such as air pollution and acid rain – and the nondescript town centre, which cannot be seen from the highway, offers nothing to merit a diversion.

This region is home to the Southern Ndebele, refugees from Shaka's Zulu Empire who settled here in the early 19th century and are celebrated today for their colourful decoration. Exquisite examples of geometrically patterned homes and intricately beaded costumes can be seen at the 19th-century **Botshabelo Mission Station ❸** 13 km (8 miles) north of **Middelburg**. You can explore on your own or take a guided tour,

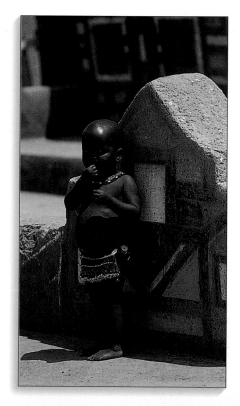

available from the open-air museum (open daily; entrance charge; tel: 013-245 9003). Nearby **Fort Merensky**, built in 1865, is a rather bizarre construction resembling a hybrid of a Gothic castle and the ruined stone city of Great Zimbabwe. You might want to take a short drive through the adjacent game enclosure, perhaps the most northerly remaining refuge for the endemic black wildebeest. About 15 km (9 miles) further north, **Loskop** (Loose Head) **Dam Game Reserve** (Apr–Oct daily 6.30am–6pm, Nov–Mar daily 6am–6.30pm) supports white rhino, giraffe, zebra, buffalo, kudu and over 200 bird species in a transitional area from the highveld to the lowveld biomes.

Back on the N4 you'll pass signs for **Belfast** and **Machadodorp**, two unremarkable towns that played important roles in the history of the Zuid-Afrikaansche Republiek. After the evacuation of Pretoria in 1900 during the Anglo–Boer War, Kruger moved his government to Machadodorp. Later that year, the last major battle of the war was fought at Bergendal, 8 km (5 miles) outside Belfast. A small memorial marks the battlefield.

Tswain Crater, 45 km (28 miles) north of Pretoria, is one of the best-preserved meteorite-impact craters in the world. The water-filled hole is 1,130 metres (3,700 ft) wide.

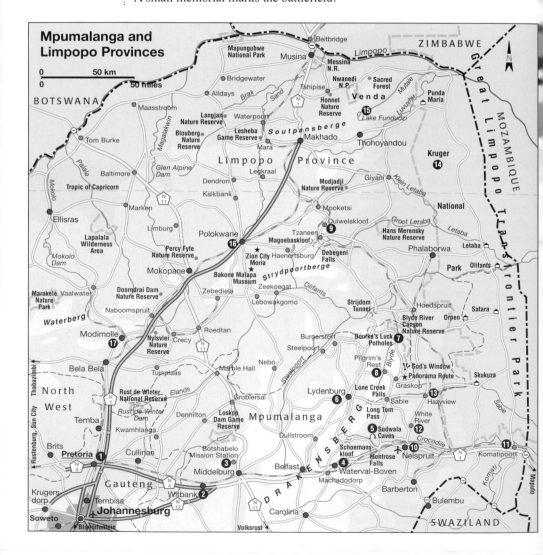

Map on page 282

On the edge of the Drakensberg escarpment, the two little railway towns of **Waterval-Boven ❹** and **Waterval-Onder** are (as their Afrikaans names suggest) respectively situated above and below a spectacular waterfall on the Elands River. In the mid-1890s, Dutch contractors employed considerable engineering skills in bringing the railway right to the point where the water plunges over the escarpment. You'll pass the steeply inclined tunnel and rack-rail as you drive; a short walk from the roadside leads to lovely views of the waterfall.

A rewarding diversion heading left over the escarpment just before reaching Waterval-Boven (R539) follows the Crocodile River for 67 km (42 miles) through the precipitous Schoemanskloof, then links up with the N4 at the confluence of the Elands and Crocodile rivers which tumble over the beautiful **Montrose Falls**.

The N4 leads on through lush farmland towards Nelspruit and Kruger National Park, past extensive citrus orchards and wayside stalls selling fruit and curios. Two km (1 mile) beyond the intersection at Montrose, a turn-off to the north takes you on a 14-km (9-mile) drive to the **Sudwala Caves ❺** (daily 8.30am–4.30pm; guided tours every 15–20 minutes; entrance charge; tel: 013-733 4152). Nobody knows why, but the caves' temperature stays at a constant 18°C (64°F) throughout the year. Their full depth has not yet been established, but you can explore the enormous chambers with their weird dripstone formations for about 500 metres (1,600 ft) into the mountainside.

The Escarpment

South Africa's Drakensberg Range swoops down along the entire length of Mpumalanga and KwaZulu-Natal, providing breathtaking views and excellent opportunities for hiking or driving. The craggy Mpumalanga section – known simply as The Escarpment – runs south from Blyde River Canyon for nearly 320 km (200 miles). It is crisscrossed with many passes pioneered by the transport-riders of the late 19th century, who provided a vital link between the land-locked Zuid-Afrikaansche Republic and the Portuguese port of Lourenço Marques (Maputo).

One of these intrepid pioneers was young Percy Fitzpatrick, who, disillusioned with his job in a Cape Town bank, opted for a job carting supplies by ox wagon from Delagoa Bay to the highveld goldfields. Fitzpatrick's closest travelling companion was a cross-breed bull terrier named Jock; the tale he wrote about their adventures, *Jock of the Bushveld* (1907), is now a classic.

Useful jumping-off points for exploring the Escarpment include sleepy little **Dullstroom**, 30 km (19 miles) north of Belfast on the R540 and set amid one of the few remaining stretches of pristine highveld countryside. Numerous small streams rise in these cool highlands, draining towards the escarpment to the east. All are stocked with trout; fly-fishing is almost as important round here as farming. As most of the trout streams are privately owned, seek advice on good fishing spots from your hotel reception.

Lydenburg

Some 58 km (36 miles) further north, **Lydenburg ❻** (Town of Suffering) is a beautiful town that belies the name given to it by survivors fleeing malaria-stricken

BELOW:
Ndebele style.

Find out how to pan for gold on a conducted tour with the Pilgrim's Rest Diggings Museum, just outside town on the Graskop road. Tel: 013-768 1060.

settlements of the lowveld. Later, it became the capital of an independent Boer republic; the town's Dutch Reformed church and old school house were built during this period. In the local museum (open daily; Mon–Fri closed noon–2pm; Sat–Sun open 1–4pm; entrance charge), you can see replicas of the Lydenburg Heads based on reassembled pottery found in the area. The masks date from AD500 and are one of South Africa's most important archaeological discoveries.

From Lydenburg, it's 56 km (35 miles) east across the Mauchberg via the scenic Long Tom Pass, once used by transport riders, to the forestry town of **Sabie**. Timber plantations cover the surrounding hill sides; most of the country's major paper mills are situated here. So dramatic is the road north from here along the Escarpment's edge that it's been named the **Panorama Route**. For once the tourist-board tag is no exaggeration. This is also waterfall country, and numerous short drives lead from town to picnic and viewing sites such as **Sabie Falls**, **Horseshoe Falls**, **Lone Creek Falls**, **Bridal Veil Falls** and **MacMac Falls** (so-called after the Scots prospectors who camped in the area during the gold rush). Visitors interested in taking photographs should bear in mind that almost all of the waterfalls face east and should therefore best be visited before midday.

The 86-km (54-mile) drive northwards from Sabie via **Graskop** to the **Blyde River Canyon** should be taken at a leisurely pace: the views are exceptional. At **Pinnacle Rock**, **Jock's View** and **God's Window**, you can stop to look out from sheer cliff outposts over the expanse of the lowveld. Other sights include the Lisbon Falls and the Berlin Falls before the road reaches **Bourke's Luck Potholes ❼**, 66 km (41 miles) from Sabie. Here, paths and footbridges take visitors to viewing sites overlooking an extraordinary series of water-eroded cylindrical potholes at the confluence of the Blyde (Joy) and Truer (Sorrow) Rivers.

BELOW:
Pilgrim's Rest.

More is to come. Northwards, the Blyde River has carved a magnificent gorge through the mountains. Viewing sites have been created at points along the canyon, providing superb views of the winding river 800 metres (2,600 ft) below. Dominated by three peaks known as the **Three Rondavels**, and by **Mariepskop**, one of the highest points in the region, the canyon is a nature reserve (open daily; free) and much of it is accessible on foot only.

Starting from the rest camp at the entrance gate, well-marked trails of varying lengths lead through the canyon's lush riverine flora of evergreen trees, prehistoric-looking cycads, giant ferns and orchids. Particularly worthwhile is the **Kadishi Trail**, which visits a waterfall notable for the stalactite-like tufa (calcium carbonate) formations that have formed below it. Large mammals are seldom seen, but the bird life is excellent including the endemic bald ibis and Gurney's sugarbird.

An alternative trip from Sabie is over Bonnet Pass along the R533 for 35 km (22 miles) to **Pilgrim's Rest ❽**, one of the oldest gold-mining towns in South Africa. Legend ascribes the discovery of gold in this valley (in 1873) to Alec "Wheelbarrow" Patterson, so called because he roamed the hills pushing all his possessions in a wheelbarrow. He stumbled across what was, at the time, the richest known deposit of alluvial gold on the subcontinent, and within no time at all a large and motley assortment of fortune seekers had flocked to the area.

Yet within a decade, most of the alluvial deposits had been worked out, and mining operations were taken over by larger companies. In 1883, the independent diggers migrated south to the new fields at **Barberton**. Underground mining continued at Pilgrim's Rest until the 1920s, but today the entire town has been restored as a national monument and living museum.

Map on page 282

Long Tom Pass got its name during the Anglo–Boer War. The Boers tried to slow the advance of the British here with the help of two mighty 150-mm Creusot field guns, nicknamed Long Toms.

Hiking trails

Some of the most rewarding views of this picturesque countryside are to be had on foot, for the Escarpment is crisscrossed by a network of impressive hiking paths. The **Fanie Botha Trail** was the first National Hiking Way trail to be opened, in 1973. It covers almost 80 km (50 miles) of magnificent mountain countryside between the Ceylon Forest near Sabie to God's Window north of Graskop. Short sections of the five-day trail can be taken one at a time.

At God's Window, the Fanie Botha Trail merges with the 65-km (40-mile) **Blyderivierspoort Hiking Trail**, offering a series of much more leisurely walks along the canyon, ending up at the Three Rondavels.

The region's early mining history can be traced along the Prospector's Hiking Trail, which links up with the Fanie Botha Trail at MacMac Falls and leads northwards for 70 km (43 miles) through Pilgrim's Rest and north to Bourke's Luck Potholes. Pilgrim's Rest is also the starting point for two other routes, the Morgenzon Trail and the Rambler's Trail, and a selection of shorter walks *(see page 360 for details)*.

Land of the Rain Queen

A 96-km (60-mile) drive from Lydenburg on the R36 brings you to a winding pass through the steep Drakensberg Cliffs via the Strijdom Tunnel that drops into the hot, baobab-studded flats of Limpopo Province.

BELOW:
Lone Creek Falls.

Soon after the tunnel, the R36 turns off to Tzaneen, 90 km (56 miles) to the west. The main road (now the R527) curves south again to many of the region's private game parks and on to Hazyview, 116 km (73 miles) away.

The well-wooded slopes around **Tzaneen** are in fact the northernmost reaches of the Escarpment. Showpiece of the area is the spectacularly beautiful **Magoebaskloof**, meandering through indigenous forest up the slopes of the Wolkberg Range. An enchanting 3-km (2-mile) walk through the forests from the main road brings you to **Debegeni Falls**, which tumble 800 metres (2,600 ft) into a deep, pot-like natural swimming pool. This is also a prosperous fruit-farming region; tea and timber plantations are abundant, too.

A further 20 km (12 miles) north towards **Duiwelskloof ❾** lies the homeland of the Lobedu people, a sub-sect of the Venda who are ruled by the mysterious queen, Modjadji. Since the 16th century, a dynasty of queens named Modjadji has held sway over the region, originally commanding awe and respect even from the warrior tribes among the Zulu and Swazi. In dry seasons she was sent gifts and offerings together with heartfelt requests to use her secret powers to bring on the rain. The adventure novelist Rider Haggard based his novel, *She* (1887), on Modjadji, and to this day the mystique of the Rain Queen remains: the reigning monarch can still only be seen and visited by favoured guests.

The 52-sq. km (20-sq. mile) **Hans Merensky Nature Reserve**, which lies on the southern banks of the Groot Letaba River about 70 km (43 miles) east of Tzaneen, has plentiful game, including leopards, hippos, lions and hyenas. Of interest is the **Tsonga Kraal Open Air Museum** that displays the Tsonga way of life and where craftsmen demonstrate their arts.

Duiwelskloof means devil's gorge – a reference to the hazards these muddy slopes posed to transport riders and wagon trains in the rainy season. Thankfully, conditions have now improved.

RIGHT:
recycling in style.

The Lowveld

Nelspruit ⑩, 355 km (220 miles) from Johannesburg, is at the base of the Escarpment; the humid, swampy atmosphere will soon make you aware that you've reached a lower altitude. Nelspruit is also the capital of Mpumalanga, one of the smallest and least-populated provinces in South Africa – but for all that it's a pretty place, its streets festooned with bougainvillaea and frangipani. The real showpiece is the **Lowveld Botanical Garden** (daily 8am–6pm; free; tel: 013-752 5531), set in lush subtropical scenery 3 km (2 miles) outside town on the banks of the Crocodile River. Rare plants include a comprehensive cycad collection.

The lowveld was once the site of the major pre-Witwatersrand gold rush. **Barberton**, 45 km (28 miles) south of Nelspruit, near the Swaziland border, is the product of those wild days of fortunes made and lost overnight. Founded in 1883, it expanded rapidly as rich gold deposits were found in the surrounding hills. Nearby Sheba Mine was once the world's richest mine, and a separate town, Eureka City, grew up beside it. Eureka is now a ghost town and a half-hour drive from Barberton leads to the ruins past old excavations and mining gear.

Nelspruit is a mere 105 km (66 miles) west of the Mozambique border and the gateway town of **Komatipoort ⑪**, sweltering in the confluent valleys of the Komati and Crocodile rivers. During the 20 years of civil war in Mozambique, Komatipoort lay dormant but for sporadic gunfire. Since then, however, the Nelspruit-Maputo road has been completely rebuilt with huge amounts of government aid, and today it's as good as any road in South Africa. The intention is to transform the region into a vibrant economic corridor of agriculture, industry and communications, and to restore Komatipoort to its old status as an important gateway to the coast.

Map on page 282

BELOW: the Three Rondavels, Blyde River Canyon.

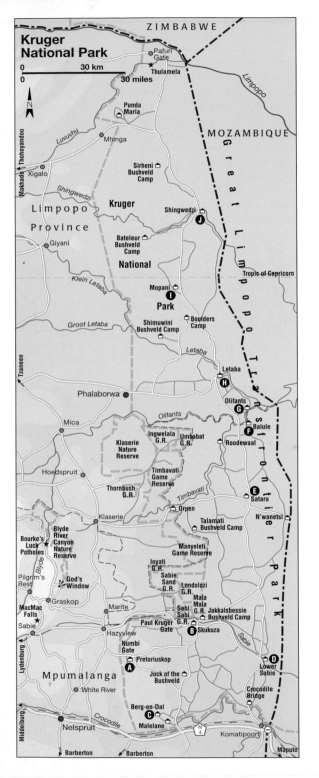

Kruger National Park

ZIMBABWE

0 — 30 km
0 — 30 miles

N

MOZAMBIQUE

Makhado Thohoyandou

Luvuvhu

Xigalo

Shingwedzi

Mhinga

Pafuri Gate

Thulamela

Punda Maria

Sirheni Bushveld Camp

Kruger

Shingwedzi **J**

Limpopo

Province

Giyani

Bateleur Bushveld Camp

National

Great Limpopo Transfrontier Park

Tropic of Capricorn

Klein Letaba

Mopani **I**

Park

Groot Letaba

Shimuwini Bushveld Camp

Boulders Camp

Letaba

Letaba **H**

Phalaborwa

Olifants **G**

Tzaneen

Mica

Olifants

Balule **F**

Ingwelala G.R.

Umbabat G.R.

Roodewaal

Klaserie Nature Reserve

Hoedspruit

Timbavati Game Reserve

Thornbush G.R.

Timbavati

Satara **E**

Orpen

N'wanetsi

Klaserie

Talamati Bushveld Camp

Blyde River Canyon Nature Reserve

Bourke's Luck Potholes

Manyeleti Game Reserve

Inyati G.R.

Pilgrim's Rest

God's Window

Sabi Sand G.R.

Londolozi G.R.

MacMac Falls

Graskop

Marite

Mala Mala

Sabie

Sabi Sabi G.R.

Mala Mala G.R.

Jakkalsbessie Bushveld Camp

Paul Kruger Gate

Skukuza **B**

Hazyview

Numbi Gate

Pretoriuskop **A**

Jock of the Bushveld

Lower Sabie **D**

Mpumalanga

White River

Crocodile Bridge

Lydenburg

Berg-en-Dal **C**

Malelane

Middelburg

Crocodile

Nelspruit

Komatipoort

Maputo

Barberton

Barberton

A 16-km (10-mile) drive north of Nelspruit on the R40 brings you to the attractive little town of **White River** ⑫. The lowveld climate here is ideal for the cultivation of exotic subtropical fruit, and you'll notice banana, papaya and mango plantations lining the roadside. Avocados, litchis, citrus and passion fruit are all farmed here, too.

After a further 24 km (15 miles), the R40 reaches **Hazyview** ⑬, a once rather down-at-heel village that has flourished over the past few years thanks to its proximity to the Kruger Park's **Numbi** (20 km/12 miles) and **Paul Kruger Gates** (45 km/27 miles). Hazyview is the site of a coterie of lodges catering to visitors who can't get bookings within the park, or want more upmarket accommodation, and day access was further improved a few years ago with the opening of the **Phabeni Gate** next to the **Albasini Ruins** (where the Portuguese ivory hunter Joao Albasini maintained a trading post in 1846–8) only 10 km (7 miles) from the town centre.

Kruger National Park

In a roundabout way, it was the mosquito and the tsetse fly which helped safeguard South Africa's herds of wild game, the highlight of any visit to the country today. Thanks to the malaria and deadly nagana cattle sickness which these insects spread, hunting parties had to be restricted to the disease-free winter months, while all attempts to settle or civilise the area were doomed. By the end of the 19th century, however, this was no longer enough to protect the land from farmers with their fences and "sportsmen" with their guns, who between them took a devastating toll of the area's game. Finally, in 1898, despite considerable opposition from his contemporaries, President Kruger granted the proclamation of the Sabie Game Reserve to conserve the area's dwindling wildlife. This was the core of what was to become the much larger **Kruger National Park** ⑭, with boundaries approximating the part of the park that lies to the south of the Sabie River.

The Kruger National Park has an extraordinarily rich and diverse animal life, which together with its tremendous size makes it one of the world's great game reserves. Some 147 mammal species have been recorded (the second-highest tally for any African national park), including lion, leopard, cheetah, wild dog, spotted hyena, elephant, black and white rhino, hippo, zebra, giraffe, warthog, buffalo and 21 antelope species. The bird checklist of 517 species is particularly strong on raptors, along with several other large birds now rare outside of protected areas, such as ground hornbill, saddle-billed stork and kori bustard. Of the other vertebrate classes, 114 reptile, 34 amphibian and 49 fish species have been recorded, while the more conspicuous invertebrates include the dung beetle (often seen rolling elephant dung along the road), a variety of butterflies, and – somewhat less endearing – significant numbers of mosquitoes in summer.

Although the park is served by an extensive network of roads and rest camps, this infrastructure barely affects the natural wildness. Some of the regulations governing activities may seem onerous, but they are directed mainly at the well-being of the wildlife. For example, the strictly enforced speed limit of 40 kph (25 mph) on dirt roads and 50 kph (30mph) on surfaced roads is designed to limit the number of road kills (and wrecks) that might otherwise result from collisions between traffic and wildlife – in any event, even at these speeds it's difficult to spot well-camouflaged wildlife, and you'd see nothing if you went any faster.

Plenty of coach tours of the Kruger National Park are available, but game viewing from a private car is just as enjoyable – and you can go at your own pace. The best game-viewing is in the morning until about 10am and in the late afternoon. Camps open at dawn (ranging from 4.30am in midsummer to 6.30am in winter) and it is well worth rising early to get the best sightings of predators,

Maps on pages 282 & 288

Anopheles mosquito, the malaria carrier. Malaria kills more than a million people every year in Africa alone.

BELOW: the Sabie River, lifeblood to big game.

A marker on the Jock of the Bushveld Road, a scenic 12-km (8-mile) route through the Kruger National Park once used by transport riders such as Percy Fitzpatrick and his dog, Jock.

BELOW: Kruger Park's monument to its founder.

which are generally most active at this time of day. The sweltering midday hours are best spent enjoying a picnic at a waterhole, or in the camps, some of which have swimming pools. Camp gates and park entrance gates close at sunset (6.30pm in summer and 5.30pm in winter) and late comers are fined. Frustratingly, this early closing time often means abandoning a game drive just when it holds most promise. However, night drives in special vehicles with knowledgeable driver-guides are on offer in the larger camps.

The South African cognoscenti try to visit the park during the dry winter months of May to September, when temperatures are relatively moderate, mosquito activity (and the risk of contracting malaria) is very low, and the thinner vegetation improves the odds of picking up predators. The very best time to visit is towards the end of the dry season, from August into early October, when the lack of any other standing water forces the wildlife to concentrate around perennial waterholes and rivers, where they can more easily be spotted.

Paradoxically, tourist numbers in the Kruger Park actually peak during the hot, wet summer months of October to April, which is favoured by international visitors as it's the best time to visit Cape Town and it coincides with the European winter. Fortunately, spring and summer are not without their attractions – the trees and flowers are at their best, bird life is abundant thanks to an influx of migratory species, and many of the animals are nursing newborn young.

Wilderness hiking trails – where face-to-face encounters with big game are a real possibility – are conducted under the supervision of experienced rangers. Trails operate out of six base camps; they last three nights and two days, starting either on Sunday or Wednesday. The number of hikers on each trail is usually limited to 10, so book well in advance.

The southern camps

Most of Kruger's game is spread fairly evenly throughout the park, but the frequency of sightings will obviously be determined by topography and vegetation. Near the southern rivers and watering holes (Skukuza, Pretoriuskop, Lower Sabie and Crocodile Bridge), hippo, elephant, crocodile, buffalo and small herds of giraffe are often spotted. The central parts (Satara, Olifants, Letaba) are inhabited by large herds of antelope and zebra, which in turn attract the larger predators such as lion and cheetah. In the north (Shingwedzi, Punda Maria), large herds of elephant and buffalo are often spotted, as well as leopard and the elusive nyala.

As well as four small bushveld camps without restaurant or shop facilities (which can provide an exciting experience of self-catered camping in the wild), there are 18 rest camps, varying in size and character. Most camps have restaurants, but guests also have the option of cooking their own food on open-air barbecues provided at the accommodation huts. Food and fuel are sold in the larger camps. The five smaller camps – Boulders, Mopani, Jock of the Bushveld, N'wanetsi and Roodewaal – are private and must be taken in their entirety by a single party. They accommodate a maximum of 15 people, and no catering is provided.

Most of the larger rest camps lie to the south of the Olifants River, which also forms the boundary

Map on page 288

between Mpumalanga and Limpopo provinces. Orpen, Malelane and Crocodile Bridge are entry-gate camps, used most often as a first base by visitors arriving shortly before the park gates close for the night. But don't let that put you off: the road between Orpen and Satara must rank as one of the very best for lion, spotted hyena and other large predator sightings, while the immediate vicinity of Crocodile Bridge is the most reliable part of the park for rhinos.

Deeper into the park, **Pretoriuskop A**, set in the thick acacia woodland of the southwest, is the oldest camp in the park, with a large and welcoming swimming pool – the surrounding roads are good for rhino and the localised sable antelope. **Skukuza B** is the biggest and busiest camp, a bustling village in its own right, but it also lies at the heart of some of the best game-viewing roads. The up-market, modern design of **Berg-en-Dal C** near the southern border of the park is quite unlike the traditional African rondavels of other camps. Set in a hilly landscape overlooking the Matjulu Dam, its extensive, well-fenced grounds are one of the few places where you can walk in the park and enjoy the flora at close quarters.

A firm favourite with many Kruger aficionados is **Lower Sabie D**, a relatively small camp set attractively on the banks of a dam on the Sabie River, in the heart of a prime viewing area. Elephants are numerous and can often be seen from the camp as they visit the Sabie River, or at the small water hole on the Skukuza Road about 1 km (⅔ mile) from camp. The drive along the river towards Skukuza should reward you with sightings of buffalo and bushbuck. It can also be good for lion and leopard, and the opportunities for bird-watching are excellent. Unfortunately, this road also carries the densest traffic in the park – if it gets too much, try the quieter but often very rewarding road loop to and from Crocodile Bridge.

Further north, **Satara E** is a large camp set in the open savannah of the park's central region. Scenically, it's not very interesting, but several good game-viewing roads emanate from it, and cheetah and lion are regularly seen within a 10-km (6-mile) radius of camp. Large seasonal concentrations of wildebeest and zebra may be seen on the road towards Nwanetsi, and if you have no intention of staying at the more northerly camps, then do try to fit in a day trip northwards as far as Olifants. The most northerly camp in Mpumalanga is the tiny but highly recommended **Balule F**, which consists of just ten huts and a similar number of camp sites about 5 km (3 miles) south of the Olifants River.

Private game reserves

In the 1960s and 1970s, a number of drought-stricken farms adjacent to the southern half of the park were turned into game farms and reserves by their enterprising owners, and so granted a new lease of life. Set in the **Sabi Sand Game Reserve**, which abuts the Kruger north of Skukuza, MalaMala, Londolozi and Sabi Sabi game reserves are among the best known of these private reserves, each offering luxurious bush-style accommodation to go with the spectacular game-watching. Many others have subsequently sprang up in their wake; prices are generally high (on a par with five-star rated hotels) but then so are the standards of service. At night, dinner is set out under the stars in a traditional *boma*, where guests can exchange their experiences of the day

BELOW: Chacma baboon and young.

Because the Kruger Park's population of elephants is culled every year, it has amassed a large ivory stockpile.

around the campfire. The use of private cars for game viewing is forbidden in these reserves, which have their own four-wheel-drive vehicles and experienced game guides to lead visitors around. Not only does this mean that more game is seen, but much can be learned from the guides, who explain the behaviour of animals, how to track their spoor and how they integrate with the natural environment. The less obvious things – trees, geology, small mammals and birds – are also shown and explained. Night drives are integral to the private game reserve experience, and come with a high chance of seeing the elsewhere elusive leopard, along with other nocturnal oddities such as bushbaby, serval, genet and civet.

In recent years, all of the eastern lowveld game parks (except those that still permit hunting) have removed the fences between themselves and between the Kruger National Park, so that wildlife moves unimpeded across the entire region. The Kruger National Park has now been amalgamated into the Great Limpopo Transfrontier Park, joining Zimbabwe's Gonarezhou National Park and Mozambique's Limpopo National Park to make Africa's largest game reserve at 35,000 sq. km (22,000 sq. miles). An important practical landmark in the development of the Transfrontier Park was the opening of the **Giriyondo border post**, 45 km (28 miles) northeast of Letaba, in 2006. Not only does this allow direct access between the Kruger and Limpopo national parks, but it means there is now a direct road corridor between Phalaborwa and the Mozambican beach resort of Xai-Xai, which could have a significant impact on tourist development for both towns.

The northern Kruger

BELOW: vernacular creation...

Unquestionably the most scenic of the Kruger camps, **Olifants ⑥** is set on a high cliff overlooking the northern bank of the eponymous river. The game

viewing from the comfort of the restaurants and public verandas here can be simply superb – ne'er was a river more aptly named than the Olifants (Elephants) – and the surrounding roads offer reliable game viewing.

Only 30 km (18½ miles) further north, **Letaba** ❶ is named after the meandering seasonal river upon whose southern bank it lies, and can also offer good in-house game viewing (elephants on the river, bushbuck in the riparian forest, and some wonderful bird life in the shady fig trees). A speciality of this area is the uncommon roan antelope. Since 1993, the camp has housed an elephant exhibition that includes the 3-metre (10-ft) long, 50-plus kg (100-lb) tusks of the so-called Magnificent Seven – a group of immense bulls who roamed the area for decades before they died of old age in the 1980s.

Coming from the south, the area around Olifants and Letaba feels pretty quiet in terms of tourist traffic. Head further north still, into the part of the park that was first proclaimed in the 1920s, and things start to take on a genuine wilderness atmosphere – amazingly, only three public camps lie in the half of the park north of Letaba, with a combined bed space far smaller than that of Skukuza alone. **Mopani** ❶, the first camp you reach coming from Letaba, is one of the newest in the park, set in an area of dry mopane woodland that can offer rather indifferent game viewing, but it makes for a convenient overnight stop.

Far more reliable for wildlife is **Shingwedzi** ❶, a medium-to-small camp set attractively on the stretch of the eponymous river above the Kanniedood Dam. The best game drive here follows the river for about 10 km (6 miles) south of the camp, through an area favoured by elephants, buffalo and handsome male kudus, to the dam wall. The bird life here is among the best in the park – look out for openbilled, yellow-billed and woolly necked storks near the water, and the spectacular

Map on page 288

BELOW: ...in a rural community.

Elephants rarely use the park's designated crosswalks.

BELOW: a very unusual encounter: leopards are seldom seen in daylight.

broad-billed roller in the riverine woodland. Further north still, Punda Maria is a small camp ideally placed to explore the superb and remote Pafuri game-viewing circuit on the Luvuvhu River near the Zimbabwe border. Ongoing archaeological research suggests that the northern Kruger is a pre-colonial treasure house, and one very interesting site is **Thulamela**, a 16th-century royal village set close to Pafuri; guided tours can be arranged from your camp.

The politics of conservation

In post-apartheid South Africa, people who had been evicted from their homes on racial grounds between 1936 and 1994 are entitled to appeal to a special court for restoration or compensation. A number of such claims have been lodged against the Kruger Park, but only one – that of the Makuleke in the far north – appears to have much substance. In 1969, the Makuleke were evicted from their ancestral grounds between the Levuvhu and Limpopo rivers and resettled on the park's western boundary, so that the fences could be extended as far as the Zimbabwean border. If found to be valid, their claim will probably be settled by means of financial compensation.

The Makuleke's story reflects something of the extraordinary zeal with which Kruger's administrators carried out their conservation mission during the apartheid era. Indeed, the image most black South Africans had of the park was that it was a kind of armed camp, run by white racists for the pleasure of a privileged elite. Incidents such as that of 1988, when – to cheers from tourists following the scene with field glasses and long lenses – rangers ran to ground a group of guerrillas, heading through the bush with a haversack of hand grenades, only reinforced this view. Because Mozambique was sympathetic to the then-outlawed ANC, the park's

sensitive eastern border with that country was patrolled by a quasi-military unit of rangers trained by instructors from the SADF's 111 Battalion. Even today, a select group of game wardens are still given paramilitary training by former counter-insurgency specialists, to defend themselves against modern-day poachers armed with automatic weapons. In addition, rangers are sometimes called on to act as impromptu border guards, intercepting illegal immigrants from Mozambique who have negotiated a hazardous passage through the bush in order to seek back-door entry into South Africa.

Maps
on pages
282 & 288

Baobab country

Leaving the Kruger Park from its northerly Punda Maria or Pafuri gates, you can follow the R524 and R525 respectively to connect with the N1 highway after about an hour's drive. Either way, the first major town you'll find yourself in is nondescript **Makhado** (formerly called Louis Trichardt, after the intrepid Voortrekker), which lies just south of the small but impressive **Soutpansberge** (Saltpan Mountains). A large variety of small antelopes and birds – including raptors – can be spotted on these richly forested slopes, while in the northern section you will also see rock shelters with vivid prehistoric wall paintings. One of the most popular ways of exploring these mountains is on the five-day Soutpansberg Hiking Trail.

North of the Soutpansberg, at the top of Limpopo Province, lies the traditional homeland of the Venda. Like the people of southern Zimbabwe with whom they have close historical and cultural links, the Venda were skilled miners and masons, and the ruins of their intricately patterned stone structures can still be seen. In earlier centuries, they traded iron, copper and ivory with Arab merchants on the east coast; historians are only now beginning to understand the cultural and economic impact of these ancient trade routes on the African hinterland.

BELOW: the "inverted" baobab looks like a fairy-tale creation.

In these remote areas, traditional rituals continue to survive; ancestral spirits guard many of the pools and forests in these beautiful mountains. Most important of the holy places is **Lake Fundudzi** ⑮. The best way to reach this quiet and beautiful spot is to hike the four-day **Mabuda-Shango Hiking Trail**, which starts from the Thathe-Vondo Forest Station, 71 km (44 miles) north of Makhado. Visitors to these holy forests and lakes should always take care to respect the beliefs of the local people, and swimming and washing in the lakes is forbidden.

From time to time, initiation ceremonies take place in Venda villages, and visitors may, by special arrangement with the local tourist office, witness the famous python dance, part of the *domba* or initiation ceremony. Lining up closely behind one another, young girls of the village mime the serpentine movement of a python to the beat of sacred drums. At Thohoyandou, fine carvings and other curios can be bought from traders along the road side. The **Honnet Nature Reserve**, 90 km (55 miles) east of Makhado, has large numbers of game roaming between the ancient baobab trees and the bush – bus tours and hiking trails are offered, but private cars are forbidden entry.

South Africa's northern border with Zimbabwe is the Limpopo River, which can be reached by follow-

ing the N1 north for about 100 km (60 miles) though **Musina** – a dull little town rescued from total anonymity by the surrounding stands of bulbous baobab trees – to the Beitbridge border post. Copper has been mined in the Limpopo Valley since prehistoric times, and the district is rich in archaeological relics.

Proclaimed a World Heritage Site in 2003, **Mapungubwe Hill** lies at the confluence of the Limpopo and Shashi rivers some 75 km (45 miles) west of Musina in the newly proclaimed **Mapungubwe** (initially Vhembe Dongola) **National Park** (open daily, no gate times enforced; entrance charge; tel: 015-534 0102). The stone ruins on this hill, which were occupied from approximately AD950–1300, are the precursor to the even more impressive ruins of Great Zimbabwe to the north, and have yielded several artefacts – including a pair of golden rhinos in 1932 – that hint at trade links with the Indian Ocean coast. In addition to the ruins, Mapungubwe National Park contains several rock-art sites and a good variety of big game and birds. It is hoped that Mapungubwe will eventually be merged with Botswana's Tuli Block and the Tuli Safari Area of Zimbabwe to become part of a transfrontier park.

The bushveld: hot, yellow plains

Heading back southward in the direction of Pretoria, the Great North Road pushes steadily on through a series of hot, yellow plains – classic cattle-ranching country. Some 112 km (70 miles) south of Makhado, you pass through plain, dusty **Polokwane** ⑯, capital of Limpopo Province, then about 70 km (45 miles) further comes nondescript **Mokopane**; while pressing on a further 90 km (56 miles) through sleepy Naboomspruit brings you to the agricultural settlement of **Modimolle** ⑰ *(see Dorps feature, page 315).*

BELOW:
a rural village.

Map on page 282

Modimolle was formerly known as Nylstroom (Nile Stream) after a latter-day Voortrekker group called the Jerusalem-gangers attempted to cross Africa in 1886 and mistook a river flowing past a pyramid-shaped hill for the Nile – somewhat naively, they were convinced they had reached Egypt. The bird life around Modimolle is among the richest in South Africa, in terms of both numbers and variety. The little **Nylsvley Nature Reserve** (daily 6am–6pm; entrance charge; tel: 014-743 1074) conserves some of the marshland 16 km (10 miles) north of the town. This key wetland attracts more than 400 species of bird, notably one of the greatest concentrations of waterfowl in South Africa, and 70 mammal species are present in the reserve.

Aeons ago, the Great Rift Valley in East Africa cracked open, pumping masses of molten rock southwards and eventually creating the Igneous Bushveld Complex – today regarded as one of the world's richest mineral areas. Traces of these ancient seismic events are still evident around the town of **Bela Bela**, founded near the largest of several hot mineral springs which erupt from the flat savannah.

Driving along the N1, it's impossible to ignore the distant mountain massif on the western horizon. This is the Waterberg, an isolated mountain range long used for cattle ranching which has only recently opened up to tourism. Various ranches offer horse-riding safaris and other kinds of activity holiday, and there are also three luxurious private reserves within the **Lapalala Wilderness Area** (tel: 014-755 4395), some 130 km (80 miles) from Nylstroom. Nearby **Marakele National Park** (tel: 014-777 1745) has been restocked with indigenous game and is now home to the world's largest breeding colony of endangered Cape vultures as well as elephant and both black and white rhino; the rich diversity of plant species includes the rare Waterberg cycad. ❏

Afrikaner polymath Eugene Marais – lawyer, farmer, natural scientist, poet and novelist – farmed in the Waterberg from 1907 to 1917. His best-known work, The Soul of the Ape, *was based on a study of local wildlife.*

BELOW: the young always lend a helping hand.

THE BULBOUS BAOBAB

African legend has it that in a light-hearted moment, the gods planted the first baobab upside down. Yet the role of these monster trees is more important than their weird shape suggests. Because their fibrous wood allows them to store huge volumes of water, they can offer critical relief in times of drought – to humans as well as animals. This perpetual supply of water ensures an abundance of leaves every spring, providing both shade and nourishment to animals and insects alike. The soft, well-insulated stems are ideal for hole-nesting birds such as barbets and hornbills. After these have been vacated, the nests are often re-employed as beehives, or retreats for snakes and lizards, so that every baobab is always abuzz with the comings and goings of its many residents. People of the Limpopo River Valley attribute fertility properties to the fruits, filled with seeds embedded in a refreshing white "cream-of-tartar" pulp; rock paintings in the region often portray women with baobab fruits instead of breasts. Baobabs can live for 3,000–4,000 years. When they die, the end is swift and dramatic. In a few months, the ancient fibres disintegrate and the tree simply collapses in on itself, disappearing so suddenly that it was once thought that baobabs ignited spontaneously and burned away.

TWO ROUTES TO CAPE TOWN

*Two overland routes from Johannesburg to Cape Town –
a journey from vast, sunburned plains to fertile
valleys graced with historic wine farms*

Map on page 300

Few tourists undertake the long overland trek through the interior between South Africa's two largest cities. And understandably so. The most direct route, the N1 via Bloemfontein, entails a daunting 1,400-km (875-mile) drive through a landscape of open farmland and semi-desert that has its apologists but offers few opportunities for sightseeing, and much the same might be said for the slightly longer N12 via Kimberley. If you need to travel directly between Johannesburg and Cape Town, the most efficient route is undoubtedly the aerial one – what's more, the arrival of several budget-friendly domestic airlines means that flying is also the cheapest option for single travellers and couples.

There is, however, a third inland road route between Gauteng and Cape Town – and it is well worth considering. True, the N14 and N7, which run via Springbok through the arid heart of the thinly populated Northern Cape, won't hold out much appeal to agoraphobics, nor will they to those visitors seeking the sort of tropical beach nirvanas that proliferate on the east coast. Furthermore, advocates of the N12/7 who bang on about it being only 200 km (120 miles) longer than the N1 are begging the question somewhat, since it would scarcely be worth undertaking this additional mileage unless you also made a few diversions that would double the total driving distance and require at least a week and better 10 days to complete. Make that commitment, however, and you'll be amply rewarded. The Northern Cape accounts for almost one-third of South Africa's surface area, but supports less than 5 percent of the national population; its wide-open spaces and perennial blue skies are possessed of an austere beauty and spirit-enriching tranquillity that reaches its apex in the fantastic granite moonscapes of Augrabies Falls National Park and the soulful red dunefields of the remote Kgalagadi Transfrontier Park on the Namibia/Botswana border.

ROUTE ONE: BLOEMFONTEIN

Travelling southwards from Johannesburg along the N1 for about 300 km (180 miles) brings you to the turn-off to the **Willem Pretorius Game Reserve** (daily 6am–6pm; entrance charge; tel: 057-651 4003), which lies between the identikit highveld towns of Kroonstadt and Winburg. This underrated reserve harbours the largest extant herd of black wildebeest (some 600), as well as introduced populations of giraffe, buffalo and white rhino. A large dam is part of the reserve and many of the 200 bird species that have been recorded here can be seen in the vicinity of the dam. Boat trips are organised and the fishing is good.

Heading further south along the N1, you reach **Bloemfontein ❶** – or more accurately a series of off-

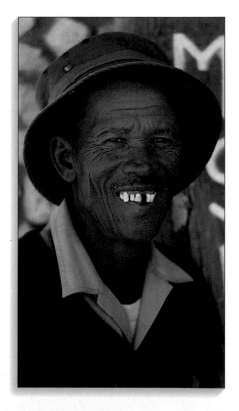

LEFT: the N1 motorway near the Karoo.
BELOW: ranger in the Kgalagadi Transfrontier Park.

*Kimberley's Big
Hole, once the
world's richest
diamond mine.*

ramps that lie a few kilometres northwest of the city centre – after another 100 km (60 miles) or so. The long-serving capital of Free State Province, Bloemfontein (also known as Manguang) means spring of flowers, a name which dates back to 1840 when the Voortrekker Johannes Nicolaas Brits built his *hartbeeshuisie* (a simple thatched dwelling with a dung floor) here, at the site of a spring encircled by clover.

Bloemfontein briefly served as capital of the Old Republic of the Free State before it was occupied by the British forces of Lord Roberts during the Anglo–Boer War (1899–1902). The occupation was a mixed blessing. The descendants of the Voortrekkers, who had braved the dangers of the wild unknown to escape the British Empire, had nothing but contempt for the Union Jack hoisted over their town. But British occupancy protected the town from the ravages of war, ensuring that its architectural heritage remained well preserved as it is to this day.

For a better understanding of the war and its background, the excellent **Anglo-Boer War Museum** (Mon–Fri 9am–4.30pm, Sat 10am–5pm, Sun 2–5pm;

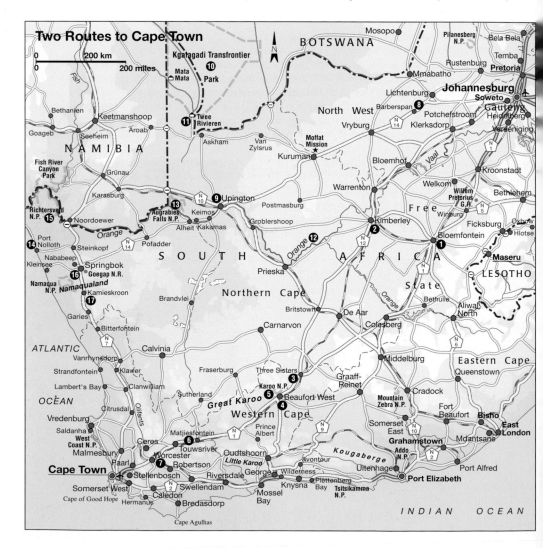

Two Routes to Cape Town

Map
on page
300

entrance charge; tel: 051-447 0079) stands alongside the **National Women's Monument**, which was unveiled in 1913 to commemorate the Boer women that died in British concentration camps.

Stroll down **President Brand Street**, which is widely regarded as one of South Africa's most beautiful streets. Most of the historic buildings are open to the public apart from the **Fourth Raadsaal**, once the parliamentary building of the Boer's Orange Free State Republic and now the provincial legislature. The Old Government Building on the corner of President Brand and Maitland streets houses the **National Afrikaans Literary Museum** (Mon–Fri 7.30am–12.15pm, 1–4pm, Sat 9am–noon; free; tel: 051-405 4034), with displays on all the leading lights of Afrikaans literature from the brilliant Eugene N. Marais *(see page 86)* to anti-apartheid novelist André Brink. Continue down to the corner of St Georges Street to reach the **Old Presidency** (Tues–Fri 10am–noon, 1–4pm, Sun 2–5pm; free; tel: 051-448 0969), and the **First Raadsaal** (Mon–Fri, Sat and Sun pm; free), the city's oldest surviving building.

The British side to Bloemfontein often surprises visitors – the Free State is, after all, an Afrikaner heartland. Yet sites such as **Naval Hill** and **Queen's Fort** (Mon–Fri), as well as the Edwardian Ramblers cricket ground with its Edwardian clubhouse, preserve the colonial heritage. Bloemfontein also holds a very significant place in black South African history, for this was the birthplace in 1912 of the South African Native National Congress – known after 1923 as the African National Congress, or ANC. The **Bloemfontein Zoo** (daily 8am–5pm; entrance charge; tel: 051-405 8498) reputedly contains more primate species than any other in South Africa, and was once famous for its liger – the sterile (and now, in this instance, stuffed) offspring of a lion and a tiger.

BELOW: the appeal court, Bloemfontein.

A cement owl, bright-eyed and inscrutable, guards the entrance to the Owl House in the peaceful village of Nieu-Bethesda.

BELOW: during the Diamond Rush, this Kimberley building was the main headquarters of the De Beers group.

Diamond country

Situated some 470 km (295 miles) southwest of Johannesburg along the N12, **Kimberley ❷** ("the town that sparkles") is also accessible from Bloemfontein following the almost dead straight 150-km (90-mile) N8 along a road bordered by vast sunflower fields. Kimberley is distinctly past its prime; indeed, when you consider that this was the country's fastest-growing town in the 1870s, its present-day atmosphere of somnolence is astonishing. Unfortunately for modern residents of Kimberley, their hometown's former prosperity was based entirely on diamonds, the supply of which petered out in the 1930s. The local economy has been boosted considerably since Kimberley was chosen over Upington as the capital of the Northern Cape, despite lying right on the eastern border of this vast province.

Whether it's worth making a special effort to visit Kimberley is debatable, but passers-through will find that the open-air **Mine Museum** (daily 8am–5pm; entrance charge; tel: 053-833 1557) does a good job of reincarnating the city as it looked in its colourful heyday. Here you can see a collection of 40 reconstructed buildings such as Barney Barnato's Boxing Academy and the Diggers' Tavern, along with a private railway coach custom-built for the directors of the all-powerful De Beers mining group. You'll also find an exquisite collection of uncut stones here, along with a copy of the largest diamond in the world (616 carats).

All the stones in the museum come from the nearby mine known as **The Big Hole**, some 800 metres (2,600 ft) deep and 470 metres (1,500 ft) wide *(see picture page 300)*. Today it's filled with water and the towers are derelict, but between 1871 and 1914, 2,722 kg (5,988 lbs) of diamonds were excavated from this giant gash in the earth. In the city centre lies an unexpected treat –

the **William Humphreys Art Gallery** (Mon–Sat 8am–4.45pm, Sun 2– 4.45pm; entrance charge; tel: 053-831 1724), which contains one of South Africa's best collections of 16th- and 17th-century Flemish and Dutch Old Masters as well as South African works. On the eastern edge of town you'll find the wealthy suburb of Belgravia, where the diamond barons built their grand houses. Several villas are open to the public, furnished just as they were in their heyday – **The Bungalow on Lodge Road**, built for a certain H.P Rudd, is open by appointment; enquire at the tourist office.

Another interesting record of the city's diamond-mining days is housed in the **Duggan-Cronin Gallery** (Mon–Sat 10am–5pm, Sun 2–5pm; entrance charge; tel: 053-842 0099) on Egerton Road. Exhibits include a collection of photographs of mine labourers taken between 1919–39 by Alfred Duggan-Cronin, a nightwatchman for De Beers.

Outside Kimberley on the Barkley West Road is the **Wildebeest Kuil** (Tues–Fri 10am–5pm, Sat–Sun 11am–4pm; entrance charge; tel: 053-833 7069), where several prehistoric rock engravings of animals can be admired in-situ. The self-guided tour includes a 25-minute introductory film and short walking trail with 10 listening posts providing audio commentary.

The Central Karoo

Southwest of Kimberley and Bloemfontein, the N12 and N1 run roughly parallel to each other for approximately 550 km (330 miles), passing through an eastern extension of Northern Cape Province, before finally they converge at Three Sisters on the border with Western Cape Province. Once little more than a dot on the map, **Three Sisters ❸** – which is named after a nearby trio of dolerite-

Map on page 300

BELOW: you can hitch a ride on this old train at the Kimberley Mine Museum.

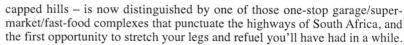

Many old farmsteads in the Karoo have been abandoned during hard times.

BELOW: the rare geometric tortoise is only found in the southwestern Cape.

capped hills – is now distinguished by one of those one-stop garage/supermarket/fast-food complexes that punctuate the highways of South Africa, and the first opportunity to stretch your legs and refuel you'll have had in a while.

Three Sisters lies in the heart of the Great Karoo, the name of which derives from a San phrase meaning Land of Great Thirst. For most visitors – and even for South Africans – these wide, rocky plains are often seen as a natural obstacle, something to overcome en route to the lush winelands or frenetic Gauteng. Yet the Karoo's bleakness has a beauty all its own. Dotted with flat-topped *koppies* (hills), it is somehow reminiscent of the South Dakota badlands; a spaghetti-western setting enhanced at sunset when the *koppies* – peculiarly light-sensitive – change colour from warm red and ochre to purple and blue. At night the cool, clear air tempts you outside to gaze at the brilliant stars of the southern hemisphere.

The origin of the Karoo is still a mystery. It is known that the soft sandstone and shales here were created some 200 million years ago, when vast quantities of mud, clay and sand were first washed into the low-lying, marshy Karoo basin. As the climate gradually warmed, the area was invaded by an ocean, trapping the remains of a temperate forest and creating significant deposits of coal, which are now mined in the northern part of the system. The entire sequence was capped some 130 million years ago by a massive volcanic outpouring of basalt lava. The softer sandstone layers underneath gradually eroded, while the hard volcanic dolerite remained, creating those characteristic flat-topped hills.

It is ironic that what was once a gigantic freshwater swamp is today drought-stricken and almost devoid of surface water. Rainfall is quite unpredictable – when it does rain, torrents fall in fierce thunderstorms, often causing destruction and erosion as the water cascades into normally dry water beds. Keep an eye out for that trademark of the Karoo, its creaking wind pumps. This ingenious but simple contraption forms the backbone of the region's economy. Erected at a borehole and then left to its own devices, the wind pump continuously churns up water from deep underground into drinking troughs for livestock.

Beaufort West

About 75 km (45 miles) southwest of Three Sisters lies the self-styled "Capital of the Karoo", the small town of **Beaufort West** ❹, whose dry climate once made it a popular winter holiday resort for asthmatic and otherwise wheezy Capetonians. Those days are long gone, but Beaufort West is still studded with its fair share of guesthouses and hotels, most of them rather modest crash pads geared towards tired Cape-bound motorists. In the town itself you can visit three neo-Gothic churches and the **Town Hall** (open daily), built in 1867. A wing of the latter is now a museum, which includes in its exhibits a section dedicated to the town's most famous son, the pioneering heart surgeon Dr Chris Barnard.

Beaufort West lies at the hub of a rich farming district known primarily for its merino sheep, a breed that was first brought to the country from the Netherlands in 1789. Today, more than 35 million of the ani-

Map on page 300

mals graze on a diet of semi-desert shrubs, herbs and succulents, which creates the utterly distinctive taste of Karoo mutton – well worth trying should you decide to stop over for lunch or dinner in the area.

Comparatively more interesting than Beaufort West itself is the **Karoo National Park 5** (daily 5am–10pm; entrance charge; tel: 023-415 2828), the main entrance to which lies about 5 km (3 miles) west of town along the N1. Established in 1979, the park covers almost 33,000 hectares (81,500 acres). Early hunters and explorers recounted tales of a land where thick swathes of grass stood shoulder-high and where the teeming herds of springbok were so huge that wagons had to be unharnessed for two or three days to allow the herd to pass by. But "civilisation" brought with it hunters and guns and ploughs and fences and fires. Two animal species – the zebra-like quagga and the bluebok antelope – were shot to extinction, and other herds were decimated and driven into the remotest regions of the arid interior. Today, nature reserves like the Karoo National Park are trying their utmost to preserve some of that fauna and its typical Karoo habitat.

Visitors are likely to see limited numbers of springbok, gemsbok and hartebeest – reintroduced here by game rangers – as well as smaller predators such as caracal, black-backed jackal and African wild cat. A unique feature is the great concentration of tortoises, of which the world's largest and smallest species can both be spotted here – these are the leopard tortoise, which weighs in at 45 kg (100 lb), and *Homopus s. signatus* (Namaqualand speckled padloper), which is just 100-mm (3-inches) long and weighs 150 grams (5 oz). The park also forms the major stronghold for the riverine rabbit, an endangered Karoo-specific species that's now thought to number just 1,500 in the wild.

BELOW: you may spot the majestic black eagle in the Karoo National Park.

In spring, the dusty landscape is covered with a colourful carpet of wild-flowers. This is a particularly rewarding time to tackle the demanding 27-km (17-mile) **Springbok Hiking Trail**, for which you should allow three days. The route is seldom fully booked, but it is closed between November and February because of the excessive heat. Nights are spent in two simple huts along the route. If you prefer to restrict your walking tour to just a few hours, you can undertake an excursion into prehistory along the **Fossil Trail**, where fossilised remains over 50 million years old can be seen. The path is also suitable for the blind and for those in wheelchairs.

Continue your journey through the "Land of the Great Thirst" towards **Matjiesfontein ❻**, some 240 km (150 miles) southwest of Beaufort West. This lovely little Victorian town has been declared a National Monument in its entirety. An enterprising Scotsman, Jimmy Logan, was the first to make profitable use of the railway station here, a refilling point for steam locomotives about to embark on the long haul north to Pretoria through the parched Karoo. It wasn't long before he was supplying the trains with water and the passengers with cold drinks and hot lamb chops. Logan's business prospered to such an extent that he was soon able to build the elegant **Lord Milner Hotel**. You can still spend the night here if you wish, and the Karoo lamb still tastes as good as it did in Logan's times. During the Boer Wars the little town was a British garrison and the hotel served as a military hospital, with a lookout post in the tower. Today, Matjiesfontein is a popular stopover on the route between Johannesburg and Cape Town; the famous luxury Blue Train also pulls in here.

About 100 km (60 miles) past Matjiesfontein, the N1 leaves the Karoo to cross the Hex River Pass and descend into the strikingly different landscape of

BELOW:
a herd of springbok
on the move.

green mountains and cultivated river valleys that characterise the southwestern Cape. Another 30 km (18 miles) brings you to the champion winelands centre of **Worcester** ❼, from where you can either head straight on to Cape Town, some 80 km (55 miles) distant, or divert towards the Boland and wine-production centres such as **Stellenbosch** or **Franschhoek** (*see Winelands pages 182–8*).

ROUTE TWO: TOWARDS UPINGTON

The otherwise memorable journey from Gauteng to Cape Town through the heart of the Northern Cape starts less than auspiciously with a 350-km (210-mile) haul west along the N14 to **Vryburg**. The only attraction of note along this flat stretch of road is **Barberspan** ❽, an important wetland that flanks the northern side of the N14 between Sannieshof and Delarayville and often harbours flocks of up to 20,000 flamingos as well as large numbers of other water birds. As for Vryburg itself, it sprang to life in 1882 as the capital of a breakaway (hence the name, which means Freetown) Boer Republic called Stellaland – and nothing much of note seems to have happened there since that republic was disbanded in 1885.

Some 150 km (90 miles) further west, the pretty town of Kuruman owes its existence to the large freshwater spring that empties a remarkable 50,000 litres (227,000 gallons) of crystal-clear water daily into a lily-covered, tree-fringed pool in the town centre. The **Moffat Mission** (Mon–Sat 8am–5pm; entrance charge; tel: 053-712 1352), which lies 6 km (4 miles) from Kuruman along the Hotazel Road, was established in 1821 by the Scots missionary Robert Moffat. Oddly reminiscent of a misplaced English village, the mission is centred on the attractive stone church – built in 1838 and still in active use –

Map on page 300

TIP

Matjiesfontein is a little Victorian gem.. Keep a look out for items such as lampposts – shipped all the way from London.

BELOW: the Lord Milner Hotel, Matjiesfontein.

The crescent-shaped pods of the camel-thorn tree are a valuable source of food for many species of animal in the Kalahari Gemsbok National Park.

where Moffat's daughter Mary married a budding young explorer named David Livingstone.

Situated on the N14 roughly 260 km (155 miles) west of Kuruman – about 8–10 hours' drive from Gauteng if you're thinking of pushing through in one day – **Upington ❾** is the second-largest town in the Northern Cape after Kimberley, and (although it probably receives fewer international tourists annually than Table Mountain would on a quiet day) it is also an important regional tourist centre. Direct flights from Cape Town or Johannesburg shorten the journey here considerably; if you're planning to head off into the Kalahari, this is a good place to rent a four-wheel-drive vehicle, or even a mobile home. At the entrance to the Eiland Holiday Resort there's an impressive 1,041-metre (3,415-ft) long date-palm avenue – indeed, coming after the increasingly arid landscapes passed through on the N14, much of Upington feels unexpectedly green and leafy, thanks to its location on the banks of the Orange River, the country's largest waterway.

Kgalagadi Transfrontier Park

The remote, immense and utterly absorbing **Kgalagadi Transfrontier Park ❿** (daily dawn–dusk; entrance charge; tel: 054-561 2000) was created in 1999 when South Africa's 9,600-sq. km (3,750-sq. mile) Kalahari Gemsbok National Park merged with its larger but less-accessible cross-border counterpart, the Gemsbok National Park in Botswana. Characterised by red sand dunes interspersed with sandy river beds, the Kalahari Gemsbok is strikingly reminiscent of Australia's Simpson Desert, but with a more varied fauna, including all three of Africa's large felines as well as an impressive selection of smaller

BELOW: Kalahari saltpan, with camelthorn tree.

predators such as black-backed jackal, bat-eared fox (very visible in winter when it is more diurnal), Cape fox, caracal, suricate and yellow mongoose.

The only entrance to the park, and the site of the largest camp, is at **Twee Rivieren ⑪** (Two Rivers), which lies close to the confluence of the Auob and Nossob rivers – or, more normally, river beds, since the Auob might go three or four years without flowing, and the Nossob several decades. It's the rainwater that collects beneath the light sand of the river beds that ensures the vegetation along them is relatively lush, attracting surprisingly large concentrations of wildlife. It's not unusual to witness a cheetah running down a springbok along the Nossob's dry bed, or a large herd of handsome gemsbok with their rapier horns silhouetted against a sky bruised by thunderclouds. Heavily maned Kalahari lions escape the midday heat beneath thorn bushes, while brilliantly spotted leopards take refuge in the tall camelthorn trees.

The park's 200-odd bird species are sure to impress most visitors – highlights include the brilliant swallow-tailed bee-eater and the noisy but sometimes elusive crimson-breasted shrike, while a wide array of raptors is most visibly represented by Bateleur, pale chanting goshawk and the shrike-sized pygmy falcon. The large camelthorn trees *(Acacia erioloba)* that define the river's course are the life-giving source of the region, providing nesting sites for sociable weavers and the many other birds, and offering shade to game and domestic stock. The tree's large crescent-shaped pods also make for nutritious food when they fall. The gum is eaten by animals and used in traditional medicine by local communities. Giraffes (one herd of which was recently reintroduced to the park after several decades absence) can wrap their long prehensile tongues around the thorny branches and strip the leaves with seeming immunity to the cruel spikes.

The best time of the year to visit is between February and April, at least that is the case in years with a good amount of rainfall, as large herds of game concentrate along the river beds (don't forget to protect yourself against the pesky mosquitoes who also thrive on the damp environment). Some, however, might prefer the cooler winter months of June to September, when daytime temperatures are generally comfortable to warm, but the nights are very cold. The month of May would be an excellent compromise. Accommodation in the park is sometimes booked solid well in advance (booking 13 months in advance is normal). The relatively comfortable main camp is located at Twee Rivieren, but you can also spend the night at **Mata Mata Camp** (118 km/73 miles to the northwest, after a particularly attractive trip), located not far from the Namibian border which is, however, closed at that point. **Nossob Camp**, 152 km (94 miles) to the north and on the border with Botswana, is less attractive. There are also three new unfenced wilderness camps in the park, of which Grootkolk and Bitterpan each consist of just four double chalets apiece and overlook a water hole.

The closest town and normal springboard for visits is Upington, from where a nippy (and bizarrely quiet) 190-km (114-miles) surfaced road leads through some impressive dunes to Askham, after which it's 60 km

Map on page 300

BELOW:
Kalahari meerkat.

(100 miles) on dirt to Twee Rivieren. Coming from Johannesburg, a more direct route runs north from Kuruman through Van Zylsrus, but this involves 358 km (222 miles) of manoeuvring on dirt roads. Either route is do-able in an ordinary saloon car, provided you drive sensibly, but the Van Zylsrus route is exhausting and without suitable experience there's a real risk of losing control of the vehicle or getting stuck in the sand. Whichever route you use, leave in time to get there before the gate closes.

The Orange River

Back in Upington, the N14 continues westward along the banks of the **Orange River** ⑫, which dominates the entire region as it makes its inexorable way to the Atlantic Ocean like a giant serpent. Carrying almost a quarter of the volume of South Africa's entire river system, the 2,000-km (1,240-mile) long Orange is the life-giving source of the entire region. Artificially irrigated vineyards and orchards are a feature of the landscape around **Keimos** and **Kakamas**, respectively 50 km (30 miles) and 90 km (54 miles) west of Upington, and the green river banks, cultivated with cotton, fruit and grapes, stand in stark contrast to the arid surroundings.

The region is famous for its delicious sultanas, and provides a good deal of the table grapes exported from South Africa to Europe. The local dessert wines and sherries are also justly celebrated, and can be sampled in Kakamas's **Oranjerivier Wine Cellars** (tastings Mon–Fri 8am–4.30pm, Sat 8.30am–noon; tel: 054-337 8800) along with an ever-improving range of dry whites and reds.

The tiny **Tierberg Nature Reserve** (open daily; free) on the outskirts of Keimos offers a good view over the river and surrounding cultivated area, and also con-

The deep pools at the base of the Augrabies Falls are home to shoals of giant barbel – up to 2 metres (6½ ft) long – sightings of which have given rise to rumours of a river monster.

BELOW: taking a ride on the Orange River.

tains some excellent specimens of the striking kokerboom (quiver tree), a type of tree aloe whose bark was used by the San to make quivers for their arrows.

Just past Kakamas, a side road branches north from the N14 and follows the bank of the Orange River to **Augrabies Falls National Park** ⓭ (Apr–Sept daily 6.30am–10pm, Oct–Mar daily 6am–10pm; tel: 054-452 9200; book accommodation in advance through SANParks, *see page 334*). Here, overlooked by a gem of a rest camp, the Orange thunders spectacularly over a 56-metre (185-ft) cliff into a deep gorge carved out of the granite bedrock. Crashing down a further 35 metres (115 ft) over a series of secondary falls and cataracts, the water sends a vast column of spray into the air, enveloping the area in a heavy mist. Two large pools at the base of the falls are thought to be at least 130 metres (425 ft) deep and contain a great wealth in diamonds carried from the vicinity of Kimberley and washed over the edge – unfortunately, it is difficult to explore or extract the gems from underneath a waterfall.

The park contains a great deal more than just the waterfall. Colourful Cape flat lizards bask conspicuously around the rocky rest camp, from where you can wander or drive along a small road network from where springbok, klipspringer, rock hyrax and a variety of dry-country birds are likely to be seen. The route to Arrow Point is particularly recommended; there's a great view from here over two canyons simultaneously. More ambitiously, the popular three-day **Klipspringer Hiking Trail** (40 km/23 miles) is almost always booked solid during school holidays, and it closes during the extreme heat of summer. Night drives and black rhino tours to otherwise inaccessible parts of the park can be booked at the rest camp – as can the Augrabies Rush, a white-water rafting excursion along an 8-km (5-mile) long stretch of river with five sets of grade 2–3 rapids.

Map
on page
300

The striped ground squirrel is not too proud to beg scraps.

BELOW: klipspringer, Augrabies Falls National Park.

BELOW: it's rare to
see an oryx braving
the journey alone.

The Diamond Coast

From Kakamas, a lonely 250-km (150-mile) trip along the N14 leads via
Pofadder – a good place to stop for petrol and a cold drink, to the medium-
sized town of **Springbok** at the junction of the N7 between Cape Town and
Namibia. Here, you'll most probably want to head south, towards Cape Town,
but it's also possible to follow the N7 northwards to Steinkopf (52 km/32
miles) and turn onto the asphalt-surfaced R382 leading over the 950-metre
(3,100-ft) high Anninous Pass, down to the coast and **Port Nolloth ⑭**. The
biggest attraction here is the sunsets – utterly magnificent when they aren't
obscured by rising sea fog. Port Nolloth used to be a copper port, but today
the primary source of income is fishing – and not just for crayfish, either. Diamonds are sucked off the seabed here in large quantities by giant vacuum
cleaner-like devices. On its journey past Kimberley, the Orange River gath-
ers up diamond-rich sediments before spewing its precious load up and down
the Northern Cape coastline, thus creating the world's richest deposits of
alluvial diamonds.

Diamonds were discovered here almost by accident when a British officer,
Captain Jack Carstens, undertook an exploratory dig while visiting his parents
in Port Nolloth in 1926. The geologist Hans Merensky later claimed to have
found 487 diamonds under one stone, and in a single month he recovered 2,762
diamonds near Alexander Bay. As news spread, fortune seekers descended on
the area in droves, prompting the government to ban private prospecting. Today,
the coast between Kleinsee and Oranjemund is controlled by De Beers Consolidated Mining Company – founded by Cecil John Rhodes in 1880 – and the
public isn't allowed off the main road.

This stretch of coast is continually worked over and shifted by the world's largest armada of earth-moving equipment, and a vast wealth of diamonds is recovered each year. The desert-besieged fishing and diamond towns of the northwest coast are still real frontier places, and the only resorts are to be found much further south at Strandfontein near the Olifants River mouth and at the Port Nolloth extension, McDougall's Bay. These are rudimentary places as resorts go, catering almost exclusively for fishermen and the rough-and-ready local sheep-farming communities. If there is such a place as the end of the line, then Port Nolloth is surely it.

From Alexander Bay, an unsurfaced road leads to the **Richtersveld National Park** ⓑ (Oct–Apr 7am–7pm, May–Sept 7am–6pm; entrance charge; tel: 027-831 1506). Founded in 1993 (which makes it one of the newest national parks in the country), Richtersveld is a wild, semi-desert region with virtually no marked routes. Whatever you need here you have to bring yourself and – no less important – take out with you again when you leave. Winter is the only time it rains here, and in summer the temperature can rise as high as 50°C (122°F) – visits should be avoided during this time as the heat is simply unbearable. It's hard to believe that so much grows in such a harsh environment, but the diversity of succulents here is so rich that botanists are struggling to get them all classified and described. Some species are known from only one locality or even one specimen and are never found again. Others, like the halfmensboom (half-human tree – *Pachypodium namaquanum*) are equally strange; the San people believed they were half-plant and half-human, and anyone who has seen the single, thick tapering stem with its crowning rosette of tightly crinkled leaves will understand why. This remote park used to be accessible to campers only, but 10 self-catering chalets were built in 2005. The park now forms part of a transfrontier park with Ai-Ais in Namibia.

Namaqualand

Back on the N7, **Springbok** ⓖ is the principal town of a vast region of sandveld known as Namaqualand, which extends northwards from the Olifants River as far as Pofadder, and is renowned for its spring wildflower displays. For most of the year, these stony plains cannot hide the wrinkles and cracks of their age-old skin, or the tattiness of their drab green-grey cover. But come spring, fields burst forth in colours gay and dazzling. Nature favours these semi-arid scrublands with one youthful flush of wildflowers that draws people from all over the world for a few days in August or September each year. Indeed, the daisies of Namaqualand are one of South Africa's greatest natural attractions.

Springbok owes its existence to the rich copper reserves in the region (some mines are open to the public), and to something much rarer round here: a spring of fresh water. The big attraction, however is the **Goegap Nature Reserve** (daily 8am–4pm; entrance charge; tel: 027-712 1880), about 15 km (9 miles) to the east. It is absolutely stunning during the flowering season, and worth a visit even outside that time of year. In the Hester Malan Wild

Map on page 300

BELOW: windmills still power many of the country's farms.

Map on page 300

Flower Garden, which forms part of the reserve, you can admire over a hundred species of aloes and succulents, many of which are indigenous to the area. It's a 17-km (10-mile) long round trip if you decide to explore the reserve in your own car, but it's actually more rewarding to book the three-hour guided tour when you arrive; it will take you to more remote and exciting corners. Caracal, gemsbok, springbok and South Africa's only population of Hartmann's mountain zebra are just a few of the animals you may encounter.

The Namaqualand wildflower extravaganza lasts for only a short time each year and never erupts in the same place all at once, so make sure you listen to the weather forecast before you plan your trip (Cape Town flower hotline: 083-910 1028) and bear in mind there are no flowers without rain. One of the most reliable sites for wildflowers is **Kamieskroon** ⓱, 68 km (42 miles) south of Springbok, which consists of little more than a petrol station, a shop, and the Kamieskroon Hotel (a seasonal hotel if there ever was one) – the latter often booked solid by wildflower enthusiasts right through from July to September.

The nearby **Skilpad Wild Flower Reserve** (only open during the flower season; entrance charge; tel: 027-672 1614) gets most of the rain and the flowers here are particularly fine. There are three hiking paths to choose from. They take around 2–4 hours each to complete and navigate through the reserve in a way to show off the best views (in season) across the carpets of flowers. There is also a route for mountain bikes and another for horse riders – though you will, of course, have to supply your own horses and bicycles. Further south, only small corrugated-iron hamlets such as Garies, Bitterfontein and Vanrhynsdorp add variety to the dusty-brown wilderness before you arrive at Citrusdal and the moister southern section of the West Coast *(see pages 178–80).* ❏

BELOW: Kalahari grasslands.

Dorps

The paint brushes of history have coloured the South African landscape with a rich diversity of villages and hamlets – or dorps, as the locals call them, from the Afrikaans word for little town.

Tranquil and traditionally minded, often poor and distinctly down-at-heel, most dorps are just pinpoints on the map – yet they can be well worth the effort it takes to track them down. There's a timeless quality to these dusty verandahs and sun-baked stone cottages set back in wide main streets, where the rhythms of life are seductively slow and measured. Here, locals greet each other by name; such things as direct telephone dialling and video shops (to say nothing of racial integration) are but a recent fad, and everything – even the corner café – closes for lunch.

Take the time to delve behind the sleepy facade and you'll find most dorps steeped in romance and folklore, still proudly bearing testament to the colourful cast of characters – outlaws, fortune-seekers, missionaries and pioneers – who helped to shape the country over the past 100 years.

Bathurst in the Eastern Cape has a particularly fine collection of classic old buildings, built by British settlers in the 1820s. Here, the Pig & Whistle – the country's oldest pub – still resounds with bawdy laughter. Lazy creepers climb the walls of the old stone churches which sheltered settler women and children when the town became the focus of a series of bloody frontier wars with the Xhosa.

One of the strangest places anywhere in South Africa is Die Hel (The Hell), an isolated hamlet in the remote Karoo valley of Gamkaskloof. First settled by farmers during the Great Trek of 1837, residents contrived to avoid contact with the outside world for more than 50 years. It was only when Boer War guerillas fleeing the British stumbled across the valley that they were discovered – some 20 families, speaking an archaic form of High Dutch, clad in goat skins and only vaguely aware that there was a war on. It took until 1963, 126 years after the settlement was established, for a road connecting the valley to the outside world to be built (until then, all provisions were brought in by pack donkey over a mountain track).

The Northern Province settlement of Modimolle, formerly Nylstroom (Nile Stream), was named by a break-away sect of Voortrekkers on a mad mission to reach the Holy Land. Having driven their wagons all the way from the Cape, the day came when the doughty trekkers saw up ahead what they thought was a pyramid (actually, a solitary hill) and assumed they were in Egypt – and that the large, flooding river before them was the Nile.

Like so many dorps in the far north of the country, Leydsdorp began life as a mining camp at the turn of the 20th century, part of a colourful wild-west culture where the local stagecoaches travelling on to Pietersburg were pulled by zebra. Today, in the local cemetery, gravestones bear silent witness to the deadly plague of malaria and blackwater fever which brought the thriving little settlement to its knees in 1924 – and condemned it to the status of a dorp forever.   ❑

RIGHT: time moves slowly on these dusty, sun-baked streets.

SWAZILAND AND LESOTHO

*These two tiny kingdoms, both enclosed within
South Africa, have a great deal to offer
the adventurous traveller*

Maps
on pages
320

L isten! The drums – African drums playing out the rhythms of the ancient
continent. They tell stories of the people who lived here long, long before
the European settlers arrived. Listen to the beat quicken as they tell of
Swaziland and Lesotho, for apart from one brief period in Swaziland's history,
neither country has ever been ruled by whites.

Lesotho dates back to the time of the first Basotho king, Moshoeshoe. He
founded the Basotho nation, uniting a medley of vanquished clans after inter-
tribal clashes convulsed much of southern Africa during the 1820s and 1830s.
From his celebrated mountain stronghold, Thaba Bosiu (Mountain of the Night),
he went on to repel countless attacks by Zulu, Boer and British invaders.

Finally, tired of fighting, Moshoeshoe turned to Britain for aid. His kingdom
was proclaimed a British protectorate in 1851, and remained so until 1966 when
it became an independent democracy with a titular king.

Swaziland's history has much in common with Lesotho's. The Swazi nation
started to take shape in the late 1600s under a powerful chief, Dlamini. He forged
a nation of Nguni-speaking clans, closely related to the Zulus further south.

The Boers subjugated the Swazi for several decades, but when Britain won the
Anglo–Boer War at the turn of the 20th century, it inherited Swaziland. Mswati
III now rules one of the world's last absolute monar-
chies – political parties are banned, and ministers are
hand-picked by the king.

PRECEDING PAGES:
sangoma in
Malealea, Lesotho.
LEFT: Swazi
dancers
BELOW: Mbabane
craft market.

Highland peaks, wild lowveld

Compared to Lesotho, Swaziland has a good, pre-
dictable infrastructure and is a much simpler country
to negotiate. The main road through the country also
forms the least circuitous route between Zululand and
the Kruger Park, so that it slots neatly into any itinerary that includes both of these areas. Once in Swaziland, it's easy to organise guided tours or to rent a car
for self-drive trips, and travel conditions are safe too
(in Lesotho, even the weather conspires against you)
– though drivers should be aware that livestock quite
often wanders onto the road.

The country's attractions divide fairly neatly into
two categories: the comforts of the Ezulwini Valley,
with its numerous smart hotels, restaurants, casinos
and craft markets; and then the impressively well-
stocked and managed game reserves.

Many of the key sights are ranged on either side of
the capital, **Mbabane ❶**, which lies in the northwest of
the country on the South African border. Founded in
the mid-1880s, Mbabane has a temperate climate that
made it attractive to British settlers, and it was made
capital of the protectorate in 1903. Today, it's a bustling
little city of 50,000, rather lacking in charm or any

unique character – indeed, a few international embassies aside, there's little to distinguish Mbabane from any similarly sized South African town. The closest thing to a tourist attraction in the city centre is the main market, on Msunduzu Street, which offers good craft bargains but also attracts its fair share of pickpockets.

Craft-hunters should head for the **Ngwenya Glass Factory** (daily 9am–5pm; tel: 442 4053; www.ngwenyaglass.co.sz), which manufactures decorative and functional glassware from recycled bottles, and **Phumalanga Tapestries**, where Albert and Marie-Louise Reck weave (and sell) tapestries based on San rock art and bird designs. You'll find both at the border post at Oshoek, 23 km (14 miles) northwest of Mbabane.

Sibebe Rock

A 15-minute drive north from Mbabane, **Sibebe Rock ❷** is the largest exposed granite dome in the world. Sibebe rises in lunar splendour from the surrounding green valleys like Africa's answer to Ayers Rock (Ulura), and it's even more impressive when you realise it's merely the tip of a batholith that extends for a full 15 km (9 miles) below the earth's surface. Not for the faint of heart or giddy of head, Swazi Trails offers a guided three-hour ascent of the main face that's billed as the steepest commercial walk (more accurately, slow-motion wobble) in the world – difficult to verify, but thus far, they claim, nobody's returned with sufficient breath left to argue the point.

About 15 km (9 miles) southeast of Mbabane on the MR3, at the end of a tortuous descent down Malagwane Hill, is the lovely **Ezulwini Valley ❸**, the centre of most tourist activity in Swaziland. A sign as you enter proudly declares "Phuma Lankga Sikose" (Long Live the King), for the 30-km (18-mile) valley

BELOW: look out for hippos at the Mlilwane Wildlife Sanctuary.

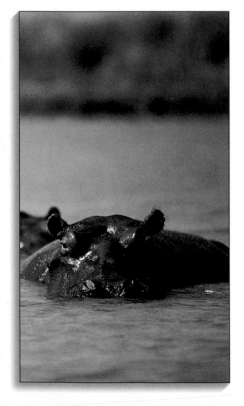

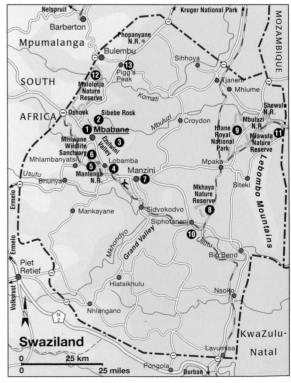

ends at **Lobamba** ❹, the traditional seat of the Swazi monarchy and modern site of parliament. The fascinating National Museum at Lobamba (open daily; entrance charge) houses several displays relating to the royal lineage and an absorbing collection of monochrome photographs from late 19th century onwards. Also of cultural interest is the nearby **Mantenga Nature Reserve** ❺ (daily 7am–6.30pm; entrance charge; tel: 416 1151/1178), whose lush riverine scrub and attractive waterfall are leered over by the foreboding Execution Rock (over which convicted murderers were shoved in pre-colonial times). As well as good tented accommodation, the reserve contains a meticulously reconstructed traditional Swazi village offering cultural tours and virtuoso musical performances.

Elsewhere in the valley, there's a good range of hotel accommodation, offering just about every holiday activity short of a beach. As well as golf, bowls, tennis, horse riding and a health centre, there are a few glitzy casinos and strip clubs that pay sleazy homage to the days when visiting Swaziland was practically synonymous with indoor pursuits frowned on by the apartheid government. You'll also find plenty of opportunity to buy Swazi crafts, both at the road side (bargaining is expected) and in more organised shops. Soapstone sculpture and wood carvings, beadwork and woven articles are the cream of the curios, while the brilliantly coloured Swazi candles – shaped like animals – are the pick of the crafts.

Midway along the valley is the **Mlilwane Wildlife Sanctuary** ❻ (daily 6am–6pm; entrance charge; tel: 528 3944), a patch of former farmland that has now been regenerated and re-stocked with game, though it remains compromised by the abundance of exotic trees, eucalyptus in particular. You can see white rhino, hippo, giraffe, crocodile, kudu, nyala and eland here, among other

Map on page 320

An adult male rhino comes well-armed for anyone who crosses his territory.

BELOW: Usutu, the largest man-made forest in the world.

animals, although the only large predators are leopards, which are rarely spotted. Bird-watching hides have been built overlooking the dams (240 species of bird have been recorded here, including plum-coloured starlings and blue cranes). As there are few predators in Mlilwane, you can explore it in your own vehicle, on horseback, or even by mountain bike, as well as taking game drives or guided walks with park rangers. Mlilwane is an easy day trip from Mbabane; there is also a pleasant rest camp if you wish to stay longer. Reservations are handled by the tour operator Big Game Parks (tel: 528 3943; www.biggameparks.org).

Swaziland's main industrial hub is **Manzini** ❼, which lies about 40 km (24 miles) southwest of Mbabane at the opposite end of the Ezulwini Valley. Founded in 1889 as Bremersdorp, Manzini served as the capital of Swaziland before it was usurped by Mbabane in 1903, and it remains the country's largest town. Although not overly endowed with character, Manzini has a bustling central market – an excellent place to buy traditional handicrafts – and on Thursday it hosts a macabre traditional medicine market.

The interior – myriad landscapes

Private and exclusive **Mkhaya Nature Reserve** ❽ (overnight visitors only; tel: 528 3943) lies about 90 km (55 miles) southeast of Mbabane, past scenery which changes from the forestry plantations of the highveld and the rolling grasslands around Manzini to dry, flat plains, dotted with thatched huts. Mkhaya itself is set in classic acacia bushveld and offers excellent game viewing, whether you choose guided walks or drives with the rangers. It is one of the best places in southern Africa to see both white rhino and the more reticent black rhino, while the likes of crested guineafowl, Narina trogon and paradise flycatcher inhabit the luxury river-front lodge.

You'll pass through much the same range of landscapes en route to Swaziland's other chief game reserve, the **Hlane Royal National Park** ❾ (open daily, 24-hour access to rest camp; entrance charge, tel: 528 3943), about 110 km (68 miles) east of Mbabane on the MR3. Hlane, pronounced shlane, covers 70,000 hectares (173,000 acres) of bushveld, spread among the toes of the Lebombo Mountains. Hlane was designated as a royal hunting ground since colonial times, but has been privately managed as a certified game reserve since 1967 – though it's still owned by King Mswati, who pops by on ceremonial occasions to bag the customary impala. Game includes hippo, elephant, white rhino, giraffe, zebra, impala and – the big news round these parts – lion, successfully reintroduced here for the first time in the country. This is a good place for bird-watching, and for raptor-watching in particular. Hlane is popular with young independent travellers because its rest camp is readily accessible from the main road, and it's one of the few reserves in southern Africa offering inexpensive no-booking-required game walks that come with a high chance of encountering rhino and the like on foot.

Another highlight for thrill-seekers is the white-water rafting run by Swazi Trails on the **Great Usutu**

TIP

A good time to visit Swaziland is in January, during the traditional *Incwala* ceremony. The new year is ushered in with much festive singing and dancing.

BELOW: the Barberton daisy was originally found in the countryside near Barberton on the Swazi border.

River ❿ south of Manzini (tel: 416 2180; www. swazitrails.co.sz). The series of Grade I–IV rapids on this river is probably the most challenging stretch of southern African white water that can safely be tackled in unguided two-berth crocodile rafts. Navigable all year through, the turbulent river runs through a starkly beautiful valley of black volcanic outcrops hemmed in by wooded hills, an excellent location for abseiling – which, if your legs are feeling up to it, can be tagged on to the rafting to make a full-day excursion.

Map on page 320

The wild north

The contiguous **Mbuluzi**, **Mlawula** and **Shewula nature reserves** ⓫, set in the far northeast, cover the slopes of the Lebombo Mountains and associated river valleys on the Mozambique border. Mbuluzi and Mlawula protect similar habitats of dense acacia woodland, coursed through by the forest-fringed sub-tropical rivers after which they are named. Large mammals are present in both reserves – giraffe, kudu, zebra – but nothing dangerous enough to inhibit exploration on foot, while the checklist of 350 bird species approaches Zululand's more publicised Ndumo and uMkhuze Game Reserve in stature and species composition. Altogether different, Shewula is the only community-owned reserve in Swaziland – running village tours that reflect modern rather than traditional rural culture out of a rustic rest camp set on a ridge offering breathtaking views across the surrounding lowveld.

Spectacular **Malolotja Nature Reserve** ⓬ (daily 6.30am–6pm in winter, 6am–6.30pm in summer; entrance charge; tel: 442 4241), about 35 km (22 miles) north of Mbabane on the road to Pigg's Peak, is Swaziland's other northern gem. Wildlife is not the main attraction here, although game includes the

BELOW: blue wildebeest, Hlane Royal National Park.

*Moshoeshoe asked
Queen Victoria to
annex Lesotho in
1851 so that his peo-
ple might be as "the
lice in the blanket of
the great Queen" – a
reference to the all-
embracing protection
of the British Empire.*

BELOW: family
outing, Makhaleng
River Valley.

endemic blesbok and black wildebeest, as well as impala and oribi antelope. The
varied bird life includes a breeding colony of the rare bald ibis on the cliffs
above the Malolotja Falls. Above all, this is superb hiking country, from deep,
forested ravines and waterfalls to high plateaux, most of which are only accessible on foot (there are some 200 km/125 miles of trails).

The reserve also contains the ancient Lion Cavern, believed to be the world's
oldest mine. Radiocarbon dating techniques have shown that red oxides and
haematite were being dug out of the earth here as long ago as 41,000BC. It is
situated about 16 km (10 miles) from the park entrance, near the still-active
Ngwenyan iron-ore mine.

Run by the National Trust Commission, accommodation at Malolotja is in log
cabins, adequately equipped with cooking facilities. There is a shop selling
basic supplies and a camp site. Further afield, the historic mining village of
Pigg's Peak ⓭ (about 24 km/14 miles further north from the reserve on the
MR1) is set amid green, rolling hills covered in pine and eucalyptus plantations; it makes an interesting half-day excursion.

Lesotho – African Switzerland

This tiny mountain kingdom is an adventurer's dream. Saw-tooth ridges and
deep, precipitous valleys glittering with tumbling rivers and falls; mud-and-
thatch villages where herders watch over their flocks – it's an African Switzerland, on African time.

The best time to go is between March and April, before it gets too cold to
swim, or from October to November, before the summer rains turn the rivers to
torrents. These are also good times to see wildflowers – the white and mauve

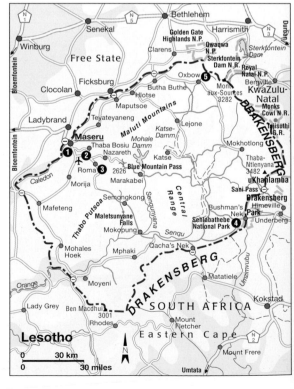

cosmos which creates great bands of colour across the landscape in autumn, and the delicate Afro-alpine species which twinkle on the grassy hills throughout spring and summer. One of the most popular modes of travel through the rugged interior is by sturdy Basotho pony (but be warned – this does require a certain level of stamina and stoicism). Trekking centres organise tours for horse riders through breathtakingly beautiful mountain scenery, in accommodation ranging from hotels to village huts. Here, conditions are fairly basic, but perfectly adequate once you get used to no running water, no flush toilets and no electricity. The other way to get round Lesotho is by four-wheel-drive vehicle, either on a self-drive basis or on a guided trip with a tour operator.

The west – mountain cities, painted caves

Most visitors will pass through or be based in **Maseru ❶**, the capital. Just across the border from the South African town of Ladybrand, it may be twice as big as its South African neighbour, but it's also twice as ugly. Nonetheless, the gift and craft shops here serve as a good introduction to the styles of local craftsmanship you'll encounter throughout the country.

Thaba Bosiu ❷, King Moshoeshoe's majestic mountain stronghold, lies about 10 km (6 miles) east of Maseru on the B20. You can visit the ruins of the king's residence and his grave after tackling the short, steep climb to the summit. It is compulsory to hire a guide (a small fee is charged) from the Tourist Information Centre at the base of the mountain.

Also worth a visit is the picturesque sandstone town of **Roma ❸**, about 35 km (22 miles) southeast from Maseru on the A3 route. Home of the National University of Lesotho, Roma was first established as a mission centre in 1863.

Maps on pages 320 & 324

BELOW: Lesotho – African Switzerland.

Map
on page
324

The sturdy Basotho pony is the product of careful breeding from bloodstock captured by the Sotho during the Eastern Cape's Frontier Wars over a century ago.

BELOW: sunset from a mountain top.
RIGHT: a gathering of the clans, Thaba Bosiu.

Educational and spiritual matters aside, it is set in a lovely wooded valley, surrounded by mountains that are often snowcapped in winter.

Lesotho's topography consists of a skirt of sandstone crowned by a massive wedge of volcanic basalt (no point in the country has an altitude less than 1,000 metres/3,300 ft). Pocking the soft sandstone are hundreds of caves, once home to those diminutive hunter-gatherers, the San – many are vividly decorated with their paintings.

One of the best-preserved rock-art sites is at Ha Baroana, about 20 km (12 miles) north of Roma near the mission settlement of **Nazareth**. This drive follows a road that winds up from the lowlands into the foothills of the Maluti Mountains, offering dramatic views back over Roma. From Nazareth, it's a 5-km (3-mile) walk from a signposted turn-off to the site. The curator charges a small fee to open the gate.

Peaks and dramatic passes

East from Maseru, a series of magnificent passes soar over the Maluti Mountains, penetrating deep into the heart of Lesotho. The Thaba Tseka road via **Marakabei** is especially scenic; **Bushman's Pass** (2,268 metres/7,440 ft) and the dramatic **Blue Mountain Pass** (2,626 metres/8,615 ft) are just two of the highlights. In between lies the Molimo Nthuse Pass, at the top of which is a pony-trekking centre from which ponies may be hired and excursions planned.

South from here lie **Semongkong** and the Maletsunyane Falls, at 192 metres (630 ft), the longest single-drop waterfall in southern Africa. You could fly to Semongkong from Maseru in about an hour, but it takes three days to ride there from the trekking centre at Molimo Nthuse Pass. By four-wheel-drive track from Roma, you could spend anything from a few hours to a few days, depending on the weather. That's Lesotho, and that's why it's such an adventurer's dream.

Isolated, inaccessible and spectacular, **Sehlabathebe National Park** ❹ is the only one in Lesotho. There's very little game there except for the occasional mountain reedbuck, grey rhebok or oribi, although it's an excellent place to see the rare lammergeyer (bearded vulture) and black eagle.

Situated in the far southeast of the country on the South African border, you can reach the park by four-wheel-drive from **Qacha's Nek** (about 100 km/60 miles), or by walking or pony-trekking from the South African border post at Bushman's Nek. Either way, there's nothing there but miles of rugged wilderness.

Europeans may find the ski resort at **Oxbow** ❺ a bit of a joke, although there's usually a foot or two of snow in midwinter. Reached via Butha Buthe, about 100 km (60 miles) northeast of Maseru on the Sani Pass road, accommodation is rudimentary; nevertheless, young, white South Africans love it. Summer visitors can take advantage of the fine trout fishing in the Malibamat'so River here – there's a good site near the Oxbow Lodge, which will advise on permits as well as arrange local guides and treks. ❏

INSIGHT GUIDES

TRAVEL TIPS

SOUTH AFRICA

TRAVEL TIPS

T RANSPORT

GETTING THERE
AND GETTING AROUND

GETTING THERE

By Air

Most flights to and from Europe are nonstop. It's best, however, to ask when you book – a stopover can make the flight (which takes about 11 hours from London) up to 1½ hours longer. Johannesburg's OR Tambo International Airport is southern Africa's transportation hub and it handles the majority of international flights to South Africa. From here, you can fly to Botswana, the Ivory Coast, Kenya, Malawi, Namibia, Zaire, Zambia and Zimbabwe, as well as Mauritius, the Comoro Islands, Madagascar and Reunion. An ever-increasing number of international flights go directly to Cape Town and Durban, a more convenient option for visitors who are coming to South Africa with intentions of exploring the Western Cape and Garden Route.

South African Airways (SAA; www.flysaa.com) flies to South Africa from Amsterdam, Bangkok, Buenos Aires, Dubai, Düsseldorf, Frankfurt, Hong Kong, Miami, Mumbai (Bombay), Munich, New York, London, Paris, Perth, Rio de Janeiro, Sao Paulo, Singapore, Taipei, Tel Aviv, Tokyo, Zurich and other cities around the world.

Since the liberalising of air routes in 1992, about 80 other airlines have started competing for the profitable South African international routes. The main operators are Air France, Alitalia, British Airways, Lufthansa, Qantas and Virgin Atlantic. A little bit of research on the internet or via your travel agent will be able to provide

information about cheaper flights available from charter airlines.

The Kruger Mpumalanga International Airport near Nelspruit opened at the end of 2002 for domestic flights. South African Airways and Nationwide Airlines currently run 10 scheduled flights a day, from Johannesburg, Cape Town, Durban and Lanseria.

KMIA was granted international status at the end of June 2003 and the first international flight landed there a week later. Check out www.kmiairport.co.za for the latest information on services.

By Sea

The days when you could take one of the weekly mail boats from Cape Town to Southampton in England for far less than the price of a flight are no more. However, there are still a number of shipping companies offering passage to the Cape. Various cruise liners call at South African ports – detailed information is available from adventurous travel agents.

RMS St Helena carries up to 128 passengers on its Cardiff (Wales) to Cape Town route, via Tenerife, Ascension Island and St Helena. There are two sailings in each direction every year. For more information, visit their website at www.rms-st-helena.com. Reservations can be made at tel: 020 7575 6480 in London or tel: 021-425 1165 in Cape Town.

By Rail

It is possible, and undoubtedly nostalgic, to enter South Africa by train from Namibia and Botswana.
• Namibia: Trans-Namib, based in

the Namibian capital of Windhoek, operates a twice weekly service to Upington via Keetmanshoop. The train leaves Windhoek at 7.40pm on Tuesday and Friday, while the return trip sets off from Upington at 5am on Sunday and Thursday, and takes around 26 hours one-way. Contact www.transnamib.com.na or call 061-298 2600.

By Long-distance Bus

This is faster and cheaper than the train, but distances are substantial and you should be ready for lengthy, if comfortable, periods sitting down and braced for rally-style bus drivers.
• Namibia: The Inter-Cape Mainline goes from Windhoek to Cape Town and Johannesburg. Windhoek–Cape Town Friday, Sunday, Monday, Wednesday, 6pm (18 hours); Windhoek–Johannesburg on the same days, changing buses at Upington, 6pm (21 hours).
• Zimbabwe: Translux Harare–Bulawayo–Johannesburg, services have been suspended due to fuel shortages in Zimbabwe.

By Car

For reasons of insurance and security, you can't go to or from South Africa by way of Zimbabwe and Mozambique in a hired car.

In Botswana, you can only drive hired cars on paved roads (except four-wheel drive vehicles).

To go to or from Namibia, Botswana, Lesotho or Swaziland you need a written statement from the hire company authorising you to take the car over the border.

Automobile Association

Services are free to international AA members, on presentation of a valid membership card, and, for a fee, to non-members. The services include car hire (Avis), international motoring advice, route maps, road travel and weather information.

Useful AA numbers
The Automobile Association of South Africa
Dennis Paxton House, Kyalami Grand Prix Circuit, Allandale Road, Kyalami, Midrand 1685, Gauteng
Membership: 083 843 22
Insurance: 0861 222229
www.aa.co.za
Roadside repairs and towing
Tel: 0838 4322

GETTING AROUND

Internal Flights

Increased competition in the country's aviation market has reduced fares on many of South Africa's most popular domestic routes. Always shop around for the best deals, especially on the busiest routes, such as Johannesburg to Cape Town.

For inexpensive tickets a British Airways affiliated airline called kulula.com offers excellent rates as low as ZAR 500 (£40/US$70) one-way between Johannesburg and Cape Town (including taxes) on about ten flights daily between major cities, as well as very reasonably priced car-rental deals and accommodation at selected Protea Hotels – all bookable online at their website: www.kulula.com.

Similar air fares are offered by other local airlines such as: Mango (www.flymango.co.za) and 1time (www.1time.co.za). Tickets for flights with both companies can be booked online.

Otherwise, if you expect to fly internally a good deal, there are various frequent-flyer schemes which will save you money, such as an African Air Pass available on SAA regional and domestic flights – it's a good deal if you plan to make four or more flights. To qualify, you need an international ticket to South Africa on any airline, and must quote your ticket number. It's valid for 45 days and can be purchased in Europe as well as in South Africa. Other domestic carriers operating scheduled services include British Airways/Comair, Nationwide Air and Sun Air.

South African Airways (SAA)
www.flysaa.com
Central Reservations (toll-free)
Tel: 0861 359 722
Cape Town: International Airport
Tel: 021-936 1111
Fax: 021-424 3777
Durban: Overport City, City Centre
Tel: 0860 808808
Fax 031-250 1010
Johannesburg: Domestic Departures, Terminal 4, International Airport
Tel: 011-978 1111
Fax: 011-978 1386

British Airways/Comair
www.comair.co.za
Central Reservations:
Tel: 0860 435 922
Johannesburg:
Tel: 011-921 0222

Nationwide Air
www.flynationwide.co.za
Central Reservations:
Tel: 0861 737 737
Johannesburg:
Tel: 011-305 3550
Fax: 011-390 1928
Cape Town:
Tel: 021-935 5600
Fax: 021-936 2062
Durban:
Tel: 031-408 9300
Fax: 031-450 2092
Kruger Mpumalanga International Airport:
Tel: 013-750 2640
Fax: 013-750 2641
Port Elizabeth:
Tel: 041-502 6300
Fax: 041-507 7291

Specialised Charter and Sightseeing Flights

If you'd like to visit South Africa's remotest corners, a light aircraft or helicopter flight could be your best bet, making the journey as much of an adventure as the destination. Obviously, chartering an aircraft will work out cheaper if you can fill every passenger seat.

Here is a small selection of specialist operators:
Civair Helicopters
PO Box 120,
Newlands 7725
Cape Town
Tel: 021-419 5182
Fax: 021-419 5183
www.civair.co.za
CHC Helicopters
Cape Town
Tel: 021-934 0560
Fax: 021-934 0568
www.chc.ca
Tours can vary from a lunch-time trip to a two-day tour.
Executive Aerospace
Tel: 011-395 9142
Fax: 011-395 9134
www.aerospace.co.za
Reliable charter service for business and leisure.
Jetair Charter
PO Box 259
Lanseria 1748
Gauteng
Tel: 011-880 8800
Fax: 0860 325158
www.jetair.co.za
Rossair
PO Box 428
Lanseria 1748
Gauteng.
Tel: 011-659 2980
Fax: 011-659 1389

Trains

Long-distance trains have clean, compact and comfortable sleeping berths. The use of the berth is included in the train fare, but a bedding ticket must be purchased, which will provide you with your sheets, pillow, etc – you can do this when making your reservation, or on the train. First-class coupés and compartments carry two and four passengers, while second-class coupés and compartments carry three and six passengers. Most long-distance trains have a dining salon and catering trolleys. It is possible to rent a whole compartment/coupé at a special price which is about 80 percent of the price of a fully occupied one. Children under seven travel free; children under 12 pay half price. Senior citizens (over 60) are entitled to a 40 percent discount.

Platform boards can be found on the departure platform on which coach and compartment numbers are listed against the names of the passengers. The train conductor is also available to assist you.

Spoornet
The passenger service of the state-owned Spoornet is now known as Shosholoza Meyl – Shosholoza ("Push Forward") being a well-known traditional song chanted by the labourers who laid the railway lines, and Meyl a derivative of imeyili, a local slang term for a long-distance train. Shosholoza Meyl operates long-distance mainline routes listed between Musina, Komatipoort, Pretoria, Johannesburg Bloemfontein, Durban, Port Elizabeth, East London and Cape Town.

TRANSPORT

ACCOMMODATION

EATING OUT

ACTIVITIES

A – Z

Car Rental Agencies

International companies with offices and representatives in South Africa include:
Avis Rent-A-Car
Tel: 011-923 3660
www.avis.com
Europcar
Tel: 0860 011344
www.Europcar.com
Hertz
Tel: 011-390 9700
www.hertz.com

Travellers who book domestic flights with kulula.com *(see flights)* can get excellent car rental deals as part of the package when they book. Other sensibly priced and reliable local car rental companies include the following:
Around About Cars
Tel: 021-780 1384.
Email: info@aroundaboutcars.com
www.aroundaboutcars.com
Imperial
Tel: 0861 131000 (toll-free) or Cape Town 021-421 5190
www.imperialcarrental.co.za
Economic Hire (only for Cape Town and Plettenberg Bay)
Tel: 041-581 5826.
Pender Car Rental
Tel: 012-460 8016 (Pretoria)
Email: rentals@pender.co.za
www.pender.co.za
Four-wheel drive jeeps, caravans, campers, camper-mobiles and similar are also available; *see page 362* for hire companies, or for further information contact the regional tourism agencies.

For reservations and enquiries, tel: 086-000 8888 or visit www.spoornet.co.za.

Long-distance Buses

Probably the most comprehensive network of domestic and international coach (long-distance bus) routes is provided by Translux Luxury Coaches, which operates daily services between key destinations such as Musina, Komatipoort, Pretoria, Johannesburg, Bloemfontein, Kimberley, Durban, Umtata, East London, Port Elizabeth, Graaff-Reinet, George, Oudtshoorn and Cape Town. It also runs cross-border coaches into Zambia, Malawi and Mozambique.
For further information on time-tables and fares, log on to www.translux.co.za. Tickets can be bought at any branch of Computicket or Shoprite-Checkers supermarket or online at www.computicket.com.

Alternatively, ring the central reservation line, tel: 0861 589 282, the Pretoria head office at 012-315 3476, or Johannesburg 011-774 3333, Cape Town 021-449 6209, Durban 031-361 7670, Port Elizabeth 041 392-1304, East London 043-700 1015, Bloemfontein 051-408 4888 or Knysna 044-382 1407.
Inter-city bus services are also offered by Greyhound Coach Lines. These follow similar routes to Translux, but with fewer international connections and the addition of a service from Durban to Johannesburg via Richards Bay.
Online bookings can be made at www.greyhound.co.za. Alternatively, ring the central reservations number, tel: 083 915 9000, the office in Johannesburg (tel: 011-276 8500; fax: 011-276 8550) or regional offices in Durban (tel: 031-334 9702), Port Elizabeth (tel: 041-363 4555; fax: 041-363 3559) or Pretoria (tel: 012-323 1154; fax: 012-323 1294).
Another reliable bus operator is Intercape, which has a slightly less exhaustive route network through eastern and central parts of South Africa, but still covers most major routes, and also has services running from Johannesburg or Cape Town through the Northern Cape towns of Kakamas, Upington and Springbok to Namibia. Intercape often offers very cheap last-minute specials, as advertised on its website: www.intercape.co.za, or contact the Cape Town head office, tel: 021-380 4400; fax: 021-380 2076.
A good-value means of getting around South Africa is the Baz Bus, a flexible hop-on, hop-off, door-to-door service that takes in the main tourist areas from Cape Town to Johannesburg, including Swaziland, Zululand, the Drakensberg, the Eastern Cape, the Garden Route and Cape Town. Backpackers are the main customers, but the flexibility and reliability of this service will be attractive to anybody who wants to explore the country at their leisure.
Full route details are posted online at www.bazbus.com. Tickets are available at backpacker hostels, or travellers can book directly at tel: 021-439 2323 (in Cape Town); fax: 021-439 2343; email: info@bazbus.co.za.

Car Hire

South Africa has a very good network of roads, some 84,000 km (52,000 miles) of which is surfaced. Even the unsurfaced roads are usually in good condition. Travelling overland, visitors will enjoy the low traffic densities outside of urban areas. South Africa drives on the left-hand side of the road. Traffic laws are strictly enforced. Speed limits are generally well signposted. The maximum speed on motorways is: 120 km/h (74 mph); rural roads: 100 km/h (62 mph); in built-up areas: 60 km/h (37 mph). Seat belts must be worn at all times by both the driver and passengers.
Traffic casualties are high in South Africa due to reckless and high-speed driving. It's advisable to drive more carefully than you would at home, and to be wary of other road users doing the unexpected – minibus-taxi or "combie" drivers have a particularly bad reputation in this regard. When driving through any rural area, particularly in Swaziland, be careful of cattle, goats and sometimes even pedestrians wandering blithely into the road. Most roads are poorly lit at night, when you ought to be careful of cyclists and also of pedestrians.
If you will be driving in national parks and reserves, bear in mind that speed limits vary from 25 km/h (15 mph) to 50 km/h (30 mph) and are strictly enforced. Because of stops for photography and the like, you should reckon on an average speed of 30–35 km/h (18–21 mph) at a push on the asphalt roads, and 25–30 km/h (15–18 mph) on gravel. More realistically, assuming that game viewing takes priority over hurtling around for the sake of it, would be to work on the basis of covering around 20 km (12 miles) per hour. Maps showing the distances from point to point can be bought at the entrance gates. Note that in most game reserves it is forbidden to get out of the vehicle except in designated areas.
Remember to take an international driving licence with you if you wish to hire a car. Car hire firms offer a wide variety of vehicles; mileage charges are usually extra. Check with the car hire firm for details. With major international car rental companies, it is often cheaper to arrange your car hire from home, but many local companies offer extremely competitive rates once you are in the country – it's not difficult to find a serviceable saloon car for around ZAR 200 (£14/US$28) including insurance and 200 km (124 miles) free daily usage.

A CCOMMODATION

HOTELS, YOUTH HOSTELS, BED & BREAKFAST

CHOOSING A HOTEL

Visitors to South Africa can expect a good choice of accommodation, from exclusive five-star hotels to modest city guesthouses, efficient motorway motels to tranquil country inns, rustic rondavels (thatched huts) in game reserves to farmhouses offering bed and breakfast. As South Africa is such an outdoor-loving nation, there's also an excellent range of camping and caravan sites, although national park and in-town campground sites are not necessarily the cheapest accommodation options. For the budget traveller, there is a superb network of private backpacker hostels.

It is advisable to book accommodation in South Africa's bigger parks well in advance, and to try and avoid the school holidays. Guided trails in the parks must also be booked, as there is often more demand than places. Campers and holidaymakers in caravans should book directly with the reserve concerned.

A hotel's star rating is a good guide to its quality and price range. Luxury hotels of four or five stars cost over £150/US$300 per night for a double room, while budget hotels of one star cost less than £50/US$100. The rest fall somewhere in between, though many hotels in the three-star category will offer special rates at not significantly higher than budget hotels when you visit out of season. It is not an indication of poor quality if a hotel has no star rating: such hotels are simply those not listed by the tourist board. Guesthouses and hostels fall into moderate and budget accommodation, while backpacker hostels typically charge around £5/US$10 per person for dormitory accommodation and around £15/US$30 for a double room, rising to £25/US$50 in Cape Town.

There are many hotel booking agencies on the Internet. In addition to the sites listed below, check out www.southafrica.net for information on all kinds of accommodation, or www.bedandbreakfast.co.za.

Hotel Chains

Southern Sun
One of the largest hotel operators in South Africa, this manages several different chains, ranging from its flagship Sun hotels (several of which are rated five star) through the upmarket but somewhat character-less Holiday Inns, right down to the budget-friendly Garden Court and StayEasy Chains. You'll find at least one establishment in each of these ranges in every large South African city, and several in Johannesburg, Cape Town and Durban.

For further details and online bookings log onto www.southernsun. com. Alternatively dial 0861-447744 toll-free (within South Africa), or 011-461 9744, or fax 011-461 9742.

Protea Hotels
This long-serving chain owns, manages or franchises more than 100 hotels countywide, several units in all major cities as well as hotels in some fairly out-of-the-way places, for instance Bathurst and Lambert's Bay. The feel of its hotels varies quite widely, since most were not custom built by Protea, but overall standards are high, and many units have more character than you'd normally expect of a chain hotel. Good-value special offers are often available at selected hotels off-season or over weekends, and full details are available on the website: www.proteahotels.co.za. Alternatively dial 0861-119000 toll-free (within South Africa), or 021-430 5300, or fax: 021-430 5320 or email info@proteahotels.com.

City Lodges
This chain of bland and mostly urban hotels is aimed squarely at local business travellers, but it also offers comfortable accommodation and good value to tourists. Its flagship range of hotels is the rather plush Courtyard chain, while City Lodges, Town Lodges and Road Lodges are each another rung down and priced accordingly. Superb deals are sometimes available online for select hotels, so it's well worth checking the website. Tel: 011-557 2600; toll-free: 0861 563437; fax: 011-557 2670; www.citylodge.co.za.

Portfolio Collection
This is not a chain as such, but rather a loosely affiliated collection of small, often owner-managed guesthouses, bed & breakfasts and game lodges, most of which offer a combination of high-quality accommodation, personalised service and a degree of individuality lacking in the chain hotels. With more than 800 individually selected establishments countrywide, Portfolio covers practically every corner of the country, and offers online booking through its website www.portfoliocollection.com. Enquiries can be directed to tel: 021-686 5400 or 689 4020; fax: 021-686 5310/5404 or email: res@portfoliocollection.com.

Coast to Coast

Again, not a chain, but an excellent information and booking service aimed at backpackers and other budget travellers. Its regularly updated 320-page Coast to Coast booklet lists practically every backpacker hostel countrywide, while a user-friendly website (www.coastingafrica.com) has links and/or booking facilities for most such establishments. Further enquiries can be directed to info@coastingafrica.com or tel: 021-786 1742.

SANParks

Formerly the National Parks Board, SANParks is the authority responsible for the country's 20 national parks, including the Kruger and Kgalagadi. All accommodation, camping and other overnight facilities within these national parks can be booked online through the website www.sanparks.org or through the head office in Pretoria (tel: 012-428 9111; fax: 012 343 0905; email: reservations@sanparks.org).

KZN Wildlife

The most important of South Africa's provincial conservation bodies is KZN (KwaZulu-Natal) Wildlife, which manages 66 game, nature and other reserves in Zululand, the Drakensberg and elsewhere in the province. Bookings for practically all accommodation and camping within these reserves (the exception being a handful of upmarket private franchises) can be made at www.kznwildlife.com, or by ringing 033-845 1000 or fax: 033-845 1001.

ACCOMMODATION LISTINGS

CAPE TOWN AND CAPE PENINSULA

CENTRAL

Arabella Sheraton Grand Hotel
1 Lower Long Street
Convention Square
Cape Town 8000
Tel: 021-412 9999
An ultra-cool glass-and-granite structure situated opposite the Cape Town International Convention Centre. A good selection of restaurants and bars nearby to suit your mood. **$$$$**

Holiday Inn Waterfront
1 Lower Buitengracht Street
Cape Town 8002
Tel: 021-409 4000
Fax: 021-409 4444
Magnificent views of the mountain and the sea, and close to the Victoria and Alfred Waterfront shopping precinct. **$$$$**

Mount Nelson Hotel
76 Orange Street
PO Box 2608
Cape Town 8000
Tel: 021-483 1000
Fax: 021-483 1782
www.mountnelson.co.za
First on anyone's list of Cape hotels, the pale pink "Nellie" is a grand colonial hotel that has been a favourite with discerning travellers for nearly a century. Even if you don't book in, taking afternoon tea here is a must. **$$$$**

The Table Bay
Quay Six, V & A Waterfront
Cape Town 8002
Tel: 021-406 5000

Fax: 021-406 5686
www.suninternational.com
A spectacular addition to Cape Town's clutch of luxury hotels; where the Clintons stayed on their 1999 state visit. Handsomely furnished rooms with satellite television and sea or mountain views. **$$$$**

Victoria & Alfred Hotel
The Pierhead
PO Box 50050
Waterfront, 8001
Tel: 021-419 6677
Fax: 021-419 7714
Email: info@vahotel.co.za
www.vahotel.co.za
Victorian elegance combined with modern four-star standards. Outstanding restaurant. **$$$$**

Breakwater Lodge
Portswood Road
PO Box 50683
Waterfront, 8002
Tel: 021-406 1911
Fax: 021-406 1070
Email: reserve@bwl.co.za
www.breakwaterlodge.co.za
This converted 19th-century prison offers comfortable rooms with all mod cons at very reasonable rates directly opposite the popular V&A Waterfront and its excellent selection of shops, restaurants and other facilities. **$$$**

Kensington Place
38 Kensington Crescent
Higgovale 8001
Tel: 021-424 4744
Fax: 021-424 1810
With only eight rooms, this

is the best small hotel in the city. Chic is a byword for the style of the rooms and of the guests. Centrally located. **$$$**

The Metropole
38 Long Street
Cape Town 8001
Tel: 021-424 7247
www.metropolehotel.co.za
Set inside a restored Victorian building, this hip hotel has a good mix of upbeat interiors, a gourmet restaurant with adjoining bar and it's close to all the action on Long Street. **$$$**

The Peninsula All-Suite Hotel
313 Beach Road
Sea Point
Tel: 021-430 7777
www.peninsula.com
Situated on the city's Platinum Mile, this hotel has large, luxurious, sea-facing rooms. **$$$**

The Village Lodge
49 Napier Street
De Waterkant
Cape Town 8001
Tel: 021-421 1106
www.thevillagelodge.co.za
A 15-bedroom boutique hotel, a private villa and several fully furnished self-catering town houses in this trendy and centrally located area. The rooftop pool at the main lodge is a highlight. **$$$**

Cape Victoria
Corner Wigtown and Torbay roads
Green Point
Cape Town 8005
Tel/fax: 021-439 7721
www.capevictoria.co.za
Top for breakfasts served

by owner Lily Kaplan. Great views; great style. **$$**

Head South Lodge
215 Main Road
Green Point
Cape Town
Tel: 021-434 8777
Fax: 021-434 8778
Email: headsouth@kingsley.co.za
www.headsouth.co.za
This is a 15-room gem. Chic and retro cool with its Tretchikoff portraits on the walls, rich-coloured fabrics and dark wood fixtures, there's a strong whiff of glamorous decadence here. Ironic and fun. **$$**

Ashanti Lodge
11 Hof Street, Gardens
Tel: 021-423 8721
Fax: 021-423 8790
Email: ashanti@iafrica.com
www.ashanti.co.za
Another long-standing and perennially popular backpackers hostel, Ashanti offers similar facilities to The Backpack and also has a good travel centre. **$**

Daddy Long Legs
134 Long Street
City Centre
Tel: 021-422 3074
www.daddylonglegs.co.za
A unique, arty, boutique backpackers hotel with a difference. Each of the 13 rooms has been individually decorated by a well-known Cape Town artist. Well priced and central to all the hotspots and tourist attractions in the mother city. **$**

THE PENINSULA

The Bay Hotel
69 Victoria Road
PO Box 32021
Camps Bay 8040
Tel: 021-430 4444
Fax: 021-438 4433
www.thebay.co.za
Clean white lines, cool tiled floors, light, bright and airy – this is a refreshingly modern alternative in a town where it's almost obligatory for luxury hotels to double up as listed monuments. Every room enjoys a spectacular sea or mountain view. **$$$$**

The Cellars Hohenort
93 Brommersvlei Road
Constantia 7800
Tel: 021-794 2137
Fax: 021-794 2149
Graceful hotel converted from the 17th-century cellars of the former Klaasenbosch wine farm. Set in large landscaped gardens. Noted restaurant and cellar, too. Swimming pool, tennis and walking trails. **$$$$**

Twelve Apostles Hotel & Spa
About 2 km (1½ miles) south of Camps Bay on the Hout Bay road
Tel: 021-437 9000
Fax: 021-437 9055
Email: salesta@rchmail.com
www.12apostleshotel.com
Since it opened in 2003, this plush boutique hotel has been hot-listed in *Conde Nast Traveller* and *Travel and Leisure*, while *GQ* has named it "Hotel with the Best View in the World" – and suffice to say that the food, service and ambience don't disgrace that spectacular view. **$$$$**

The Constantia
Spaanschemat River Road
Constantia 7864
Tel: 021-794 6561
www.theconstantia.com
Spacious, well-appointed rooms in the heart of the Constantia winelands. Country-style accommodation and a full English breakfast so good, it will keep you going all day. **$$$**

Hout Bay Manor
Main Road, Hout Bay
Tel: 021-790 0116
www.houtbaymanor.co.za

Built in 1871, this hotel is a national monument that underwent a major refurbishment and now provides a more contemporary feel. Affordable luxury with all the modcons, gourmet food and luxury amenities you'll want during your stay. **$$$**

Lord Nelson's Inn
St George's Street
Simon's Town
Tel: 021-786 1386
Fax: 021-789 1009
Email: nsnelson@mweb.co.za
This delightful small but long-serving inn offers unpretentious, homely and very reasonably priced accommodation and meals within walking distance of Boulders and its penguin colony, and a short drive from the Cape of Good Hope Nature Reserve. **$$**

Cape Point Cottage
59 Cape Point Road
Castle Rock, Simon's Town
Tel: 021-786 3891
www.capepointcottage.co.za
Only five minutes from the Cape Point Nature Reserve, this cottage can be booked as a self-catering cottage or

on a bed-and-breakfast basis. Unpretentious and perfect for nature lovers. **$**

Green Elephant
57 Milton Road, Observatory
Tel: 021-448 6359
Email: greenele@iafrica.com
This stalwart backpacker hostel lies in the trendy suburb of Observatory and is ideal for travellers who value laid-back socialising as much as active sightseeing – though there is a great selection of day trips and activities are also offered. Colourful murals adorn each guest room. **$**

Simon's Town Backpackers
66 St George's Street
Simon's Town
Tel: 021-786 1964
Email: capepax@kingsley.co.za
www.capepax.co.za
Situated within walking distance of a railway station, several historic buildings and good but inexpensive restaurants, and the iconic Boulders Beach, this boasts one of the most scenic and convenient locations of any of the 40-odd backpacker hostels in and around Cape Town. **$**

WESTERN CAPE

SALDANHA

Saldanha Bay Protea Hotel
51B Main Road, Saldanha, 7395
Tel: 022-714 1264
Fax: 022-714 4093
www.proteahotels.com
This refurbished harbour-front hotel is well-equipped and makes a useful upmarket base from which to explore the nearby West Coast National Park. **$$–$$$**

CAPE COLUMBINE

Beach Camp
Tel: 082-926 2267
Email: info@ratrace.co.za
www.ratrace.co.za
This private camp set within the nature reserve offers inexpensive tented and A-frame accom-modation, along with

guided sea-kayak trips, dive training and trips, boat trips to the nearby seal and seabird colonies, and hikes into the Cederberg. **$**

LAMBERT'S BAY

Lambert's Bay Hotel
72 Voortrekker Street
PO Box 249, Lambert's Bay 8130
Tel: 027-432 1126
Fax: 027-432 1026
Comfortable harbour-facing accommodation in this quaintly attractive village known for its bird colonies and fine seafood restaurants. **$$**

CEDERBERG

Bushmans Kloof Wilderness Reserve & Retreat
43 km (27 miles) from Clanwilliam,

towards Wupperthal through Parkhuis Pass
Tel: 027-482 2627
www.bushmanskloof.co.za
A luxury oasis in the middle of nowhere. Guests can expect tranquillity, gourmet cuisine, game drives, unspoilt vistas with incredible surrounding rock art. Enjoy some serious pampering in the sumptuous spa. **$$$$**

Kagga Kamma
Between Citrusdal and Ceres streets
Tel: 021-872 4343
Fax: 021-872 4524
Email: info@kaggakamma.co.za
www.kaggakamma.co.za
This private reserve in the southern Cederberg is less notable for its game perhaps than its craggy scenery, rock art and resident San village. Accommodation is in luxury chalets or tents, and there's a restaurant and swimming pool. **$$$$**

STELLENBOSCH

D'Ouwe Werf
30 Church Street
Stellenbosch, 7600
Tel: 021-887 4608
Fax: 021-887 4626
www.ouwewerf.com.
Founded more than 200 years ago, this plush inn set in the heart of old Stellenbosch is notable for its Cape Dutch architecture, period decor, personalised service, sumptuous traditional Cape cuisine and quality wine list. All in all, a gem. **$$$$**

PRICE CATEGORIES

Price categories are for a double room without breakfast:
$ = under US$50
$$ = US$50–100
$$$ = US$100–200
$$$$ = more than US$200

Lanzerac Manor
Lanzerac Street
Tel: 021-887 1132
www.lanzerac.co.za
This 300-year-old manor house is set amongst award-winning vineyards, beautifully landscaped gardens and centuries-old oak trees. Five-star suites, Cape Malay cuisine and a wellness centre and spa. **$$$$**

Devon Valley Hotel
Devon Valley Road
PO Box 68
Stellenbosch 7600
Tel: 021-865 2012
Fax: 021-865 2610
www.devonvalleyhotel.com
Set on the Sylvanvale Estate (a boutique vineyard known for its Pinotage reserve and vine-dried Chenin Blanc), this medium-sized hotel has a scenic winelands atmosphere, a fine restaurant, no-smoking rooms, facilities for disabled guests, and a pool. The small and beautifully located Sugarbird Manor, owned by the World Wildlife Fund, functions as an annexe. **$$$**

Stumble Inn
12 Market Street
Stellenbosch 7699
Tel/fax: 021 887 4049
Email: stumble@iafrica.com
This lively, central and well-established back-packer hostel sprawls over two houses, and facilities include a swimming pool, satellite TV, and discounted wine-tasting tours. **$**

Grande Roche Hotel
Plantasie Street
PO Box 6038
Paarl 7622
Tel: 021-863 5100
Fax: 021-863 2220
www.granderoche.co.za
One of the best hotels in South Africa. A superb setting in a vineyard, sumptuous accommodation, good service. Bosman's, the hotel restaurant, has classically trained staff serving *haute cuisine* and there is a prize-winning cellar. Swimming pool, tennis and gym. **$$$$**

Picardie Guest Farm
Laborie Street
Tel: 021-863 3357
www.picardie.co.za
A small farm at the foot of Paarl Mountain with three types of accommodation: luxury bed & breakfast, self catering or a more informal backpackers unit is available. **$$**

Roggeland Country House
Roggeland Road
Dal Josafat
PO Box 7210
Northern Paarl 7623
Tel: 021-868 2501
www.roggeland.co.za
A superb eight-bedroom Cape Dutch-style guesthouse set in the shadow of the Drakenstein Mountains. The atmosphere, the restaurant and the service have placed it firmly in the ranks of the 50 best country-

house hotels in the world. The cuisine is South African. **$$**

Le Quartier Francais
16 Huguenot Road
Franschhoek 7690
Tel: 021-876 2151
Fax: 021-876 3105
An exceptional upmarket guesthouse set in the heart of this scenic village. It's small and built round a garden courtyard with a pool. Well placed for tours of the winelands, and the restaurant is highly acclaimed. **$$$$**

Auberge Clermont
Robertsvlei Road
Tel: 021-876 3700
www.clermont.co.za
Located on an historic wine and fruit farm, accommodation in the six luxury rooms (including a honeymoon suite), a self catering villa and a spacious loft. Breakfast is served under the 18th-century oak trees or in the courtyard. **$$**

The Marine
Marine Drive
PO Box 9
Hermanus 7200
Tel: 028-313 1000
Fax: 028-313 0160
Email: Hermanus@relaischateaux.com
www.collectionmcgrath.com
Built in 1902 but vastly

expanded and renovated since, Hermanus's finest now consists of 42 individually decorated bedrooms and suites offering commanding views across Walker Bay or the Overberg Mountains. Enjoy a choice of two fine restaurants, along with a sun terrace and the Seafood Express Café. **$$$$**

Salmonsdam Reserve
Tel: 028-314 0062
www.capenature.org.za
The basic hutted accommodation here is set in a wonderful location and is very inexpensive. **$**

Arniston Hotel
Beach Road
Tel: 028-445 9000
www.arnistonhotel.com
This refurbished hotel and social meeting place in the middle of this sleepy fishing village offers comfortable sea-facing rooms. Enjoy a gin and tonic on the terrace overlooking the ocean. Friendly staff. **$$$**

De Hoop Nature Reserve
Tel: 028-425 5020
Fax: 028-425 5030
Email: bredasdorp@capenature.co.za
www.capenature.org.za
There's plenty of low-key and inexpensive accommodation dotted around this reserve including 11 self-catering cottages and a camp site. **$–$$**

Klippe Rivier Country House
Klippe Rivier Farm
Swellendam
Tel: 028-514 3341
www.klipperivier.com
A Cape Dutch homestead that has been converted into luxury suites, while a secluded cottage is perfect for honeymooners. Lovely gardens and a swimming pool. **$–$$**

BELOW: enjoying a stay on Plettenberg Bay.

GARDEN ROUTE AND LITTLE KAROO

MOSSEL BAY

Protea Hotel
Old Post Office Square
Tel: 044-691 3738
Fax: 044-691 3104
Email: book@oldposttree.co.za
www.oldposttree.co.za
Built as a warehouse
in 1846, this historic
hotel has an attractive
waterfront location in
the town centre and
consists of 30 smartly
decorated rooms with
all the usual modern
amenities. The attached
Café Gannet serves good
seafood. **$$$**
Santos Express
Train Lodge
Tel/fax: 044-691 1995
www.santosexpress.co.za
This unusual and popular
backpacker-orientated
lodge consists of a
genuine train carriage
set immediately above
the lovely Santos Beach.
It has a good pub and
restaurant, and is a
useful source of local
travel advice. **$**

GEORGE

Acorn Guest House
4 Kerk Street
George
Tel: 044-874 0474
www.acornguesthouse.co.za
A renovated Victorian
house conveniently
situated near the best
restaurants and sights of
George. The guesthouse
has comfortable bedrooms,
a pool deck and wireless
internet. **$$**

OUDTSHOORN

Eight Bells Mountain Inn
PO Box 436
Mossel Bay 6500
Tel: 044-631 0000
Fax: 044-631 0004
www.eightbells.co.za
Family-run country inn set
amid stunning mountain
scenery on the R328

roughly halfway between
Mossel Bay and Oudtshoorn.
A wide variety of sports
facilities is available. **$$$**
Protea Hotel Riempie
Estate
Baron Van Rheede Street
PO Box 370
Oudtshoorn 6620
Tel: 044-272 6161
Fax: 044-272 6772
www.riempieestate.co.za
Cosy country atmosphere
and tranquil setting in
the heart of ostrich
country. **$$**
Backpackers Paradise
Baron Van Rheede Street
Oudtshoorn 6625
Tel: 044-272 3436
Email: paradise@isat.co.za
www.backpackersparadise.net
This well-established and
central backpacker hostel
offers dorms, double
rooms, camping, internet
facilities and ostrich
barbecues. A good travel
and adventure centre is
attached. **$**

WILDERNESS

Cinnamon Boutique
Guest House
Beacon Road
Tel: 044-877 1324
www.cinnamonhouse.co.za
A lovely guesthouse that
offers elegance and luxury
at every turn with mountain
and sea views. It is a
relatively close walk to the
beach. **$$$**
Ebb & Flow Rest Camp
Tel: 044-877 1197 bookings
through SANParks
Camping sites and a
variety of inexpensive
cabins and chalets are
available at this idyllic rest
camp set on the banks
of the Touws River about
1 km (⅔ mile) upstream
of its mouth. **$$**
The Pink Lodge on
the Beach
45 Die Duin
Tel: 044-877 0263
www.pinklodge.co.za
Have breakfast on the
terrace overlooking the
ocean and watch whales
and dolphins in the
distance (in season).

Comfortable accommo-
dation in a bright-pink
house. **$$**

KNYSNA

Knysna River Club
Sun Valley Drive
PO Box 2986
Knysna 6570
Tel: 044-382 6483
Fax: 044-382 6484
Email: knysna.riverclub@pixie.co.za
www.knysnariverclub.co.za
The recipient of several
awards, this small resort
consists of 35 fully
equipped and serviced self-
catering log chalets
perched on the grassy
verge of Brenton Lagoon.
Facilities include a
restaurant, swimming pool
and canoeing. **$$$$**
Knysna Quays
Protea Hotel
Waterfront Drive
PO Box 33
Knysna 6570
Tel: 044-382 5005
Fax: 044-382 5006
www.proteahotels.com
Good-quality mid-range
accommodation. Air
conditioning, telephone in
rooms, facilities for
disabled guests, swimming
pool and restaurant. **$$$**
Eden's Touch
Tel: 083-253 6366
Fax: 086-617 8844
Email: info@edenstouch.co.za
www.edenstouch.co.za
This idyllic retreat, which
lies a short distance from
the N2 some 20 minutes'
drive east of Knysna
consists of just five large
wooden chalets set on a
fynbos-covered slope
fringed by privately
protected indigenous
forest. Facilities include
a kitchen and satellite
television in all units, and
there's plenty of scope for
horse riding, cycling and
rambling in the surrounding
farmland. **$$$**
Knysna Backpackers
42 Queen Street
Knysna 6570
Tel: 044-382 2554
www.knysnabackpackers.co.za
Set in a Victorian manor,

this is among the more
sedate of the half-dozen
backpacker hostels
scattered around central
Knysna, and it offers
private rooms as well as
dorms. **$**

PLETTENBERG BAY

The Plettenberg
40 Church Street
PO Box 719
Plettenberg Bay 6600
Tel: 044-533 2030
Fax: 044-533 2074
www.collectionmcgrath.com
A grand hotel in the English
country-house style. One of
a small group of Relais and
Chateaux hotels. Guests can
enjoy very good food and
service and amazing sea
views. There is a swimming
pool and luxury spa also on
the property. **$$$$**
Bitou River Lodge
Tel/fax: 044 535 9577
Email: info@bitou.co.za
www.bitou.co.za
Voted South Africa's Best
B&B/Guesthouse in 2003
2004 and 2005, this
luxurious owner-managed
guesthouse consists of just
five rooms set along the
forested banks of the Bitou
River – canoes available –
about 10 km (6 miles) from
Plettenberg Bay. **$$$**
Albergo
6–8 Church Street
Plettenberg Bay 6600
Tel: 044-533 4434
www.albergo.co.za
This relaxed hill-side
backpacker hostel, set
within walking distance of
the central shopping area
and beach, offers dorms,
camping and private rooms,
while the attached "one-
stop action shop" is a good
place to arrange local
activities and day trips. **$**

PRICE CATEGORIES
Price categories are for a
double room without
breakfast:
$ = under US$50
$$ = US$50–100
$$$ = US$100–200
$$$$ = more than US$200

TSITSIKAMMA

Tsitsikamma Lodge
N2 National Road, Tsitsikamma
PO Box 10, Storms River 6308
Tel: 042-280 3802
Fax: 042-280 3702

Email: info@tsitsikamma.com
www.tsitsikamma.com
A hunting lodge with good-value log cabins in a forest setting. Within easy reach of nearby forest and river walks. Three deluxe honeymoon suites with spa baths and fireplaces are available. The lodge won the AA Award for the Best Leisure Hotel in South Africa for two years running. **$$$**

Storms River Mouth Rest Camp
Bookings through SANParks.
Set on the fantastically rugged coastline around the mouth of the Storms River, this excellent national park rest camp consists of beach-front camp sites and a variety of moderately priced wooden huts and chalets. There are walking trails, a good restaurant and well-stocked shop. **$–$$$**

EASTERN CAPE

PORT ELIZABETH

Shamwari Game Reserve
PO Box 113
Swartkops
Port Elizabeth 6210
Tel: 042-203 1111
Fax: 042-235 1224
Email: reservations@shamwari.com
www.shamwari.com
This excellent (and very expensive) private game reserve has won numerous international awards for its superior accommodation and guided game drives that offer the opportunity to see all the so-called Big Five along with recently reintroduced African wild dogs. Choose from six air-conditioned luxury lodges. **$$$$**

Lovemore Retreat
434 Sardinia Road
PO Box 15818
Emerald Hill 6011
Tel: 041-366 1708
Fax: 041-366 2304
There's a sad lack of decent accommodation in Port Elizabeth, so thank heaven for this luxurious coastal guesthouse on the outskirts of town. Offers swimming pool, jacuzzi and steam bath; tranquil beach and nature walks, too. **$$$**

City Lodge
Corner of Beach and Lodge Road
Summerstrand
PO Box 13352
Humewood 6013
Tel: 041-586 3322
Fax: 041-586 3374
Value-for-money accommodation overlooking Humewood Beach. Air conditioning, telephone in rooms, facilities available for disabled guests, restaurant and pool. **$$$**

Addo Elephant National Park
Tel: 042-233 8600
Bookings through SANParks
Chalets and rondavels; camping and caravanning; restaurant, shop, petrol at the rest camp at the park entrance. **$–$$$**

Base Camp
58 Western Road
Port Elizabeth 6001
Tel: 041-582 3285
Email: pebasecamp@yahoo.com
Top-notch modern backpacker hostel boasting a central location, good accommodation, and several excursions including discounted trips to Addo Elephant National Park. **$**

CRADOCK

Mountain Zebra National Park
Tel: 048-881 2427
Fax: 048-881 3943
Bookings through SANParks
The rest camp here offers pleasant and affordable self-catering accommodation, as well as camping facilities. **$$**

New Masonic Hotel
Stockenstroom Street
PO Box 44
Cradock 5880
Tel: 048-881 3115
Fax: 048-881 4402
Friendly hotel offering basic accommodation. **$$**

GRAAFF-REINET

Drostdy Hotel
30 Church Street
PO Box 400
Graaff-Reinet 6280
Tel: 049-892 2161
Fax: 049-892 4582
Email: info@drostdy.co.za
www.drostdy.co.za
Elegant award-winning hotel set in an immaculately restored old Cape Dutch style building and Victorian addition, whose period atmosphere and decor is offset by modern conveniences such as air conditioning, telephones in rooms and a swimming pool. The restaurant is a great place to sample traditional Cape cooking. **$$$$**

Urquhart Park
Tel: 049-892 2136
Set on the R63 fringing the town centre, this attractive municipal resort offers camping facilities, as well as comfortable and inexpensive huts and chalets. **$–$$**

NIEU-BETHESDA

Owl House Backpackers
Martin Street
Tel: 049-841 1642
www.owlhouse.info
Email: backpackersinfo@owlhouse.com
An inexpensive B&B is available near the idiosyncratic Owl House, the staff of which can also point you to some good local hiking and rock-art sites. **$**

GRAHAMSTOWN

The Cock House
10 Market Street
Grahamstown 6140
Tel/fax: 046-636 1287/95
Email: cockhouse@imaginet.co.za
www.cockhouse.co.za
Set in a restored 1820s building, this popular award-winning guesthouse is ideally located for exploring the City of Saints' many historical sites and museums. **$$$**

Grahamstown Caravan Park
Tel: 046-603 6072
This municipal site offers camping and affordable self-catering accommodation in green gardens on the southwestern edge of the town centre. **$–$$**

KING WILLIAMS TOWN

Grosvenor Lodge
48 Taylor Road
PO Box 61
King William's Town 5600
Tel: 043-604 7200
Fax: 043-604 7205
www.grosvenor.co.za
A homely hotel with air conditioning, telephone and restaurant. **$$**

HOGSBACK

Hogsback Inn & Mountain Cabins
Main Road
Tel: 045-962 1006
Email: hotel@hogsbackinn.co.za
www.hogsbackinn.co.za
With a cosy highland atmosphere, this old-fashioned, sensibly priced country inn offers good hotel accommodation and also has a self-catering log cabin available to guests as well as varied activities such as horse riding, fishing, hiking, mountain biking and birdwatching. **$$**

Away With The Fairies
Ambleside Close
PO Box 60
Hogsback 5721
Tel: 045-962 1031
Email: hogsbackl@iafrica.com
Set in spacious grounds inhabited by monkeys and various colourful birds, this excellent backpacker hostel has rooms, dorms, camping space and a restaurant – a great base for exploring the forested Amatola Mountains on a budget. **$**

PORT ALFRED

Halyards Hotel
Albany Road
Tel: 046-604 3300
www.riverhotels.co.za
The centrepiece of the Royal Alfred Marina, this highly regarded hotel is a

fine example of Cape Cod architecture and it consists of 49 smart, comfortable rooms, most of which have sea views. Conference facilities also available. **$$$$**

EAST LONDON

**Premier Hotel
King David**
Corner Currie Street &
Inverleith Terrace
PO Box 18172
Quigney
East London 5211
Tel: 043-722 3174
Fax: 043-743 8019
Email: kingdavidhotel@iafrica.com
www.kingdavidhotel.co.za
This hotel is convenient for both East London's city centre and its beaches. The 80 well-equipped rooms and suites include

air conditioning and telephones. No-smoking rooms are available. Popular with business travellers because of its proximity to the business district. Also close to the beach. **$$–$$$**

**Esplanade Hotel
Beachfront**
PO Box 18041
Quigney
East London 5211
Tel: 043-722 2518
Fax: 043-722 3679
Simple yet comfortable accommodation on the main beach front. **$$**

**East London
Backpackers**
11 Quanza Street
Quigney
East London 5021
Tel: 043-781 1122
Email: info@elbackpackers.co.za
Popular and long-serving backpacker hostel close to the beach-front esplanade. **$**

WILD COAST

Cremorne Estate
Po Box 104
Port St Johns
Tel/fax: 047-564 1110
www.cremorne.co.za
Rustic log cabins with a superb location on the lush banks of the Umzimvubu River, opposite Port St Johns. Good facilities. **$$**

Kob Inn
Box 18137
Quigney, 5211
Tel: 047-499 0011
Fax: 047-499 0016
www.kobinn.co.za
This comfortable family-oriented hotel has a beach-front location on the Qora River mouth. Well situated for beach activities, fishing and country walks. **$$**

DURBAN AND KWAZULU-NATAL (KZN) COAST

DURBAN

Southern Sun Elangeni
Durban Beachfront
Durban 4000
Tel: 031-362 1300
Fax: 031-332 5527
www.southernsun.com
Breathtaking views of Durban's Golden Mile. Three excellent restaurants and all luxury hotel and business facilities. **$$$$**

Royal Hotel
267 Smith Street
Box 1041
Durban 4000
Tel: 031-333 6000
Fax: 031-333 6002
www.theroyal.co.za
Voted the best city hotel in South Africa for five consecutive years, the bland modern exterior hides a large, luxurious and comfortable interior that prides itself on offering the "Last Outpost of the British Empire" experience. Seven restaurants, including the Ulundi which specialises in fabulous curries. Air conditioning, fitness centre and pool. **$$$$**

Essenwood House
630 Essenwood Road
Berea
Durban 4001
Tel/fax: 031-207 4547
Email: info@essenwoodhouse.co.za
www.essenwoodhouse.co.za
This colonial-era homestead, set in large gardens overlooking the city centre and ocean, offers personalised service and a high standard of accommodation in its six en-suite rooms. **$$–$$$**

Goble Palms
120 Goble Road
Morningside
Durban 4001
Tel/fax: 031-312 2598
Email: info@goblepalms.co.za
www.goblepalms.co.za
Luxurious owner-managed four-bedroom guesthouse set in a Victorian homestead with great sea views. **$$$**

Holiday Inn Garden Court Durban
Marine Parade 167
PO Box 10809
Durban 4056
Tel: 031-337 3341
Fax: 031-337 5929
All sea-facing bedrooms in

a hotel just 400 metres/yds from the beach. Also close to the central business district. **$$–$$$**

Tekweni Backpackers Hostel
169 Ninth Avenue
Morningside
Durban 4001
Tel: 031-303 1433
Email: info@tekwenibackpackers.co.za
www.tekwenibackpackers.co.za
One of the oldest and best backpacker hostels in Durban, the Tekweni sprawls over three houses near to Florida Road (good selection of restaurants) and offers a good selection of rooms and dorms. It's the home of Tekweni Ecotours, whose varied programme of cultural and wildlife tours earned it the Mayor's Award for Community Excellence in 1999. **$**

KZN COAST

Selborne Hotel, Spa and Golf Estate
PO Box 2
Pennington 4184

Tel: 039-688 1800
Fax: 039-975 1811
Email: info@selborne.com
www.selborne.com
Just 40 minutes' drive south of Durban, this smart country house-style hotel is decorated with antiques and fine oil paintings and set in tropical gardens that are a bird-spotter's delight. Good golf course, too. **$$$$**

Karridene Protea Hotel
Old South Coast Road
PO Box 20
Illovo Beach 4155
Tel: 031-916 7228
Fax: 031-916 7237
Email: sales@karridene.co.za
www.karridene.co.za
A modern hotel with good sports facilities. The rooms have air conditioning and telephone. Facilities for those who are disabled.

PRICE CATEGORIES

Price categories are for a double room without breakfast:
$ = under US$50
$$ = US$50–100
$$$ = US$100–200
$$$$ = more than US$200

Swimming pool and restaurant on site. **$$$**
Beach Lodge Hotel
Marine Drive
PO Box 109
Margate 4275
Tel: 039-312 1483
Fax: 039-317 1232

www.beachlodge.org.za
Comfortable rooms and self-catering apartments. The restaurant serves traditional German cuisine. Swimming pool. A few minutes' walk to the beach. **$$$**

Oribi Gorge Hotel
Tel/fax: 039-687 0253
Email: oribigorge@worldonline.co.za
www.oribigorge.co.za
Situated at Fairacres, this moderately priced hotel offers comfortable rooms in pretty grounds that

afford a wonderful view over Oribi Gorge. **$$**
Oribi Gorge Reserve
Tel: 039-679 1644
Bookings through KZN Wildlife. Seven cottages and huts, aimed at budget self-caterers. **$**

ZULULAND

UMHLANGA ROCKS

Beverly Hills Hotel
54 Lighthouse Road
PO Box 71
Umhlanga Rocks 4320
Tel: 031-561 2211
Fax: 031-561 3711
www.southernsun.com
Set right on the coast, just 10 minutes' drive from Durban. Air conditioning, telephone, non-smoking rooms available, restaurant and swimming pool. **$$$$**
Oyster Box Hotel
2 Lighthouse Road
PO Box 22
Umhlanga Rocks 4320
Tel: 031-561 2233
Fax: 031-561 4072
www.oysterbox.co.za
Quiet and very comfortable, this superb family-run hotel is set right on the beach. It has a good restaurant too, specialising in fresh seafood and enormous steaks. Closed for renovations until late 2008. **$$$–$$$$**

TUGELA MOUTH

Harold Johnson Nature Reserve
Tel: 0324-861 574
Bookings through KZN Wildlife. Camping and caravan site on the river mouth. **$**

RICHARDS BAY

Protea Hotel Richards Bay
Corner Launder & Davidson roads
PO Box 10105
Meerensee

Richards Bay 3901
Tel: 035-753 1350
Fax: 035-753 1361
info@proteahotelrichardsbay.co.za
Pleasant if unexceptional beach-front hotel offering good accommodation and services geared primarily towards business travellers. **$$–$$$**

MTUNZINI

Umlalazi Nature Reserve
Tel: 035-340 1836
Bookings through KZN Wildlife. A string of 13 five-bed log cabins set in the coastal forest, and there's also a camp site. **$–$$**

ESHOWE

George Hotel
36 Main Street
PO Box 24
Eshowe 3815
Tel: 035-474 4919
www.eshowe.com
Committed to several local community projects, this country-style hotel is the pulse of tourist activity in Eshowe. In addition to comfortable mid-range accommodation in the main building, it offers backpacker rooms and dorms in an annexe, while the on-site Zululand Eco-Adventures offers a variety of day/overnight tours and activities. Facilities include a pool and restaurant. **$–$$**
Eshowe Caravan Park
Tel: 035-474 4664
The municipal camp site has a wonderful location on the edge of the Dhlinza Forest Reserve. **$**

CULTURAL LODGES

Shakaland
PO Box 103
Eshowe 3815
Tel: 035-460 0912
Fax: 035-460 0824
Email: res@shakaland.com
www.shakaland.co.za
Commodious traditional beehive huts with air conditioning, en-suite bathrooms and other modern amenities, which compliment an excellent cultural programme that starts at 4pm for overnight visitors. **$$$$**
Simunye
PO Box 248
Melmoth 3835
Tel: 035-450 3111
Fax: 035-450 2534
www.simunyelodge.co.za
This fabulous (albeit somewhat rustic) lodge has a down-to-earth bush feel and a great Zulu cultural programme – starting at 3.30pm when visitors are transported there by ox-cart from a meeting point on the R66. **$$$$**
KwaBhekithunga
Tel: 035-460 0929
Low-key family-run cultural lodge offering cosy accommodation in beehive huts and a most worthwhile cultural programme that places substance over style. **$$$**
KwaZulu Cultural Museum
PO Box 523, Ulundi 3838
Tel: 035-870 2051
Tel: 035-870 2054
Email: amafahq@mweb.co.za
www.amafa.co.za
Relatively inexpensive accommodation in beehive huts on the site of Cetshwayo's last kraal and the Anglo-Zulu Battle of Ondoni. **$$**

ST LUCIA

Kingfisher Lodge
187 McKenzie Street
PO Box 291
St Lucia Village 3936
Tel/fax: 035-590 1015
Email: stluciakingfisherlodge@mweb.co.za
www.kingfisherlodge.net
Smart family-run seven-room B&B set in lush gardens that run down to the estuary shore – great for birds, hippos and duikers. **$$$**
Bhangazi Complex Cape Vidal
On the coast 30 km (18½ miles) north of St Lucia village
Tel: 035-590 9012
Bookings through KZN Wildlife. Located on a beautiful cape covered in tall dunes and coastal forest, this rest camp consists of 33 well-equipped log cabins sleeping from 2–20 each, as well as space for 50 tents. **$–$$$**
Charters Creek & Fanie's Island
Located on the western shore of the estuary, about 20 km (12½ miles) from the N2
Tel: 035-550 9000 (Charter's Creek) or 9035 (Fanie's Island)
Bookings though KZN Wildlife. This pair of rustic, low-key, low-cost camps on the western bank of the estuary are ideally suited for birdwatching and walking in areas that host a fair amount of (mostly harmless) wildlife. **$$**
Bibs International Backpackers
310 McKenzie Street
PO Box 51
St Lucia Village 3936
035-590 1056
www.bibs.co.za
Long-standing and popular backpacker hostel offering

dorms, private rooms, camping and various excursions in the leafy heart of St Lucia village. **$**

HLUHLUWE-IMFOLOZI

Bonamanzi Game Park
10 km (6 miles) south of Hluhluwe village
Tel: 035-562 0181
Fax: 035-562 0143
Email: info@bonamanzi.co.za
www.bonamanzi.co.za
This private reserve offers accommodation in tree houses and various lodges, as well as guided walks and 4x4 drives in a game area harbouring hippo, zebra and a variety of antelope and birds. **$$$$**

Hilltop Camp
Tel: 035-562 0848
Bookings through KZN Wildlife. Set within Hluhluwe Game Reserve, this modern, motel-like rest camp consists of 65 en-suite chalets and huts set on a rise offering expansive views across green hills dotted with wildlife. A good restaurant and shop are attached. **$$$**

Mpila Camp
Tel: 035-550 8476/7
Bookings through KZN Wildlife. Set within Imfolozi Game Reserve, this rustic self-catering camp offers a variety of hutted accommodation as well as some superb elevated safari tents that regularly receive nocturnal visits from spotted hyena, porcupine and other small carnivores. The small shop has limited supplies, so it's best to bring whatever food you need with you. **$$**

Isinkwe Bush Camp & Backpackers
Situated at Bushlands about 20 km (12½ miles) from Hluhluwe Game Reserve
PO Box 493
Hluhluwe 3960
Tel: 035-562 2258
Email: info@isinkwe.co.za
www.isinkwe.co.za.
This tranquil budget bush camp offers self-catering

chalets, backpacker rooms and dorms, camping space, meals and day trails, as well as operating excellent guided 4x4 trips into Hluhluwe-Imfolozi on a twice-daily basis. **$–$$**

uMKHUZE RESERVE

Phinda Resource Reserve
Bookings through CCAfrica
Private Bag X27
Benmore 2010
Tel: 011-809 4300
Fax: 011-809 4400
Email: bookings@ccafrica.com
www.ccafrica.com
The four immaculate luxury lodges within this superb private game reserve bordering uMkhuze all offer 4x4 excursions with knowledgeable guides, and a good chance of close encounters with lion, cheetah, leopard, elephant, rhino and much else besides. The food is world-class. **$$$$**

Zulu Nyala Lodge
PO Box 163
Hluhluwe 3960
Tel: 035-562 0169
Fax: 035-562 0646
Email: zulures@zulunyala.com
www.zulunyala.com
This private game reserve is adjacent to Phinda and supports many of the same species. Accommodation in either of its two up-market tented camps includes guided 4x4 drives and good food. **$$$$**

Ghost Mountain Inn
Tel: 035-573 1025
Email: gmi@ghostmountaininn.co.za
www.ghostmountaininn.co.za
Pleasant mid-range hotel situated on the lush outskirts of uMkhuze Town some 20 km (12½ miles) from the game reserve entrance gate. **$$$**

Mantuma Rest Camp
Tel: 035-573 9001
Bookings through KZN-Wildlife
Set in the heart of the game reserve, this acacia-shaded camp consists of a variety of huts, chalets and cottages catering for 2–7 people each. There's also a camp site at the reserve entrance gate. **$$**

MAPUTALAND

Rocktail Bay
Bookings through
UK tel: +44 164 728 1665 or
USA tel: +1 203-762-8050
Set on the pristine and practically deserted coastline north of Kosi Bay, this small, upmarket beach resort must be just about the most remote in South Africa, and it's also one of the most sumptuous. **$$$$**

Tembe Elephant Park
Tel: 031-267 0144
Fax: 035-266 8718
Email: info@tembe.co.za
www.tembe.co.za
Packages at this small privately run luxury tented camp set within KZN Wildlife's Tembe Elephant Sanctuary include all meals and guided 4x4 drives to seek out the park's elephant, rhino, lion and other wildlife. **$$$$**

Sodwana Bay
Bookings through KZN Wildlife
This rest camp consists of 33 log cabins sleeping 5–8 adults apiece, as well as 350 camping sites. **$$**

Ndumo Rest Camp
Tel: 035-591 0058
Bookings through KZN Wildlife
This small and inexpensive camp near the entrance gate consists of just seven two-bed huts as well as space for eight tents. **$**

Thonga Beach Lodge
Tel: 035-474 1473
Email: res@isibindiafrica.co.za
www.isibindiafrica.co.za
Operated in conjunction with the local Mabibi community, this appealing "bush meets beach" lodge has chic but organic architecture, excellent service and a pristine beach location. Snorkelling, fishing, deep-sea diving and kayak excursions onto Lake Sibaya are offered.

Kosi Forest Lodge
Tel: 035-474 1473
Email: res@isibindiafrica.co.za
www.isibindiafrica.co.za
Set in sand forest overlooking Lake Shengeza in the Kosi Bay wetlands, this relaxed bush camp is popular with birdwatchers and offers excursions to

hippo-infested Lake Amanzamnyama and the dramatic Kosi Bay mouth.

ITHALA RESERVE

Fugitives' Drift Lodge
PO Rorke's Drift
Kwazulu Natal 3016
Tel: 034-642 1843
Fax: 034-271 8053
Email: info@fugitvesdrift.com
www.fugitivesdrift.com
En-suite cottages and a six-bedroom guesthouse set within a 1,600-hectare (4,000-acre) game reserve, overlooking Isandlwana and Rorke's Drift. There is an attractive mature garden and a large swimming pool. Horse riding, hiking and fishing trips may be arranged. **$$–$$$**

Pongola Country Lodge
14 Jan Mielie Street, Pongola 3170
Tel: 034-413 1352
Fax: 034-413 1353
www.pongolacountrylodge.com
This homely and affordable hotel in the village of Pongola is ideally situated for exploring Pongola Nature Reserve and other local attractions. **$$**

Ntshondwe Lodge (Ithala)
Tel: 034-983 2540
Bookings through KZN Wildlife
This large modern rest camp in Ithala Game Reserve consists of a full-service restaurant with fantastic views and a variety of huts and chalets overlooking the sweeping plains below. **$$**

Stilwater Hotel
Dundee Road, Private Bag X9332
Vryheid 3100
Tel: 034-981 6181
Fax: 034-980 8846
www.stilwaterhotel.co.za
This hotel makes a good base from which to tour Northern KwaZulu-Natal. Air conditioning, telephones, restaurant and swimming pool. **$$**

DRAKENSBERG

PIETERMARITZBURG

**Game Valley
Lodge Otto's Bluff**
PO Box 13010
Cascades 3202
Tel: 033-569 0011
Fax: 033-569 0012
Luxury game-lodge hotel.
$$$$
Protea Hotel Imperial
224 Loop Street
PO Box 140
Pietermaritzburg 3200
Tel: 033-342 6551
Fax: 033-342 9796
Email: reservations@imperialkzn.co.za
www.imperialhotel.co.za
This Victorian gem offers
comfortable
accommodation and good
food in the heart of the
historic city centre. **$$$**

HOWICK

**Hartford House
Summerhill Stud Farm**
Mooi River
Tel: 033-263 2713
Fax: 033-263 2818
Email: info@Hartford.co.za
Superb guesthouse situated
on a large estate on the
Drakensberg foothills near
Mooi River, Horse riding,
walking, birdwatching, trout
fishing and top-notch
country cooking. **$$$$**
Hilton Hotel
Hilton Road
PO Box 35
Hilton 3245
Tel: 033-343 3311
Fax: 033-343 3722
www.hiltonhotel.co.za
Country-style atmosphere.
Restaurant, telephones, no-
smoking rooms available
and swimming pool. **$$$**
**Midmar Public Resort &
Nature Reserve**
Tel: 033-330 2067
Bookings through KZN Wildlife.
Situated on Midmar Dam,
this resort offers 63
cottages/huts, camping
and caravan sites,
restaurant and bar,
swimming (no bilharzia),
fishing, sailing, water-
skiing, tennis, squash,
bowls and riding. **$–$$**

Zivuya Mountain Lodge
PO Box 265
Howick
Tel: 033-234 4032
www.zivuya.co.za
Eco-style backpackers
lodge with river-front
setting in the hills around
Dargle, outside Howick.
$

UKHAHLAMBA PARK

**Drakensberg Sun
Cathkin Peak**
PO Box 335
Winterton 3340
Tel: 036-468 1000
Fax: 036-468 1224
A spectacular upmarket
mountain resort in the
central Drakensberg.
$$$$
Champagne Castle Hotel
Tel: 036-468 1063
Fax: 036-468 1306
Email: champagnecastle@futurenet.co.za
www.champagnecastle.co.za
Set right at the base of
the "barrier of spears"
topped by Champagne
Castle Peak, this spacious
hotel is ideally located for
hiking, horse riding, and
exploring the local rock
art. **$$$**
**Orion Mont-aux-Sources
Hotel**
Mont-aux-Sources
Private Bag X1670
Bergville 3353
Tel: 036-438 8000
Fax: 036-438 6201
Central reservations: 0861-99199
Email: gmmont@orion-hotels.co.za
www.oriongroup.co.za
Situated at the entrance
to Royal Natal Park,
arguably the most scenic
piece of real estate
anywhere in the
Drakensberg, this quiet
upmarket hotel also has
good sports facilities and
a swimming pool, and the
surrounding slopes are
rich in walking
possibilities. **$$$**
Sani Pass Hotel
Sani Pass Road
PO Box 44
Himeville 4585
Tel: 033-702 1320
Fax: 033-702 0220
www.sanipasshotel.co.za

Set at the foot of the Sani
Pass in 800 hectares
(2,000 acres) of southern
Drakensberg countryside.
Good for sports and activity
holidays, facilities include
sauna, swimming pool,
golf, horse riding, tennis
and squash courts. **$$$**
Ardmore Guest Farm
PO Box 122
Champagne Valley
Winterton 3340
Tel: 036-468 1314
Fax: 036-468 1241
Email: info@ardmore.co.za.
www.ardmore.co.za
This small, homely and
very friendly owner-
managed guesthouse lies
on grassy green farmland
overshadowed by the
peaks of Champagne
Castle. It's attached to
the celebrated Ardmore
Ceramic Art Studio, which
is well worth a look. The
superb home-cooked four-
course meals are very
reasonably priced.
$$–$$$
ATKU Drakensville Resort
PO Box 53
Jagerspruit 3354
Tel: 036-438 6287
Fax: 036-438 6524
Email: reservations@drakensville.co.za
www.drakensville.co.za
This popular and
attractively located family
resort in the northern
Berg, near Royal Natal,
offers a wide range of self-
catering accommodation,
as well as camping
facilities, a good
restaurant and bar, and
plenty of walking
opportunities. **$$**
**Giant's Castle
Game Reserve**
Tel: 036-353 3718
Bookings through KZN Wildlife
The main camp here
consists of 45 huts and
cottages of various sizes,
ideally placed for trout
fishing, hiking and viewing
the nearby rock art. **$$**
Spioenkop Nature Reserve
Tel: 036-488 1578
Bookings through KZN Wildlife
Five cottages and huts,
one bush camp, camping
and caravan site, pool,
boat rides, tennis, riding.
$–$$

Inkosana Lodge
PO Box 60
Winterton 3340
Tel/fax: 036-468 1202
Email: inkosana@inkosana.co.za
www.inkosana.co.za
Offering double rooms,
dorms and camping
facilities at backpacker-
friendly rates, Inkosana,
with its knowledgeable
staff, is a perfect base
from which to hike the
central Drakensberg on a
budget. **$**
Sani Lodge
PO Box 485
Underberg 3257
Tel: 033-702 0330
Email: info@sanilodge.co.za
www.sanilodge.co.za
This enduringly popular
backpacker lodge has a
superb location at the
base of Sani Pass, and the
owner-manager is a mine
of information about
neighbouring Lesotho. A
variety of package tours
include two-day guided
hikes to South Africa's
highest peak; a regular
road shuttle from Durban
and Pietermaritzburg. **$**

FREE STATE

Cranberry Cottage
37 Beeton Street
Ladybrand 9745
Tel: 051-924 2290
Fax: 051-924 1168
www.cranberrycottage.co.za
Delightful guesthouse in a
renovated Victorian home.
Very good food, too. Well-
placed for a stopover if
you're doing the Eastern
Highlands Route. **$$**
**Golden Gate Highlands
National Park**
Bookings through SANParks
Lodge, chalets, huts;
caravanning and camping;
restaurant and shop;
swimming pool, tennis,
golf, bowling, horse riding;
one overnight and half a
dozen shorter trails. **$$**
Mount Nebo Holiday Farm
Nebo Farm, PO Box 178
Ficksburg 9730
Tel: 051-933 3947
Fax: 051-933 3281
Two-bedroom thatched

cottage accommodation set in an Old English-style rose garden on this large cherry estate. Telephone in rooms, restaurant, sports facilities and swimming pool. **$$**

Park Hotel
23 Muller Street
PO Box 8
Bethlehem 9700
Tel/fax: 058-303 5191
Basic hotel with air conditioning, telephone in

rooms, no-smoking rooms available, facilities for disabled guests, restaurant and swimming pool. **$$**
Rustlers Valley Backpackers
Rustlers Valley Farm

Ficksburg 9730
Tel/fax: 051-933 2286
A groovy New Age hang-out for backpackers and budget travellers set in lovely Eastern Highlands scenery. **$**

GAUTENG

JOHANNESBURG

Aloe Ridge Hotel
Muldersdrift
PO Box 3040
Honeydew 2040
Tel/fax: 011-957 2070
www.aloeridgehotel.com
Luxury hotel set in a game reserve with semi-authentic Zulu village, 40 km (25 miles) from Johannesburg. Air conditioning, telephones, restaurant. Fishing, squash, tennis courts and pool. **$$$$**
The Grace
54 Bath Avenue
Rosebank 2196
Tel: 011-280 7200
Fax: 011-280 7474
www.grace.co.za
Luxurious little country-house-style hotel with impeccable service; handily placed for the shopping and nightlife facilities of Rosebank. **$$$$**
Heia Safari Ranch
Muldersdrift
PO Box 1387
Honeydew 2040
Tel: 011-919 5000
Fax: 011-659 0709
www.heia-safari.co.za
Comfortable hotel set in a nature reserve, 40 km (25 miles) from Johannesburg. Telephones, restaurant, fishing, swimming pool, tennis court. **$$$$**
Protea Hotel Balalaika Sandton
Maud Street
PO Box 783372
Sandton 2196
Tel: 011-322 5000
Fax: 011-322 5021
www.balalaika.co.za
Tranquil setting and good facilities in the exclusive suburb of Sandton. **$$$$**
Rosebank Hotel
Corner of Tyrwhitt and Sturdee avenues

PO Box 52025
Saxonwold 2132
Tel: 011-447 2700
Fax: 011-447 4554
Email: rosebank@rosebankhotel.co.za
www.rosebankhotel.co.za
Friendly, prestigious suburban hotel; three restaurants, conference facilities and bar. **$$$$**
Sandton Sun & Towers
Corner of Alice and Fifth streets
PO Box 784902
Sandton 2146
Tel: 011-780 5000
Fax: 011-780 5002
A luxurious hotel with excellent facilities in the heart of Johannesburg's most exclusive business and residential suburb. **$$$$**
The Saxon
36 Saxon Road
Sandhurst, Sandton
Tel: 011-292 6000
Fax: 011-292 6001
www.thesaxon.com
Prestigious hide-out favoured by Nelson Mandela, with high-class decor and cuisine, and rooms the size of aircraft hangars. **$$$$**
Ten Bompas
10 Bompas Road
Dunkeld West
Johannesburg
Tel: 011-325 2442
Fax: 011-341 0281
www.tenbompas.com
A rambling family home in one of the city's leafiest suburbs has been transformed into a funky boutique hotel, where each of the 10 suites has a different African theme. Swimming pool and garden. **$$$$**
The Westcliff
67 Jan Smuts Avenue
Westcliff 2193
Tel: 011-481 6000
Fax: 011-480 6010
www.westcliff.co.za
Spread out over a ridge (chauffeured golf cars

provide transport), here is opulence and luxury in slightly self-conscious "neo-African" surroundings. Wonderful views from the terrace and pool over the lush northern suburbs. **$$$$**
Garden Court OR Tambo Airport Hotel
2 Hulley Road
Isando
Private Bag X5
Kempton Park 1627
Tel: 011-392 1062
Fax: 011-974 8097
Email: gcjhbairport@southernsun.com
Only 1 km (⅔ mile) from the airport. Air conditioning, telephones, non-smoking bedrooms available, facilities for the disabled. Swimming pool. Pets can be accommodated. **$$$**
Southern Sun Grayston
Corner of Graystone Drive and Rivonia Road
PO Box 781743
Sandton 2146
Tel: 011-783 5262
Fax: 011-783 5289
Email: grayston@southernsun.com
Beautiful gardens. Air conditioning, telephones, non-smoking bedrooms available, à la carte restaurant, facilities for the disabled. Swimming pool. **$$$**
City Lodge
Johannesburg International Airport
4 Sandvale Road
Edenvale
PO Box 8404
Edenglen 1613
Tel: 011-392 1750
Fax: 011-392 2644
Warm and friendly inexpensive hotel close to the airport. Air conditioning, telephones, non-smoking bedrooms available, and facilities for disabled guests. Swimming pool. **$$–$$$**
City Lodge Sandton
Corner of Katherine Street and

Grayston Drive
PO Box 781643
Sandton 2146
Tel: 011-444 5300
Fax: 011-444 5315
Value-for-money hotel in upmarket Sandton. Air conditioning, telephones, non-smoking bedrooms, facilities for disabled guests. Swimming pool. **$$–$$$**
Airport Backpackers
3 Mohawk Street
Kempton Park 1619
Tel/fax: 011-394 0485
Email: airbackp@mweb.co.za
www.airportbackpackers.co.za
This well-established hostel offers good facilities close to the airport, free airport pick-ups, and a good travel centre. **$**
Backpackers Ritz
1a North Road
Dunkeld West
Johannesburg 2196
Tel: 011-325 7125/2520
Fax: 011-325 2521
Email: ritz@iafrica.com
www.backpackers-ritz.com
The oldest backpacker lodge in the city, and still a reliable and convenient base, offering dorms, double rooms, and free pick-up from anywhere in Jo'burg. **$**

PRETORIA

Sheraton Pretoria Hotel & Towers
Corner Church & Wessels streets
Arcadia
Tel: 012-429 9999

PRICE CATEGORIES

Price categories are for a double room without breakfast:
$ = under US$50
$$ = US$50–100
$$$ = US$100–200
$$$$ = more than US$200

Fax: 012-429 9300
This smart new hotel is probably the largest in the city centre, boasting 175 rooms, and also the only one to approach five-star standards. **$$$$**

Holiday Inn Pretoria
Corner of Church and Beatrix streets
PO Box 40694
Arcadia
Pretoria 0007
Tel: 012-341 1571
Fax: 012-440 7534
Right in the centre of Pretoria. Air conditioning, telephones, no-smoking bedrooms available, facilities for disabled guests, restaurant. Swimming pool. **$$$–$$$$**

Farm Inn Hotel
Lynnwood Road next to Silverlakes Golf Estate
PO Box 71702
Die Wilgers 0041
Tel: 012-809 0266
Fax: 012-809 0146
www.farminn.co.za
Unusual accommodation in an African stone-and-thatch palace in a private game sanctuary. Telephones, restaurant. Hiking trails, fishing, horse riding and swimming pool. **$$$**

Garden Court Hatfield
Corner of End and Pretorius streets
PO Box 14050
Pretoria 0028
Tel: 012-342 1444
Fax: 012-342 3492
Centrally located with comfortable rooms. Air conditioning, telephones,

non-smoking bedrooms available, facilities for disabled guests. Swimming pool. **$$$**

La Maison
235 Hilda Street
Hatfield
Pretoria 0083
Tel: 012-430 4341
Fax: 012-342 1531
Email: lamaison@intekom.co.za
www.lamaison.co.za
This five-bedroom hotel has an excellent reputation for its cuisine, which is prepared by the hands-on owner-manager, a qualified chef. Telephones, restaurant and swimming pool. **$$$**

Marvol House
358 Aries Street
Waterkloof Ridge
Pretoria
Tel: 012-346 1774
Fax: 012-346 1776
Small, very comfortable guesthouse in the whitewashed-and-gabled Cape Dutch style. Set on a ridge, with two swimming pools, gym, Jacuzzi and sauna. **$$$**

Protea Hotel Lesedi
PO Box 699
Lanseria 1748
Tel: 012-205 1394/5
Fax: 012-205 1433
Email: sales@lesedi.com
Comfortable accommodation based on traditional African architecture in a Lesedi cultural village in Broederstroom on the road towards Hartebeespoort Dam. **$$**

Word of Mouth Backpackers
430 Reitz Street
Sunnyside
Pretoria 0002
Tel: 012-343 7499
Fax: 012-343 9351
Email: wom@mweb.co.za
www.wordofmouthbackpackers.com
Popular backpacker hostel in a central location, with good facilities and comfortable dorms and rooms. **$**

PILANESBERG PARK

The Palace of the Lost City
PO Box 308
Sun City 0316
Tel: 014-557 1000
Fax: 014-557 3111
www.suninternational.com
Critics deplore its flamboyant, glitzy presence in one of the poorest regions of the country. A top-class hotel in an imported "tropical jungle" setting, complete with artificial beach and wave pool. **$$$$**

Manyane Resort
PO Box 6651
Rustenburg 0300
Tel: 014-555 1000
Fax: 014-555 7555
Email: goldres@iafrica.com
www.goldenleopard.co.za
This resort at the entrance gate of the same name has good chalet accommodation, camping space, a restaurant, a

shop, a swimming pool, and a wonderful walk-in aviary. **$–$$$**

MADIKWE RESERVE

Tau Game Lodge
Tel: 011-314 4350/4349
Fax: 011-314 1162
Email: taugame@mweb.co.za
www.taugamelodge.com
Built in 1995, this classy lodge consists of 30 thatched chalets, each with its own wooden deck and en-suite bathroom with open-air shower, set in a vast natural water hole that attracts a variety of game. **$$$$**

Madikwe River Lodge
Tel: 014-778 9000
Fax: 014-778 9020
Email: lodge@madikwe.threecities.co.za
www.madikweriverlodge.com
This tranquil and exclusive lodge consists of 16 secluded split-level thatched chalets tucked into the cool forest fringing the Groot Marico River. **$$$$**

Mosetlha Bush Camp
PO Box 78690
Sandton 2146
Tel: 011-444 9345
Email: info@thebushcamp.com
www.thebushcamp.com
This rustic, unfenced bush camp accommodates a maximum of 16 people in nine double cabins. It emphasises intimacy and bush simplicity, and doesn't have electrical power. **$$$$**

MPUMALANGA & LIMPOPO

MIDDELBURG

Loskop Dam Game Reserve
Private Bag X1525
Middelburg 1050
Tel: 013-759 5300
Fax: 013-752 7012
Fifty-three km (32 miles) north of Middelburg. The reserve offers caravan and camping facilities plus fishing; adjoining reserve offers more sheltered accommodation. **$–$$**

SABIE

Jock of the Bushveld
Main Road, Sabie 1260
Tel: 013-764 2178
www.jock.co.za
Central resort offering camping space, dorm accommodation and chalets to backpackers and other budget travellers. **$$**

Villa Ticino Guesthouse
Louis Trichardt Road
PO Box 823, Sabie 1260
Tel/fax: 013-764 2598
www.villaticino.co.za

This small bed and breakfast accommodation offers comfortable and good food and is surrounded by lush gardens only 100 metres/yds from the town centre. **$$**

BLYDE RIVER CANYON

Swadini Forever Resort
On the Lowveld side off the R531 from Acornhoek to Hoedspruit
Box 281, Hoedspruit 1380
Tel: 012-423 5600
www.foreversa.co.za

Chalets and huts, caravanning and camping, restaurant and shop; sporting facilities. **$–$$$**

Forever Resorts Blyde Canyon
Off the R532 between Graskop and Tzaneen
Private Bag X368
Ohrigstadt 1122
Tel: 012-423 5600
www.foreversa.co.za
With 75 chalets, caravanning and camping sites, two restaurants, a shop, sport facilities and several trails, this is an excellent base from which

to explore the Panorama Route. **$–$$**

PILGRIM'S REST

Royal Hotel
Tel: 013-768 1100
Fax: 013-768 1188
www.pilgrimsrest.org.za
This atmospheric hotel offers accommodation in converted miners' cottages, decorated in period style, as well as forming a useful base for exploring the Panorama Route. **$$$**

Mount Sheba
Lydenburg Road
Pilgrim's Rest
Mpumalanga
Tel: 013-768 1241
Fax: 013-768 1248
www.mountsheba.co.za
Situated in the mountains above Pilgrim's Rest, this small thatched lodge boasts wonderful views, walking trails through forested slopes alive with small game, and superb four-course meals by candlelight in its Chandelier Restaurant. **$$$**

TZANEEN

The Coach House
Old Coach Road, Box 544
Tzaneen 0850
Tel: 015-306 8000
Fax: 015-306 8008

www.coachhouse.co.za
Set in lushly forested countryside, this elegant, luxury country-house style hideaway has won several awards, and has a highly regarded restaurant. **$$$$**

Magoebaskloof Hotel
Road R71, Magoebaskloof 0731
Tel/fax: 015-276 5400
www.magoebaskloof.co.za
Small, friendly hotel. Telephones, restaurant, facilities for disabled guests and sports facilities including a swimming pool. **$$$**

NELSPRUIT

Crocodile Country Inn
PO Box 496, Nelspruit 1200
Tel: 013-733 3040
Fax: 013-733 4171
www.crocinn.co.za
Situated alongside the N4 20 km (12½ miles) west of Nelspruit, this country-style hotel offers comfortable accommodation and good food in leafy grounds centred on a large swimming pool, only 45 minutes' drive from the Kruger Park. **$$$**

HAZYVIEW

Pine Lake Inn
Main Hazyview Road, PO Box 94
White River 1240
Tel: 013-751 5036

Fax: 013-751 5134
A high-quality resort set in beautiful countryside. Air conditioning, telephones, non-smoking rooms available, restaurant. Fishing, golf course, swimming pool, hiking trails, horse riding, bowling green, squash and tennis courts. **$$$$**

Sabie River Sun
Main Sabie Road, PO Box 13
Hazyview 1242
Tel: 013-737 7311
Fax: 013-737 7314
Email: sarah@southernsun.com
Luxury hotel located close to Kruger National Park. Air conditioning, telephones, non-smoking rooms available, restaurant. Fishing, swimming pool, bowling green, squash and tennis courts. **$$–$$$**

Böhm's Zeederberg Country House
PO Box 94
Sabie 1260
Tel: 013-737 8101
Fax: 013-737 8193
www.bohms.co.za
Set in the Sabie Valley, near Kruger Park. Air conditioning, telephones, restaurant and swimming pool. **$$$**

Hazyview Protea Hotel
R40 Road, Mpumalanga
Tel: 013-737 9700
Fax: 013-737 9800
www.hazyview.co.za
Comfortable hotel 15 km (10 miles) from the Kruger National Park. Air conditioning, telephones, no-

smoking rooms available, restaurant. Swimming pool, sauna and tennis court. **$$$**

Kruger Park Backpackers
Main Road, Hazyview 1242
PO Box 214
Tel/Fax: 013-737 7224
www.krugerparkbackpackers.com
As well as dorms, private rooms and camping, this place runs budget day and overnight trips into Kruger Park. **$**

KRUGER PARK

The numerous rest camps in this vast park are described in the Places section on pages 288–295. Bookings for all camps are through SANParks, which can also provide up-to-date details of rates and facilities.

PRIVATE RESERVES

Inyati Game Lodge
PO Box 38838
Sandton 2146
Tel: 011-880 5907
Fax: 011-788 2406
www.inyati.co.za
Set on the Sand River in the Sabie Sand Game Reserve, this lodge offers accommodation for up to 18 guests and dinner is served in "bush bomas", while dancers accompanied by drums perform traditional ceremonies. Cottages; meals available. **$$$$**

Londolozi Game Reserve
Bookings through CCAfrica
Private Bag X27
Benmore, 2010
Tel: 011-280 6655
Fax: 011-280 6610
www.londolozi.co.za
Situated on the Sand River in the Sabie Sand Game Reserve, this lodge is renowned for its top-of-the-

BELOW: it is easy to forget your wild environs when you're tucked away in a luxury lodge.

PRICE CATEGORIES

Price categories are for a double room without breakfast:
$ = under US$50
$$ = US$50–100
$$$ = US$100–200
$$$$ = more than US$200

range quality, comfort and service, amid the wild African bush and its unique wildlife, and is especially highly rated for leopard sightings. Facilities at Tree Camp (eight guests), Granite Private Suites (rock cabins, maximum of six guests) and Varty Camp (en-suite luxury chalets, maximum of 24 guests). **$$$$**

Mala Mala
PO Box 55514
Randburg 2125
Tel: 013-442 2267
Fax: 013-442 2318
www.malamala.com
This internationally renowned game lodge, situated in the Sabie Sand Game Reserve 10 km (6 miles) from Kruger Park (Paul Kruger Gate), offers safari drives to view the Big Five, walks, luxurious camps and a personal guide who looks after the guests' every need, including wake-up calls and after-dinner drinks. 26 cottages with 24-hour room service; restaurant and bar; swimming pool and laundry service. On the same property (and bookable through the same address) is Harry's Camp (10 Ndebele-styled bungalows and an emphasis on outdoor living) and Kirkman's Camp (15 rooms or cottages offering a spectacular view of the river and the surrounding bush and wildlife). **$$$$**

Manyeleti Game Reserve
PO Box 786064
Sandton 2146
Tel: 011-341 0282
Fax: 011-341 0281

www.honeyguidecamp.com
This 230-sq. km (88-sq. mile) reserve is situated between Timbavati and Sabie Sand on the western boundary of Kruger Park. Khoka Moya Trails operate two camps in the reserve: Khoka Moya Camp and Mantobeni Safari Camp, both of which lie 20 km (12 miles) from Kruger Park (Orpen Gate), and offer open-car safari drives by day and night, and hiking trails to view the abundance of game. Four huts; meals available; swimming pool and bar. **$$$$**

Sabi Sabi Private Game Lodge
PO Box 16
Skukuza 1350
Tel: 013-735 5656
Fax: 013-735 5165
Has a reputation for friendly hospitality and high standards. Rich and varied wildlife can be experienced on safari drives, and even near the camp itself. Facilities at Bush Lodge (25 chalets) and River Lodge (20 chalets) in the Sabie Sand Game Reserve. **$$$$**

Timbavati Game Reserve
PO Box 67865
Bryanston 2021
Tel: 011-793 2436
Fax: 011-793 2394
Situated north of Sabie Sand on the western boundary of Kruger Park between Phalaborwa and Orpen Gates, this 750 sq. km (290 sq. miles) unspoilt bushveld abounds in wild animals and birds, most famously magnificent white lion. Within the reserve,

several lodges offer excellent opportunities for spotting game, be it on drives in open safari cars or on walking trails. They include Motswari, 97 km (60 miles) from Kruger Park (Orpen Gate), and M'bali Game Lodge, 9 km (5 miles) from Motswari. **$$$$**

Tshukudu Game Lodge
On the R40 between Hoedspruit and Mica
PO Box 289
Hoedspruit 1380
Tel: 015-793 2476
www.tshukudulodge.co.za
This family-owned and run establishment is an excellent getaway spot. Accommodation is in thatched rondavels, and game drives in open-top Land Rovers are supplemented by walks with habituated wildlife, including lion and elephant. **$$$$**

BELA BELA

Mabula Game Lodge
Rooiberg Area
Private Bag X1665
Bela Bela 0480
Limpopo Province
Tel: 014-734 7000
Fax: 014-734 0001
www.mabula.com
Set in 8,000 hectares (19,800 acres) of private game reserve, two hours north of Johannesburg. Offers game drives, walking trails, horse riding, swimming pool, sauna, fitness centre, tennis and squash courts. Air conditioning, telephones,

non-smoking rooms available. **$$$**

MODIMOLLE

Protea Hotel Shangri-La
Eersbewoond Road
PO Box 262, Modimolle 0510
Tel: 014-718 1600
Fax: 014-717 3188
www.shangri-la.co.za
Small and traditional. Telephones, restaurant, swimming pool. **$$–$$$**

MOKOPANE

Protea Hotel The Park
1 Beitel Street, PO Box 1551
Mokopane 0600, Limpopo Province
Tel: 015-491 3101
Fax: 015-491 6842
Set in peaceful parklands. Air conditioning, telephones, non-smoking rooms available, restaurant and pool. **$$**

MAKHADO

Bergwater Hotel
5 Rissik Street, PO Box 503
Louis Trichardt 0920
Tel/fax: 015-516 0262/3
Small, simple with good service. Air conditioning, telephones, non-smoking rooms available, restaurant. **$$**

Mapungubwe National Park
Bookings through SANParks
www.sanparks.org
There are four camps. *See* SANParks website for details.

OVERLAND ROUTES

WILLEM PRETORIUS

Willem Pretorius Rest Camp
PO Box Ventersburg 9451
Tel: 057-651 4004
Fax: 057-651 4005F
Flats, rondavels, huts; caravanning and camping. Amenities include a restaurant and shop; golf, tennis and bowls. **$–$$**

BLOEMFONTEIN

Southern Sun Bloemfontein
Corner Nelson Mandela Blvd and Melville Drive
PO Box 12015
Brandhof 9301
Tel: 051-444 1253
Fax: 051-444 0671
A somewhat bland but well-managed upmarket hotel set right in the city centre.

Facilities include air conditioning, non-smoking rooms, facilities for the disabled, a restaurant and pool. **$$$**

City Lodge Bloemfontein
Corner Nelson Mandela Blvd and Parfitt Avenue
PO Box 3552
Bloemfontein 9300
Tel: 051-444 2974
Fax: 051-444 2192
Functional mid-range hotel, aimed mainly at business

travellers, set in landscaped grounds close to the city centre. Air conditioning, facilities for disabled guests and swimming pool. **$$**

Bishop's Glen
PO Box 9
Glen 9360
Tel/fax: 051-861 2210
Email: bishopsglen@connix.co.za
Good-value and atmospheric accommodation in a 19th-century mission set on a

working stud farm (with adjacent game ranch) about 15 km (10 miles) north of Bloemfontein following the Glen/Maselpoort turn-off from the N1. **$$**

Innes Guesthouse
29 Innes Avenue
Suite 149
Private Bag X01
Brandhof
Bloemfontein 9324
Tel: 051-433 1555
Email: innes@internext.co.za
www.innes.co.za
This peaceful ten-bedroom guesthouse is set alongside a small nature reserve, and offers the rare opportunity to watch wildlife wander past the veranda only 5 minutes' drive away from the city centre and all its amenities. **$$**

Golden Gate National Park
A variety of affordable self-catering and camping is available at Glen Reenen Rest Camp, while a higher standard of accommodation can be found at Brandwag Hotel, and the Highlands Mountain Retreat offers isolation in rustic log cabins. It's all bookable through SANParks.

KIMBERLEY

Gum Tree Lodge
Old Bloemfontein Road (R64)
PO Box 777
Kimberley 8300
Tel: 053-832 8577
Fax: 053-831 5409
Email: lawrie@global.co.za
www.gumtreelodge.com
This historic backpacker hostel, which lies along the R64 towards Bloemfontein, about 5 km (3 miles) from the city centre, can host up to 150 people in its dorms and private rooms (some en suite). Facilities include a good restaurant and swimming pool. **$$$**

Milner House
31 Milner Street
PO Box 10219
Beaconsfield
Kimberley 8315
Tel: 053-831 6405

Email: info@milnerhouse.co.za
www.milnerhouse.co.za
This comfortable and friendly six-bedroom guesthouse, set in lush gardens centred on a swimming pool in the old suburb of Beaconsfield, lies close to most tourist attractions and amenities. **$$$**

Diamond Protea Lodge
124 Du Toitspan Road
PO Box 2068
Kimberley 8300
Tel: 053-831 1281
Fax: 053-831 1284
Email: dplkim@global.co.za
This small, central hotel offers rooms with air conditioning and telephones, facilities for disabled guests and bar. **$$–$$$**

KAROO

Lord Milner Hotel
Tel: 023-561 3011
Email: milner2@mweb.co.za
www.matjiesfontein.com
There is no better place to break up a long drive than this atmospherically restored Victorian resort, whose period character is rendered somewhat surreal by its isolation amid open arid plains. **$$$**

Lemoenfontein Game Lodge
Tel: 023-415 2847
Email: lemoen@mweb.co.za
www.lemoenfontein.co.za
This game farm set amid wild Karoo rockscapes harbours more than 20 game species and its 13 chalets lie only 5 km (3 miles) from the N1 between Three Sisters and Beaufort West. **$$–$$$**

Matopo Inn
7 Bird Street
Beaufort West 6971
Tel: 023-415 1055
About the best of Beaufort West's several guesthouses and small hotels, all of which offer a place to break up the long drive between Jo'burg and Cape Town... and little else. **$$**

Karoo National Park
Bookings through SANParks.

Excellent rest camp only a few km from the N1 with chalets, camping facilities, restaurant, shop and various walking and hiking trails. **$–$$**

KURUMAN

Eldorado Motel
Main Street
PO Box 313
Kuruman 8460
Tel: 053-712 2191/2/3
Fax: 053-712 2194
This motel has comfortable rooms with air conditioning, and telephones. Swimming pool. **$$**

UPINGTON

Protea Hotel Upington
24 Schroder Street
PO Box 13
Upington 8800
Tel: 054-337 8400
Fax: 054-337 8499
Email: reservations@uphotels.co.za
Centrally located and blandly comfortable accommodation, with a good restaurant, bar and swimming pool. **$$–$$$**

Le Must River Manor
12 Murray Avenue
Upington 8801
Tel: 054-332 3971
Email: manor@lemustupington.com
www.lemustupington.com
This absolute gem consists of a lovingly restored and lavishly decorated Cape Dutch homestead set in flowering gardens that run down to the banks of the Orange River. **$$–$$$**

Die Eiland
Tel/fax: 054-334 0286
Excellent municipal resort offering comfortable chalet accommodation and camping space on a wooded island on the Orange River. **$**

KGALAGADI

All reservations through SANParks. There are three main rest camps: Twee Rivieren (the South African

entrance to the park), Mata-Mata and Nossob. All three have hutted accommodation, camping sites, cooking facilities, and reasonably well-stocked shops. There's also a restaurant (advance booking sometimes necessary) and swimming pool at Twee Rivieren. There are six smaller and more exclusive unfenced camps, offering more of a bush experience. **$–$$$**

ORANGE RIVER

Waterwiel Lodge
Voortrekker Street
PO Box 250
Kakamas 8870
Tel: 054-431 0838
Fax: 054-431 0836
Small hotel with air conditioning, telephone in rooms and a pool. **$$**

AUGRABIES FALLS

All reservations through SANParks. An excellent rest camp next to the entrance gate and overlooking the main falls offers a variety of chalet and hutted accommodation, as well as camping. Facilities include a restaurant and shop, while the front desk can arrange night drives and rafting trips on the Orange River. **$–$$**

Augrabies Falls Backpackers
PO Box 20
Augrabies 8874
Tel: 054-451 0177
Fax: 054-451 0218
Email: info@kalahari.co.za
www.kalahari.co.za
Situated 10 km (6 miles) from the park entrance, this isolated backpacker hostel is one of the best

PRICE CATEGORIES

Price categories are for a double room without breakfast:
$ = under US$50
$$ = US$50–100
$$$ = US$100–200
$$$$ = more than US$200

budget options anywhere in the Kalahari, and the attached Kalahari Adventure Centre offers rafting, extended Karoo trips, and safaris to Kgalagadi Transfrontier Park. **$**

Kokerboom Motel
Biesjesfontein, Springbok 8240
Tel: 027-712 2685
www.jcbotha.co.za

This cool, spacious hotel on the outskirts of Springbok has a good restaurant and a camp site that becomes seriously crowded in wildflower season. **$$**
Kamieskroon Hotel
Old National Road

Kamieskroon 8241
Tel: 027-672 1614
www.kamieskroonhotel.com
Family-owned hotel in Namaqualand. Specialises in eco-tourism and photographic workshops during wildflower season. **$$**

SWAZILAND & LESOTHO

International dialling code +268

MBABANE

Mountain Inn
PO Box 223
Mbabane
Tel: 404 2781
Fax: 404 5393
Email: mountaininn@realnet.co.sz
www.mountaininn.sz
This attractively located hotel on the outskirts of town consists of 60 en-suite rooms and a good restaurant set in green gardens overlooking the Ezulwini Valley. **$$$**
City Inn
Allister Miller Street
Tel/fax: 404 2406
Email: cityinn@realnet.co.sz
Small, comfortable and very reasonably priced accommodation in the city centre. **$$**

EZULWINI VALLEY

Royal Swazi Spa, Ezulweni and Lugogo Suns
PO Box 784487
Sandton 2146
Gauteng
Tel: 011-780 7800
Fax: 011-780 7726
www.suninternational.com
This trio of glitzy upmarket hotels is most popular for its casinos – bookings and enquiries can be directed through Sun International's head office in South Africa. **$$$–$$$$**
Mantenga Tented Camp
PO Box 100, Lobamba
Tel: 416 1049
Fax: 416 2618
Email: reservations@mantengalodge.com
www.mantengalodge.com
This superb bush-style

tented camp is great value, consisting of about 15 en-suite thatched units tucked unobtrusively into thick riverine woodland on the Mantenga River. A cultural experience is offered, and a coffee shop serves great snacks and meals. **$$**
Mlilwane Wildlife Sanctuary
PO Box 311
Malkerns
Tel: 528 3944
Fax: 528 3924
Email: reservations@biggame.co.sz
www.biggame.co.sz
Overlooking a water hole with resident hippo, the rest camp in the centre of this small reserve offers a variety of inexpensive accommodation in dormitories, basic huts and more commodious en-suite rooms, as well as camping. A good restaurant is attached. **$–$$**
Sondzela Backpackers
PO Box 311
Malkerns
Tel: 528 3944
Fax: 528 3924
Email: reservations@biggame.co.sz
www.biggame.co.sz
A popular stopover on the Baz Bus route, this rustic backpacker hostel sits on the border of Mlilwane Wildlife Sanctuary and is under the same management. Dorms, private rooms, camping, bar and good food. **$**

THE INTERIOR

Mkhaya Game Reserve
PO Box 311, Malkerns
Tel: 528 3944
Fax: 528 3924
Email: reservations@biggame.co.sz
www.biggame.co.sz
Excellent and decidedly non-

package-orientated luxury tented camp consisting of just half-a-dozen luxurious open-air "rooms" with en-suite facilities strung along a thick stand of riverine scrub. Rates include all meals and game drives (which come with a high chance of seeing rhino). **$$$$**
Hlane Royal National Park
PO Box 311
Malkerns
Tel: 528 3944
Fax: 528 3924
Email: reservations@biggame.co.sz
www.biggame.co.sz
Comfortable and very affordable hutted accommodation, camp sites and decent restaurant, set in spacious, bird-filled grounds overlooking a water hole where rhino come by on a daily basis. **$–$$**

THE NORTH

Piggs Peak Hotel & Casino
PO Box 385
Piggs Peak, Swaziland
Tel: 437 1104
Fax: 437 1382
www.piggspeak.co.sz
This smart hotel is just across the Swazi border in richly forested high country to the north of Malolotja Nature Reserve. **$$$**
Mbuluzi Game Reserve
Tel: 383 8861
Fax: 383 8862
Email: mbuluzi@swazi.net
Accommodation within this reserve consists of just a handful of isolated but luxurious self-catering chalets overlooking the Mbuluzi River and offering great opportunities to view rare birds and watch big game on foot. Especially good value for families. **$$$**

Phophonyane Lodge
Tel/fax: 437 1319
Email: lungile@phophonyane.co.sz
www.phophonyane.co.sz
Situated on what is in effect a private sanctuary abutting Malolotja Nature Reserve, this comfortable self-catering lodge protects a spectacular waterfall and a long stretch of riverine forest in an area rich in bird life. **$$**
Shewula Mountain Camp
Tel: 605 1160
Email: shewula@realnet.co.sz
Bookings through Swazi Trails. The rustic accommodation here has fantastic views into the riverine valleys and is part of a community project offering insights into contemporary rural Swazi culture. **$**
Malolotja Nature Reserve
PO Box 1797, Mbabane
Tel: 416 1151
www.sntc.org.sz
Inexpensive log cabins and camping in a compelling, hiker-friendly montane wilderness running along the South African border. **$**

LESOTHO

Lesotho Sun
Private Bag A68, Maseru
www.suninternational.com
Modern, comfortable and central. **$$$–$$$$**
Malealea Lodge
PO Box 119
Wepener 9944
Tel/fax: 051-436 6766
www.malealea.co
This self-catering lodge situated in the central Thaba Putsoa Range also offers facilities for backpackers and campers, It specialises in pony treks, but the staff can organise just about anything you want to do in Lesotho. **$–$$**

E ATING OUT

RECOMMENDED RESTAURANTS, CAFÉS & BARS

LOCAL CUISINE

Many South African specialities are derived from Malaysian cuisine – a legacy from the 17th century, when Indonesian slaves imported by the Dutch were sometimes used as cooks in white households. In and around Cape Town particularly, mildly spicy Malay dishes have established a firm foothold on the menus of restaurants and hotels. *Bobotie* is a sweet and spicy dish of ground meat. *Bredie* is traditionally a casserole of mutton and vegetables. *Sosaties* are skewers of mutton or pork with small onions. Chutney is a sweet-and-sour fruit conserve which is served as a condiment with curries. *Koeksisters* are only advised for those with a very sweet tooth; they are doughnut-like cakes fried in fat, then immersed in syrup.

In Durban and the surrounding area, the cuisine has a distinctively Indian flavour. Indentured labourers imported from India to work in the sugar-cane trade in the 1860s brought with them their wonderful curries – spicy casseroles made of vegetables, legumes, lamb, chicken or beef on saffron rice. They're accompanied by such condiments as bananas, tomatoes, chutneys, and particularly grated coconut, which is said to take away some of the bite of very hot curries. Catering to timid foreign tastes, curries are also served mild and medium-hot.

It may look like dry sticks of wood, but biltong – strips of salted, spiced and air-dried beef – delights the hearts of all South Africans. Venison biltong is a particular delicacy: when a game farmer produces his own, it leaves commercially prepared beef biltong in the dust.

The *braai* (barbecue) is as much a part of the South African way of life as sunshine and sport. There's hardly a picnic spot, camp site or bungalow in the national parks that hasn't got a barbecue and grill. Many hotels also *braai* in their gardens on weekends. An important ingredient of the *braai* is *boerewors*, a large sausage made of mutton and beef. The best specimens can be purchased at small rural butchers in Free State or Mpumalanga, who make them with the same recipes used by their grandmothers.

Thanks to the country's various climatic and soil conditions, all kinds of fruit are grown in South Africa. On the Cape, there are marvellous grapes, apples and pears; while Mpumalanga and KwaZulu-Natal produce tropical fruits such as paw-paws, avocados, mangos, lychees, pineapples, bananas, and many others. You can get fruit fresh, as juice, or as delicious fruit rolls – fruit pulp dried in thin layers and rolled up – ideal snacks for long car trips.

When you visit game reserves and national parks, find out beforehand whether restaurant facilities exist, because many of the smaller ones are only geared to self-caterers. If you're going to be on the road the whole day, it's a good idea to take along your own supply of cold drinks, food, nuts and dried fruit. Feeding the animals is not only forbidden, but also highly irresponsible.

Even the smallest towns in South Africa can be relied upon to have one decent grill-style restaurant. Medium to large towns will typically have a wide variety ranging from fast-food outlets such as Kentucky Fried Chicken, McDonalds and similar (as well as Nando's, a local chain specialising in Mozambique-style spicy peri-peri chicken) to proper sit-down restaurants specialising in grills, seafood and Italian dishes – ask your hotel or the local tourist office for recommendations. The restaurants in and around the main cities that are listed below reflect the rich diversity of cuisines available in modern South Africa.

BELOW: Mama Africa is located on Cape Town's bustling Long Street.

CAPE TOWN AND THE CAPE PENINSULA

CAPE TOWN

The Africa Café
110 Shortmarket Street
Heritage Square
Tel: 021-422 0221
Authentic African cuisine. **$**

Anatoli
24 Napier Street
Tel: 021-419 2501
www.anatoli.co.za
Particularly good for Turkish *meze* (a selection of small dishes). Dinner Tues–Sun. **$$**

The Atlantic Grill
The Table Bay Hotel
Victoria & Alfred Waterfront
Tel: 021-406 5688
Meals on a par with those of any world-class hotel. Breakfast and dinner daily, Sunday jazz brunch. Closed in winter. **$$$**

Aubergine
39 Barnet Street
Gardens
Tel: 021-465 4909
www.aubergine.co.za
Set in a 19th-century town house, this is the place for traditional Cape favourites with a distinctly French slant. Lunch Mon–Fri, dinner Mon–Sat, and Sun in summer. **$$**

Baía
V&A Waterfront, Shop 6262
Upper Level Victoria Wharf
Tel: 021-421 0935
Classy seafood with a Portuguese leaning. An impressive wine list. Lunch and dinner daily. **$$$–$$$$**

Beluga
The Foundry
Prestwich Street
Green Point
Tel: 021-418 2948/9
www.beluga.co.za
Good for game fish and smoked ostrich. Fine wines. Restaurant: lunch, dinner; café: breakfast, teas, lunch, dinner. Mon–Sat. **$$**

Bukhara
33 Church Street
Tel: 021-424 0000
Excellent north Indian cuisine. Lunch Mon–Sat, dinner daily. **$$$**

Café Paradiso
110 Kloof Street Gardens
Tel: 021-423 8653
Chef Freda van der Merwe dishes up exceptional Mediterranean-style cuisine in this relaxed and friendly café-brasserie, much loved by the local élite. **$$**

Col'cacchio
Seeff House
42 Hans Strydom Avenue
Foreshore
Tel: 021-419 4848
Superb pizzas make this a locals' favourite. **$**

Fork
84 Long Street
City centre
Tel: 021-424 6334
Think contemporary tapas-style food in a laid-back bistro setting. Excellent local wine list and professional service. Lunch and dinner Mon–Sat. **$$**

Ginja
121 Castle Street
Cape Town CBD
Tel: 021-426 2368
Funky fusion-style dishes with some interesting South African twists. Dinner Mon–Sat. **$$**

Haiku
33 Church Street
City centre
Tel: 021-424 7000
A hotspot new-age Asian tapas venue in sexy surroundings. Pricey but worth every cent. Lunch and dinner Mon–Fri. Dinner only on Sat. **$$$$**

Jardine
185 Bree Street
City centre
Tel: 021-424 5640
An exceptional fine-dining experience. Sit and watch George Jardine take action inside his open-plan kitchen and prepare specials that include a beetroot tart or a seared sirloin with a béarnaise sauce. Lunch and dinner Tues–Sat. **$$$$**

JB Rivers Café and Cocktail Saloon
Cavendish Square
Tel: 021-683 0840
New Orleans-style spicy Cajun food plus a multitude of intriguing cocktails. **$$**

Leinster Hall
7 Weltevreden Street
Gardens
Tel: 021-424 1836
Lovely historical manor house right in the city centre. Food is classic *haute cuisine*. **$$$**

Limoncello
8 Breda Street
Gardens
Tel: 021-461 5100
Fantastic pasta and salads in tiny Italian trattoria. Lunch Mon–Fri, dinner Mon–Sat. **$**

Mama Yama
15 Shortmarket Street
off St Georges Mall
Tel: 021-423 0605
Trendy express sushi bar set in a beautiful Art-Deco building with a pleasingly plain interior. **$$**

Mama Africa Restaurant and Bar
178 Long Street
Tel: 021-424 8634
Stylishly ethnic. Check out the bar for the biggest reptile in town. **$**

Nelson's Eye
9 Hof Street
Gardens
Tel: 021-423 260
Find the best steak and seafood grills at this Cape Town institution. Lunch and dinner Tues–Fri, dinner only Sat–Mon. **$$**

Saigon Vietnamese
Corner of Kloof and Camp streets
Gardens
Tel: 021-424 7670/669
Authentic Vietnamese restaurant. Lunch Fri–Sun, dinner daily. **$**

The Sweetest Thing
82 St Georges Street
Simons Town
Tel: 021-786 4200
A harbour-side patisserie that delivers mouthfuls of classic French perfection in the form of teatime treats. Open daily, mornings and afternoons. **$$$–$$$$**

Willoughby's
Lower Level, Victoria Wharf
V & A Waterfront
Tel: 021-418 6116
Best sushi. Lunch, snacks and dinner daily. **$$**

CONSTANTIA

Buitenverwachting
Klein Constantia Road
Tel: 021-794 5190
www.buitenverwachting.co.za
The name means "beyond expectation" and that's a fair description of this wonderful restaurant set on a stunning wine estate. Impressive wine list. Closed Mondays and in August. **$$$**

Cape Malay Restaurant
The Cellars-Hohenort
93 Brommersvlei Road
Tel: 021-794 2137
Traditional Cape Malay restaurant in a luxury hotel. Best of the country's indigenous cuisine. **$$$**

La Colombe
Uitsig Farm
Spaanschemat River Road
Tel: 021-794 2390
www.lacolombe.co.za
First-class Provençal food with Cape flavours. Always busy. Estate wines. Lunch Mon, Wed, Sun; dinner Mon, Wed, Sat. **$$**

Constantia Uitsig
Spaanschemat River Road
Tel: 021-794 4480
This wine-farm restaurant offers fine Provençal cooking where fish and game are specialities. **$$$**

AROUND CAPE TOWN

Blues
The Promenade
Victoria Road
Camps Bay
Tel: 021-438 2040
Californian-style cuisine in a spacious, airy room overlooking one of the world's most pristinely beautiful beaches. Always packed, so book ahead. **$$**

Harbour House
Kalk Bay Harbour
Tel: 021-788 4133
Perched above rocks and

crashing waves serving up simple seafood. Perfect for a lazy lunch. Lunch and dinner daily. **$$–$$$**

I Gugu Le Africa
Corner of Spine and Iwandle roads
Khayelitsha
Tel: 082-423 8479
In the townships, a traditional Xhosa and Cape-style buffet. **$**

La Perla
Beach Road
Sea Point
Tel: 021-434 2471
Italian restaurant. The

place for seafood. **$$**

Mainland China
45–7 Main Road
Claremont (opposite mosque)
Cape Town
Tel: 021-683 7298
Simple Chinese fare, some of the best in town. Lunch Wed–Mon, dinner daily. **$$**

Posticino
3 Albany Mews
323 Main Road
Sea Point
Tel: 021-439 4014
A welcoming local pizzeria with a vibrant atmosphere

and some of the best pizza and pasta in town. Lunch and dinner daily. **$$–$$$**

Salt
Ambassador Hotel
Victoria Road
Bantry Bay
Tel: 021-439 7258
Possibly the best seat on the Atlantic Seaboard if you want spectacular sea views (diners are suspended over the ocean) and good food. Delicious local wines by the glass that are affordable too. Breakfast, lunch and

dinner daily. **$$–$$$**

Sandbar
31 Victoria Road
Camps Bay
Tel: 021-438 8336
The hottest place to be or be seen. Laid-back setting overlooking Camps Bay beach. **$$–$$$**

Wijnhuis
Kildare Centre, Kildare Road
Newlands
Tel: 021-671 9705
Seafood, pasta and steaks. Good local wine. Breakfast, lunch, dinner daily. **$$**

WESTERN CAPE

FRANSCHHOEK

La Petite Ferme
Pass Road
Tel: 021-876 3016
Nice French café serving midday meals, coffee and cakes. **$$**

Le Quartier Français
16 Huguenot Street, Franschhoek
Tel: 021-876 2151
Fine cuisine which reflects

the continental influences of the region's original French settler families. **$$$**

ELSEWHERE

Boschendal Restaurant
Groot Drakenstein
Tel: 021-870 4274
Situated on the wine estate of the same name near Franschhoek, this offers

first-class South African cuisine in elegant surroundings. **$$$**

Knysna Oyster Company
Long Street
Thesen's Island, Knysna
Tel: 044-382 6942
Cheap-and-cheerful joint serving oysters cultivated in Knysna Lagoon and the local draught beer. **$**

Laborie Restaurant and Wine House
Taillefert Street, Paarl

Tel: 021-807 3095
Gourmet Cape cuisine with exquisite wines, naturally. **$$$**

Die Strandloper
Saldanha Road, Langebaan
Tel: 022-772 2490
One of a clutch of great little west-coast restaurants serving a huge range of grilled, smoked and curried fish and seafood in the open air, right on the beach. **$**

GAUTENG

JOHANNESBURG

Gramadoelas at the Market
Market Theatre Precinct
Wolhuter Street, Newtown
Tel: 011-838 6960
www.gramadoelas.co.za
A magnet for overseas visitors who come for the superb South African cuisine, including such delicacies as crocodile. Beautiful mock-18th century decor. **$$**

Bistro 277
Cramerview Shopping Centre
277 Main Road, Bryanston
Tel: 011-706 2837
www.bistro277onmain.co.za
Never mind the shopping-mall setting, this large, airy space is an oasis for local foodies, who go into raptures over the fine Provençal cooking. **$$$**

Cranks
Rosebank Mall
Tel: 011-880 3442

Funky decor, an informal vibe, large portions and reasonable prices are a hallmark of this justifiably popular Thai restaurant, conveniently located at the entrance to Rosebank Mall. **$$**

Kapitan's Café
11a Kort Street
Central Johannesburg
Tel: 011-834 8048
Specialising in delicious curries, this establishment was a favourite haunt of attorneys Nelson Mandela and Oliver Tambo in the 1950s. Open lunch times only. **$**

Le Canard
163 Rivonia Road
Morningside
Sandton
Tel: 011-884 4597
www.lecanard.co.za
Award-winning French and international cuisine in a gracious house and garden setting. Also with a notable wine list. **$$$**

Linger Longer
58 Wierda Road West
Wierda Valley W, Sandton
Tel: 011-884 0465
Despite the silly name, this luxurious restaurant serves exceptional (and quite serious) French cuisine. **$$$**

Moyo
Melrose Square
Tel: 0861 006696
www.moyo.co.za
Sumptuous pan-African cuisine from both sides of the Sahara complemented by a superb and varied list of local wines make this one of Johannesburg's most innovative fine-dining venues. **$$$**

Osteria Tre Nonni
9 Grafton Avenue
Craighall Park
Tel: 011-327 0096
Always abuzz with Italian families tucking into authentic dishes from Tuscany and Umbria. **$$**

Pomegranate
79 Third Avenue, Melville

Tel: 011-482 2366
Trendy Melville is the setting of this converted warehouse, whose innovative fusion menu is strong on fish, game meat, vegetarian dishes and Asiatic touches.

Wandie's Place
Makhalamele St
Soweto
Tel: 011-326 1700
www.wandies.co.za
A mandatory lunch-time stop on most Soweto tours, Wandie's has a lively informal atmosphere and offers a self-service buffet of popular local African dishes. **$$**

PRICE CATEGORIES

Price categories are for a meal for one including one glass of house wine:
$ = under US$10
$$ = US$11–20
$$$ = US$21–30
$$$$ = more than US$30

PRETORIA

Café Riche
Church Square, City Centre
Tel: 012-328 3173
Open from 6am until after midnight, this laid-back street café has a historic location on Church Square. The extensive menu of pastries, snacks and meals has a strong South African character. **$–$$**

Cuban Café
129 Duxbury Road, Hatfield
Tel: 012-362 1800

This slick restaurant and cigar bar has a contemporary Cuban decor and a varied Caribbean and Mediterranean menu that will delight meat lovers, but is also strong on seafood platters and vegetarian fare. **$$**

La Madeleine
122 Priory Road
Lunwood Ridge
Tel: 012-361 3667
Sensational Provençal food. Simplicity is the watchword of Daniel Leusch's cooking, and it's won him many laurels. **$$$**

The Odd Plate
262 Rhino Street
Hennops Park
Centurion
Tel: 012-654 5203
Training ground for Prue Leith's College of Food and Wine, set in a fine old building. **$$**

SURROUNDINGS

The Carnivore
Muldersdrift Estate
69 Drift Boulevard, Muldersdrift
Tel: 011-957 2099

Very aptly named and not a place for vegans. At this vast carvery the meat (mostly game) is spit-roasted over a huge charcoal fire in the middle of the restaurant. It's wise to starve for a few days before coming here. **$$**

Da Vincenzo
29 Montrose Road
Barbeque Downs, Kyalami
Tel: 011-466 2618
www.davincenzo.co.za
Authentic home-made Italian cuisine on a thatched house with a country setting between Johannesburg and Pretoria. **$$–$$$**

DURBAN AND THE EASTERN CAPE

DURBAN

Aangan
86 Queen Street
City centre
Tel: 031-307 1366
Excellent South Indian vegetarian restaurant with an informal atmosphere. **$**

Fabulous Moroccan Restaurant
37 St Thomas Road
Off Botanic Garden Road
Berea, Durban
Tel: 031-201 7292
www.fabulousrestaurant.co.za
Durban's only North African restaurant serves a wide selection of tangy meat, poultry and vegetarian dishes in airy bright medina-style surroundings. **$$**

Jewel of India
Elangeni Hotel

63 Snell Parade
Tel: 031-337 8168
One of the city's finest Indian eateries, situated in the beach-front Elangeni Hotel. **$$$**

Joe Kool's
137 Lower Marine Parade
North Beach
Tel: 031-332 9697
Popular beach-front bar and restaurant. Where Durban's surfers come when there's no surf. **$**

La Dolce Vita
Durban Club
Smith Street, city centre
Tel: 031-301 8161
Classy Italian cooking in a romantic setting, with verandah tables overlooking the bay. **$$**

New Café Fish
Durban Yacht Mole
off Victoria Embankment
Tel: 031-305 5062

Indoor and outdoor dining at this recently revamped seafood restaurant on stilts, plus a pub area. **$$**

Oyster Bar & Zenbi Sushi
Victoria Embankment
Tel: 031-307 7883
Specialising in prawns, sushi, oysters and other seafood, this open-plan harbour-front restaurant has an airy atmosphere, a great view, and a quality wine list. **$$–$$$**

Thirsty's Dockside Tavern
King's Battery, New Point
Waterfront Harbour
Tel: 031-337 9212
Curries and good pub food. Great value and even better views. **$**

Ulundi
Royal Hotel
267 Smith Street
Tel: 031-333 6000
One of Durban's most renowned curry restaurants set in smart, colonial-style surroundings. **$$$$**

ENVIRONS

Marco's
45 Windermere Road
Morningside
Tel: 031-303 3078
Buzzing, picturesque courtyard, serving imaginative contemporary South African cuisine. **$$**

Razzmatazz
Cabana Beach Hotel
10 Lagoon Drive
Umhlanga Rocks

Tel: 031-561 5847
This restaurant is known for its good game and seafood dishes with a rotating selection of daily specials. **$$**

PORT ELIZABETH

Bella Napoli
Hartman Street
Tel: 041-585 3819
A casual and informal restaurant serving Italian and Mediterranean cooking and seafood specialties. There are also Vegetarian alternatives and a Sunday lunch buffet. **$**

Old Austria
24 Westbourne Road
Tel: 041-373 0299
Atmospheric upmarket restaurant housed in a Victorian rectory. Combines rich Viennese food with a varied selection of seafood dishes. **$$$**

The Ranch Steakhouse
Russell Road
Tel: 041-585 9684
Mainly for steaks, any size, but some Greek and Turkish alternatives too. **$$**

Royal Delhi Restaurant
10 Burgess Street
Tel: 041-373 8216
This family-run Indian restaurant has been serving the best curries in town for longer than a decade, and its also strong on seafood and vegetarian fare. **$$**

A CTIVITIES

THE ARTS, NATURE EXCURSIONS, OUTDOOR PURSUITS AND SPECTATOR SPORTS

ARTS

Theatre

Cape Town and Peninsula
Baxter Theatre Complex
University of Cape Town, Main Road, Rondebosch
Tel: 021-685 7880
www.baxter.co.za
Contains a theatre, concert hall and Studio Theatre.
Maynardville Open-Air Theatre
Corner of Church and Wolfe streets, Wynberg
Tel: 021-761 8922
Shakespeare and dance performances under the oak trees in summer.
Artscape (Nico Malan) Theatre Complex
DF Malan Street, Foreshore, Cape Town
Tel: 021-421 5470
Performing arts centre housing an opera house and several theatres.
Oude Libertas Open-Air Amphitheatre
Stellenbosch
Tel: 021-809 7473
www.oudelibertas.co.za
Theatre on the Bay
Link Street, Camps Bay
Tel: 021-438 3301
www.theatreonthebay.co.za

Durban
Dockyard Supper Theatre
Musgrave Road, Waterford
Tel: 031-201 9147
Daily dinner and live-music venue.
Elizabeth Sneddon Theatre
University of KwaZulu-Natal, Durban
Tel: 031-260 2296
Playhouse Theatre
231 Smith Street, Berea

Tel: 031-369 9555
Drama and dance.

Gauteng
Civic Theatre
Loveday Street, Braamfontein
Tel: 011-877 6800
Contains four stages: the Main Auditorium, the Tesson, the Thabong and the Pieter Roos auditorium.
Johannesburg Market Theatre
The Market Theatre Complex, Bree Street, Newtown, Johannesburg
Tel: 011-832 1641
www.markettheatre.co.za
Contains three stages: the Main Auditorium, the Barney Simon Theatre and the Laager Theatre. The home of protest theatre in South Africa.
Pro Musica Theatre
Civic Theatre Complex, Florida Park, Roodepoort
Tel: 011-674 1357
www.promusicaproductions.co.za
Venue for drama, ballet and visual arts with an acclaimed resident orchestra, Pro Musica.
State Theatre
Church Street, Pretoria
Tel: 012-392 4066
www.statetheatre.co.za
Seven auditoriums with everything from symphony orchestras and opera to contemporary drama.
Victory Theatre
Louis Botha Avenue, Orange Grove
Tel: 011-483 2793
Alternative Theatre
Windybrow Theatre, Nugget Street, Hillbrow
Tel: 011-720 0003
www.windybrowarts.co.za
Alternative and fringe performances.

Arts & Crafts

With its rich mix of cultures, South Africa has an abundance of artists

and craftsmen: painters, graphic artists and sculptors working in wood, bronze and metal; potters who produce work of high artistic quality and craftsmanship; artists who work with leather; jewellery-makers, porcelain sculptors, glass-blowers, woodworkers and furniture-makers; and weavers and spinners producing hand-knitted garments, painted fabrics and individually styled designer clothes.

The African motif evident in animal products, textured fabrics and earth colours has lately been married to Western sensibility to produce sophisticated decorative products.

In rural areas, traditional crafts abound. The Ndebele paint their houses with certain specific patterns, and produce magnificent beaded jewellery as well as copper and bronze bracelets; while the filigree-like chains of Zulu beadwork have an entirely different character. Craft shops also stock grain baskets or sieves of grass and reeds, as well as stylised wood carvings of animals.

The Venda produce brightly coloured clay pots, while the Toriga weave mats from coloured sisal. In Mpumalanga, along the Panorama Route, you can find leiklip, a soft, shale-like stone with light and dark layers, which is used to make ashtrays and animal carvings.

When considering a purchase, ask about the item's provenance. Old (antique) South African beadwork and San (Bushman) curios are very rare.

Arts and crafts routes enable the visitor to see the artists and view their work in their studios, to meet them over a cup of tea and to experience the environment they live in; perhaps even to buy a piece of art. Ask the local tourist association for more detailed information and maps regarding arts and crafts routes and markets in the area you're visiting.

Western Cape
Contact Captour for arts and crafts routes maps.
Constantia Craft Market
Alphen Common, Main Road, Constantia, Cape Town
First and last Saturday of the month and first Sunday, 8am–2pm.
Grand Parade Market
Cape Town
Every Wednesday and Saturday.
Greenmarket Square Market
Cape Town
Monday–Saturday 9am–5pm.
Cape Town's largest and best-known market offers clothes, jewellery, antiques, leather goods and more.
Green Point Market
Green Point Stadium, Cape Town
Sunday and bank holidays, 9am–5pm.
Hout Bay Craft Market
Village Green, Hout Bay
Tel: 021-790 3474
Every Sunday 9am–5pm.
Kei Carpets
Wesley (90 km/56 miles on R72 from Port Alfred)
Tel: 040-577 1024
www.keicarpets.co.za
Fine hand-knotted carpets. Guided tours can be arranged. Wesley Crafts and Bira Crafts are here too and worth a look.
Noordhoek Art Route
Near Hout Bay
First Sunday of the month
10am–5pm.
**Plettenberg Bay
Arts and Crafts Route**
Plettenberg Bay
Fourteen shops and galleries.
Treasure Coast Art Route
Marina da Gama to Seaforth, Cape Peninsula
Includes 21 artists and galleries.
First Sunday of the month
10am–5pm.
**Victoria & Alfred Waterfront
Arts and Crafts Market**
Dock Road, Cape Town. Daily.
Whale Coast Art Route
Hangklip-Kleinmond-Stanford
Tel: 021-700 929

Eastern Cape
Bathurst Market
Bathurst. First Saturday of the month
9am–3pm.
Beacon Bay Arts and Crafts
East London
First and last Saturday of the month
9am–1pm, tel: 043-753 1660.

Ikhwesi Lokusa Workshop
Umtata
The Xhosa are noted for the high quality of their handicrafts. Pottery, leather, jewellery, etc. are produced here by disabled people.
Izandla Pottery
Outskirts of Umtata
The best pottery in the region emanates from this studio where it is also possible to see the potters at work. Next door is Hilmond Weavers, one of the largest hand-weaving shops, producing wall carpets and pillowcases from the pure mohair spun by the pupils of a local school for the blind.
**Lattimer's Landing
Flea & Craft Market**
East London
Sunday 10am–4.30pm.
The Provost Craft Market
Grahamstown
Weekdays 10am–5pm.

KwaZulu-Natal
Amphimarket
Lower Marine Parade, Durban
Every Sunday 9am–4pm.
The Amphitheatre is transformed into a flea market where you can also watch Zulu dancers.
Church Square Market
Church Street, Durban
Tel: 031-392 1400
Daily 8am–4pm. Curios, clothing – a little bit of everything.
Essenwood Craft Market
Essenwood Park, Essenwood Road, The Berea
Tel: 031-202 5632
Every Saturday arts and crafts, plus tea garden and live music. 9am–2pm.
Midlands Meander
www.midlandsmeander.co.za
A collection of 150 craft shops, cottage industries and restaurants scattered around the KZN Midlands north of Howick.
South Plaza Market
Corner of Aliwal and Walnut streets, Durban
Tel: 031-301 9900
Monday–Friday 8am–4.30pm, Sunday 7.30am–5pm.
Victoria Street Market
Durban
Daily. Haggling is expected here: you can get discounts of up to 30 percent when buying jewellery, wood-carvings, hand-embroidered clothing or Indian spices. Don't feel guilty: these reductions will have been calculated by the salesmen as part of the sale price.

Gauteng
African Craft and Rooftop Market
Rosebank Mall, Johannesburg
Sunday. One of the best in Johan-

nesburg for African artefacts and crafts – from as far afield as the Ivory Coast and Ghana. Craft market open 9am–5pm daily; rooftop market Sunday only.
Artists under the Sun
Zoo Lake, off Jan Smuts Avenue, Johannesburg
First Sunday of the month.
Bruma Flea Market
Bruma Lake, Johannesburg
Tuesay–Sunday 9am–5pm.
Hundreds of stalls to choose from – including plenty selling good-quality African crafts.
Bryanston Organic Village Market
Culross Road (off Main Road), Bryanston, Johannesburg
Around 100 stands selling hand-sewn clothes, jewellery, African batik and pearl creations, minerals and crystals, glass, leather, woodwork, and even organically grown vegetables. Everything offered here is made of all-natural materials.
Thursday–Saturday 9am–3pm; Tuesday nearest the full moon, 6–9pm. For more information, tel: 011-706 3671.
Crocodile Creek Crafts Village
Top Crop Centre, DF Malan Drive, Muldersdrift, Johannesburg
Daily. Crafts include furniture, clothes, ceramics and more.
Hatfield Flea Market
Hatfield Shopping Centre, Pretoria
Sunday and bank holidays, 9.15am–5.30pm.
Market Theatre Flea Market
Market Theatre, Johannesburg
Saturday 9am–4pm. The best-known bazaar in Johannesburg, worth a visit for people-watching.

Mpumalanga
Promenade Centre Flea Market
Louis Trichardt Street, Nelspruit
Every Saturday 8am–1pm; moonlight markets last Friday of the month 6–10pm.
White River just north of Nelspruit, is home to a number of well-known South African wildlife artists including sculptors, woodcutters, weavers and potters. Ask SATOUR for further information.

Limpopo Province
**Ditike Craft Shop and
Tourism Centre**
Thohoyandou
Sells clay pots, carvings, basket-ware and articles woven out of grass or reed of high craftsmanship for which the Vha-Venda are known.
Polokwane Flea Market
Polokwane
First and last Saturday of the month, set in the Library Gardens, 9am–5pm.

Free State

Art Market
King's Park, Bloemfontein
First Saturday of the month
8am–1pm.
Cinderella Castle
Clarens
Curio shop in a building made of beer
bottles.
Kroon Market
Kroonstad
Last Saturday of the month
8am–2pm.
Westdene Flea Market
Brill Street, Bloemfontein
Second Saturday of the month
8am–1pm.

NATURE EXCURSIONS

Birdwatching

Southern Africa is great for bird-
lovers. More than 800 species
belonging to 22 of the 27 living
orders have been recorded, and
more than 60 species are unique or
all-but-unique to the country. One of
the reasons for the astounding
diversity in bird life is the great
variety of vegetation zones.

Below are a list of the major
vegetation zones and the nature
reserves which are best suited to
observing the birds in that
particular region.

The Eastern Woodlands (or
Bushveld) have the richest avifauna.
Key sites are Kruger Park and the
KwaZulu-Natal reserves of Ndumu,
Mkuze, Hluhluwe and Umfolozi, of
which Ndumu is particularly highly
regarded, as well as the lower-lying
reserves of Swaziland. For further
information contact SANParks or KZN
Wildlife *(see page 334)*.

Birds of the **Eastern Mistbelt
forests** can be seen in Game Valley
(Safari World) near Cramond, tel:
033-569 0011, and in the Karkloof
Nature Reserve. Another interesting
area for forest birds is
Magoebaskloof between Polokwane
and Tzaneen. For more information,
contact the Directorate of Forestry,
Limpopo Province, Private Bag
2413, Makhado 0920, tel: 015-291
4689.

The birds of the coastal
evergreen forests of the **southern
Cape** can be seen in the Tsitsikama
Forest National Park near Port
Elizabeth, and in several small
forested reserves near Knysna.
Information is available from
SANParks.

Birds of the **Highveld** can be seen
anywhere along the road, but a stay

at Barberspan near Delareyville in
North-West Province should be very
rewarding; it is the largest waterfowl
sanctuary in the region. Information
is available from the Barberspan
Nature Reserve, PO Barberspan
2765, tel: 053 948 1854.

The **Willem Pretorius Game
Reserve** between Winburg and
Kroonstad in the central Free State
is also worthwhile for the
ornithologist. For more details,
contact the Willem Pretorius Game
Reserve, Ventersburg 9451,
tel: 057-651 4004.

Mountain birds, including several
endemics, are most easily accessible
in the **Golden Gate Highlands
National Park** near Bethlehem, in the
eastern Free State and the beautiful
reserves of the Natal Drakensberg –
for further details contact SANParks
and KZN Wildlife respectively.

The **arid regions** have an
extremely rich bird life. The Karoo
National Park, near Beaufort West
in the Cape, and the Kgalagadi
Transfrontier Park, in the northern
Cape, are among the most
convenient reserves to find the
birds adapted to these harsh
conditions. For more details,
contact SANParks.

Namaqualand on the Cape West
Coast is a bird-watcher's and
botanist's paradise in September
when the otherwise arid plains are
carpeted with flowers. The Hester
Malan Nature Reserve near Springbok is worth a visit (daytime only).

The **Fynbos** of the southwestern
Cape has several endemic species of
birds, which can be seen in the Cape
of Good Hope Nature Reserve and
the Helderberg Nature Reserve near
Somerset West (day visits only).

A useful organisation for all
matters ornithological pertaining to
South African is Birdlife South Africa,
which can be contacted at P.O. Box
515, Randburg 2125, tel: 011-789
1122; fax: 011-789 5188; email:

info@birdlife.org.za;
www.birdlife.org.za.

The superb magazine Africa Birds
& Birding is published bi-monthly and
can be bought at any branch of the
CNA or subscribed to online at
www.africageographic.com
Safaris for Bird Lovers
Wilderness Safaris, PO Box 5219,
Rivonia 2128, tel: 011-807 1800;
fax: 011-807 2110.

Botanical Excursions

Considering its size, South Africa's
wealth of flora is remarkable: there
are 24,000 flora species, compared
with 10,000 in Europe. Keen
amateur botanists may be
interested to know that The Botanic
Institute issues computer printouts
which list every species according
to family, together with their
common names.

The Dendrological Society, one of
the largest arboreal organisations in
the world, also issues national lists
of native (green) and imported
(yellow) trees, which you should
keep on hand, as all of the number
and name-plates in nature
preserves and botanic gardens
accord with this information.
Contact the Dendrological Society of
South Africa, PO Box 104, Pretoria
0001; www.dendro.co.za.

The Botanical Society organises
regular excursions for foreign
visitors. Contact the Botanical
Society of South Africa,
Kirstenbosch, Private Bag X10,
Claremont 7735, tel: 021-797
2090; fax: 021-797 2376; email:
info@botanicalsociety.org.za;
www.botanicalsociety.org.za

Of South Africa's many state and
private nature preserves,
Richtersveld, south of Namibia, is
of interest because it is richer in
succulents than any other park in
the world and half of the species
are endemic.

BELOW: during the spring and summer birds from all over the world visit the Cape.

South Africa's botanic gardens worth visiting are listed below according to region.

Cape Region
Caledon: Caledon Wildflower Garden; Namaqualand wildflowers.
Cape Town: Kirstenbosch Botanic Garden, Rhodes Drive, Constantia. Open April–August daily 8am–6pm, September–March daily 8am–7pm; guided tours Tuesday and Saturday 11am. One of the most important botanic gardens in the world, it is home to most of the 22,000 plant varieties native to South Africa, notably the entire *fynbos* family, of which the protea are members. A bus runs from the city centre three times a day.
Kleinmond: The Harold Porter National Botanic Garden contains plants of the winter rainfall region.
Stellenbosch: Hortens Botanicus, Neethling Street, has a rare collection of local succulents and orchids. Open Monday–Friday 9am–5pm, Saturday 9am–11am.
Worcester: Karoo National Botanic Garden is located on Roux Road on the N1 motorway, 3 km (2 miles) north of Worcester. In spring (Sept–Oct), this garden is a veritable sea of flowers.

The North
Johannesburg: Johannesburg Botanic Garden includes a herb garden. The Wilds, Houghton Drive, Houghton, is a conservation area devoted to local flora, containing numerous species of wildflower from Namaqualand.
Nelspruit: Nelspruit Botanic Garden contains African trees. Open in summer Monday–Friday 7.30am–6pm, in winter Monday–Friday 8am–5pm.

Pretoria: Pretoria National Botanic Garden has various biomes, particularly those of the drier regions of southern Africa (Madagascar, Namibia).
Roodepoort: National Botanic Garden contains flora of the Highveld (Bankenveld).
Sun City: the Botanic Garden is devoted to "the dramatic and bizarre elements of the plant world".

KwaZulu Natal
Durban: Durban Botanic Gardens, between Syndenham Road and Botanic Gardens Road, Lower Berea, are open daily from 9am. A special feature is the world-famous orchid house, containing 3,000 species from around the world.
Pietermaritzburg: the Natal National Botanic Gardens contain exotic trees and flora of KwaZulu-Natal.

Free State
Bloemfontein: the Botanic Garden is mainly given over to plants native to the Free State, but it's also known for a fossilised tree trunk said to be at least 150 million years old. The orchid house in Hamilton Park, with its sliding roof and computerised air-conditioning system, is worth a visit. Three thousand orchids are arranged in a fairy-tale landscape of waterfalls, footbridges and ponds.
Harrismith: Drakensberg Botanic Garden on Platberg presents a cross-section of flora from the Drakensberg Mountains, as well as several lovely walking trails.

Caves

You need a permit to enter a cave on state-owned land. Caves are generally dry, with an average

temperature of 16°C (60°F); visitors are advised that histoplasmosis (cave disease) is a danger. It is best to arrange itineraries and access through clubs, which gladly welcome overseas visitors. The following societies can help:
South African Speleological Association
www.caves.co.za
Cave Research Organisation of South Africa
PO Box 7322, Johannesburg 2000
Tel: 011-640 4394

The **Cango Caves** near Oudtshoorn are the best-known South African limestone caves. A small section of the subterranean cave complex is open to the general public on guided tours. The main attractions are the imposing sculptures formed by stalactites and stalagmites.

The caves are open December–February and April 8am–5pm, tours every hour; May–November and March 9am–3pm, tours every two hours. There is a museum on site featuring plants, animals and rock formations from the caves.

The **Sudwala Caves** in Mpumalanga near Waterval Boven are a network of large interlocking chambers, one of which is used for musical recordings because of the incredible acoustics in the chamber, which measures 67 metres (220 ft) in diameter and 37 metres (120 ft) in height. Within the caves, the temperature remains a constant 17°C all year round. Guided tours take place daily, 8.30am–4.30pm. On the first Saturday of each month a six-hour tour is available to the more remote chambers like the fairy-tale Crystal Room.

Outside the caves is a world-famous Dinosaur Park. The first of Sudwala's model dinosaurs was commissioned to illustrate the age of the caves (100 million years). Now there are many dinosaurs representing species drawn from around the world; life-size, they inhabit the hill side to the side of the caves and are well worth a visit. The Dinosaur Park is open every day from 8.30am–5pm.

The **Echo Caves** on the road from Ohrigstad to Tzaneen are the least well known of the limestone caves. The advantage is that fewer people visit them and you may be lucky enough to enjoy this underworld with just your guide. The caves are so-called because the local people used one of the flowstones as a drum to warn of approaching Swazi. As these caves extend for some 40 km (24 miles),

BELOW: much of South Africa's flora can be viewed from easily accessed trails.

TRANSPORT

the sound travelled for surprisingly long distances and the people could take refuge in the caves.

From an archaeological point of view, the caves are fascinating as finds here corroborate the legend that, long ago, strangers in long white robes came to look for gold and to barter with the inhabitants. Some of the finds are exhibited at the Museum of Man on the turn-off from the tar road to the Echo Caves. Both the Echo Caves and the Museum of Man are open daily from 8am–5pm.

Beach Holidays

South Africa has a coastline some 3,000 km (1,900 miles) long. Along this are beaches of all shapes and characters. In northern KwaZulu-Natal, you will find beautiful and practically deserted beaches stretching for miles; isolated stretches can also be found along the Wild Coast. At the other end of the scale are the main tourist beaches complete with restaurants, entertainment, lifeguards – and thousands of sun worshippers during the holiday seasons.

The KwaZulu-Natal Coast
There are wonderfully remote and isolated sandy beaches all the way from Kosi Bay near the Mozambique border south to the Tugela Delta. Many, unfortunately, aren't equipped with shark nets, and some can only be reached in a four-wheel drive vehicle. Nonetheless, daring swimmers entrust themselves to the calm waters of the Kosi Bay Delta, Sodwana Bay, Mapelane, St Lucia, Cape Vidal and Richard's Bay.

Under no circumstances should anyone swim in the lakes or lagoons (especially St Lucia Lake), though, as there's danger from crocodiles and hippos. Campground swimming pools are a safer alternative.

From Zinkwazi Beach to Port Edward, the larger beaches are effectively protected from sharks. The nets are only lifted during heavy rainfall and during the sardine runs in July.

North of Durban, Umhlanga Rocks, Umhloti Beach and Ballito Bay are the most beautiful stretches of coast. In the holiday season, Durban's beaches are popular resorts, but if you do bathe here, keep an eye on your possessions.

The numerous tidal pools are also very popular: at high tide, the hollows

in the rocks fill with water. A favourite is the one found at Thompson's Bay (situated north of Ballito Bay).

On the south coast, in the rock pools along the marvellous beaches, you can find sea urchins, anemones and other sea creatures close at hand. A particularly lovely one is on Treasure Beach.

Dune forests often reach all the way down to the beach in the northern region of the south coast, providing shady trails for hours of beach walks.

Between Port Shepstone and Port Edward, on the border of Transkei, there are 11 large beaches which are protected against sharks.

The Eastern Cape
The Eastern Cape's shores are known as the Romantic Coast for a number of reasons: their many bays, their not-too-crowded sandy beaches, and their shallow lagoons and rivers where you can sail, canoe, or water-ski. However, swim with care in this area: there aren't any shark nets and sharks are particularly fond of river deltas, especially after heavy rainfall, when the water is muddy.

Between Mzamba and the Umngazi Delta, there is excellent swimming and the beach near Port St Johns is also very beautiful. East London offers three large beaches and a tidal pool near Fullar's Bay. Between Kidd's Beach and the Great Fish River, there are several good places to swim, and Kidd's Rock has another pretty tidal pool.

Also between the deltas of the Boesman's River and the Kariega, there is over a mile of small beaches of various sizes where you can swim safely and enjoyably. Kenton-on-Sea is one of the loveliest bathing spots in South Africa.

Kei Mouth is at the end of the Kei River, which forms the Transkei border. This broad delta is perfect for swimming and all sorts of water sports; it's also popular for deep-sea and coastal fishing. The tropical coastal forest is ideal for long walks; those in the mood for adventure can take one of the old ferries over to Kei.

Just south of Kei Mouth, Morgan's Bay lies in a particularly impressive stretch of coastal landscape with high cliffs; spray from the breaking waves is thrown up to a height of almost 30 metres (100 ft). The forests and coastal regions are home to a wide variety of birds and, from Haga-Haga, you can embark on interesting coastal walks or an excursion to one of the many tidal pools.

The Garden Route
In Port Elizabeth, Kings Beach, Humewood and McArthur Pool, overseen by lifeguards, are the safest places to swim.

The stretch of coastline north of St Francis Bay, notably Jeffrey's Bay, is especially good for swimming. This is also a popular area for surfing; St Francis Bay is a particular favourite.

Mossel Bay has many sheltered lagoons, such as Hartenbos, Little and Great Brak rivers, and beaches down to Victoria Bay, with calm waters.

Between Mossel Bay and Plettenberg Bay, Great Brak River is a little village on the coast, 20 km (12 miles) east of Mossel Bay, with a lagoon and sandy beach surrounded by wooded hills.

Herold's Bay is located on the N2 National Road, some 25 km (15 miles) southwest of George. A small, sheltered holiday village, it offers a sandy beach and large tidal pools for safe sea bathing.

At Sedgefield, on Swartvlei, you can bathe either in sheltered lagoons or on magnificent sand beaches.

Buffels Bay, near Knysna, is known for its picturesque beaches, which extend to Brenton-on-Sea.

The beach at Noetzie, east of Knysna, can only be reached on foot or in a four-wheel drive vehicle (the lagoon, too, is safe for swimming).

Oyster Bay is a holiday village with broad sandy beaches, 26 km (16 miles) southwest of Humansdorp. In the nature preserve between Oyster Bay and Cape St Francis, you can observe the antics of the sea otters.

St Francis Bay is a magnificent spot on the coast of the Indian Ocean, with broad sandy beaches and excellent facilities for swimming and water sports. The lagoon on the Seekoei and Swart rivers is known for its extensive bird life, including flamingos and swans by the hundreds. The old, 28-metre (91-ft) tall lighthouse on Seal Point, dating from 1876, is still operational.

Jeffrey's Bay lies a few miles to the north. Its "super tubes" are on a par with St Francis Bay's "Bruces" – that is, surf you can rely on the year round. But Jeffrey's Bay also offers plenty for less sporty, more contemplative souls. Every tide casts a treasure-trove of shells upon the beautiful beaches; you may even find the chambered nautilus and pansies (have a look at the displays in the town library). The town also has a strong arts and crafts contingent.

Kenton-on-Sea is 56 km (35

ACCOMMODATION

EATING OUT

ACTIVITIES

A – Z

miles) south of Grahamstown, between the Bushman River and Kariega, which flow into the sea at a distance of over a mile from each other. The coast between these two deltas has sandy beaches, tidal pools and bizarre rock formations. Some 10 km (6 miles) to the west, near Kwaaihoek, is a replica of the Diaz Cross.

Southwestern Cape
West of Mossel Bay are several popular beaches near Infanta, Witsand and Stilbaai. There are spectacular walks along the cliffs of Cape Hangklip at Hermanus. From June to November, you can spot whales in Walker Bay and other inlets in the area.

The western coast near False Bay has several lovely beaches, especially south of Simonstown. On the Atlantic coast, the water is too cold for swimming. Nonetheless, Sandy Bay is a nudist beach with a popular gay section. Camps Bay has a long, sandy beach, grassy lawns and a saltwater swimming pool, located at the feet of the Twelve Apostles.

Clifton offers four magnificent short sandy beaches, separated from each other by huge blocks of granite.

Sea Point is a thickly populated suburb with a pleasant beach promenade almost 3 km (2 miles) long and a large saltwater pool.

On the west coast, the beaches of Strandfontein (at the level of Vanrhynsdorp) are the most popular with swimmers. The coast before McDougall's Bay, near Port Nolloth, is protected by shallow reefs, and is also ideal for swimming.

Spas

Limpopo Province
Bela Bela, 100 km (62 miles) from Pretoria on the N1, is a renowned mineral resort with a modern health complex that includes various pools and hydrotherapy facilities. There is also a nature reserve (with a variety of game) where you can take lovely walks. Accommodation is in chalets, flats, a caravan park and camping site. Contact Bela Bela Tourist Information, tel: 014-736 3694.

There are waterfalls of varying height scattered throughout this region: near Sabie is the Bridal Veil falls, plus Horseshoe, Lone Creek and Sabie falls; near Graskop are the Mac Mac falls, plus Lisbon and Berlin falls. All of them are worth a detour.

Garden Route
To get to the Karoo Sulphur Springs, near Cradock, take the R32 towards Middelburg. There are lovely trails and paths through this area.

Cape Peninsula
Montagu Springs have been touted for their curative powers for more than 200 years. These mineral springs are located almost 3 km (2 miles) north of Montagu, in the Cogmans Kloof (Gorge) Nature Preserve. There are many hiking trails in the vicinity, tel: 021-614 1050; www.montagusprings.co.za.

Central Cape
Aliwal Spa, on the R30 between Bloemfontein and East London, has mineral springs and thermal baths, plus four open-air and two indoor

pools, a bio-kinetic centre and a children's water playground. Bus tours take visitors to see nearby San drawings. For information, contact the Northern Cape Tourism Authority, tel: 051-633 2951.

Geological Sites
The classical geological formations of South Africa are of interest to scientists throughout the world. Geological strata (including very old rocks), which in other parts of the world are hidden way down below, are often visible on the surface – creating a sort of hands-on geological history book. The major geological areas are:

Barberton Mountain Land in Mpumalanga – microscopic fossils of the earliest known forms of life found in the chert rocks.

Witwatersrand Basin around Johannesburg – the richest goldfield in the world.

Bushveld Complex north of Pretoria – volcanic layers containing the world's largest reserves of platinum, chrome and iron ore.

Pilanesberg near Sun City – one of the largest extinct volcanoes on earth.

Cape Supergroup in the southern margin – spectacular sandstone mountain ranges including the most famous landmark of all, Table Mountain.

The Karoo stratae, covering nearly half of South Africa, is a massive layered cake of sandstone and rock with a capping of basalt representing the widespread lava flows that accompanied the break up of Gondwanaland. The picturesque mountain landscapes that characterise the Drakensberg and the Lesotho Highlands are carved wholly within the basalt capping.

Preserved within the sandstone and rocks of the Karoo basin is an unbroken record of vertebrate evolution, from fishes through amphibians and reptiles, including dinosaurs. The Karoo is one of the world's largest fossil graveyards from the age of reptiles and is regarded by scientists as one of the natural wonders of the world.

In the **Karoo National Park** near Beaufort West on the N1 between Cape Town and Bloemfontein, there is a fossil trail which takes the visitor back through 250 million years of geological history. This 400-metre/yard long trail is suitable for wheelchairs and the visually impaired. Information is available from the SANParks.

BELOW: it's easy to keep boredom at bay on South Africa's beaches.

The Rubidge fossil collection on the **Farm Wellwood** in the Graaff Reinet area is, in all probability, the finest private collection in the country.

In Mpumalanga, a geological route has been developed for hobby geologists: the **Kaapse Hoop Hiking Trail** in the Barberton/Nelspruit area has boards with geological explanations en route. More of these popular trails are in preparation.

For further information, contact The Geological Society of South Africa, (GSSA) at Chamber of Mines Building, 5th Floor, Johannesburg; PO Box 61809, Marshalltown 2107, tel: 011-492 3370; fax: 011-492 3371; www.gssa.org.za. The society also publishes two journals: *The South African Journal of Geology* and *The Geo-Bulletin Quarterly*.

Geological Museums

Geological Museum
Johannesburg
Tel: 011-833 5624
Geological Survey Collection
Transvaal Museum, Pretoria
Tel: 012-322 7632
Alexander McGregor Museum
Kimberley
Tel: 053-839 2700
South African Museum
Cape Town
Tel: 021-481 3800

Mines

Diamonds are, without a doubt, the most exciting precious stones, and the purest, for they're made entirely of carbon. Under enormous pressure, at high temperatures, the stones are formed in the earth's interior over millions of years and forced up towards the surface by volcanic eruptions.

Kimberley, with its Big Hole, is South Africa's most famous diamond mine. Dug in 1871, the world's largest man-made hole is 400 metres (1,300 ft) deep and 500 metres (1,600 ft) in diameter. Up to 30,000 adventurers dig for the shining stones as if possessed. The **Kimberley Mine Museum** brings pioneer days again to life, as does the small restored city dating from the mine's foundation. The Diamond Museum will make even hardened hearts beat faster. Open daily 8am–6pm (closed on Good Friday and Christmas); small admission charge.

The world-champion diamond was found in 1905 in the **Cullinan Premier Mine**, east of Pretoria. The Cullinan weighed 3,106 carats

(about 600 grams/1.3 lbs) and was as large as a child's fist. Four of the nine diamonds cut from this stone ornament the British crown jewels, among them the 530-carat Great Star of Africa, the largest-ever cut diamond. Guided tours of the Cullinan Premier Mine are held Monday–Friday at 9am and 10.30am. Pretoria Tourism, tel: 012-308 8909.

The **Rustenburg Platinum Mine**, in North-West Province, is the largest in the world. It is possible to visit the mine, but necessary to book in advance. Rustenberg Regional Tourism Information, tel: 014-597 0904; www.tourismnorthwest.co.za.

The **Blue Mine**, to the west of Springbok in Namaqualand, was expanded up until the end of the 19th century. It can be reached on foot.

Phalaborwa, 68 miles (110 km) from Tzaneen on the R71, just outside Kruger Park, is the centre of a rich mining area and an open-cast copper mine which can be visited after prior arrangements on Friday afternoon.

There is also a museum here which shows the archaeological, ethnological and mining history of the region. For more information, contact Limpopo Province Tourism Board, tel: 086-073 0730; www.golimpopo.com.

Archaeological Sites

The South African Archaeological Society will assist with information on archaeological sites that can be visited by the public. Visitors are welcome to attend the monthly evening lectures and the monthly outings. Further detailed information is available from the South African Archaeological Society, tel: 021-481 3886; email: secretary@archaeology.org.za. Also note that the society has an excellent website: www.archaeology.org.za.

Northwest Province

Norlim: the famous limeworks where the Taung skull *(Australopithecus africanus)* was found are situated in this town. The site is open to the public and the position where the skull was found is marked with a little monument.

Cape Region

Cape Town: in the lower levels of the Golden Acre shopping complex are the remains of Wagenaar's Dam, built in the 17th century after the Dutch East India Co. established a settlement at the Cape.

Wonderwerk Cave: this important solution cavity is situated on the road between Kuruman and Danielskuil in the Kuruman hills, in the northwestern Cape. The site is signposted, but the cave itself is protected by a gate and fence. The key can be obtained from the custodian who lives on the farm. The site has been intermittently inhabited for over half a million years and has provided valuable information on Early, Middle and Late Stone Age ways of life.

Postmasburg (northwestern Cape): just to the northwest of the town, within its municipal boundaries, lies Blinkklipkop, an ironstone outcrop with an ancient specularite mine. It has been mined for probably a few thousand years by the indigenous people of the local area.

Barkley West: Canteen Koppie on the Vaal River, approximately 2 km (1 mile) southeast of the town. This site contains a vast amount of Stone Age implements. It is worth a visit if you are interested in stone implements.

Driekopseiland: this site is in the bed of the Riet River in the northwestern Cape. It consists of large sheets of glacial striated bedrock on which over 3,000 rock engravings are visible.

Free State

Willem Prinsloo Game Reserve: this reserve near Winburg contains the ruins of early Tswana Iron Age settlers. Easily accessible, the ruins are on and next to the road that meanders along the low range of hills on the reserve.

Florisbad: this famous site is situated near Bloemfontein and has a recreation facility. Appointments to visit the archaeological or palaeontological part of the site can be made via the National Museum of Bloemfontein, tel: 051-447 9609; www.nasmus.co.za.

KwaZulu-Natal

Umgungundlovu (which means "the secret place of the elephant"), situated in northern Natal between Melmoth and Babanango, was once the military headquarters of the Zulu king, Dingane. It was built around 1828 and destroyed by fire in 1838 on the orders of the king. The archaeological excavations have exposed numerous hut floors. Part of the site is being reconstructed.

Ulundi (the high place) is close to and southwest of the modern town of Ulundi. This was King Cetshwayo's capital, destroyed by the British Army during the Zulu wars of the late 19th century. It has been partially restored and also doubles as a holiday resort where visitors can rent a traditional Zulu hut.

The Drakensberg in KwaZulu-Natal, the Free State and Lesotho have numerous caves and shelters with exquisite rock paintings; sites are often remote and inaccessible and most easily visited by hikers. Directions and permits can be obtained from the officials of these various parks and resorts. Information: Natal Parks Board.

Gauteng

A park right in the heart of Johannesburg contains the **Melville Koppies**, believed to have been occupied by man 100,000 years ago. An ancient iron-smelting furnace can be seen on top of the hill. Eighty percent of all plant species in the Witwatersrand region can be found in this park, including medicinal and poisonous varieties. The reserve is open on the fourth Sunday of each month when guided tours are offered. Information and a guidebook are available from the Johannesburg Parks & Recreation Department, PO Box 6428, Johannesburg 2000, tel: 011-782 7064.

The Sterkfontein Caves, not far from Krugersdorp are limestone caves where archaeological history was made with the discovery of the famous "Mrs Ples" (*Plesianthropus transvaalensis*), the so-called missing link. Guided tours take place every half hour, Tuesday–Sunday 9am–4pm, tel: 011-956 6342; www.cradleofhumankind.co.za.

Mpumalanga

The **Museum of Man** on the turn-off to the Echo Caves in Mpumalanga is an archaeological excavation site with interesting remains reaching back well in excess of 100,000 years. This Iron Age site is situated in Kruger National Park on the road between Phalaborwa Gate and Letaba Rest Camp. It is well signposted and guided tours are available. A kiosk on the site provides information on the site's history and archaeology.

In the Kruger National Park, there are many sites with rock paintings in the **Stolznek area** in the south of the park. In the far north are the remains of the fascinating Stone Age city-state, **Thulamela**. Ask at your rest camp's reception about tours.

Ermelo lies 120 km (75 miles) from Waterval Boven, in Mpumalanga, on the R36. There are a number of interesting archaeological sites in the vicinity: the corbelled stone houses of a tribe that is now extinct; the Goliath Foot Print, a footprint of 1.24 metres (4 ft) which can be seen on a rock in a beautifully wooded area on the farm called Arthur's Seat near Lothair; and the many San drawings on the Welgelegen farm. Since all these lie on private property, permission to view them must be obtained beforehand. For information, contact the Mpumalanga Tourism and Parks Agency, tel: 013-759 5300; www.mpumalanga.com.

STEAM TRAIN JOURNEYS

A number of vintage trains have been preserved as tourist attractions, drawing steam-train enthusiasts from all over the world.

The Transnet Heritage Foundation, part of the Transnet Museum in Johannesburg, organises a number of **steam-train safaris** each year to different parts of the country to enable visitors to see steam locomotive yards and depots. They last 14 days and the price includes meals and bus tours to places of interest en route. Photo stops are held at scenic places. These steam-train safaris are run on trains belonging to Union Limited Steam Safaris, a company which offers its own programme of steam-train journeys. These include day rambles from Cape Town to Franschhoek and Ceres, and a six-day Garden Route tour on the Union Limited Golden Thread.

For more information, contact Friends of The Rail, tel: 012-548 4090; www.friendsoftherail.com.

In addition, the Transnet Museum recently took over the **Outeniqua Choo-Tjoe** (Western Cape), which usually travels between George and Knysna, Monday–Friday, taking 2½ hours each way and winding through the most breathtaking mountain scenery. The current route runs between George and Mossel Bay only. Tickets can be bought at the stations in George and Mossel Bay. For booking and information, tel: 044-801 8288.

The **Magaliesberg Express**, PO Box 3753, Johannesburg 2000 (tel: 011-888 1154) departs Johannesburg Station on the first Sunday of the month at 9.15am bound for the Magaliesberg, a journey of just under 2 hours, arriving back in Johannesburg at 5.45pm. There is a lounge car with full bar services and souvenir shop. On arrival, *braai* fires are lit and meat and salad dishes are on sale. Eating utensils and folding chairs must be brought by the passengers.

Since 1906, the narrow-gauge **Apple Express** has been chugging between Port Elizabeth and Thornhill in the fruit-growing area of the Langkloof. It travels once or twice a month, and there are also some trips to Loerie and back. For booking and further information, contact the Port Elizabeth Apple Express, tel: 041-583 2030; fax: 041-583 3413.

The **Banana Express** (KwaZulu-Natal) travels between Port Shepstone (on the south coast), historic Paddock and the spectacular Oribi Gorge Nature Reserve. For those seeking a longer steam-train journey, there are occasionally rides to Harding too. For information and tickets, tel: 082-781 2492.

Rovos Rail operates a luxury steam train (the **Pride of Africa**), which offers one of the most opulent rail journeys in the world. There are four main routes: Pretoria to Cape Town (lasting two days, with sightseeing stops at Kimberley and historic Matjiesfontein); Pretoria to Victoria Falls (return trip lasting five days); Cape Town to Knysna (lasting three days, with sightseeing excursion to Oudtshoorn); and Pretoria to Kruger National Park (with additional bus transfers).

Rovos Rail also operates an epic **12-day safari** from Cape Town to Dar-es-Salaam in Tanzania (via Pretoria, Victoria Falls and Lusaka). For more details, contact: Rovos Rail, PO Box 2837, Pretoria 0001, tel: 012-315 8242; fax: 021-323 0843; www.rovos.co.za.

South African National Railway and Steam Museum, Randfontein Estates Gold Mine, near Krugersdorp, tel: 011-888 1154/5/6. The museum offers train rides once a month to Magaliesburg.

Umgeni Steam Railway Excursions, operated by volunteers at the Natal Railway Museum, Hilton Station, Pietermaritzburg, organises trips to Howick on the second Sunday of each month, except during August and September. For more information, contact Umgeni Steam Railway, tel: 082-353 6003.

Steam trains are in regular use in the **Kimberley region** in the Northern Cape. There are departures to De Aar (250 km/155 miles) or to Kraankuil at the halfway point. Contact: Northern Cape Tourist Information, tel: 053-832 2657.

OUTDOOR PURSUITS

Hiking

The best way to discover South Africa's lofty mountains, long, sandy beaches, indigenous rainforests and plantations is on foot. Opportunities range from short rambles suitable for families with young children to week-long expeditions and guided wilderness trails in big-game country. A **network of self-catering overnight hiking trails** traverses the country from the **Augrabies Falls National Park** in the Northern Cape to the **Western Cape mountains** and the **Soutpansberg** in Limpopo Province. While some trails follow the coastline, others traverse challenging peaks which are often covered in snow during the winter. Some wind through the aromatic *fynbos* vegetation of the Western Cape, others through the grasslands of the Free State. Hiking trails vary in length from two to eight days, although shorter alternatives are usually available on long routes.

Heading the list of South Africa's most popular trails is the **Otter Hiking Trail** along the southern Cape coast, while the **Blyderivierspoort** and **Fanie Botha hiking trails** in Mpumalanga are other favourites. Of the several wilderness areas available to outdoor enthusiasts seeking solitude and tranquillity, those in the **Drakensberg** are the most dramatic. Although footpaths exist, backpackers are not obliged to stick to a particular route, nor are any facilities provided.

Backpacking requires a degree of experience and self-reliance and, depending on weather conditions, nights are spent either under the stars, in caves or, in many instances, in a small backpacking tent. Other wilderness areas include the **Cedarberg**, **Groot-Winterhoek** and **Boesmanbos** (Western Cape), the **Baviaanskloof** and **Groendal** (Eastern Cape), **Ntekenda** in KwaZulu-Natal and the **Wolkberg** in the north. For many hikers, however, the ultimate outdoor experience is a **guided wilderness trail** such as those conducted in several game reserves of the Natal Parks Board and Kruger National Park (information under Large Parks and Reserves).

If you are keen on hiking in South Africa, advance planning is essential since it is almost impossible to get a booking at short notice for popular hiking trails. Contact your nearest South African Tourism Board office for a copy of *Follow the Footprints*, which lists trailing opportunities, as well as information regarding duration, capacity, cost, facilities and reservation addresses.

On full payment following a reservation, usually a year in advance, a map is issued which serves as a confirmation of the booking besides giving useful information on climate, geography, flora and fauna of the trails. Keep it safe, as you may need it again.

Hiking trails in the national parks and KwaZulu-Natal must be booked through SANParks and KZN Wildlife respectively *(for contact details see page 334)*. A booklet with all other hiking trail booking details is available from the Hiking Federation of South Africa, tel: 083-535 4538; email: christine.frost@pfizer.com; www.hiking-south-africa.info.

Drifters offer hiking tours in the spectacular **Cedarberg Mountains** on the Cape West Coast, along the **Garden Route** and **Eastern Cape**, the **Wild Coast**, the **Drakensberg**, **Mpumalanga** and the **Fish River Canyon** in Namibia. The price for 3–8 day hikes includes transport from Johannesburg, a professional guide, accommodation and most meals. For detailed brochure and information write to PO Box 48434, Roosevelt Park 2129, tel: 011-888 1160; fax: 011-888 1020; www.drifters.co.za.

Mountaineering

South Africa's mountains and marvellous cliff formations are particularly inviting to mountain climbers. Rock climbers incline towards Limpopo Province, or the Cedarberg or du Toits Kloof Mountains in the Cape. Often, the best mountains for climbing are privately owned. Local climbing clubs apply for permits to climb these from the farmers who own them, so it is a good idea to contact these clubs.

The **Magaliesberg Mountains** lie only 2 hours by car from Johannesburg. On the range's north side, the rock faces have been eroded in places into picturesque gorges, lined with clear mountain brooks and giant trees (difficulty rating up to 8b on the French scale). Limpopo Province also offers tempting and difficult faces with walls up to 400 metres (1,300 ft) high. For information, contact the Mountain Club of South Africa, tel: 011-786 8367.

KwaZulu-Natal's **Drakensberg Mountains** have a more Alpine character; there are several 3,000-metre (9,800-ft) peaks to scale. The highest mountain in the range is just over the Lesotho border, the 3,482-metre (11,386-ft) Thabana Ntlenyana. Most of the climbing mountains in KwaZulu-Natal lie within nature reserves; before beginning, climbers have to register with the Natal Parks Board.

Montesiel, between Durban and Pietermaritzburg, is held to be the best region in South Africa for hobby climbers.

BELOW: even remote areas of South Africa are accustomed to catering for hikers.

Cape Province contains the most popular and best-known mountains for climbers. Leader among these is **Table Mountain** (1,084 metres/ 3,556 ft), which boasts more than 500 routes. Northwest of Cape Town, the **Cedarberg Range** enchants visitors with its wonderful rock formations. Along the Garden Route, the **du Toits Kloof Mountains** (Bain's Kloof and Sir Lowry's Pass) are also climbers' favourites.

For further information, contact the Mountain Club of South Africa, 97 Hatfield Street, Cape Town, 8001, tel: 021-465 3412 (10am–2pm, Friday until 7.30pm); fax: 27-21-461 8456; email: info@mcsa.org.za; www.mcsa.org.za.

Four-wheel Drive Camping

Four-wheel drive vehicles are advisable for journeys into Botswana or the more remote beaches of northern KwaZulu-Natal. Rental vehicles are available fully equipped with a long-distance tank, special jack, fridge, one–two tents on the roof rack and camping requisites (bedding, cutlery, gas stove and gas lamps). The rental price normally includes insurance and unlimited mileage. In general it is safer to use international companies or to follow recommendations from friends.

Rental Companies
Campers Corner Rentals
11 Mimosa Street, Randburg, 2194, Gauteng
Tel: 011-787 9105
Fax: 011-787 6668
www.campers.co.za
U-Drive-Rent-a-Car
Box 23802, Joubert Park 2044
Tel: 011-392 5852
Fax: 011-392 5854
www.udrive.co.za

As camping equipment is seldom available for rent, tents are best brought from home. Alternatively, it can be bought cheaply at South African chain stores such as Makro (tel: 0860 300999; www.makro.co.za) or Cape Union Mart (tel: 021-464 5800; www.capeunionmart.co.za).

Gliding

The north of the country is renowned for its good gliding conditions – endless blue skies, stable weather all year round with lots of sunshine and thermals that facilitate very long glides. Gliding tours are offered and clubs may be helpful in organising

equipment privately; there are no commercially organised hiring facilities.

Information
Aero Club of South Africa
Tel: 011-805 0366
Lifestyle Travel
PO Box 67, Randburg 2125, Gauteng
Tel: 011-705 3201/2; fax: 705 3203
Lifestyle Gliding Adventures take you up on a soaring experience from the Parys airfield. The rates vary depending on the number of passengers.
Magaliesburg Gliding Club
PO Box 190, Tarlton 1749, Gauteng
Tel: 011-716 5229
Witwatersrand Gliding Trust
PO Box 6875, Johannesburg 2000
Tel: 011-615 2461

Hang-gliding

To practise hang-gliding in South Africa, you need to be a member of the South African Aero Club, thereby incurring a liability insurance, but temporary membership is available. Also, check whether your licence system is valid here. The Aero Club will be helpful in that respect. Contact the Aero Club of South Africa, tel: 011-805 0366.

Equipment may be a problem if you need to hire it. Clubs may be able to help, but there are no regular hiring facilities. For further information, contact the national body, or clubs directly:
South African Hang Gliding & Para-gliding Association
Tel/fax: 012-668 1219
www.sahpa.co.za
Hang-gliding is very, very popular in northern areas as a result of good weather all year round.

Cycling

As there are no cycling paths, the sport is more hazardous than in Europe. However, traffic on the smaller roads is not heavy. Despite the distances involved, people do cycle from Johannesburg to Cape Town, from Durban to Johannesburg, along the Garden Route and most of all around the Western Cape, which is wonderfully suited for fun cycling as it has magnificent scenery and there is no rain during the summer months (October–April).

Hiring of bikes
Downhill Adventures
Shop 10 Overbreek Building,
Corner Kloof and Long streets
Tel: 021-422 0388

Fax: 021-423 0127
www.downhilladventures.com

Information
The South African Cycling Federation
PO Box 271, Table View 7349,
Cape Town
Tel: 021-557 1212
www.sacf.co.za
Mountain Bike Association
Tel: 011-964 2301
Cycling South Africa
www.cyclingsa.com
The official cycling body in South Africa.
Mountain Biking in South Africa
www.mtbonline.co.za
News and links to local mountain bike clubs.

Golf

Some 300 registered golf courses are scattered around the country, offering a wide range of challenges. Many also incorporate the natural habitat to stunning effect. Most of the leading courses are reviewed on the websites www.southafricagolf.com or www.golfinginsouthafrica.co.za.

From the **Milnerton** or **Mowbray** greens, you have a splendid view of Table Mountain, while the **Wild Coast Course** is laid out with sea water, dunes and plants. The **Royal Cape** and **Royal Johannesburg** are graced by beautiful old trees, dating from 1882 and 1890 respectively. The **Royal George** and the **Durban Country** are said to be the most beautiful golf courses.

It's advisable to call the club secretary and ask for a confirmed starting time and dress codes. For further information on golf courses that are part of holiday resort accommodation, consult SATOUR's publication on golf.

BELOW: riding is affordable here.

For further information – possibly the planning of a golf safari – contact South African Golf Tours, tel/fax: 021-712 1949; www.southafricangolftours.com.

Horse Riding

The diversity and spaciousness of the South African landscape, together with the temperate climate, lends itself well to horse riding. Riding is within reach of many more people here than in Europe since it is more affordable.

Trails are available throughout the country, offering visitors a chance to experience it at a "grass-roots level" where the sensations of what South Africa is about are really immediate and alive. For more details, contact the Association for Horse Trails & Safaris in Southern Africa, tel: 011-788 3923.

Trails in the Drakensberg take you through scenic grandeur, across natural streams and grassy plains along the escarpment. The area appears untouched by the 21st century. You may come across rural dwellings or Basotho (the people of Lesotho) pursuing the rhythm of their traditional lifestyle.

Drifters, PO Box 484, Roosevelt Park 2129, tel: 011-888 1160; fax: 011-888 1020; www.drifters.co.za.

Hollybrooke Farms (tel: 011-793 4634; cell: 082-552 1285; email: info@hollybrooke.co.za; www.hollybrooke.co.za) offers horseback excursions along the Magalies River in the untrammelled thornbush of the Skeerpoort Valley, less than an hour's drive from Johannesburg or Pretoria. A range of other activities are available, as is accommodation.

Equus Horse Safaris, tel: 011-788 3923, and **Horizon Horse Trails**, tel: 014-755 4003, both offer horse-riding holidays in the craggy, isolated Waterberg range, 2 hours' drive north of Pretoria. Trails in the Cape are equally scenic but offer a very different landscape that includes lush green surroundings, rolling hills, forests and vineyards.

Sleepy Hollow Horse Riding, tel: 021-789 2341, www.sleepy hollowhorseriding.co.za, gives you the chance to ride in the beautiful surroundings of the Noordhoek Valley. Join their sunset and champagne rides, moonlight rides with an evening meal, morning rides with a hearty farmhouse breakfast afterwards and lessons. The 2-hour beach ride is highly recommended in winter.

Marathons

Road running – ranging in distance from 10 to 90 km (6 to 55 miles) – is one of South Africa's most popular sports. Events are held in most major towns and cities at weekends.

The highlight of the year is the 90-km (55-mile) **Comrades Marathon** which alternates annually between Durban and Pietermaritzburg on 31 May. The race has an 11-hour time limit and attracts over 10,000 participants. The runners have to endure a 700-metre (2,300-ft) altitude difference. The 50-km (31-mile) **Two Oceans Marathon** on the Cape Peninsula every Easter Saturday also attracts many runners. Another popular event is the **City to City Marathon** from Johannesburg to Pretoria.

Contact **Athletics South Africa** (ASA), Athletics House, 3 11th Avenue, Houghton Estate, tel: 011-880 5800; www.athletics.org.za, and **Comrades Marathon Association**, PO Box 100621, Scottsville 3209, KwaZulu-Natal, tel: 033-897 8650; www.comrades.com.

Canoeing

South Africans engage with enthusiasm in all forms of canoeing: white water, slalom, sprint and long distance. Olympic canoeists and trainers regard the Highveld as a good training area because of the sunny climate and high altitude (Johannesburg lies at 1,700 metres/yards). There are also some very challenging rivers in South Africa. Some clubs hire out equipment. For information, contact:

Canoeing South Africa PO Box 212005, Oribi 3205, KwaZulu-Natal, tel: 031-764 3022; www.canoesa.org.za.

River Rafting

This is another popular way to enjoy the many large African rivers, especially the Orange River. For 4–6 days let this gentle giant take you in rubber rafts or canoes through the most spectacular, unspoilt Richtersveld – cooking on open fires and sleeping under the remote beauty of the African desert sky – a unique way of letting go of the stresses of "civilisation". The wonderful thing is that no canoeing experience is required and even children can take part (especially in the rubber-raft trips).

Rafting and Canoeing Trips South African River Rafters Association Cape Town: tel: 021-712 5094 **Felix Unite** (Tugela, Orange and Breede rivers – canoes) Tel: 021-404 1830 Fax: 021-448 4915 www.felixunite.com This is the very best agency for finding out all you need to know about rafting and canoeing in South Africa.

Diving

Diving South Africa's coastal waters is a great way to explore the rich marine life (2,000 species) from the icy west coast (the Benguela current of the Atlantic) to the subtropical east coast (the Agulhas current of the Indian Ocean).

On the Atlantic coast, divers can harvest rock lobster (crayfish), perlemoen, black mussels and others. Where the warm Agulhas current can be felt further up the Eastern Cape coast, the marine life changes: flame coral, starfish, feather stars and other exotic and colourful sea creatures abound. People without diving experience might consider making use of diving courses offered here to acquire diving qualifications. For further information contact:

South African Underwater Union PO Box 557, Parow 7500 Tel: 021-930 6549 Fax: 021-930 6541 **Sea Fisheries Research Institute** Tel: 021-402 3911 **South African Heritage Resources Survey** (formerly the National Monuments Council) Tel: 021-462 4502 Fax: 021-462 4509 www.sahra.org.za. For information about wreck diving.

From Cape Vidal (on the level of St Lucia Lake) to the Mozambique border, an aquatic reserve stretches for 5 km (3 miles) out into the sea. Divers are drawn by the world's southernmost coral reefs and the colourful marine life. At Sodwana Bay are the Sodwana Dive Retreat and Sodwana Lodge Charters. These diving resorts offer training, sale and hire of equipment, speciality diving (such as night dives) and accommodation. The area has a beautiful sandy beach with a dune forest. The bay is sheltered by a ridge jutting seaward from the dune headland. Contact **Sodwana Bay Scuba Centre**, tel: 035-571 0117; fax: 035-571 0055; www.sodwana diving.co.za.

The region between Umhlanga Rocks and Salt Rock, with its shallower reefs close to the coast, lends itself especially to spear fishing. Vetch's pier is more for beginners.

Trident Diving School in Durban (tel: 031-305 3081; fax: 031-301 7867) organises dives to the Aliwal Shoal 4 km (2 miles) off the coast of Umkomaas just south of Durban.

The dive businesses in East London are good places to organise trips further afield – countless reefs between the Great Fish River and Kidd's Beach provide excellent diving opportunities. Many vessels have foundered along this stretch of coast, adding plenty of extra interest for intrepid divers. For more information, tel: 043-722 6015.

The area around Port Alfred is only suitable for experienced divers. Information can be obtained from the **Kowie Underwater Club** in Port Alfred. Less experienced divers can brave the deep around Algoa Bay. The **Dolphin Underwater Club** in Humewood offers courses.

At the Tsitsikamma National Park, east of Plettenberg Bay, a snorkelling trail and a scuba-diving trail have been established so you can explore this silent world. For more information, contact SANParks *(see page 334)*.

The numerous rugged stretches of coast in the southwestern Cape make diving a fascinating proposition almost everywhere. You may well discover old wrecks between Danger Point and Waenhuiskrans; more information can be obtained from the Cape Overberg Tourism Association, tel: 0281-41466. Closer to Cape Town, Cape Hangklip is another popular diving area.

Fishing

Trout fishing is pursued by many South Africans all over the country. You need a licence – not transferable from province to province – which is issued by a magistrate's court or (sometimes) by the office of the nature reserve where the stream is located. Obviously, you also require the prescribed trout tackle. The season is all year round, peaking in autumn and spring. In the north, the favourite areas are Dullstroom, Pilgrim's Rest, Graskop, Sabie and Lydenberg, all in Mpumalanga.

The KwaZulu-Natal trout areas are all along the Drakensberg Escarpment and rivers in the Umgeni and Himeville districts. In the Cape popular trout-fishing areas are around Stellenbosch, La Motte, Bain's Kloof and Maden Dam near King Williams Town.

For information, contact the **Federation of South African Fly Fishermen**, tel: 011-467 5992; www.fosaf.org.za.

Rock and Surf Angling
This is a favourite pastime all along South Africa's interesting coastline with its varied conditions concerning water temperatures, winds and currents, all of which affect the type of marine life. Fishing permits are required for particular areas such as Table Bay (obtainable from harbour authorities). No licences are required to fish off the KwaZulu-Natal coast or in estuaries, but taking rock life such as crayfish does.

Popular coastal strips include Durban Harbour, North and South Pier, St Lucia, Mapelane, Cape Vidal, Mission Rocks, Umfolozi and Sodwana Bay. The best season here is June–November.

The Garden Route coastline, the peninsula coastline and False Bay and from Gordon's Bay around Cape Hangklip are popular areas. The season is all year round.

Game and Deep-sea Fishing
This has a special thrill for many anglers. June marks the famous Sardine Run which is accompanied by hundreds of game fish, while in the Cape the two main runs are the tunny run in October and the runs of snoek in autumn and winter. For further information contact: **False Bay Marlin and Tuna Club**, www.fbmt.za.net.

The best areas of the KwaZulu-Natal coast include the south coast, off Durban harbour and the north coast at Sodwana, Richards Bay and St Lucia (season December–June). Cape areas include Hout Bay, Simonstown and Hermanus, where the season stretches mid-October–November and March–mid-May. In KwaZulu-Natal the best season for marlin and sail fish is November–April, while in the Cape the long fin and yellow-fin tunny are in season September–April.

Sailing

With a 3,000-km (1,860-mile) coastline of sandy beaches, bays, lagoons, cliffs and rock shorelines, the South African seas offer the sailing enthusiast the full spectrum of challenges in conditions from the Cape of Storms to calm seas bathed in sunshine. On average the winds are in the 15–25 knots range.

Yacht-club facilities are excellent, from clubs with 50 to those with 3,000 members. Most yachts in South Africa belong to the cruising category in the 10–15-metre (50–80-ft) range, of which the majority are built locally to stringent standards. Offshore sailing requires that you belong to a recognised yacht club and that you comply with harbour regulations (licence, permits, registration, etc.). Local yacht clubs include the following:
Royal Cape Yacht Club
PO Box 772, Cape Town 8000
Tel: 021-421 1354/5
www.rcyc.co.za
Point Yacht Club
3 Maritime Place, Durban 4000, KwaZulu-Natal
Tel: 031-301 4787
www.pyc.co.za
The following listed organisations offer courses in sailing, scenic chartered tours, and activities such as fishing:

BELOW: fishing fleets have found new custom with tourists.

TRANSPORT

ACCOMMODATION

EATING OUT

ACTIVITIES

A – Z

Good Hope Sailing Academy
PO Box 32296, Camps Bay 8040
Tel/fax: 021-424 4665
www.goodhopesailingacademy.co.za
They offer everything from lunch and
sunset charters to five-day cruises in
13-metre (45-ft) and 16-metre (53-ft)
sailing boats off the Cape coast and
in the best wetland and wildlife
sanctuaries.

Dinghy Sailing
Dinghy sailing (that is, sailing in a
boat under 6 metres/20 ft with
raisable centreboard) is popular
mainly on the inland dams. Clubs
welcome visitors and may be helpful
in getting you a sail. The Vaal Dam is
the largest venue (420 km/260
miles), with 700 km (430 miles) of
shoreline, and the season is year
round. The major event is the Lion
Week Vaal Dam in October.
North Vaal Sailing Authority
Tel: 011-824 2402
Fax: 011-827 0853
www.sailrsa.org.za

Surfing

South Africa has beautiful sandy
beaches and great surf. Durban,
South Africa's surfing centre, hosts
most of the surfing competitions
since weather and water are warm all
year round. Further south lies
Jeffrey's Bay, well known for its
dangerous but exhilarating waves.
Even more challenging are the St
Francis Bay waves known as
"Bruce's". However, they are not as
consistent as the waves at Jeffrey's
Bay; many only work on a few winter
days a year. West of Port Elizabeth,
the long breakers abound right down
to Cape Town's big solid waves.
While the landscape is spectacular,
the waters are freezing. Major events
are the National Amateur
Championships (July, venue changes)
and the Gunston 500 (July, Durban).
Equipment and information on local
conditions is available from surf
shops in urban centres.
Surfing South Africa
Tel: 021-674 2972
www.surfingsouthafrica.co.za

Windsurfing

South Africa's sunny weather,
together with the many beautiful
sandy beaches and the huge
expanses of water of the inland
dams, offer many opportunities for
the windsurfing enthusiast. Not only
are temperatures ideal, wind
conditions, too, facilitate the sport.
Access to the water is very good and
South Africa's rescue operations are

very well organised. All you need
worry about is whether you can
handle the strength of the wind.
Some areas require permits for
offshore windsurfing. Below are
some of the popular areas in
Mpumalanga, KwaZulu-Natal and the
Western Cape.
The North: Bona Manzi Dam (near
Bronkhorstspruit), Vaal Dam,
Ebenezer Dam (near Tzaneen).
KwaZulu-Natal: Midmar Dam;
suitable coastal areas are few:
Warner Beach (Scottburgh),
Amanzimtoti (for experienced
windsurfers), lagoon at Zinkwazi,
northern Richards Bay, lagoon at
Mtunzini.
Cape: Plettenberg Bay, Struisbaai,
Swartvlei (inland near George), and
many more. For information, contact
Windsurfing Africa, tel: 021-783
8056; www.windsurfingafrica.org.

Inland Water Sports

Sailing, windsurfing, speed-boating
and water-skiing can be enjoyed at
the Midmar Dam, northwest of
Pietermaritzburg on the N3, and at
the Hartebeespoort Dam, north of
Johannesburg on the R511.

SPECTATOR SPORTS

Football

The most popular game in South
Africa as elsewhere on the
continent, football is played at a
high level in the first-division league.
The national side Bafana Bafana
("The Boys") is one of the strongest
on the continent, and it includes
several players who have made a
huge impact on the European club

scene, notably Benni McCarthy
(Porto), Quinton Fortune
(Manchester United) and Lucas
Radebe (Leeds United, retired).
South Africa has made the last four
in the Africa Nations Cup on three
occasions since sanctions were
lifted – a record that includes one
won and one lost final – and it also
competed in the last two World Cup
finals without making it past the first
round. South Africa will host the
Football World Cup in 2010. For
more information, contact the South
African Football Association at PO
Box 910, Johannesburg, 2000, tel:
011-494 3522; fax: 011-494 4111;
www.safa.net

Cricket

This is one of the major team
sports in South Africa. The standard
is very high, and the game is
strongly promoted. A quota system
has helped open up the game to all
South Africans – many players "of
colour" now play at a provincial
level and several have made an
impact on the international stage,
most prominently Xhosa fast bowler
Makhaya Ntini and opening bat
Herschelle Gibbs, both ranked in
the KC World Top Ten in their
respective disciplines for much of
their career. South Africa hosted the
Cricket One-day World Cup in 2003
but failed to reach the "super six"
stage, despite being ranked second
in the world in this form of the
game.
    The game was introduced to the
continent by the British colonials. The
fact that since 1858 the Queen's
Birthday has been officially
celebrated by a cricket match
testifies to its long popularity among
the English community.

BELOW: the wind and waves can be exhilarating but dangerous.

For more information, contact:
Cricket South Africa, PO Box 55009, Northlands 2116, Gauteng, tel: 011-880 2810; www.cricket.co.za or www.ucbsa.cricket.org.

Horse Racing

Competitive horse riding is a popular spectator sport. Some of the major horse-racing events attract large, glamorous crowds, most famously the Rothmans July Handicap.

Rugby

Despite the years of sanctions against South African sport, rugby remained strong and competitive at the provincial level and it made a strong international comeback after sanctions were lifted, one that has waned somewhat since it won the World Cup on home soil in 1995. For more information, contact: **South African Rugby Football Union**, PO Box 99, Newlands 7725, Cape Town, tel: 021-659 6722; fax: 021-686 3907; www.sarugby.net.

ADVENTURE ACTIVITIES

Over its first ten years of democratic rule, South Africa also established itself as a leading destination for adventure activities, and at least one company in most major tourist centres will offer a variety of adrenaline-charged (and more sedate) day trips to various local attractions. Some of the more useful local contacts follow:

Cape Town & Western Cape
Adventure City
229 Long Street, Cape Town 8001
Tel: 021-424 1580
Email: info@adventure-village.co.za
Air Team Paragliding
Tel 082-257 0808
Email: airteam@
tandemparagliding.co.za
www.tandemparagliding.co.za
Ashanti Travel Centre
11 Hof Street, Gardens 8001
Tel: 021-423 8721
Email: ashanti@iafrica.com
Venture Forth
9 Unyawo Business Park,
Cape Town 7405
Tel: 021-511 4615
Email: info@ventureforth.co.za
www.ctsm.co.za
Day Trippers
414 Voortrekker Road
Maitland 7405
Tel: 021-511 4766

Email: info@daytrippers.co.za
www.daytrippers.co.za
Pro Divers Shop
88B Main Road, Sea Point 8001
Tel: 021-433 0472
Email: info@prodiverssa.co.za
www.prodiverssa.co.za
Shiraz Travel Centre
Stellenbosch
Tel: 021-882 8362
Email: clive@shiraztravel.co.za
Table Mountain Walking Safaris
4 Henshall Road, Hout Bay 7806
Tel: 082-339 7047
Email: info@tablemountainsafaris.co.za

Garden Route
Deep South Eco-Adventures
21 The Island, Knysna 6570
Tel: 044-382 2010
Email: info@deepsoutheco.com
www.deepsoutheco.com
Garden Route Adventure Centre
1 Marsh St, Mossel Bay 6505
Tel: 044-691 3182
Email: marquette@pixie.co.za
www.gardenrouteadventures.com
Heads Adventure Centre
George Rex Drive, PO Box 1401,
Knysna, 6570
Tel: 044-384 0831
Email: hippodivecampus@gmail.com
www.headsadventurecentre.co.za
Ocean Blue Adventures
PO Box 1812, Plettenberg Bay 6600
Tel: 044-533 4897
Email: info@oceanadventures.co.za
www.oceanadventures.co.za
Oudtshoorn Adventure Centre
148 Baron Van Rheede Street,
Oudtshoorn 6625
Tel: 044-272 3436
Email: paradise@isat.co.za
www.backpackersparadise.hostel.com
Seal Adventures Shop
1 Knysna Quays Protea Hotel,
Knysna 6570
Tel: 044-382 5599
Email: seals@mweb.co.za
www.sealadventures.co.za
Storms River Adventures
Darnell Street, PO Box 116, Storms
River 6308
Tel: 042-281 1836
www.stormsriver.com

Eastern Cape
Amadiba Adventures
PO Box 588, Port Edward 4295
Tel: 039-305 6455
Email: amadiba@euwildcoast.co.za
www.amadibaadventures.co.za
Red Cherry Adventures
PO Box 15710, Emerald Hill, Port
Elizabeth 6011
Tel: 041-581 5335
Email: team@cherryadventures.co.za
www.cherryadventures.co.za
Ikhayalam Tours
25 Windermere Road, Port Elizabeth

Tel/fax: 041-582 5098
www.ikhayalamlodgeandtours.co.za

Durban, Zululand & The Drakensberg
Adventure Dives
14 Vickers Place, Durban North 4051
Tel: 083-657 0965
Fax: 031-573 2840
Email: info@adventuredives.co.za
www.adventuredives.co.za
Bibs Tours & Adventures
310 McKenzie Street, PO Box 51,
St Lucia Village 3936
Tel: 035-590 1056
Email: info@bibs.co.za
www.bibs.co.za
Calypso Dive and Adventures
uShaka Marine World, Durban
Tel: 031-332 0905
www.calypsodiving.co.za
Inkosana Lodge & Trekking
PO Box 60, Winterton 3340
Tel/fax: 036-468 1202
Email: inkosana@inkosana.co.za
www.inkosana.co.za
Skydive Durban
La Mercy Airfield
Tel: 072-214 6040
www.skydivedurban.co.za
Tekweni Ecotours
PO Box 39438, Queensburgh,
Durban 4093
Tel: 031-462 9017
Email: info@tekweniecotours.co.za
www.tekweniecotours.co.za
Zululand Eco-Adventures
36 Main Street, PO Box 24,
Eshowe 3815
Tel: 035-474 4919
Fax: 035-474 2691
Email: info@eshowe.com
www.eshowe.com

Gauteng, Mpumalanga & Northern Province
Footprints in Africa
425 Farenden Street, Pretona
Tel: 083-302 1976
Email: info@footprintsinafrica.com
www.footprintsinafrica.com
Jozi Tours and Safaris
Tel: 011-882 6845
Email: tours@jozitours.co.za
www.jozitours.co.za
Kruger Flexi-tours
PO Box 19389, Nelspruit 1200
Tel: 013-744 0993
www.krugerandmore.co.za
Sabie Extreme Adventures
185 Main Street, Sabie 1261
Tel: 013-764 2118
www.sabiextreme.co.za

Swaziland
Swazi Trails Mantenga Craft Centre
Ezulwini Valley
Tel: 416 2180
Email: tours@swazitrails.co.sz
www.swazitrails.co.sz

A–Z

A HANDY SUMMARY OF PRACTICAL INFORMATION, ARRANGED ALPHABETICALLY

B udgeting for your Trip

The following are some prices in US dollars ($). However, they must be taken as an approximate guide; inflation is a factor in South Africa as elsewhere.

Airport transfers: shuttle from Johannesburg International Airport to central Johannesburg: US$30 (first passenger) and US$5 (additional passengers), to Pretoria: US$50 (first passenger) and US$6 (additional passengers); taxi to central Johannesburg US$35 upwards; taxi from Cape Town International Airport to central Cape Town: US$35.

Car hire: (international company). VW Golf: about US$30 per day for up to 14 days. Minibus: about US$100 per day. Prices include collision damage waiver, other insurance and VAT.

Excursions: full-day Cape Peninsula tour from Cape Town: starting from US$55 per person; three-day Johannesburg–Kruger Park bus tour including most meals, entry fees and accommodation (shared room, per person): US$500; three-day Johannesburg–Sun City bus tour including most meals and accommodation in double room: US$400 per person.

National Parks. Entry fees: US$5–12 per person. **Lodges:** US$50–150 double.

Petrol (gasoline): US$0.80–1 per litre.

Taxis: Fares vary from town to town. For safety, stick to metered taxis and avoid informal, minibus-style cabs. Meters start at about US$1.20, plus US60¢ per km (tip expected).

Trains: (one way). Johannesburg–Cape Town, normal train: US$75–200; Blue Train, Cape Town–Pretoria, luxury compartment (per person, meals included): US$1,200 upwards. Johannesburg–Durban: US$40–50.

Business Hours

Business hours are from 8.30am to 4.30pm. Most shops stay open from 8.30am to 5pm Monday to Friday and until 12.30pm on Saturday. Some greengrocers, pharmacies, book shops and supermarkets may stay open later. Cafés (essentially small general stores) may operate from 6am to midnight seven days a week. Some big shopping centres stay open till 5pm on Saturday and from 9am to 1pm on Sunday. Beach-front shops in Durban stay open all day on Sunday.

C limate

The Cape Peninsula has a typically Mediterranean climate while the weather on the highveld (the area around Gauteng) is moderate. The lowveld (including Kruger Park) and the east coast of KwaZulu-Natal are subtropical.

The seasons are exactly opposite to those in the northern hemisphere, with Christmas coming right in the middle of the hottest season, when temperatures often exceed 30°C

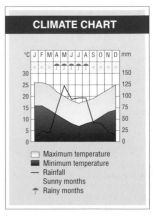

CLIMATE CHART

°C J F M A M J J A S O N D mm

☐ Maximum temperature
■ Minimum temperature
— Rainfall
  Sunny months
☂ Rainy months

(86°F) in the shade in many parts of the country.

Thanks to the sunshine which each year graces the coastal resort areas with 300 more hours of sun than the Canary Islands, any time of year is the right time to travel, but autumn (March–April) and spring (September–October) are particularly pleasant, as the weather's not too hot.

Rainfall is an uncertain quantity. South Africa is characterised as an arid region (the rate of evaporation is higher than that of precipitation), and two-thirds of the country receives less than 500 mm (19 inches) of rainfall a year. In the interior, the precious rain falls mostly in the summer months (November–April), generally in brief but violent showers. The Western Cape receives its precipitation in winter (June–September). Along the southern coast, it could rain at any time of year. The high humidity in KwaZulu-Natal can also make for some truly muggy days.

Snow falls nearly every year in the high mountains, but seldom results in more than a powdery dusting along the ground. The reason for this is lack of humidity rather than the temperature, which regularly dips below freezing. Check the weather forecast on www.weathersa.co.za.

Crime & Safety

During the last few years, there has been a sharp increase in crime in the large cities. Although incidents of violent crime against tourists are not the norm, sensible precautions should be taken.

Keep cameras, expensive watches and jewellery concealed when walking about in built-up areas, especially in Johannesburg. If you need to stop to consult a map or guide book, don't draw attention to yourself by looking lost on a street corner – walk into a shop or bank.

Walking the streets, particularly alone, at night is not recommended. Car windows should be kept closed and doors locked at all times when driving in Johannesburg. If you are unsure about the safety of a particular area, consult the local tourist information office.

Any loss of valuables should be immediately reported to the police. The telephone number in all large cities is 10111.

Customs & Entry

All visitors need to bring a valid passport (expiring at least six months after date of entry, and with two full empty pages) and a return or onward ticket, but visitors from the EU, the

USA, Canada, Australia, New Zealand, Singapore, Japan, Liechtenstein and Switzerland can travel to South Africa for up to 90 days without a visa. However, if any visitors, regardless of passport, travel through Swaziland, a visa is required, which you can get at the border. Visitors from other countries can receive a South African visa free of charge, but must apply at least four weeks before their date of departure. Holidaymakers from countries including Australia, the USA, and Canada (but not the UK, France, Germany or the Netherlands) require a visa for Lesotho.

Transit visas are issued to travellers who plan to go through South Africa to neighbouring countries, whether by air, train or car. Applicants must be able to show a return ticket and a visa for their final destination.

Multiple-entry visas are recommended for all visitors who want a South African visa and also plan to visit Lesotho or Swaziland or other surrounding countries, and return to South Africa (for their return flight, for example). If you don't decide on such an excursion until you actually get to South Africa, you'll need to apply for a re-entry visa before leaving the country. This takes at least a week, and can be obtained from the Department of Home Affairs in Cape Town (www.home-affairs.gov.za) or its regional offices in every major city.

A temporary residence permit is issued on arrival when you give your reason for, and length of, your stay. If you should want to stay for longer than three months, you'll have to have this permit renewed at the Department of Home Affairs, one of its offices, or a police station; try to do this 10–14 days before the previous permit expires.

Disabled Travellers

A disabled person with a measure of patience and a sense of humour will enjoy touring South Africa, even though facilities are not always readily available. However, the new South African government is attempting to improve matters and has set up the National Accessibility Scheme. As well as creating a database of accessible amenities and attractions, the scheme promotes awareness of disabled needs throughout the tourism industry. Contact the South African Tourism Board (*see under Tourist Offices, page 370*) or one of the following for details:
National Portal Accessibility
www.napsa.org.za
Deaf Federation of South Africa
20 Napier Road, Richmond, Johannesburg

Tel: 011-482 1610
Fax: 011-726 5873
www.deafsa.co.za
QuadPara Association of South Africa
Tel: 031-767 0348
www.qasa.co.za
SA National Council for the Blind
Tel: 012-452 3811
Fax: 012-346 4699
www.sancb.org.za

E lectricity

The standard current throughout the country is 220/230 volts. Only sockets with three-pronged plugs are used, so to use European or American appliances you'll have to get an adaptor (which you can find in any electrical appliance shop on the Cape). Some of the larger hotels will loan adaptors to you on request.

Embassies/Consulates

Australia: Rhodes Place, State Circle, Yarralumla, Canberra ACT, 2600
Tel: 02-6272 7300
Fax: 06-6272 7364
www.sahc.org.au
Canada: 15 Sussex Drive, Ottawa KIM 1M8
Tel: 613-744 0330
Fax: 613-741 1639
www.southafrica-canada.ca
United Kingdom: South Africa House, Trafalgar Square, London WC2N 5DP
Tel: 020-7451 7299
Fax: 020-7451 7283
www.southafricahouse.com
United States: 3051 Massachusetts Avenue NW, Washington DC 20008
Tel: 202-232 4400
Fax: 202-265 1607
www.saembassy.org
Consulates:
New York: 333 East 38 Street, New York, NY 10016
Tel: 212-213 4880
Fax: 212-213 0102
www.southafrica-newyork.net
Los Angeles: 6300 Wilshire Boulevard, Suite 600, CA 90048
Tel: 310-651 0902
Fax: 310-651 5969
Email: info.losangeles@foreign.gov.za

Emergencies

Ambulance and Police: 10111
Fire Brigade: 10111
Medical: 10177

H ealth & Medical Care

Cholera and smallpox vaccinations are no longer required. Yellow-fever inoculations are only necessary for those travelling from an infected yellow-fever zone.

Malaria tablets are strongly recommended if you're planning to visit the north of the country, including the Lowveld and Kruger National Park, and northern KwaZulu Natal. Consult your doctor about suitable anti-malarial precautions which you'll need to start taking several weeks before you fly. Typical symptoms are similar to flu, and should show within a week or two.

The best prophylactic is not to get bitten: use insect repellent liberally, especially in the early evenings, wear long-sleeved tops and long trousers in the evening, and try to make sure you sleep in mosquito-proof quarters, particularly when travelling in northern areas. Use mosquito coils, which you can buy in any supermarket. The critical period is from November to May or June, depending on how late the rains have fallen.

Ticks are found in long grass and can carry tick bite fever (if it should be an infected one that bites you). When walking in long grass it is advisable to wear trousers tucked into boots or long socks.

Snake bites are not very common, because snakes generally try and slither away from visitors as fast as they can. Before you take a needle and serum and do yourself any undue damage, you should first head for a doctor or clinic – wherever you are in South Africa, medical aid is generally no further than two hours away. The best serum is vigilance: don't sit on any fallen tree or stone without first checking that there are no snakes underneath; walk firmly and look where you're going. If you get bitten then check what kind of snake the culprit was – you can recognise a snake bite by the two adjacent pricks. Don't panic, but calm the patient, lie him or her down and be reassuring – a snake bite is not necessarily a death sentence.

Put cooking salt and an icepack on scorpion bites to reduce the pain.

Bilharzia is found in virtually every inland body of water in the north, KwaZulu-Natal and Eastern Cape (except in rapidly flowing water or lakes at high altitudes). Don't wade or swim in ponds or brooks. When in doubt, ask about local conditions.

As for "traveller's tummy", or diarrhoea, you won't suffer ill effects from consuming fresh fruit, vegetables, lettuce, fruit juices, ice cream or water from the tap in South Africa.

Aids is one of the biggest killers in South Africa. HIV infection is widespread. Avoid high-risk activities such as unprotected sex.

Internet

Inexpensive internet access should be available at any upmarket city hotel or beach resort, as well as at most backpacker hostels, and at internet cafés in the larger towns and cities. Internet facilities may not exist in smaller towns, and there certainly won't be access in game reserves, so you should catch up on any outstanding correspondence before you head out to the sticks.

Media

Television
South Africa has had television only since 1976. Currently, the South African Broadcasting Corporation provides three television channels, called SABC 1, 2 and 3, which broadcast mostly in English, but also in eight African languages and in Afrikaans. Broadcasts are dominated by a mix of imported and local soaps, sitcoms, quiz shows and made-for-TV (or very old) movies. The only other non-pay channel is ETV, a recent introduction that generally shows more recent films than SABC but is otherwise more of the same. Most but by no means all major sporting events involving South Africa are shown on one of the above channels, but other international sport generally isn't.

The advent of satellite and cable television has increased the choice for viewers who can afford it. M-Net is a private subscription channel, accessed with the help of a decoder that broadcasts reasonably new films, documentaries and imported sitcoms, while a subsidiary service called DSTV has dozens of choices including two movie channels, various news channels (CNN, BBC World, Sky) and five sports channels that broadcast pretty much every major international rugby, cricket, football, tennis and golf event. Most hotels ranking three stars or higher have DSTV in the room, the main exception being game lodges and other places that preserve a bush atmosphere.

Radio
South Africa has radio stations broadcasting in all 11 official languages. As well as SABC's public stations, there are dozens of commercial and community stations.

Print
Newspapers are sold in supermarkets, news agencies, corner grocery stores and on the street. The most responsible and least sensationalist of the established dailies is the *Business*

Day. In most parts of the country, however, the local newspaper published by the Argus Group (*Cape Argus*, *Pretoria News*, *Johannesburg Star*, etc) dominate the market. Weeklies include the gossipy *Sunday Times*, quality *Sunday Independent* and outspoken *Mail & Guardian* – the latter, published on Friday, also contains good arts coverage and entertainment listings. European papers and magazines can be found at the booksellers CNA – at high prices and up to a month old – as can the southern African editions of the *Weekly Telegraph*, *International Express* and *Guardian Weekly*.

Money

The currency is the South African rand (ZAR), which consists of 100 cents. Lesotho and Swaziland have their own currencies, which are interchangeable with the rand.

Visitors can take ZAR 5,000 in cash each in and out of the country; there's no limit on foreign currencies or traveller's cheques. You can exchange extra rand into other currencies at the end of your trip, but you have to prove that you brought the money in with you: don't forget to save your exchange receipts.

Traveller's cheques are the safest form of currency. Cheques in US dollars, euros and pounds sterling will yield the highest rate of exchange. Banks are the best place to exchange cheques or cash; you can take care of this directly at the airport upon arrival. Major hotels also exchange money.

Most hotels, shops, restaurants and travel agencies accept international credit cards such as Visa, MasterCard (Eurocard), Diners Club and American Express. These cards can also be used to draw up to ZAR1,000 cash daily from ATMs outside most branches of major banks such as First National Bank, Standard Bank and Nedbank.

VAT refunds
You won't have to pay value-added tax (VAT) if you have your purchases sent directly to your home address. When purchasing diamond jewellery or precious metals from a shop which is a member of the Jewellery Council of South Africa, Johannesburg (tel: 011-334 1930; www.jewellery.org.za), the tax is recorded on a separate receipt and credit-card slip. When leaving the country, have your departure confirmed at the Jewellery Council counter; the Council will then send a form back to the shop, which will destroy the credit-card slip. This

practice, however, is only possible with a shop which is a Council member.

P ostal Services

You can buy stamps at post offices, book shops such as CNA, supermarkets and a host of other outlets. If travelling to rural areas, buy a supply in advance, as post offices can be few and far between.

Post office opening times: Monday–Friday 8.30am–4.30pm, Saturday 8am–noon. Smaller, rural branches close 1–2pm. The South African Post Office is not the most reliable postal service in the world, nor the speediest – domestic mail and letters to/from Europe can take anything from a few days to two weeks, and longer waits are commonplace for North America, Australia and elsewhere in Africa.

If sending mail other than postcards (especially anything of value), it is probably wiser to use one of the many private postal services available. PostNet is the most widespread of these and details of their nearest bureau can be found in the telephone directory.

Public Holidays

1 January New Year's Day
21 March Human Rights' Day
27 April Freedom Day
1 May Workers' Day
16 June Youth Day
9 August National Women's Day
24 September Heritage Day
16 December Day of Reconciliation
25/26 December Christmas Day/ Goodwill Day
Movable dates: Good Friday, Family Day (Easter Monday)

T elephones

Direct Dialling Dial 27 for South Africa, then 21 for Cape Town, 31 for Durban, 12 for Pretoria, or 11 for Johannesburg.

International calls from South Africa must be prefixed with "00", while all domestic calls must be dialled as a full ten-digit number including the regional code (eg, 011 for Johannesburg), even if you dial from within the region.

Telephone calls are fairly cheap. To use public telephones, it's best to purchase a telephone card (from post offices and supermarkets in ZAR 10, 20, 50, 100 and 200 denominations). Local, national and international calls can be made from public telephone boxes. Hotels generally charge two to three times more than the official rate.

Time Zone

South Africa stays on GMT +2 all year round.

Tourist Information

All larger towns and cities have a Tourist Information Bureau (sometimes called the Publicity Association), which can be identified by a large white "I" on a green background, and will be able to provide city maps, information on current events, museums and other points of interest. The Municipality provides information in very small places. You will find numbers listed in the telephone directory under Publicity Association or Municipality, as well as in publications and websites put together by the provincial tourist boards.

The contact details and (in many cases excellent) websites of the provincial authorities are listed below. These provincial websites generally include listings for or links to more local sources of tourist information within that province.

Eastern Cape Tourist
Tel: 043-701 9600
Fax: 043-701 9649
Email: info@ectourism.co.za
www.ectourism.co.za
Free State Tourism Marketing Board
Tel: 086-110 2185
Fax: 051-400-9593
www.freestateprovince.co.za
Gauteng Tourism Agency
Tel: 011-639-1600
Email: tourism@gauteng.net
www.gauteng.net
KwaZulu-Natal Tourism Authority
Tel: 031-366 7500
Email: tkzn@iafrica.com
www.kzn.org.za
Mpumalanga Tourism Authority
Tel: 013-752 7001
Email: taelo@mtpa.co.za
www.mpumalanga.com
Northern Cape Tourism Authority
Tel: 053-832 2657
www.northerncape.org.za
Limpopo Tourism Board
Tel/fax: 015-781 0644
Email: webmaster@ limpopowildlife.co.za
www.limpopotourism.co.za
North-West Parks & Tourism Authority
Tel: 018-397 1500
Email: info@tourismnorthwest.co.za
www.tourismnorthwest.co.za
Western Cape Tourism Board
Tel: 021-426 5639
Fax: 021-426 5640
Email: info@tourismcapetown.co.za
www.capetourism.org

Tourist Offices (SATOUR)

South African Tourism Board
Head Office: Private Bag X10012, Sandton 2146, Johannesburg
Tel: 083-123 6789
Fax: 011-895 3001
www.southafrica.net
Australia & New Zealand:
Level 1, 117 York Street, Sydney 2000 NSW, Australia
Tel: 02-9261 5000
Fax: 02-9261 2000
United Kingdom, Republic of Ireland, Scandinavia: 5 & 6 Alt Grove, Wimbledon, London SW19 4DZ
24-hr brochure line: 08701-550044
Tel: 020 8971 9350.
United States (Eastern): 500 Fifth Avenue, 20th Floor, Suite 2040, New York, NY 10110 ·
Tel: 212-730 2929
Fax: 212-764 1980
United States (Western):
Tel: 310-643 6481
Fax: 310-643 0333
Zimbabwe: Office 106, Sanlam Centre, Newlands, Harare
Tel: 04-746 487
Fax: 04-746 489

W ater

You can drink tap water anywhere in South Africa – even in the big game parks. In some coastal areas it may be tinted by iron deposits, but it's still potable.

Websites

In addition to the many websites listed elsewhere in this book, the following general websites might be useful to travellers:
www.anc.org.za – the official mouthpiece of the ANC has plenty of coverage of contemporary issues.
www.africageographic.com – news and features from the country's leading wildlife and ecological magazine.
www.coastingafrica.com – comprehensive coverage of South Africa's backpacker hostels and related facilities.
www.iafrica.com – current news and features by a leading local internet provider.
www.gaysouthafrica.org.za – the official gay and lesbian site for South Africa.
www.getawaytoafrica.com – website of South Africa's most popular travel magazine.
www.mg.co.za – online version of the Mail & Guardian newspaper.
www.sanparks.org – information and booking facilties for the country's 20 national parks.

www.platterwineguide.co.za – online version of Platter's popular wine guide.
www.southafrica.net – official site of the South African tourist board.
www.southafrica.co.za – useful general site with up-to-date information about weather, exchange rates and tourist attractions, as well as good maps.
www.sundaytimes.co.za – good news and sport coverage from the *Sunday Times* newspaper.
www.womensnet.org.za – news and links for women's issues in South Africa.

What to Bring

As in any warm climate, you'll be most comfortable in light cotton clothing. Most hotels offer a next-day laundry and pressing service, and big cities also have coin-operated launderettes. Holiday centres require only casual dress, although for dinner in a hotel or restaurant one generally dresses more formally.

In winter (June–August), it's generally still comfortably warm in KwaZulu-Natal (Durban). The rest of the country tends to be around 20°C (68°F) in the day's sun; however, at night and in the early morning, it can be extremely cold. Warm clothing is an absolute must.

On the Cape and the Highveld (Johannesburg) it can become quite cool, especially in the evenings. Always take a jacket or anorak out with you.

When hiking in the game reserves, wear dull colours such as beige, brown, khaki or olive green. This isn't only to keep you from being too noticeable to the animals; flies and insects are more attracted to white or colourful clothing. Long-sleeved shirts are also a protection against insect bites.

Rain is termed "lovely weather" in South Africa – an indication that the country's citizens would like to see more of it. When it does rain, however, it pours, and one is quickly soaked through to the skin. It's wise to take a raincoat or umbrella with you.

Topless bathing for women is acceptable on some beaches, but not all, so ask around or check what other people are doing first. It is not generally the done thing at hotel pools; bikinis are perfectly acceptable.

In addition, don't forget to pack high-factor sun screen and a wide-brimmed sun hat, which you should wear at all times when outdoors, especially on the beach and for hiking trips.

What to Read

Abraham Esau's War: A Black South African War in the Cape, 1899–1902; Cambridge University Press. The Boer War seen from a black perspective and focusing on the context of Cape Colony social culture and political life at the turn of the 20th century.
A Bed Called Home: Life in the Migrant Labour Hostels of Cape Town by Mamphela Ramphele; Ohio University Press. The writer, an anthropologist, interviewed a number of the city's hostel dwellers for this profound study of poverty and ways in which the victims can create better lives for themselves.
Country of My Skull by Antjie Krog; Random House. Few books provide so compelling an introduction to the iniquities of apartheid as this multiple award-winning and highly personal account of the Truth & Reconciliation Commission hearings that took place under the Mandela government.
Field Guide to the Mammals of Southern Africa by Chris & Tilde Stuart; Struik Publishers. Easy-to-use and thorough field guide to the varied furry inhabitants of Africa south of the Zambezi.
John Platter South African Wines; Zebra Publications. The South African wine-lover's bible, with listings for practically every vineyard countrywide, and many thousands of individual wine ratings, yet still just about compact enough to slip into a large pocket.
Mandela: The Authorised Biography by Anthony Sampson; Harper Collins. The most thorough available overview of the life and times of South Africa's much-loved former president.
My Traitor's Heart by Riaan Malan; Bodley Head. This candid 1990 account of a liberal Afrikaner's perspective on apartheid feels somewhat time-warped today, but it's fascinating reading all the same.
Newman's Birds of Southern Africa by Kenneth Newman; Struik Publishers. This comprehensive field guide includes colour plates, descriptions and distribution details for every bird species ever recorded south of the Zambezi.
Shaka's Children: A History of the Zulu People by Stephen Taylor; Harper Collins. Readable and erudite account of the rise of Shaka and subsequent fortunes of the Zulu Nation.
South Africa: A Modern History by T.R.H. Davenport; Palgrave MacMillan. First published in 1977, this definitive, short – well, 700-page – history of South Africa is now in its fifth edition, with up-to-date coverage of the post-apartheid era and a fresh introduction by Archbishop Desmond Tutu.

Soweto Style by Mark Lanning, Neil Rooke and Glynis Horning; Struik Publishers. This handsome large-format book captures the inventive and creative side of everyday life in South Africa's most notorious township.
Strange Days Indeed by Shaun Johnson; Bantam. Anthology of Johnson's newspaper columns from 1986 to 1994, as the country struggled to form a democracy.
The Boer War by Thomas Packenham; Weidenfeld & Nicolson. Masterly and thorough account of the protracted Anglo-Boer hostilities in whose aftermath South Africa took its modern shape.
The Illustrated Long Walk to Freedom ed. Paul Duncan; Little, Brown. Revised version of Nelson Mandela's epic, first published when he emerged from prison. This Mandela biography also serves as an arresting account of modern South Africa's miserable, sectarian history.
The Official Field Guide to the Cradle of Humankind by Brett Hilton-Barber & Lee Burger; Struik Publishers. Worthwhile overview of the archaeological and palaeontological marvels of the Sterkfontein Caves and surrounds in western Gauteng.
The Roots of Black South Africa by David Hammond-Tooke; Jonathan Ball. Fascinating study of southern Africa's cultural traditions.
The Vanishing Cultures of South Africa by Peter Magubane; Struik Publishers. Superb coffee-table tome whose exceptional pictures evoke several dying aspects of traditional South African culture.
Tomorrow Is Another Country by Allister Sparks; University of Chicago Press. Former newspaper editor Sparks – an outspoken critic of the apartheid government – provides a detailed and readable account of the CODESA talks that led to the 1994 election.
Winnie Mandela: A Life by Anne Marie du Preez Bezdrop; Zebra Press. The former wife of Nelson Mandela is among the most divisive political figures in present-day South Africa, and – whether you admire or despise her outspokenness and capacity for courting controversy – her life story makes for utterly compelling reading.

Other Insight Guides

Insight Guides to Africa include *East African Wildlife, Egypt, Gambia & Senegal, Kenya, Namibia, Tanzania & Zanzibar* and Insight Pocket Guides to *The Nile, Kenya* and *Cape Town*. Insight FlexiMaps, laminated for ease of use and durability, cover *South Africa* and *Cape Town*.

TRANSPORT
ACCOMMODATION
EATING OUT
ACTIVITIES
A – Z

ART & PHOTO CREDITS

PICTURE SPREADS

Map Production:
Polyglott Kartographie and Laura Morris
© 2006 Apa Publications GmbH & Co.
Verlag KG (Singapore branch)

INSIGHT GUIDE
SOUTH AFRICA
Art Director **Klaus Geisler**
Picture Research **Hilary Genin**
Cartographic Editor **Zoë Goodwin**
Production **Linton Donaldson**

INDEX

Numbers in italics refer to photographs, in bold refer to major entries.

A
B
C
D
E
F
G
H
J
a
b
c
d
f
g
h
i
j
k
l

Insight Guides Website
www.insightguides.com

*Don't travel the
planet alone.
Keep in step with
Insight Guides'
walking eye,
just a click away*

INSIGHT GUIDES
The classic series that puts you in the picture